The Art of Rigging

Volume 3

Publisher:
CG Toolkit
www.cgtoolkit.com

Kiaran Ritchie, Oleg Alexander, Karim Biri.
ISBN: 0-9768003-2-2

Credits,

Authors:
Kiaran Ritchie, Oleg Alexander, Karim Biri,

Contributors:
Emrah Emrasi, Kursad Karatas, Pat Presley, Cluster animation Studio
Glen Southern, Motion Analysis Studios, Boxx, Remington Scott
Eric Aten, Matt Bauer, Christopher Johnson, James Bowers, Larry Jacks
Anet Hambarsumian, Bo Wright, Bo Wright, Mario Perez

This is the final book in The Art of Rigging series. In past volumes, we have covered the fundamentals of character rigging, intermediate MEL scripting and a sprinkling of advanced topics (to help push the reader's imagination).

We want to introduce you to the mindset in which this book (and indeed, the entire series) was created. There is a lot of talk about 'next-generation' graphics applications. Todays 3d applications, astounding as they are, will undoubtedly become obsolete. The CG industry relies on constant change and unrelenting progress. This can scare artists from investing the time it takes to learn the more esoteric areas of a piece of software. What many artists fail to realize is that while software will inevitably progress, the basic concepts of 3d animation have already been established. Knowing this, the prospect of diving into areas like cloth, hair and fur become more attractive.

This book is about exploring the often overlooked modules that give Maya its prestige. Any and every 3d application can do inverse kinematics, polygon modeling and keyframe animation. These 'features' have become staple ingredients in every 3d artist's toolset. The future belongs to increasing complexity and sophistication. Setting yourself apart from the crowd, as a TD, is now a matter of mastering the advanced topics.

The Art of Rigging series is about giving people the power and inspiration to get started making believable, production worthy results. That's why we include tons of 3d models, MEL scripts and video lectures. We just believe that learning 3d animation, like any craft, requires that the student have access to the right tools. The book you hold in your hands was carefully crafted to give you a solid understanding, with no excuses. Everything we created in the book is included on the DVD. Just like every book from CG Toolkit, this one includes a DVD with ample video lectures and 3d assets.

We have been working on The Art of Rigging series for almost two years. To be candid; this is our favorite book in the series.

We at CG Toolkit want to thank everybody for supporting our endeavors. Because the response from The Art of Rigging has been so good, CG Toolkit has been able to expand into other areas. Without revealing too much, we just want to assure our readers that CG Toolkit plans to continue making top-quality books that cover the most exciting topics in computer graphics. Without your help, this expansion would be impossible.

Thank you, and enjoy...
CGtoolkit Team

Table of Contents

Chapter 1
Cloth Fundamentals

▶

Introduction:

Believable cloth is one of the most complicated and chaotic effects to animate. No other effect is as expensive to compute or devilishly complicated to animate, with perhaps the exception of fluids.

The problem with animating cloth is directly related to its complex nature. Real cloth is an artificial material comprised of a network of natural or artificial fibers (thread and yarn). These threads are woven together by a loom machine to form a cohesive pattern. Creating different fabrics (like denim, satin, or silk) is done by varying the pattern and changing the material that the thread is made of. This process produces the myriad of different fabrics we see all over the place.

Cloth is, basically, just a bunch of threads woven together to form a solid surface. When forces are applied to a piece of cloth, its shape is determined by how these threads pull and stretch each other. Loosely woven cloth will fall into a shapeless clump, while tightly woven fabrics (like canvas) can retain their shape under pressure. When cloth forms into folds and wrinkles, this is because the threads were not strong enough to resist bending. When animating cloth, it can help to keep this in mind.

In computer graphics, cloth is animated by simulating the complex interaction between threads as they undergo stresses (like collisions, friction and gravity). This is done using what is referred to as a spring-mass solver. A spring-mass solver creates an array of particles across the surface. These particles are usually positioned at each vertex, and are connected by several different types of springs (shear, stretch and bend springs). The particles are then subjected to forces, and the springs (like the threads in a fabric) keep the whole system together.

Cloth simulation is an amazing thing to witness. While it can be tricky to setup and tweak, if you follow the guidelines in this chapter you should have no problem getting professional results, every time. Specifically, we will cover:

- Introduction to Cloth Simulation
- Modeling Garments
- Animating Cloth
- Preparing Cloth for Rendering

Introduction to Cloth Simulation:

Cloth simulation is a very important part of many modern productions. Every visual effects studio has, at some point, required cloth simulation. In fact, most visual effects studios employ full-time technical directors (often referred to as 'finishing TDs') whose sole job it is to setup and simulate cloth. Knowing how to tame a cloth simulator will make you a valuable asset in today's CG industry.

Before we dive into the nitty-gritty stuff, it helps to know exactly how cloth simulation came about and what software solutions exist. There is no single dominant cloth simulator, and in fact, some studios use several *different* simulators for a single production. Fortunately for us, all cloth simulators are based on the same basic principles. This makes learning and using different simulators a breeze.

Cloth Simulators:

Cloth simulation is a relatively new technology in the animation world. The first commercial cloth simulator, ClothReyes, was released in 1997 by Reyes Infographica Inc. ClothReyes was released as a plugin for 3ds Max at a time when cloth simulation was still a dream for most production houses. Since 1997, many commercial cloth simulators have come to market for every major animation package.

Users of 3ds Max have access to several cloth solutions. In addition to ClothReyes, 3ds Max users can simulate cloth with the built-in reactor dynamics or the open source (and completely free) plugin, SimCloth. While these solutions may work perfectly for your needs, the best, most stable, and flexible cloth simulator for 3ds Max is Clothfx. This cloth simulator has been included since version 7.0. As with many of 3ds Max's features, Clothfx started life as a 3rd party plugin under the old name of 'Stitch'. Clothfx is very similar to the cloth simulator discussed in this book (including the ability to create garments from panels) and is fully capable of creating amazing results.

For those of you who are using Softimage's 3d software, XSI includes two native cloth solutions. For simple cloth effects, XSI Cloth provides nice stable results and the ability to add/remove vertices from the simulation so that pieces of a single mesh can be simulated (like a sleeve) while neighboring vertices are enveloped. For more complex cloth animation, XSI Advanced includes the Syflex cloth simulator. Syflex has been used with success on countless feature films, cinematics and television series because of its stability and speed (more on this soon).

Maya users have two options for animating cloth, Maya Cloth or the Syflex plugin. The Maya Unlimited package includes the Maya Cloth module. Maya Cloth uses the curves-to-panels-to-garment paradigm that has seen much success in many major productions. Maya Cloth gained popularity after its first major use in the feature film, Stuart Little (1999). Since then, many production houses around the world have used it to create amazingly complicated cloth animations.

The Syflex plugin is a very impressive, powerful and fast cloth simulator (www.syflex.biz, $2200). Syflex relies on the user to model their own garments (does not use curves-to-panels-to-garments) and works best with clean polygon surfaces. Syflex is usually much easier to setup than Maya Cloth while providing a *very* stable simulation. Syflex can even be used to create realistic soft bodies (like a tire tube), flesh (for muscle simulations) as well as hair, ropes and chains. For this reason, almost every major visual effects studio has incorporated Syflex into their pipeline.

It is inevitable that you will want to compare Syflex with Maya Cloth. The following table should help you:

#	Syflex	Maya Cloth
Garment Creation	Syflex provides no modeling tools. Garments are created with regular polygon modeling techniques and users must be careful to construct clean surfaces. UV's must be prepared and layed-out prior to simulation.	Maya Cloth provides artists with a method of modeling garments based on traditional real-world sewing techniques. Garments are automatically tessellated for good folding and provide perfect UV layouts for flawless texturing (very useful for cloth).
Speed of Simulation	Very fast with simple meshes. Simulation times will slow as mesh density is increased and self-collisions are calculated, but it is definitely a fast solver.	Most garments can be simulated at 1-15fps (with moderate density). An improperly tuned solver/cloth property will greatly increase the time per frame.
Quality of Simulation	Syflex produces very convincing results quite easily, although many users report spending more time ridding the simulation of the annoying "rubbery" look.	If tuned properly, Maya Cloth will provide physically accurate results. If not tuned properly, it can blow-up and cause much frustration.
Ease of Use	Your grandmother could use this cloth simulator.	Maya Cloth is not difficult to use. The workflow is complicated, but it makes sense.
Stability	Syflex's algorithms adaptively adjust to prevent explosions. It is very stable.	If setup properly, Cloth is very stable and works as advertised. It does take some practice to avoid creating cloth bombs though.

#	Syflex	Maya Cloth
Additional Features	Syflex Includes : -A Caching System -Several Constraints -Several Dynamic Forces (wind, gravity, damp etc...) -Paintable Per-vertex Properties -Collisions -C++ SDK.	Maya Cloth Includes: -A Caching System -Several Constraints -All of Maya's Dynamic Forces -Paintable Per-Vertex Properties -Collisions
Integration	Syflex is very well integrated into Maya.	Maya Cloth is extremely well integrated. You can connect cloth to any Maya force field, hair, particles or even fluids.
Price	$2200 USD (non-commercial licenses are available)	Included with Maya Unlimited

The Bottom Line:

As you can see, Maya Cloth and Syflex are quite similar but have some important differences. Deciding which one to use really depends on several factors and is not a clear-cut decision. The bottom line is that having and knowing how to use both simulators can be a great help. The good news is that if you know how to use Maya Cloth, Syflex will be immediately familiar. And if you have both, you can leverage their strengths and weaknesses as your production requires. Many studios use Maya Cloth for modeling garments and creating irregular tessellation (more about this later) while using Syflex to simulate.

Because Maya Cloth covers garment construction, draping, simulation, tweaking, caching, constraints and collisions, learning Maya Cloth will give you the tools to master any other cloth simulator. Remember, at the core, they are all spring-mass solvers. The only difference is in how the software engineers implemented the algorithms. Mastering cloth simulation is simply a matter of learning all the dials, and knowing how to tweak them.

The rest of this chapter will dive into the details of getting professional results from the powerful Maya Cloth module.

Modeling Garments:

The first step in any cloth simulation is, of course, modeling your clothing. The success or failure of your efforts rely heavily on how well your cloth object is constructed. Here are a few things to remember about modeling cloth:

- Cloth objects must be polygonal meshes. No other surface types are supported.
- Cloth objects absolutely must have adequate tessellation to enable proper bending/folding during simulation.
- Cloth objects must be thin. The surface must be only a *single polygon thick* during simulation. Worry about adding thickness *after* simulation.
- Cloth objects should not contain any 'extra' pieces. Props (like buttons and zippers) can be attached later and will only interfere with the simulation.

Now that you have a better idea of what a cloth object should be like, let's move on and discuss the two major modeling techniques (garments and cloth objects).

Garments vs. Cloth Objects:

Maya Cloth's modeling paradigm is centered around the idea of a 'garment'. A Maya Cloth 'garment' is a procedurally generated polygonal mesh. Garments provide amazing modeling and simulation benefits, but they are not the only method of creating cloth. You can convert any Maya object into a cloth object. Cloth objects have some limitations, but they are still very useful. To understand how you can use 'cloth objects' and 'garments' together, let's first take a look at how a 'garment' is created.

Important Note: From here onwards, a *garment* will refer to a piece of cloth created from panels and stitching, a *cloth object* is any Maya object that was converted into cloth.

A garment is constructed from a panel, which is, in turn, constructed from NURBS curves. This allows a setup artist to create panels of clothing from real-world patterns. The workflow is remarkably similar to that of a real-world clothier. It goes like this:

1.) Determine the 'look' you want and do some research to find an appropriate pattern for the particular garment (tank-top, t-shirt, cape, jeans etc...) FIGURE 1.1.

2.) Create an image of the pattern in Photoshop. Import this image and place it on a reference plane over your character FIGURE 1.2. Ensure your character is in its 'dress-up' pose with arms held outwards (the 'da Vinci' pose).

3.) Using the CV or EP curve tool, draw a curve over each edge in the pattern. The curves *must be planar* and *must form a closed loop* FIGURE 1.3. If they do not, panel creation is impossible. Display the Edit Points for the curves (`Display > NURBS Components > Edit Points`) and then use point snapping (V key) to place the control points.

Figure 1.1.

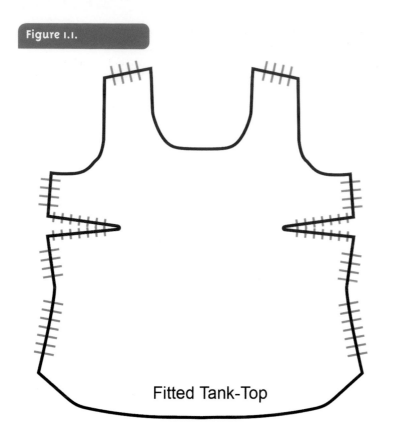

Fitted Tank-Top

Figure 1.3.

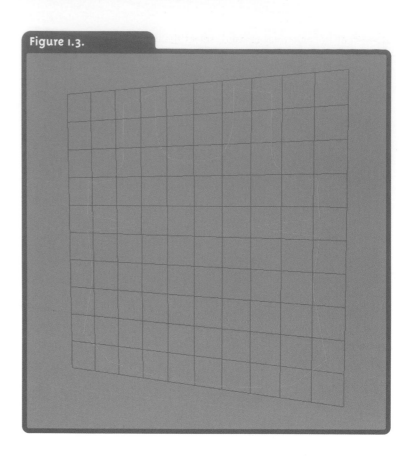

Figure 1.2.

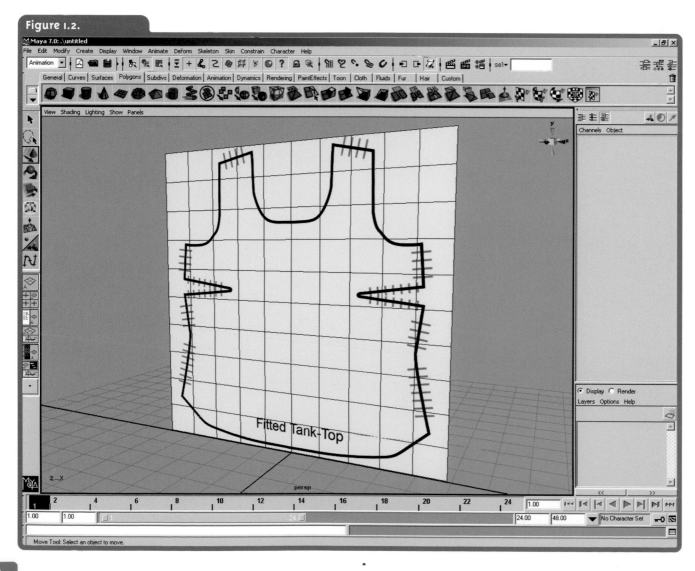

Fitted Tank-Top

4.) With all of the curves created, select them all and execute `Cloth > Create Panel`. If the curves have been placed correctly, a shirt icon should appear in the middle of the curves FIGURE 1.4.

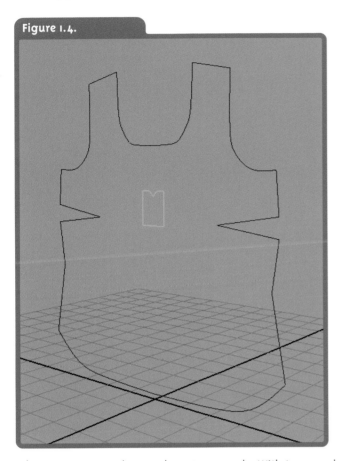

Figure 1.4.

5.) A garment must have at least two panels. With two panels created and placed around your character, you are ready to create the garment. Select one of the panels and execute `Cloth > Create Garment` FIGURE 1.5. This will create a polygonal mesh.

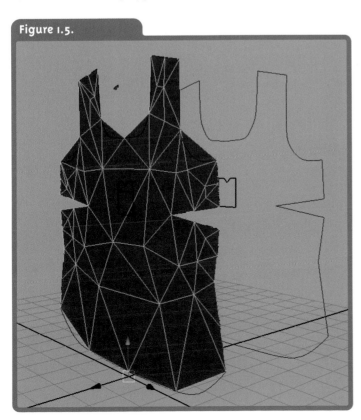

Figure 1.5.

6.) Now you can begin stitching the seams together. Select two curves along a seam and execute `Cloth > Create Seam`. This will 'sew' them together FIGURE 1.6. Continue sewing the garment together where necessary, ensuring that you don't accidentally sew across any arm, leg or head holes.

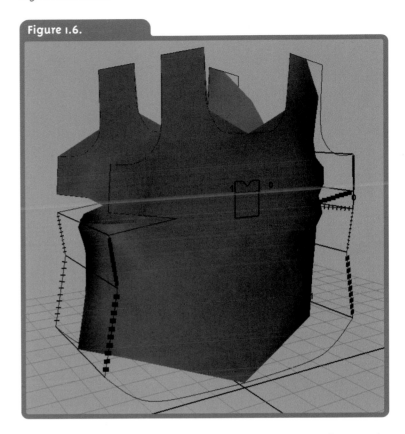

Figure 1.6.

7.) With the garment sewn together, you can move on to adjusting the resolution FIGURE 1.7. before draping and fitting the cloth.

These seven steps demonstrate the high-level method of modeling clothing that Maya Cloth provides you. The workflow may seem foreign to you at first, but that's probably because you've never touched a sewing machine. I'm no expert with a needle myself, but I can assure you that this is exactly how real-world garments are created. It goes: patterns, to panels, to stitching. It's really that simple.

With a garment created in this manner, Maya creates something called a 'stitcher' node. This node controls the tessellation on the resulting polygonal mesh. By adjusting the 'base resolution' attribute on the stitcher node, you can adaptively tessellate the garment to make it as dense (or light) as is necessary FIGURE 1.8. You can even change the density *after* stitching it all together, but be warned, changing the resolution of the mesh requires that you re-simulate/cache to see the effects. For this reason, it is necessary to test different resolutions *before* running your final simulation.

Aside from providing an easy and accurate method of creating clothing, garments have another real advantage, *irregular tessellation*. When you adjust the resolution on the stitcher node, Maya tessellates the geometry in a very chaotic and irregular manner FIGURE 1.9. Because a cloth surface can only bend along its edges, having edges that run in odd directions will enable the cloth to assume any shape.

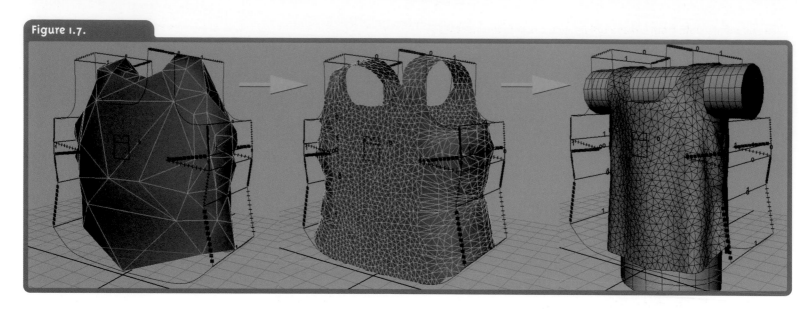

Figure 1.7.

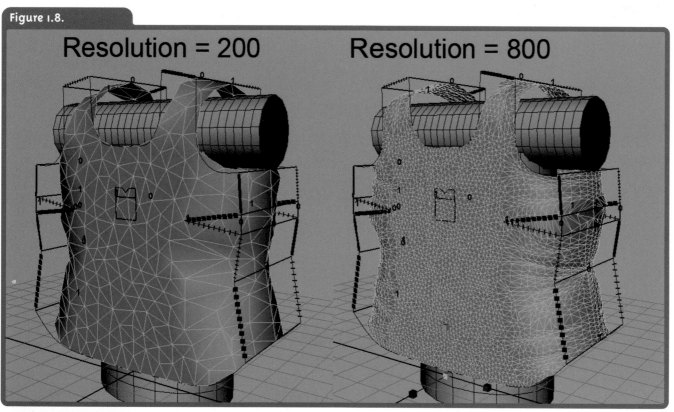

Figure 1.8.

Resolution = 200   Resolution = 800

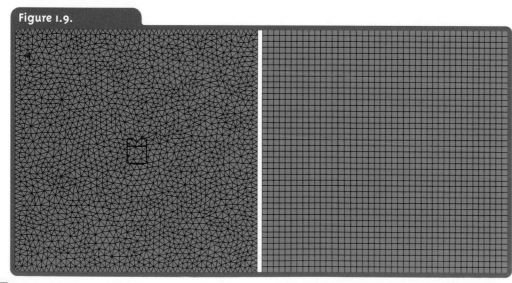

Figure 1.9.

When you create cloth from a Maya object, you cannot take advantage of the adaptive and irregular tessellation, nor can you model the cloth accurately from a pattern. When you create a cloth object, Maya will automatically apply a triangulation operation to the mesh. This can create square looking stress lines that do not look natural when folding FIGURE 1.10. For this reason, it is best to use the garment method wherever possible to create your cloth surfaces.

Figure 1.10.

This is exactly why many studios use Maya Cloth to model their garments, even if the final simulation will be performed with a different simulator, like Syflex. Maya's garments are fast to build, easy to accurately model, and very nicely tessellated for cloth purposes. As an added bonus, the UVs will inherit directly from the 2d panels thus giving you a *perfectly flattened* arrangement with zero distortion FIGURE 1.11. That alone should be enough to convince you that garments really are the bee's knees.

Figure 1.11.

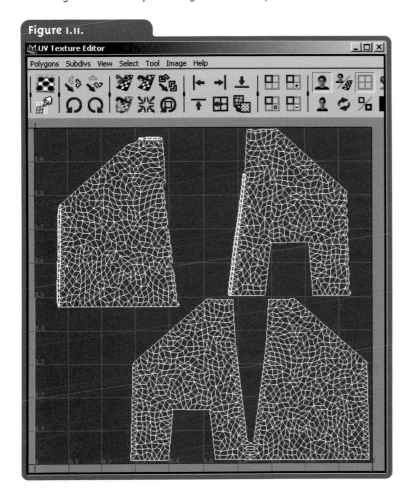

Draping and Fitting the Clothing:

Once your garment has been sewn around your character, it's time to make it look like the character is actually *wearing* your garment. At this point, the garment should be 'floating' around your character with very minimal (or no) interpenetrations. It will look very puffed-up and probably quite awful. Don't worry, the draping and fitting stage will turn this weird, stiff-looking polygon object into a form-fitting piece of clothing FIGURE 1.12.

If you notice the cloth is poking through your character's mesh, you may need to go back to the drawing board and resize your panels. Do all of the re-sizing now, before you waste a bunch of time draping and simulating only to realize that your garment doesn't fit properly. FIGURE 1.13 shows a garment that looks 'suctioned' to the character because the panel curves were too small.

To fit and drape the garment, follow these steps:

1.) **Assign Collision Objects:** Select your character's mesh and choose Cloth > Create Collision Object. Now when your character moves, it will affect the cloth, rather than pass through it. Do this for all of the objects that must collide with the cloth.

2.) **Adjust Collision Objects:** There are some very important parameters that you should be aware of on your collision objects:

Collision Offset: adjust this value to specify how far (in centimeters) you want your cloth object to stay from the collision object. The default is 1 centimeter but you will likely want to adjust this. If you find your cloth object is being pushed outwards during the draping phase, chances are the collision offset is too large and is pushing the cloth surface. Likewise, if the cloth is penetrating your collision object, you can try increasing this offset to push the cloth away. To help you visualize the collision offset, select the collision object and choose Cloth > Create Collision Offset/Depth Mesh. You will see a templated copy of the mesh is displayed around the collision object FIGURE 1.14. If needed, you can paint the offset, per-vertex, by choosing Cloth > Paint Collision Properties Tool. As you paint the collision offset, the templated offset-mesh will update to show you exactly how deep the offset is at any given vertex FIGURE 1.15. To hide the offset mesh, choose Cloth > Remove Collision Offset/Depth Mesh.

Collision Depth: This value specifies the distance (in centimeters) that a vertex on the cloth object will be allowed to penetrate while still being repelled by the collision object FIGURE 1.16. If a vertex passes this threshold, it will effectively pass-through the collision object. If you find vertices are passing through your collision object and not being repelled, increase this value, but do so carefully. If this value becomes too large, it may cause vertices that pass through the collider to be 'sucked' over to the wrong side.

Collision Priority: If two collision objects converge on a piece of cloth, this value will tell the solver which collider has priority. This can help you manage cloth that is 'pinched' between two objects. If two collision objects are affecting the same vertex, the one with the lowest value will take priority. Using integer values between 1 and 3 to specify your collision priorities will do the trick.

Figure 1.12.

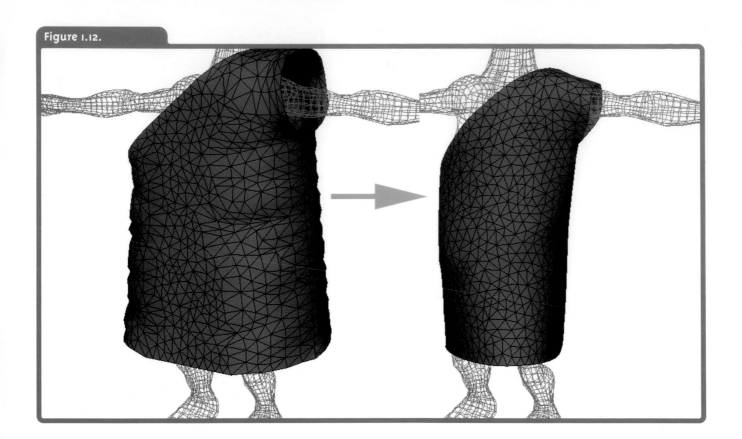

Figure 1.13.

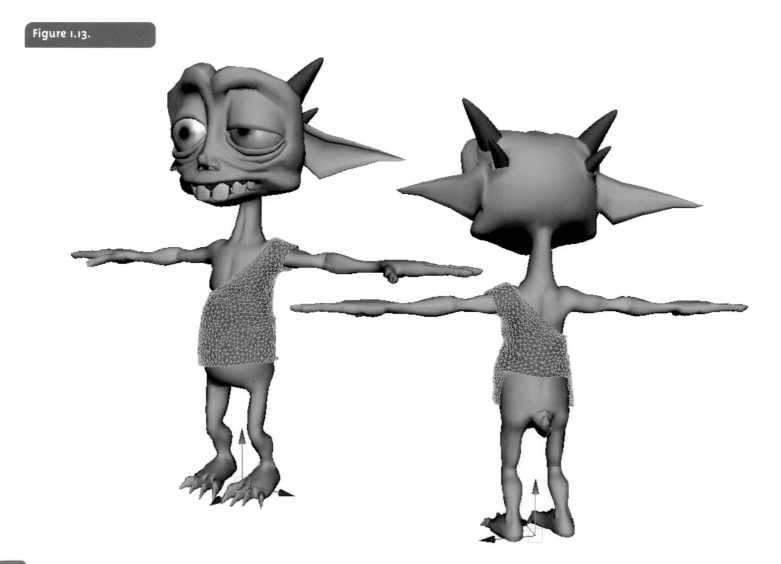

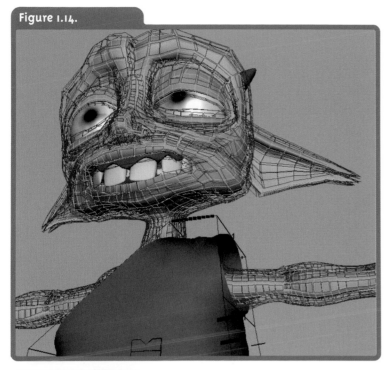

Figure 1.14.

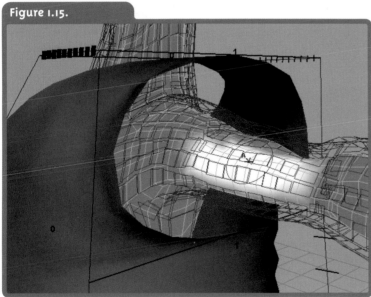

Figure 1.15.

Figure 1.16.

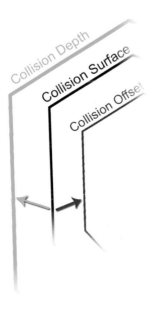

Collision Depth

Collision Surface

Collision Offset

Depth Map Enable: This feature is disabled by default. If you find that you are having real difficulties preventing vertices from passing through the collision object (and adjusting the collision depth is creating more problems), then you may need to adjust the collision depth on a per-vertex basis. By enabling this feature, Maya will actually scan the surface and calculate the ideal collision depth for each vertex at every frame. This can be computationally expensive, but it may solve complex collision issues.

Depth Map Weight: This value specifies a weight factor for the depth map. Leave it alone unless you don't notice any difference after enabling the depth map. If necessary, increase it slightly but be aware that high values may cause solution instability.

Static/Dynamic Friction Multiplier: You can use these to adjust the friction of your collision objects on a per-object basis. Static friction is the cloth-to-cloth friction while dynamic friction refers to friction between the cloth and a separate collision object.

3.) **Adjust Solver Scale:** The 'Solver Scale' attribute on the cpSolver node is extremely important FIGURE 1.17. It affects all of the internal calculations in a global manner. With the solver scale set to 1, Maya assumes that you have modeled your cloth object at real-world scale. At a value of one, if you want a shirt to behave realistically, it should be modeled at the same size as a real shirt (about 60cm). Because your production may be using a different scale, it is often necessary to adjust this value. Calculating the appropriate solver scale is easy. Simply measure the object in Maya (you can use a distance tool) and record this as the 'Maya size'. Now determine how large you want the object to appear when animated. This is the 'real size'. To calculate the solver scale, simply divide the 'real size' by the 'Maya size'. So if my model shirt is 10cm (Maya size) tall and I want it to behave as though it were 60cm (real size) tall, then the solver scale should be set to a value of 6.0 (6 = 60 / 10).

4.) **Do a Local Simulation:** Finally! At this point, we are ready to drape the garment. Select Simulation > Start Local Simulation. Local simulations are extremely useful. They allow you to run the simulation, without playing-back the scene. This means you can tweak the setup to your hearts content while you prepare it for the final animation. While running the local simulation, you should see, over a couple of frames, the garment pull together and wrap around the collision object. Once the garment stops moving, stop the local simulation. If everything went as planned, the garment should be ready to simulate. If you are happy with how it looks, select the mesh and choose Simulation > Save Initial Cloth State. This will set the cloth object so that it will start from that point. If after doing a local simulation, the garment has exploded, ballooned, twisted or otherwise simply not worked, chances are you need to adjust something from steps 1-3. Undo to remove the effects of the local simulation and begin debugging. The trick is figuring out where something went wrong. Take a look at how the cloth is behaving and logically think your way through it. Usually you simply forgot to adjust one of the many different settings on the collision object, solver or garment.

Once the garment is draped over the model and properly fitted, you've already won half the battle. The other half, is simulation. This involves adding constraints, setting forces, running the simulation and finally tweaking the results.

Figure 1.17.

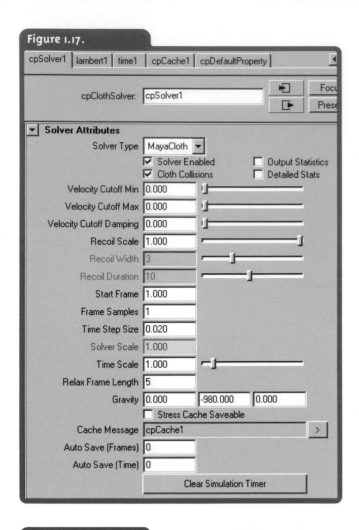

| cpSolver1 | lambert1 | time1 | cpCache1 | cpDefaultProperty |

cpClothSolver: cpSolver1

Focu

Prese

▼ Solver Attributes

Solver Type MayaCloth ▼

☑ Solver Enabled   ☐ Output Statistics
☑ Cloth Collisions   ☐ Detailed Stats

Velocity Cutoff Min   0.000
Velocity Cutoff Max   0.000
Velocity Cutoff Damping 0.000
Recoil Scale   1.000
Recoil Width   3
Recoil Duration   10
Start Frame   1.000
Frame Samples   1
Time Step Size   0.020
Solver Scale   1.000
Time Scale   1.000
Relax Frame Length   5
Gravity   0.000   -980.000   0.000
☐ Stress Cache Saveable
Cache Message   cpCache1   >
Auto Save (Frames)   0
Auto Save (Time)   0

Clear Simulation Timer

Figure 1.18.

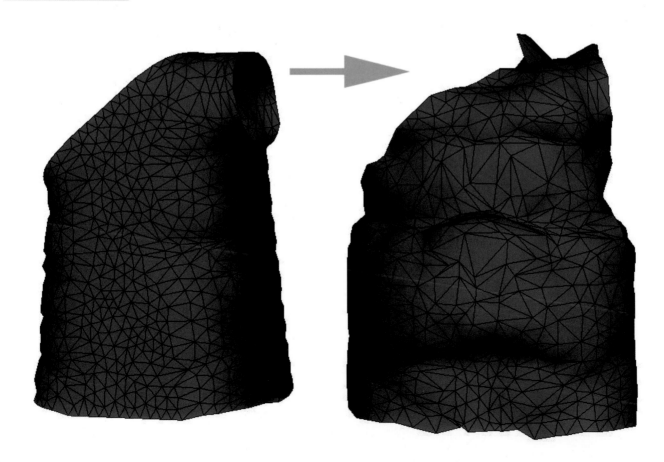

In this exercise, we will be creating a garment for our Goblin character. You may recognize this character from The Art of Rigging Volume 1 where we discussed how to rig him for animation FIGURE 1.19.

Well, now that he has been animated, we need to give him some clothing. The first step in creating any garment is, of course, figuring

Figure 1.19.

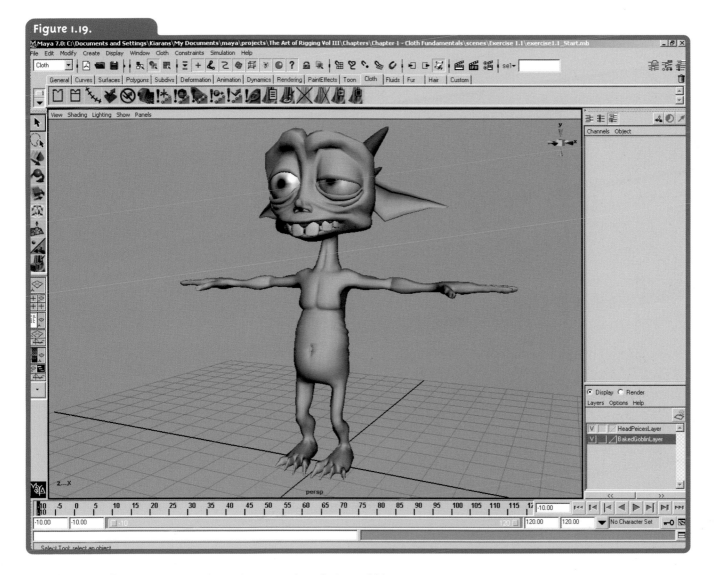

out what type of garment you want to create. We thought it would be cool to dress the goblin like a caveman. After a couple of test sketches, I did a paint-over on the goblin FIGURE 1.20. This is a simple garment that will comprise of only two individual panels; a front and a back.

The following exercise will show you how we created the Goblin's caveman-esque outfit. We start by drawing the pattern from curves, then creating the panels, stitching everything together and then draping it over the character.

I. Cloth simulation requires some preparation. Before you attempt to add clothing to an animated character, it is important that the animation is properly prepared. Your character must start in their 'dress-up' pose (with arms at 90 degrees, facing forward) FIGURE 1.20. There must be at least a 10 frame buffer between this pose and the point at which the actual animation begins. This gives the cloth time to sync-up with the starting pose of the animation. For the goblin, we have animated a walk cycle. To prepare him for clothing, he starts in his dress-up pose at frame -10 and blends into his walk cycle by frame 0 FIGURE 1.21. This way, when we are finished with the simulation, the cloth will look natural at the starting frame (having already been simulated for 10 frames). Open exercise1.1_ Start.mb to see the Goblin prepped for simulation. Notice he begins his walk cycle at frame 0 and continues walking until frame 120 (completing five full cycles).

2. Set the playback to frame -10. The Goblin should be in his dress-up pose, looking like he wants us to give him some clothes. Now, let's create the front panel curves. Import goblinGarmentCurves. mb from the DVD. You should see a set of curves in front and behind the Goblin. These are the finished panel curves FIGURE 1.22. Notice that each edge of the panel is a separate curve and that all of the curves are both planar and form a closed loop. These are the requirements for creating a panel.

Figure 1.20.

Figure 1.21.

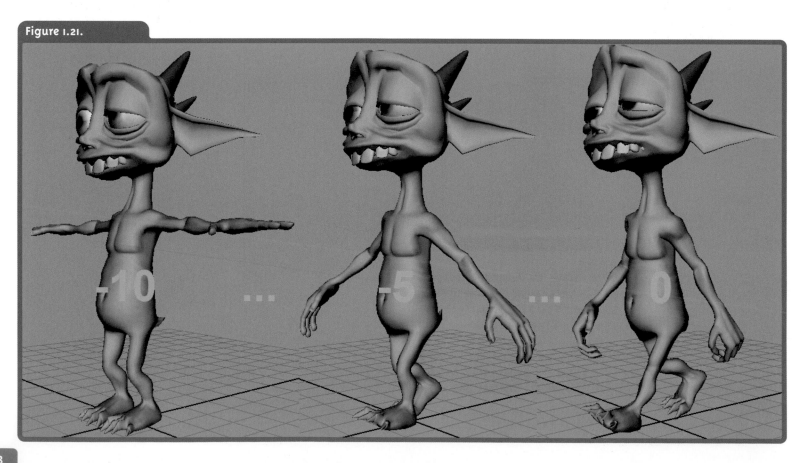

3. While you could skip this step, I encourage you to try and create these curves yourself. Template the imported curves while you draw your own. Drop into the front viewport, activate the CV curve tool and open the tool options. Set the 'Curve Degree' to 'Linear'. You don't have to use linear curves, but for simple garments, straight-edged panels are easier to work with. Now place one edge of the panel by placing two CVs and hitting *Enter*. Each edge must be its own curve! To start

as reference. When you are done, group each set of curves and name the groups 'frontPanelCurves' and 'rearPanelCurves' FIGURE 1.24.

4. With the curves created in an orthographic viewport, you will now need to manually position them around the Goblin. Drop into the perspective view and translate/rotate the groups of curves into place FIGURE 1.25. Again, use the imported curves as reference for where to place them.

Figure 1.22.

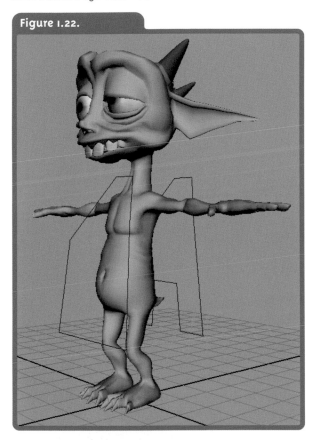

the next edge, hold the C key to curve snap the first CV to the last CV on the previous edge FIGURE 1.23. Keep working in this manner until you have constructed both the front and rear panels. Notice that the rear panel is slightly different. It has an indentation at the bottom where the Goblin's tail will fit. If you get stuck, use the imported curves

Figure 1.24.

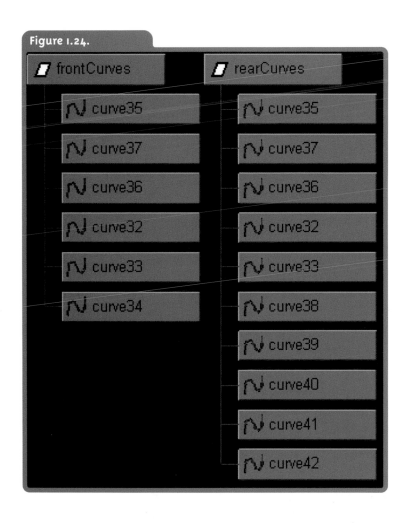

Figure 1.23.

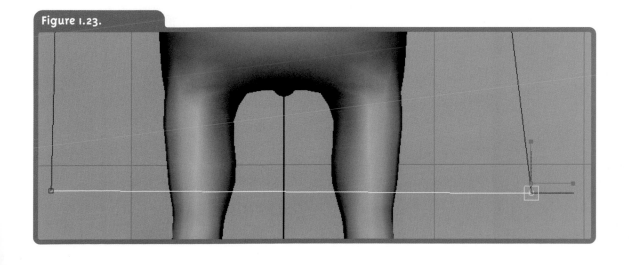

5. Believe it or not, the hard part is done. Open exercise1.1_A.mb to see the Goblin with the properly positioned panel curves. Now select all of the curves in the front panel and choose `Cloth > Create Panel`. A T-shirt icon should appear in the middle of the curves. Do the same for the rear panel FIGURE 1.26.

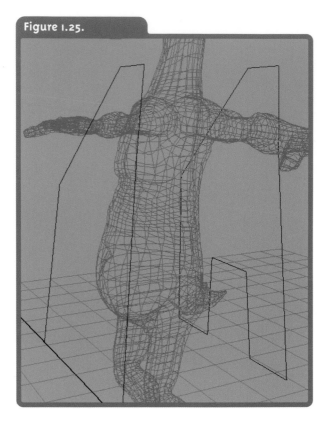

Figure 1.25.

6. Open exercise1.1_B.mb to see the finished panels. Now to create the garment, select one of the panel icons and choose `Cloth > Create Garment`. You should see the panel becomes tessellated FIGURE 1.27.

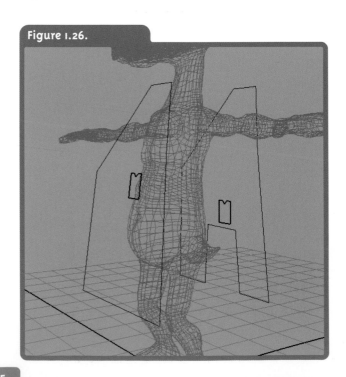

Figure 1.26.

7. At this point, we have a flat polygon garment. Not very exciting. Let's stitch-up the front/rear panels to create the full garment. There are three places that need seams; the left and right sides and the top piece (over the shoulder). To create a seam,

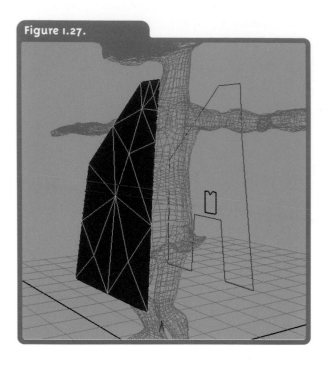

Figure 1.27.

select the corresponding panel curves on the front and rear panels and choose `Cloth > Create Seam`. After doing this, you should have a very primitive looking garment FIGURE 1.28.

8. Open exercise1.1_C.mb to see the fully seamed garment. At this point, the garment is quite blocky. We will be needing a lot more resolution to see any detailed folding or collisions. Adjusting the resolution of a cloth garment is simple. Select the garment and find the cpStitcher node attached to it. This node contains the Base Resolution

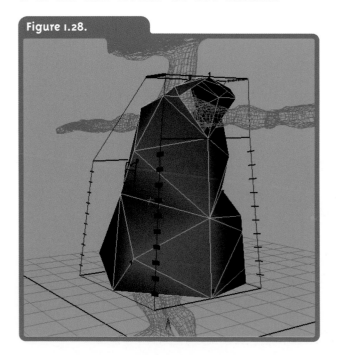

Figure 1.28.

attribute. Set this to a value of 800 to re-tessellate the garment and give it plenty of resolution FIGURE 1.29.

9. Open exercise1.1_D.mb to see the properly tessellated garment. Now let's setup the solver scale so we can drape the clothing on the character. To calculate the solver scale, we divide the 'real size' (50cm) by the 'Maya size' (4.3cm) FIGURE 1.30. This gives us a value of 12.5 (if you don't follow, please read the previous section on calculating solver

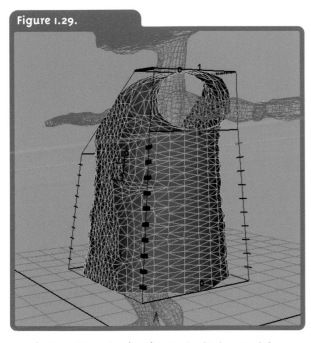

Figure 1.29.

scale). Plug this value (12.5) into the 'Solver Scale' attribute on the cpSolver node FIGURE 1.31.

10. To prevent the garment from passing through the Goblin, let's setup the collisions. Select the Goblin's mesh and choose Cloth > Create Collision Object. The mesh will automatically be set to collide with all garments on the current solver.

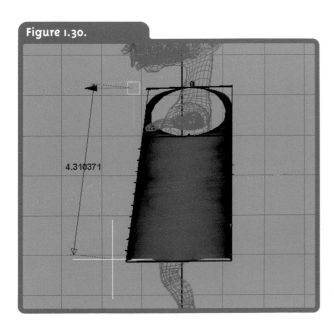

Figure 1.30.

4.310371

Figure 1.31.

INPUTS
 cpSolver1
 time1
 cpCache1
 cpStitcher1
ion Obj Debug Enable | off
           Start Frame | 1
        Frame Samples | 1
        Time Step Size | 0.02
           Time Scale | 1
          Solver Scale | 12.5

11. Open exercise1.1_E.mb to see the garment with the proper solver scale and collision object. At this point, we are ready to start draping the garment. Draping is done with the *local* simulation. While simply playing-back the scene *will* drape the cloth, it will also create a cache and, at frame 10, the animation will begin. At this point, we do not want to simulate the walk cycle. We only want to drape the cloth onto the stationary character. To start the local simulation, choose Simulation > Start Local Simulation. You should see the garment moving around the character, but it's not going to be perfect FIGURE 1.32. Hit Esc to stop the local simulation.

12. If the local simulation appears to stop (or nothing happens), hit *Esc*. At this point, the garment will *not* be draping properly. *Ctrl+Z* to undo the local simulation. The reason for this is simple; we have not adjusted our collision properties. Select the goblin mesh and choose

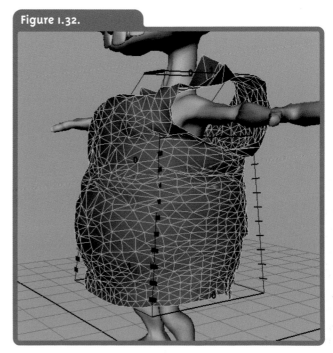

Figure 1.32.

Cloth > Create Collision Offset/Depth Mesh. You should see a large purple mesh encompass the Goblin FIGURE 1.33. This represents the mesh that the cloth is *actually* colliding with. Because the collision offset is so large, the garment is penetrating before it has a chance to collide. Let's fix this. Grab the Goblin mesh and set the Collision Offset to 0.1 and the Collision Depth to 0.2. Now the offset representation should be much closer to the real mesh FIGURE 1.34.

13. Open exercise1.1_F.mb to see the garment with the properly adjusted collision object. Start the local simulation again. This time, the cloth should wrap around the Goblin. It may take a minute, but don't stop the local simulation until the cloth has settled on the character and stopped moving. If

the cloth is misbehaving or crashing through the Goblin, you have a couple of options.

- On the solver node, set the frame samples to a value between 2 and 10. The higher this value, the more accurate the simulation is (but the longer it will take).
- If adjusting the frame samples does not help, you can adjust the time step. Set this to a value between 0.02 and 0.005. This attribute works with the frame samples to determine how accurate the simulation is. Again, lowering this value will cause the simulation to slow down.
- If adjusting the accuracy of the simulation does not help, you can try adjusting the Relax Frame Length attribute. By default, it is set to 5. Increase it to a value of 10 and see if that helps.
- Work methodically. Draping cloth can be time consuming, but you just have to trial/error your way through it; 90% of the time the solver just needs a little coaxing to get it working right.

14. When you are happy with the way the cloth is draping, make one last check to ensure that there are no stray vertices (vertices stuck to each other or penetrating the collision objects). You can manually tweak the vertices if there are very minor problems. When all is good, select the mesh and choose Simulation > Save as Initial Cloth State FIGURE 1.35. Now the cloth will always start from that position.

15. Open exercise1.1_Finished.mb to see the final draped garment on the Goblin FIGURE 1.36.

At this point, the garment is prepared for the final simulation. Simulating the garment usually requires a lot of back and forth tweaking. By setting-up constraints, fields, and collisions, the simulation can achieve the precise look you are going for. Before we dive into the details of simulating, there is one more thing to take care of with regard to the garment.

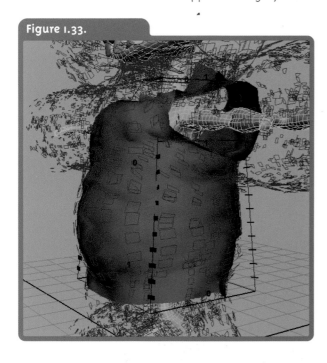

Figure 1.33.

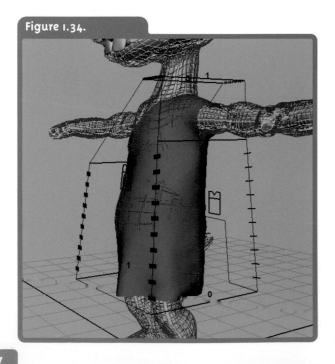

Figure 1.34.

Figure 1.35.

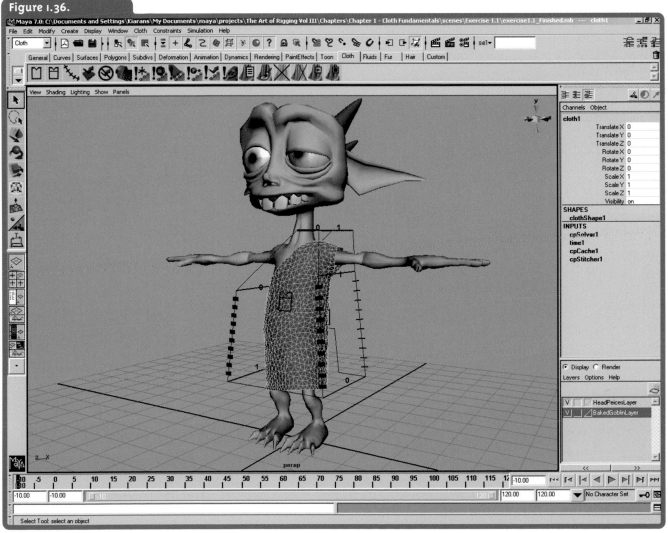

Figure 1.36.

Creating the 'Renderable' Cloth Garment:

How do you get that 'garment' and turn it into a realistic looking piece of cloth? This is probably the most common problem novices have with cloth simulation. You've got your garment stitched, draped and ready for simulation. The simulation was a breeze, the clothing looks fabulous, but there is still one glaring problem FIGURE 1.37. The cloth looks like paper because it's completely flat!

Simulating thick cloth is a guaranteed disaster. There are two options for adding thickness to your garments. Both methods are always applied *after* the simulation is cached:

Figure 1.38.

Now when the simulation garment deforms, the render garment will come along for the ride. In FIGURE 1.39, the green-wireframe mesh has been wrap deformed by the lower resolution gray-wireframe cloth object.

Figure 1.37.

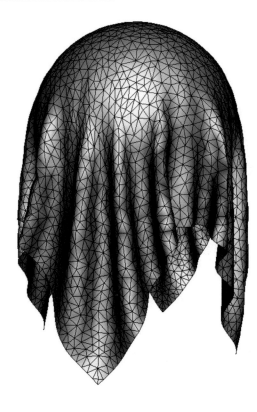

1. Extrude: Once the garment is simulated and cached, select all of the faces and extrude them outwards slightly before applying a smooth operation FIGURE 1.38. The animation will remain intact, and the cloth will look thick. With this method, you can generate thick cloth in seconds, *but* the cloth will still look like a thick version of the original garment (no added details). For further refinement of the mesh, you have to go with the second method.

2. Wrap Deformer: While the garment is draped (and before simulation), you can duplicate the mesh. This copy can then be wrap deformed to the original garment. The advantage of using this method is that you can then edit the copy in any way you like. It's usually best to quadrangulate and extrude the mesh. Detail may be added by modeling trim and adding props like zippers and buttons. Once the render version of the garment is fully modeled, delete the history and wrap deform (Deform > Create Wrap) the high-resolution garment to the simulation garment.

Figure 1.39.

Here are some tips for creating nice looking render garments:

■ Quadrangulate the garment (Polygons > Quadrangulate) before you smooth. This will result in a much smoother-looking mesh. The polySmooth operation does not work as well on a triangulated mesh and will generate ugly smoothing artifacts FIGURE 1.40. By quadrangulating before you smooth, these artifacts will disappear.

Figure 1.40.

Triangles > Smoothed > Rendered

Quads > Smoothed > Rendered

■ Add trim around the garment. Depending on the look you are going for, you may wish to have a trim around the openings on your garment FIGURE 1.41. Snap a curve around the opening, then extrude a cube face along the curve. Tweak the curve to line-up with the garment, and then wrap the trim along with the rest of the garment.

Figure 1.41.

Figure 1.42.

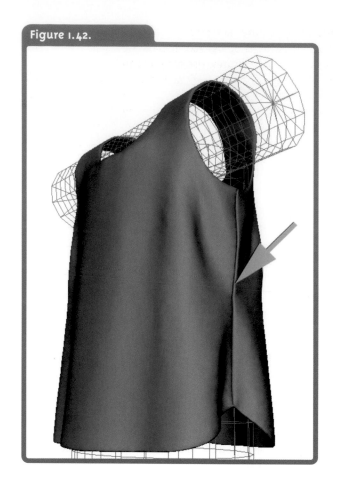

- Model creases into the seams. Wherever two panels were seamed together, there will be a perfectly straight loop of edges. Grab one of the edges, expand the selection (`Edit Polygons > Selection > Contiguous Edges`). With the whole loop selected, apply a small bevel. Now select the newly created line of faces and extrude them into the garment slightly. Voila! When smoothed, this will look like a very convincing seam in the fabric FIGURE 1.42.

- Layout the UVs. After you extrude the surface, open the UV texture editor and select all of the UVs. From the texture editor menu choose `Polygons > Layout UVs`. Reset the options and turn 'Separate' to 'Off'. When you hit 'Apply' the UVs should be nicely arranged in the 0-1 space with absolutely zero distortion FIGURE 1.43.

Figure 1.43.

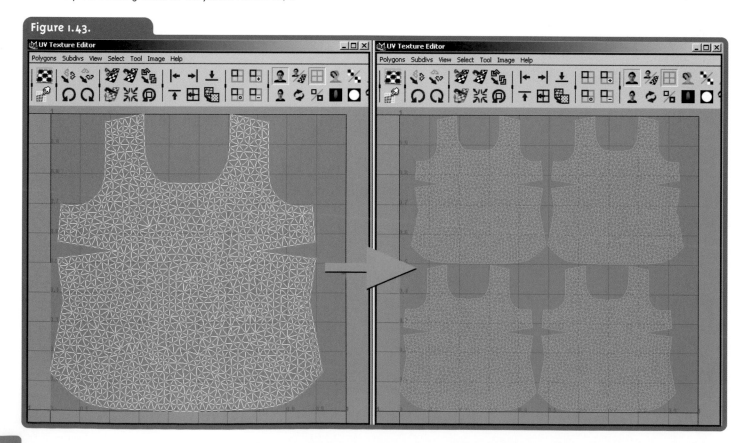

- Use a repeating texture. Remember, real fabrics are constructed from repeated patterns of weaved threads. Get creative with one of Maya's procedural textures. Use the procedural to create a base pattern. When you are happy with how it looks, you can bake the texture (`Edit > Convert to File Texture`) from the hypershade menu. Now bring it into Photoshop to add any custom designs or coffee stains. FIGURE 1.44 shows a texture created from a simple shader network with a cloth procedural and some fractals. Because the UVs are perfectly arranged, repeating textures usually look great on garments.

Figure 1.44.

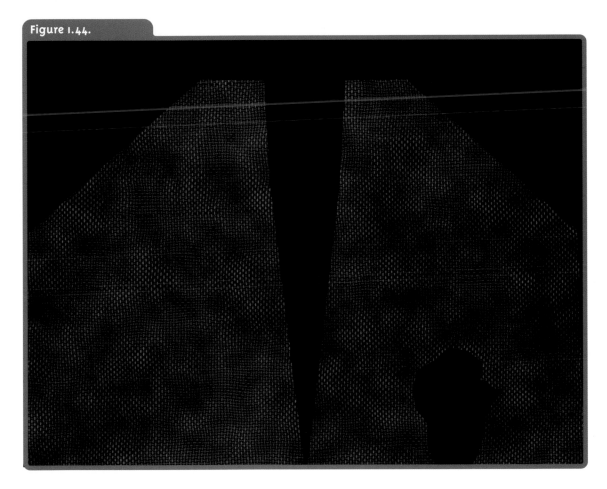

- Add lots of extra stuff! Buttons and zippers are the most obvious but many garments can really get a boost of realism simply by adding a few pockets or a collar. If it suites the character, cut some small holes where the material has worn-out or make some of the openings uneven and ratty.

Obviously, the wrap deformer method provides the most flexibility. You can re-work the cloth model to add the details that will make the cloth look truly remarkable. You may notice that the wrap deformer can be somewhat slow to calculate. In chapter four, we will counter this problem by baking the deformations. This allows the creation of clean, stable cloth animations with no CPU-sucking node-history.

Using the techniques outlined above, we are going to create a renderable version of the Goblin's garment. This version will include modeled seams, trim around the openings, proper UV layout, thickness, and better topology for smoothing.

Once we have created the render garment, we will set it to be deformed by the simulated garment (via a wrap deformer). The workflow goes like this:

A. Duplicate the simulated garment from its initial state.
B. Make changes on the duplicate.
C. Setup the wrap deformer.

So we begin the process exactly where we left-off in exercise 1.1, with a draped garment, ready for simulation…

1. Open exercise1.2_Start.mb. This is the exact same file from the end of the last exercise. In this file, we have the Goblin creature with his draped garment ready for simulation FIGURE 1.45. It is extremely important that you are happy with the way the garment is draped before you duplicate

it to create the render (high-res) garment. If you change its initial state, the render garment will not be deformed precisely with the simulation garment which will cause inaccuracies after they are wrap deformed.

2. Let's finalize the draping of the Goblin's cloth. I want the cloth to hang more loosely on the Goblin. Increase the Density of the cloth property to a value of 0.02. This will create a more 'heavy', dynamic looking cloth surface FIGURE 1.46. Do another local simulation until the cloth stops sagging, then save the initial state. If the local simulation causes the cloth to misbehave, *CTRL+Z* to undo and try it again (sometimes the first local simulation will bug-out).

3. Open exercise1.2_A.mb to see the Goblin after adjusting the draping. We are now ready to begin work on the render garment. Select the cloth object and duplicate it. Rename the new mesh 'goblinRenderGarment'. Export this mesh (File > Export Selection, with no history) and bring it into a new scene. Keeping the garment in a separate scene is a good idea FIGURE 1.47.

Figure 1.45.

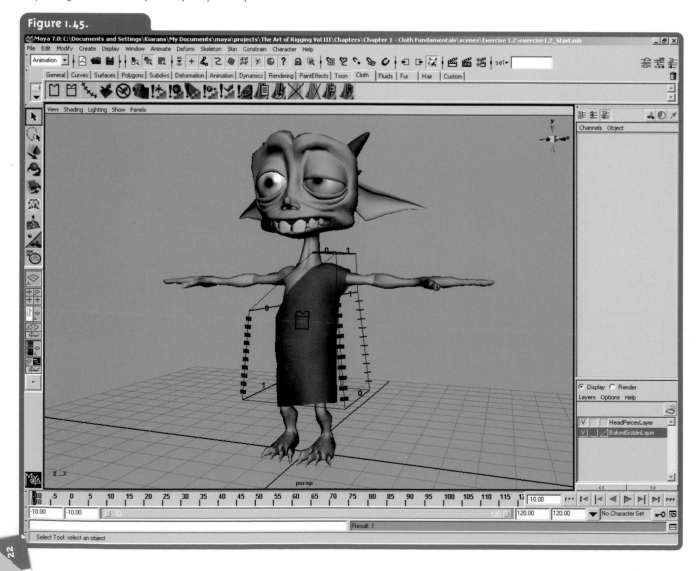

Figure 1.46.

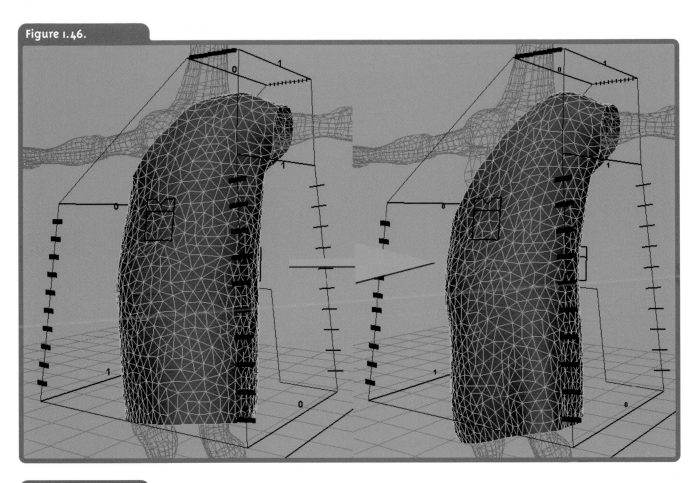

Figure 1.47.

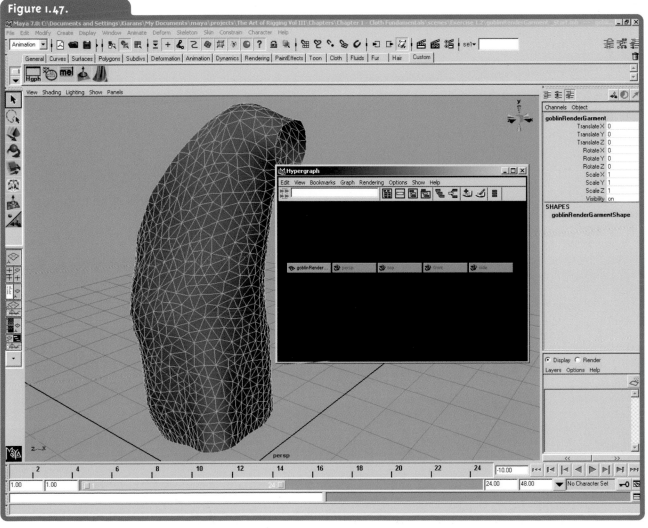

4. Open goblinRenderGarmentStart.mb. This file contains only the duplicate garment mesh. Now let's get to work on it. First, select the mesh and apply `Polygons > Quadrangulate`. Now that the mesh is mostly quads, it should look much better when smoothed FIGURE 1.48.

FIGURE 1.48.

Figure 1.49.

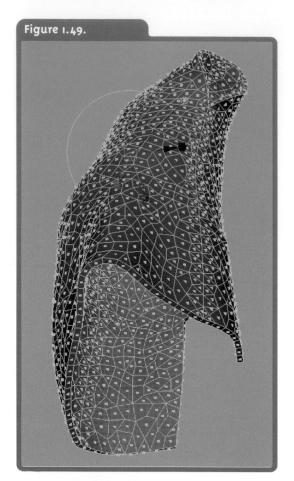

Figure 1.48.

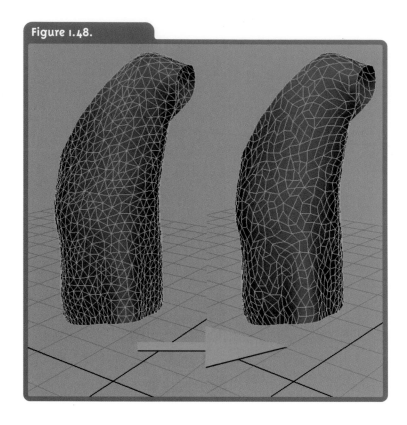

5. To add thickness, select all of the faces and apply `Edit Polygons > Extrude Face`. You can use the manipulator to pull the extrusion to the desired thickness or type a value of 0.035 into the 'Local Translate Z' attribute on the polyExtrudeFace input FIGURE 1.49.

6. Open goblinRenderGarment_A.mb to see the garment after adding thickness and quadrangulating. To break-up the surface, let's model some seams where we stitched the panels together. Select the row of edges running down the garment, under the arm opening. This is where the two panels were stitched together. Apply a bevel with an offset of about 0.8. Now select the newly created faces (in the bevel) and extrude them inwards about -0.02 units FIGURE 1.50. Do the same for the other two seams on the garment (down the right side, and along the shoulder).

7. Open goblinRenderGarment_B.mb to see the garment with the modeled seams. Now before we get any further, let's lay-out the UV's. Open the texture editor and select all of the UV's on the mesh. Choose `Polygons > Layout UVs` (default options, check 'Separate' off). The UVs should be nicely arranged like in FIGURE 1.51. If you extruded seams,

Figure 1.50.

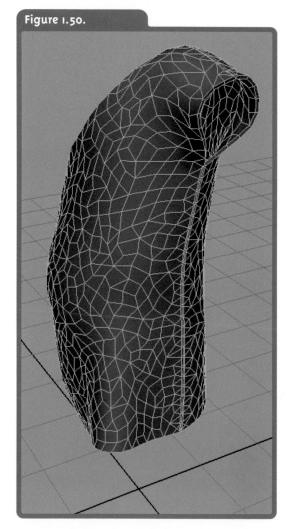

Figure 1.51.

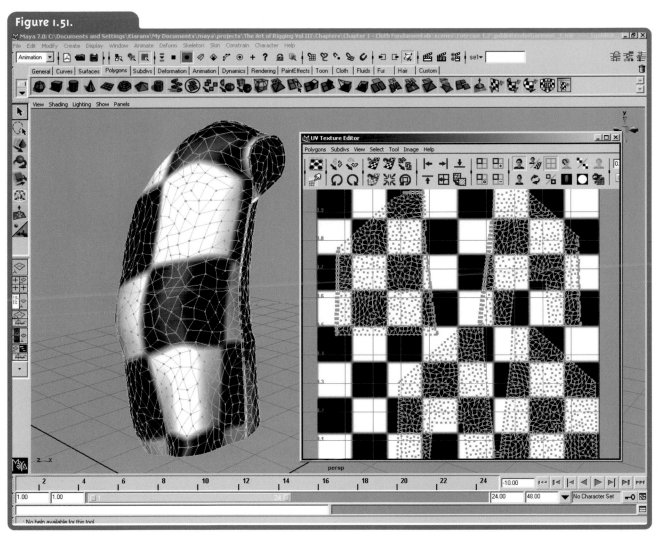

Figure 1.52.

you will have to layout the UVs along these seams manually. Once the mesh is properly unwrapped, delete the history and move on.

8. Open goblinRenderGarment_C.mb to see the garment with the properly layed-out UVs. Now let's create some trim. You can model trimming however you like, but this method has worked well for me: Make the garment Live. Draw a NURBS curve directly on the surface around each opening. Create a polygon cube. Snap it to the beginning of the curve and then scale it to the width you want your trim to be FIGURE 1.52. Now you can extrude one of the cube's faces along the length of the curve. Adjust the number of divisions on the extrude history node to create your trim surface FIGURE 1.53. You can tweak the shape of the trim by editing the curve. You can find all of the curves I used (before extrusion) in the goblinTrimCurves file on the DVD.

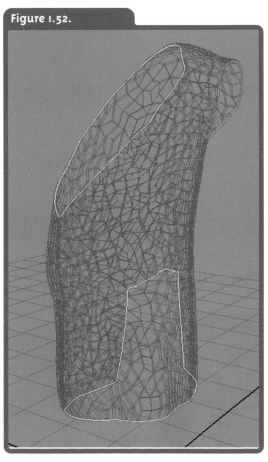

Figure 1.53.

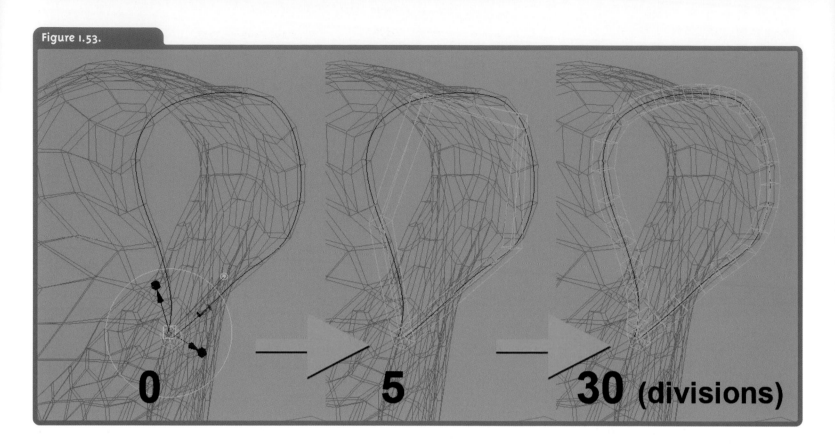

0 ─▶ **5** ─▶ **30** (divisions)

9. Open goblinRenderGarment_Final.mb to see the finished garment with trimming around the openings. At this point, we are finished the render garment and are ready to connect it to the simulation garment. Open exercise1.2_A.mb. This file contains the Goblin with the draped simulation garment. Now import goblinRenderGarment_Final. Place the render garment (with the trimming) and the simulation garment into separate layers FIGURE 1.54.

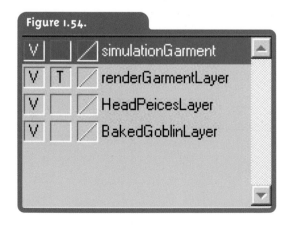

Figure 1.54.

10. Open exercise1.2_B.mb to see the Goblin with the imported render garment. To make the render garment deform with the simulation garment, we are going to use a wrap deformer. Select the render garment, shift select the simulation garment and choose `Deform > Create Wrap > Options`. To improve the performance of the wrap deformer, set the Max Distance to a value of 0.2. To finish the setup, wrap deform the trimming to

the simulation garment FIGURE 1.55. You can verify that the deformer is working correctly by moving some vertices on the simulation garment, and observing the effect on the render garment.

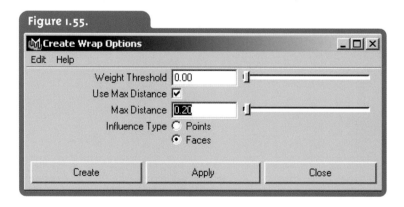

Figure 1.55.

11. That completes the creation and setup of the Goblin's render garment. When the flat garment is now simulated, the high-resolution, 'thick' garment will deform along with it. Open exercise1.2_Finished.mb to see the final setup.

Once you have the simulation garment draped and fitted, and the render garment has been prepared and setup, you are finally ready to simulate. Simulation can be an involved process. Once you get familiar with the workflow, simulating garments can actually be a lot of fun!

Simulation:

We are finally ready to finish the clothing. The last step in cloth animation is running the simulation. This will step through each frame in the animation, while the solver calculates the position of each vertex in the mesh. These vertex positions are then stored into a cache file that is saved on the hard drive. Once the cache is finished, playback will be in real-time. No further calculations are needed.

To control exactly how the cloth is animated, you must tailor the simulation to your particular animation. This involves adding collision objects, setting the cloth properties, adjusting the solver, adding forces and creating constraints. Successfully simulating a garment can be troublesome if you don't have a good understanding of all the options available to you. This section includes full discussions of the many different tools for controlling cloth. Once the big picture is clear, we will tackle an example by simulating the Goblin's garment (continuing the walk-cycle from the last exercise).

The Solver:

The cpSolver node is where the magic happens. The solver node is responsible for all of the actual calculations. All of the global controls (those that affect the entire simulation) are housed here for your convenience. There are several parameters on the solver to be aware of:

The Starting Frame: The Start Frame attribute controls the frame at which the simulation will start. The cloth will simply remain stationary during playback until this frame is reached. Often times, the character may start in the dress-up pose before blending into the beginning of the animation at frame 0. If this is the case, lower the start frame so the simulation begins when the character starts moving.

The Solver Accuracy: This is very important. Remember that the solver works by calculating the position of every vertex at each frame. It does this by iterating through each frame and calculating the displacement due to forces (like collisions and gravity). If the animation is particularly fast, then there may be a large difference from one frame, to the next. This means that the solver may not 'see' what happens in-between. If you notice that the cloth surface is passing through collision objects (even though the collision offset is adequate), the solver may need more accuracy. You can adjust the Frame Samples attribute to tell the solver how many times to calculate the cloth between each frame. For quick animations, 5 samples per frame is usually adequate. The Time Step Size works in conjunction with the Frame Samples to determine how many samples are calculated every second. Try lowering the Time Step Size by tiny amounts to increase the solver accuracy. Remember, this will slow the simulation. It can be useful to animate these values so that the simulation is extremely accurate during quick movements, and more responsive when there is little or no movement.

Gravity: The solver node contains its own gravity field. Because gravity is almost always needed, it is integrated directly into the solver. The forces are in cm/s*s units, so an earthly gravitational force is -980 which is -9.8m/s*s. This value will scale appropriately with the solver scale, so it is not necessary to manually adjust it unless you want a custom

effect. FIGURE 1.56 shows a piece of cloth with gravity set to -200 and -980 respectively.

Figure 1.56.

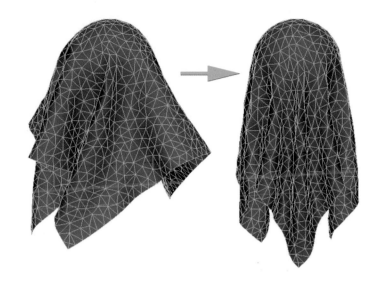

Relaxing: Do not make the mistake of forgetting about the Relax Frame Length attribute on the solver node. This specifies the number of frames at the beginning of the simulation to 'relax' the garment. A relaxed garment is given a rubbery property and ignores some forces applied to it (but will react to collisions). This is primarily used for pulling a stitched garment together after seaming. Once the garment is draped onto the character, relaxation is no longer needed and will actually *interfere* with the simulation. Remember to set this value to '0' after draping your garment to prevent unwanted relaxation at the beginning of the simulation.

Velocity Cutoff: This feature is not always needed, but at times, when the cloth is at rest, you may notice slight vibrations or 'popping' vertices. There are three attributes on the solver node used to control these stray vertices. The Velocity Cutoff Min and Max specify a minimum and maximum speed (in distance/seconds). Any vertex that is traveling within that range will be damped according to the Velocity Cutoff Damping value. What values you use here will be dependent on the scene scale and playback speed. First, find the distance that the popping vertices are moving between each frame (X). Then divide X by the current frame rate (1/24 for film, 1/30 for TV). For example, if the popping vertices are moving between 0.04 and 0.09 units, between frames (and you are animating at 1/30 fps), the Velocity Min should be set to 1.2 and Max to 2.7 (1.2 = .04/(1/30)). Just like with all minor solver adjustments, you should keyframe these values for the duration of the problem (rather than the entire simulation).

Solver Scale: This value controls the scale of the entire simulation. This value should be adjusted during the draping phase. If the cloth object is not being draped, then remember to adjust it before simulation. See page 11 for a full explanation of Solver Scale.

Time Scale: Like the Solver Scale, this value affects the entire simulation. It does so by controlling the input from the 'time' node in the dependency graph. Higher values will cause the simulation to run faster. Smaller values will cause the simulation to run at a fraction of the scene time. It is very rare that you will need this feature. Just know that it is there and that it should be set to '1' for a normal simulation.

Adaptation Control: Sometimes, the solver may have trouble computing a solution. If the simulation is carefully setup, and all of the involved geometries are clean and well prepared, it is unlikely to fail. Should the solver encounter a problem, it will turn to the Adaptation Control to determine what it should do. In addition to doing nothing, or stopping the simulation, you can tell the solver to 'adapt' to the problem by automatically adjusting the Frame Samples and/or Time Step. Most problems can be manually tweaked away, but this feature becomes useful for batch processing where a human may not be present to babysit the simulation.

Recoil: At times, a cloth object may appear to 'slide' across a stationary collision surface and may even *gain* momentum. The recoil attribute can help control this unwanted behavior by allowing you to dampen the energy from collisions. This is a much welcomed new feature in Maya 7.0. Recoil is very simple. By adjusting the Recoil Scale, you can scale the amount of energy that is retained by a vertex after a collision. A value of 0.5 will damp half of the energy from collisions. You can gain more control over the recoiling with the Recoil Width and Recoil Duration. Adjust the Recoil Width to tell the solver how many rows of edges are affected by the damping (from the point of collision). The Recoil Duration specifies the number of solver steps, after the collision, that will be affected by the damping. Recoil can also be cheated by applying drag and friction to the cloth, but the new recoil features in Maya 7.0 are far better suited to this task.

Enable / Disable: It will be necessary to disable the solver if you want to setup any further animation without hindrance. This is done with the Solver Enabled attribute. Additionally, collisions can be enabled/disabled with the Cloth Collisions attribute.

The solver node contains the 'brains' of the simulation. Complete familiarity with all of its available features will make animating cloth much easier. I have seen many people disregard Maya Cloth for its apparent 'bugginess' when, in actuality, their issues could have been resolved by committing the ½ hour that it takes to know how the solver works. Once the solver has been mastered, the rest is cake.

Collisions:

Cloth animation is useless without collisions. Fortunately, they are very simple to setup. We have already discussed collisions in the Draping and Fitting section, but there are some additional caveats to be aware of. Here are some important points to remember when setting-up collisions for cloth animation:

Only Edges Matter: Collisions are calculated whenever an edge on the cloth object comes into contact with an edge on the collision geometry. The solver does not understand the concept of a 'surface'. It can only *see* wireframes. This is both good and bad. It's good because the solver only has to sample the edges of the mesh (thus allowing for fast cloth simulation). On the flip-side, this can lead to situations where the cloth object and the collision object will penetrate where there is inadequate resolution. Just keep this in mind while constructing collision surfaces. It can help to think of the surface as a pasta strainer. Areas without edges are like holes that can allow your pasta/cloth object to slip through. FIGURE 1.57 shows a collision object that is penetrating the cloth due to inadequate tessellation.

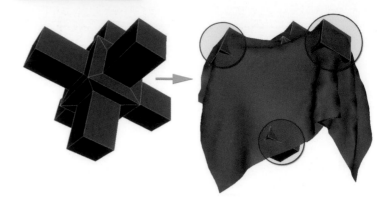

Figure 1.57.

Only Polygon Surfaces Collide: Cloth cannot collide with NURBS hulls or subdivision surfaces. If you try to make a NURBS or subdivision surface a collision object, Maya will first convert it to polygons. It is best to avoid this altogether and stick with polygons from the beginning (for the best control over edge placement).

Collision Depth and Offset: See the previous section on Draping and Fitting Clothing for a complete discussion of these parameters. These almost *always* must be manually adjusted for each particular collision object.

Friction: Friction is the term used in physics to describe the loss of energy that occurs when two surfaces slide against one-another. When an object is assigned to collide with a piece of cloth, there are several custom attributes that are added to the collider's shape node. The Static Friction and Dynamic Friction attributes are scale factors that determine how much friction is added to the system. The static friction is the friction between the cloth itself. A low static friction will give you the slippery, satin-esque behavior. Dynamic friction is the friction used between two moving surfaces (the cloth and its collision object). Because these are scale factors, values between 0 and 1 will reduce the friction, while values greater than 1 will scale it proportionately. The final static and dynamic friction values are computed by multiplying the friction values from the collision object, by the friction values from the cloth property. For this reason, it is best to only adjust the friction values on the collision objects and leave the property values at their default of 1. It can get confusing if you start adjusting the friction on both nodes.

Collisions are a vital part of every cloth simulation. The collision depth and offset parameters are the culprits behind many frustrations with Maya Cloth. Knowing how to tweak all of these values will help you yield predictable results from your collision objects.

Cloth Properties:

The cloth property node houses all of the attributes that are specific to a particular *type* of cloth FIGURE 1.58. Typically, all cloth animations should start with the default cloth property. This property is guaranteed to react in a predictable manner given a properly tuned solver. It behaves in a manner typical of a light cotton fabric. Once the cloth is behaving properly with the default property, you can begin to customize it to suit the particular garment. Every effect from silk, to rubber or even paper can be simulated by adjusting the properties of the cloth.

Figure 1.58.

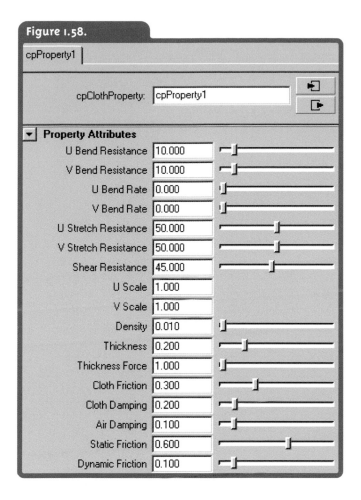

Figure 1.59.

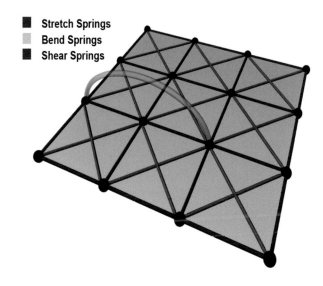

■ Stretch Springs
■ Bend Springs
■ Shear Springs

Shearing springs flow along the diagonal edges of the mesh and across faces. When the cloth is pulled parallel to the direction of its threads, its shear strength determines how it will hold together.

It is the combination of these three properties, along with the mass of the individual particles that define how a fabric will behave under stress. The following attributes can be adjusted on the cloth property node to tweak the behavior of the cloth:

Quick Note: Keep in mind, the U and V values correspond to the 2D directions across the cloth surface. Unless you want the cloth to behave in an anisotropic manner, keep the values the same.

U/V Bend Resistance: Controls the resistance to bending along the U and V directions. Quite simply, higher values yield stiffer cloth. FIGURE 1.60

U/V Bend Rate: This one may not be obvious. As a piece of cloth is bent, and the bend angle is decreasing, its resistance can be lessened. Imagine bending an iron bar. When it is straight, the force must be very large to bend the pipe. Once it is in a bent shape, it has less resistance to bending. The U/V bend rate will adjust the resistance based on the angle between the cloth vertices. A value of 0 will provide a constant resistance (regardless of the angle) while a value of 1 will cause the resistance to be much greater when the cloth is straight (and weaker when bent).

U/V Stretch Resistance: Controls the resistance to stretching along the U and V directions. Lower values yield stretchy cloth FIGURE 1.61.

Shear Resistance: Shearing resistance cannot be applied in an anisotropic manner (U/V). Higher values will prevent triangles from shearing under parallel, opposite forces. FIGURE 1.62

U/V Scale: This value will scale the actual size of the panels. A value of 0.5 will make a cloth panel half the size. You can use this to make minor tailoring adjustments after sewing the garment, but do not rely on it.

Density: Very important. This value controls the mass of the particles in the cloth object. Increase this value from 0.01 to 0.1 to create heavy looking cloth that will droop over your collision objects FIGURE 1.63.

As you know, canvas folds differently than satin, but what is it that makes some fabrics react differently? Recall that all man-made fabrics are comprised of threaded yarns. If the yarns are tightly woven and stiff (like those in a piece of canvas), the fabric will resist *bending*. Materials like paper towel *bend* very easily, but resist *shearing*. Materials like rubber will resist shearing, yet it will bend *and* stretch quite easily. These three properties; bending, stretching and shearing, can define the multitude of different fabrics we see in the real world.

It can help to understand how the cloth solver internally represents these properties. The shear, bend and stretch properties are applied to their own individual springs that are connected (like a web) across the entire cloth surface between each vertex and its neighbors. This is why it is called a *spring*-mass solver. The springs are used to connect the vertices (the masses) in a way that forces them to behave like a fabric. There are three types of springs (FIGURE 1.59) that are affected by the three main cloth properties:

Stretching springs flow along the *straight* edges of the mesh between each vertex. When force is applied to a vertex, the stretching spring determines how much it will displace in relation to its neighbors. Weak stretching springs will allow a vertex to move away from its neighbors, thus stretching the cloth.

Bending springs connect two vertices that are separated by a single vertex. These springs pull the cloth together. When force is applied to the cloth in a direction perpendicular to the surface of the cloth, bending can occur. This puts bending springs under tension and depending on their strength, the cloth will bend or remain stiff.

Figure 1.60.

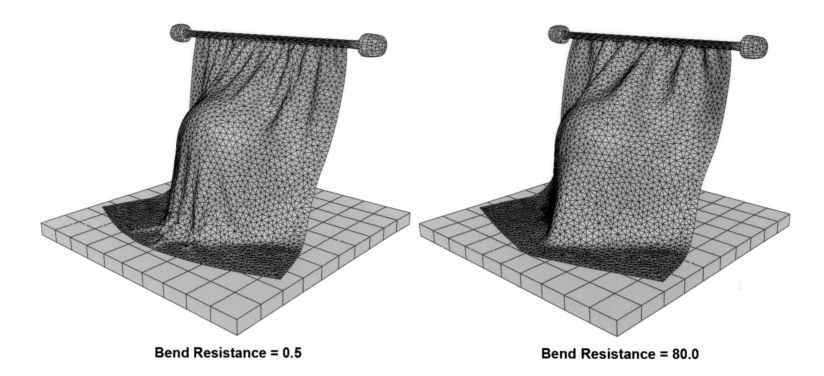

Bend Resistance = 0.5   **Bend Resistance = 80.0**

Figure 1.61.

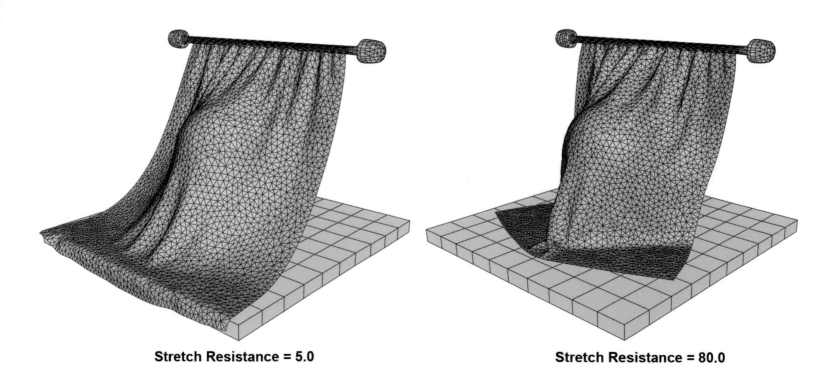

Stretch Resistance = 5.0   **Stretch Resistance = 80.0**

Figure 1.62.

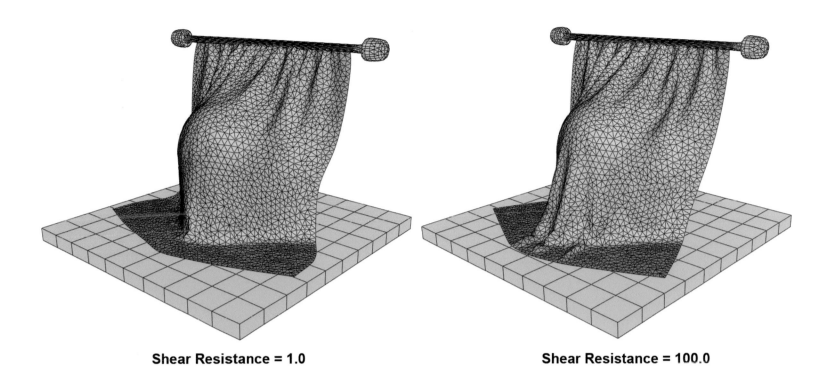

Shear Resistance = 1.0

Shear Resistance = 100.0

Figure 1.63.

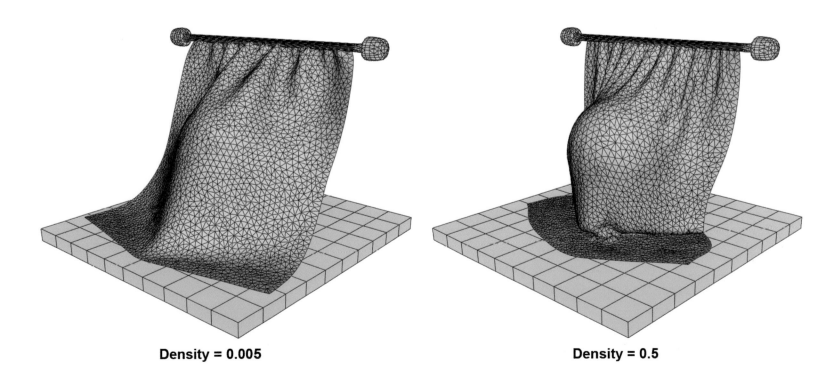

Density = 0.005

Density = 0.5

Thickness: Because the simulation garment is completely flat, it has no way of telling how thick it should behave when self colliding. This value specifies a thickness in centimeters so that the cloth will know at what distance it should begin colliding with itself. This value *is* scaled by the solver scale so you must calculate it appropriately. Take the solver scale and divide it by the real-world thickness of the garment to arrive at the proper value. For a piece of cloth 1cm thick and a solver scale of 10, the thickness should be set to 0.1 (0.1 = 1/10).

Thickness Force: This specifies the strength of the force that pushes cloth away from itself during a self collision. Basically, how much the cloth will resist being squished when colliding with itself. For heavy cloth, increase this to as much as 80 to maintain the thickness and prevent the cloth from completely collapsing on itself FIGURE 1.64.

Figure 1.64.

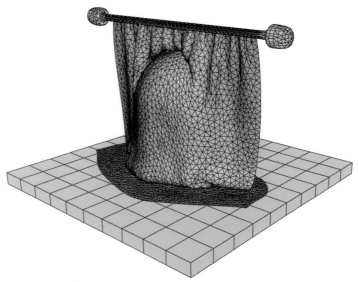

Thickness Force = 100.0 , Thickness = 0.5

Figure 1.65.

Cloth Friction: Controls the self-friction of the cloth. Fabrics like satin have very low self-friction which accounts for their slippery behavior. Similarly, a piece of cellophane has an extremely high self-friction which explains why it sticks to itself. Values range from 0 to 1.

Cloth Damping: Damping can be thought of as microscopic friction. As a real piece of fabric moves, tiny threads rub against each other converting the kinetic energy to heat. Combined with air resistance, this dissipates the total kinetic energy of the system. You can see this in the real world when a flapping flag stops moving after the wind dies. Greater values cause the cloth's kinetic energy to dissipate quickly.

Air Damping: This specific type of damping simulates the affect of air on the cloth. In an empty vacuum, the only type of friction on the cloth would be self inflicted. Of course, in the real world, air is all around us. Air damping is applied to the cloth on a per-particle basis. It is dependent on the direction of movement of the particle in relation to the normal of the surface. Basically, if the cloth is moving head-on, it is not very aerodynamic and thus will be heavily dampened by the air. Similarly, if the cloth particle is traveling perpendicular to the direction of the surface normal, its streamlined nature will lessen the effects of air damping. FIGURE 1.65 demonstrates how air damping can be used to create a parachute effect.

Static Friction and Dynamic Friction: These values are multiplied by their corresponding attributes on the collision object to arrive at a final friction factor. See the Collisions section for the specifics about how these values work.

Use our guide to help you experiment with different cloth property settings. Avoid changing multiple attributes at once. This will allow you to see the effect of each attribute as you tweak them. With a little practice, these parameters will become second nature. A seasoned cloth animator can quickly determine what attribute to use to achieve any particular effect.

The following table (opposite page) shows the recommended ranges for all of the cloth property values. Use values outside of this range with caution as it may cause solver instability (ie. cloth bombs).

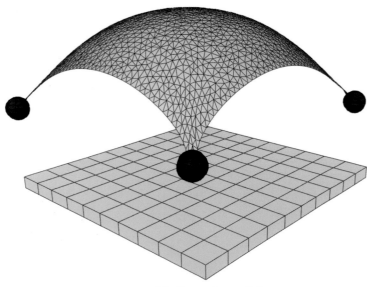

Air Damping = 0.8

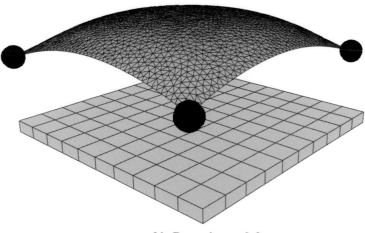

Air Damping = 0.2

Property Attribute	Min	Max
Bend Resistance U/V	10	60
Bend Rate U/V	0	0.1
Stretch Resistance U/V	50	200
Shear Resistance	30	200
Scale U/V	1	1
Density	0	0.1
Thickness	0.1	0.7
Thickness Force	30	75
Cloth Friction	0.2	0.6
Cloth Damping	0.2	0.6
Air Damping	0	0.1
Static Friction	0.6	0.7
Dynamic Friction	0.1	0.3

To get you started with creating different cloth types, Maya includes a library of common materials (silk, denim, cotton etc...). Select the property node and look under the Material Library tab in the attribute editor. Click the folder icon to bring-up a list of available properties FIGURE 1.66. Once you have created a property that you wish to store, you can add it to the library for future use. Additional cloth properties can be found in the Maya/7.0/extras/clothproperties directory.

Figure 1.66.

MayaCloth Material Library

```
cpCotton
cpDefault
cpDenim
cpSilk
cpTShirt
```

OK   Cancel

With time, you may wish to get your hands dirty by setting properties on a per-vertex basis. This can be done with the Paint Cloth Properties Tool (Simulation > Properties > Paint Cloth Properties Tool). You will find all of the regular property attributes in addition to the Bend Angle property that is unique to the painting tool. The Bend Angle property allows you to manually place creases and wrinkles in your cloth object. Simply paint a white line with the Bend Angle attribute and run a local simulation. The cloth should pull together to create a crease FIGURE 1.67.

The cloth property node may seem intimidating at first with its long list of attributes, but a methodical workflow can and will tame this beast. Maya Cloth is a robust package partly because its ample number of cloth properties enable it to simulate a wide range of cloth types.

Figure 1.67.

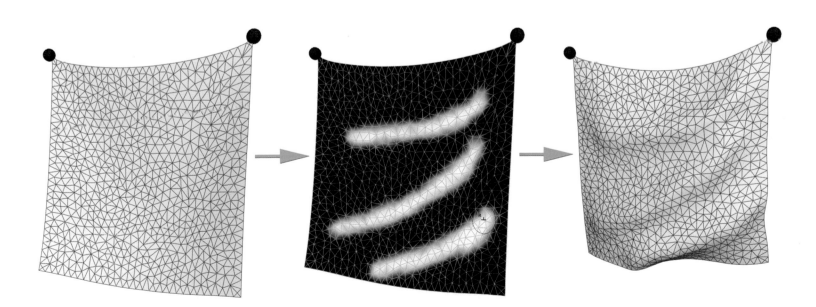

Constraints:

The final piece in the cloth simulation puzzle, constraints are used to gain absolute control over the behavior the garment. Like the animation constraints, cloth constraints can set limitations on or change the behavior of an object. Using constraints, you can pin cloth to a character, pull a character's shirt off, or even add wind to make the garment flap around. Constraints are well documented in Maya's help files, but it's not always obvious exactly how they can be used. The following table should help you discover how constraints can be 'harnessed' (pun intended).

# Constraint Type	Use	Examples
Transform	Select any number of vertices and attach them to any Maya transform node (like a locator). The constrained vertices behave as though they are parented to the transform. This constraint is useful wherever the cloth must be pulled around or pinned into a hierarchy.	- Pulling a character's shirt off. - Pinning a flag to a flagpole.
Mesh	Select any number of vertices and constrain them to a polygon surface. This constraint has the added advantage of pinning each constrained vertex to the *closest point* on the mesh. When the parent mesh is deformed, the constrained vertices will behave as though they are attached. This constraint looks particularly nice when it is made soft (see constraint options below).	- Attach a pair of pants to a character's waistline. - Glue the shoulder straps of a tank top to prevent them from falling off.
Cloth	Select any number of cloth points, then shift select a separate cloth object to create a cloth constraint. The vertices will be constrained to the closest points on the target cloth object. This constraint is used to pin the specified vertices on one cloth object to another cloth object. During simulation, the constraint will pull the vertices to the target cloth object while maintaining the offset as specified on the constraint node. You can also pin cloth vertices to itself by simply not selecting a target object before creating the constraint.	- Pin a dynamic ribbon to a garment. - Attach a pocket to a shirt.

# Constraint Type	Use	Examples
Button	Select any piece of geometry and constrain it to the nearest point on the cloth object. The button constraint creates a transform node that gets parented under the cloth object. Now you can parent any objects under this transform and they will follow the cloth. Use the UCoord and VCoord attributes on the constraint node to manually position the button.	- Attach buttons to a jacket. - 'Sew' a label to a shirt. - Glue any non-cloth object to your cloth.
Collision	The collision constraint is used to gain per-vertex control over the collisions on your cloth objects. Select some cloth points, and create the constraint. There are two boolean attributes on the constraint node, Cloth Collisions and Rigid Collisions. Turn Cloth Collisions off to disable cloth-to-cloth collisions. Turn Rigid Collisions off to disable cloth-to-collision object collisions. You can also specify collision object filters (Constraints > Collision > Create Collision Object Filter) to disable/enable certain collision objects from affecting the vertices.	- Use this to 'cheat' collisions not visible to the camera. - Prevent any unwanted or troublesome collisions.
Field	Select any number of cloth points and shift select a dynamic field. This constraint will connect the dynamic field to the specified cloth points. Typically, you will have to set the field magnitude to very high values (200 – 1500) to see the effects.	- Add wind to your clothing (air field). - Create interesting effects with the turbulence field. - Create 'underwater' cloth by adding a drag field.

As you can see, the cloth constraints are quite varied. Between the six constraints, any typical kind of cloth manipulation can be tackled with ease. Many of the constraints have additional options FIGURE 1.68. The following attributes are very useful for tweaking the behavior of constraints:

Figure 1.68.

SHAPES	
transformConstraintShape1	
Local Position X	0
Local Position Y	0
Local Position Z	0
Local Scale X	1
Local Scale Y	1
Local Scale Z	1
Size	0.06
Constraint Weight	1
Is Soft	off
Stiffness	100
Damping	10

Size: This attribute changes the size of the constraint icons on the viewport. It has no other effect.

Constraint Weight: How much does the constraint affect the cloth? Values range from 0 (no effect) to 1 (full effect)).

Is Soft: This attribute is available on the mesh and transform constraints. When turned on, the constraint will blend into the surrounding cloth points making for a much more pleasing effect. A soft constraint is also attached via springs. This can help alleviate the very harsh look of a non-soft constraint.

Stiffness: This value specifies how stiff a soft constraint spring is. Typically, values from 500 – 3000 will yield good results.

Damping: Like stiffness, this value only applies to soft constraints. Set the damping to control how the constraint rebounds from forces. This will usually take a little experimentation.

Caches:

Caching the simulation writes the vertex animation to a file on the hard drive. By default, a cache file is created whenever you play the scene. Each frame is first calculated, and then appended to the end of this file. Once a cache has been created, the animation will playback in realtime.

If you are not happy with the results of the simulation and wish to tweak some parameters, you must first delete the old cache (Simulation > Delete Cache), before running the simulation again.

Often times, a simulation may work perfectly up until a certain frame where a problem crops-up. In these cases, it is better to truncate the cache rather than delete it all and start from scratch. Scrub to a frame before the problem arises and choose Simulation > Truncate Cache. All cached data after the current frame will be deleted. Now tweak and run the simulation from the current frame to append the new simulation onto the old cache.

Once you are happy with the cached simulation, you can save a copy of it so that subsequent caches do not overwrite it. Select the cache node and open the attribute editor. Enter a name for the cache file and hit the disk icon to save it. Similarly, you can open other cache files from here to switch between different saved simulations.

Be careful when managing .mcc (.MayaClothCache) files. It can sometimes take a long time to calculate a lengthy simulation, making them quite precious. It is very easy to accidentally overwrite a cache file.

While cache file size is not usually an issue, you can compress a cache file to make it more compact (Simulation > Compress Cache). This will not, however, make it any faster/slower to read. Compressed cache files cannot be truncated and then re-simulated because they lack velocity data. Only compress a cache if the file size becomes an issue and when you are sure the animation is final.

Exercise 1.3	Simulating the Goblin's Garment

The last exercise in this chapter corresponds with the final step in animating the Goblin character's tunic: simulation. This exercise takes-off precisely where exercise 1.2 left-off: with a draped and fitted garment ready for simulation.

At the end of exercise 1.2, we set up a wrap deformer so that the Goblin's smoothed render garment will deform along with the simulation garment. During simulation, we will hide this render garment in a separate layer. Once finished, the render garment layer can be revealed to show the final tunic.

1.) Open exercise1.3_Start.mb. This file contains the Goblin character exactly how we left him at the end of exercise 1.2. Notice that there are individual layers for the simulation and render garments. Ensure that your playback speed is set to Play Every Frame and hit the play button. The scene will quickly move from frame -10 to frame 0 as the Goblin blends from his dress-up pose, to the beginning of the walk cycle. During this time, the cloth will *not* react. In fact, it only begins simulating at frame 0. But by that time, the Goblin has already moved into a pose that is penetrating the cloth (FIGURE 1.69)!

2.) It's obvious that we need to tell the solver to begin simulating at frame -10. Find the solver node and change the Start Frame from 0 to -10. Rewind the scene, but before you try to simulate again, select the cloth and choose Simulation > Delete Cache. You may wish to use the cloth shelf to speed things up because the cache must be removed whenever you wish to tweak the simulation FIGURE 1.70.

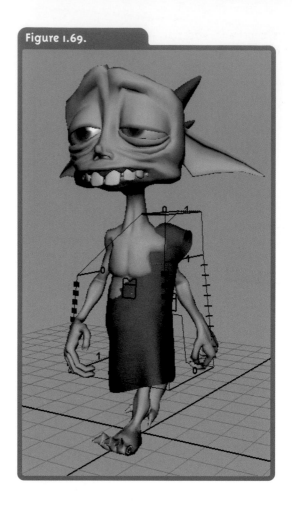

Figure 1.69.

along the curve. So to pull the cloth along a specific path, we must tweak the curve. Grab the locator and move it to the right side of the Goblin's neck. Now re-model the curve into a path that will pull the strap up the shoulder and over the clavicle FIGURE 1.72.

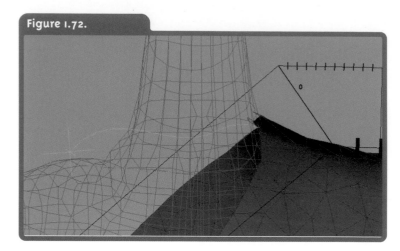

Figure 1.72.

5.) Open exercise1.3_A.mb to see the finished drag controller (after simulation). When you are ready, do a local simulation to actually pull the cloth up. Stop the local simulation when the strap is closer to the neck and delete the drag control FIGURE 1.73. Drag controls may seem confusing at first, but once you give them a try, you should find they are actually quite simple (and useful). If the

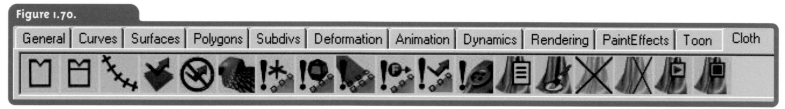

Figure 1.70.

| General | Curves | Surfaces | Polygons | Subdivs | Deformation | Animation | Dynamics | Rendering | PaintEffects | Toon | Cloth |

3.) With the solver Start Frame properly adjusted, hit the play button again to run the simulation. This time, the garment should begin simulating at frame -10. It may take a few moments, but when the simulation gets to frame 5 (with his arms at his side), you will notice that the garment slips off his shoulder and tumbles to the floor. We can't have a naked Goblin walking around, (the neighbors will start asking questions) so we need to constrain the shoulder strap such that it sticks to the Goblin. Rewind and delete the cache.

4.) Before we apply the constraint, let's pull the Goblin's shoulder strap further up his shoulder so that it looks like it's resting on his clavicle and not the edge of his shoulder. To do this, we will use a Drag Control. Select about 5 vertices across the edge of the strap and choose Simulation > Manipulators > Drag Control. This will create an orange pyramid pointing along a curve with a locator at the end. This strange device will allow us to pull the sleeve of the garment. The orange pyramid is attached to the vertices and will travel

drag controller has pinched any vertices, simply manually adjust them and choose Simulation > Set Initial Cloth State.

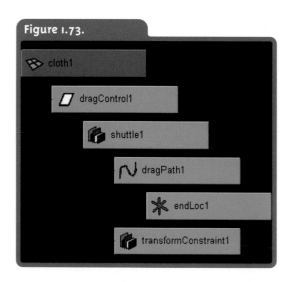

Figure 1.73.

cloth1
  dragControl1
    shuttle1
      dragPath1
        endLoc1
          transformConstraint1

6.) Open exercise1.3_B.mb to see the shoulder strap after being repositioned. To glue the shoulder strap on, let's use a mesh constraint. Start by zooming-in on his shoulder and selecting about 5-10 vertices across the strap. Now shift select the Goblin mesh and choose Constraints > Mesh. You should see the constrained vertices surrounded by small boxes FIGURE 1.74. These indicate that they are connected to a constraint. Rename the constraint to something like: 'shoulderMeshConstraint'.

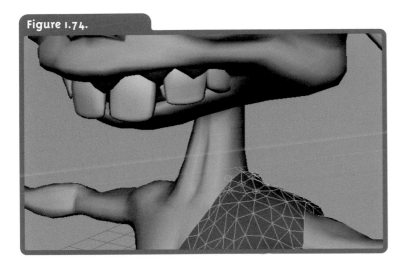

Figure 1.74.

7.) Open exercise1.3_C.mb to see the shoulder strap with the constraint applied to it. Try running the simulation again. The garment should now stay 'pinned' to the shoulder as the Goblin lowers his arms. At first glance, it seems we are already getting a pretty nice simulation. However, under closer scrutiny, you will notice that the shoulder constraint is causing a very harsh deformation FIGURE 1.75. By default, both 'mesh' and 'transform' constraints are created as *hard*. To soften their effects, we can turn on the IsSoft feature.

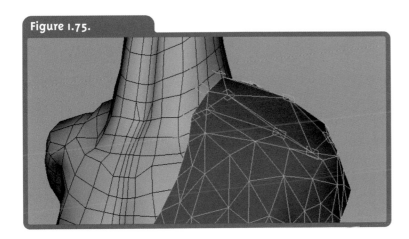

Figure 1.75.

8.) Select one of the box icons surrounding the constrained vertices and open the channel box. Find the IsSoft attribute and set it to 'on'. Now we have a soft constraint. Rewind, delete the cache and try the simulation again. This time, the shoulder strap remains attached, but will slip down as far as the Goblin's elbow FIGURE 1.76.

By default, the soft constraint was not strong enough to keep the cloth up.

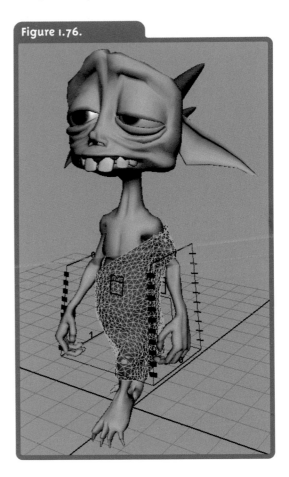

Figure 1.76.

9.) Rewind and delete the cache (this is the last reminder). Set the Stiffness value on the mesh constraint to a value of 1000 and the Damping to 75. This will force the constraint to stick to the mesh.

10.) Open exercise1.3_D.mb to see the Goblin with the finished shoulder strap constraint. Run the simulation (or load D_Solve.mcc from the DVD into the cache node) and observe that the strap remains fixed to the shoulder without any harsh deformations (the deformations are softer because the constraint is soft) FIGURE 1.77. The initial solve is already looking pretty good. The cloth is colliding properly and folding realistically as the Goblin goes through his walk cycle. Depending on the production, this may be all you need, but for demonstration purposes, let's take it a bit further.

11.) The cloth could benefit from some slight turbulence. Any real-world garment will flap around slightly during an outdoors walk due to slight air currents. Let's create a little wind to give the cloth a more dynamic feel. Under the Dynamics menu set choose Fields > Air FIGURE 1.78. This will create an air field that we can connect to the cloth. Select all of the vertices on the cloth, shift select the air field and choose Constraints > Field (in the Cloth menu set).

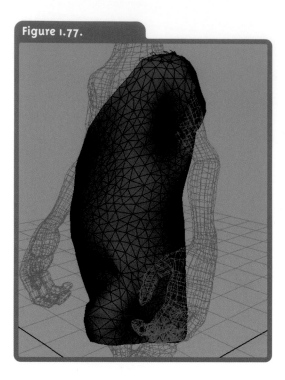

Figure 1.77.

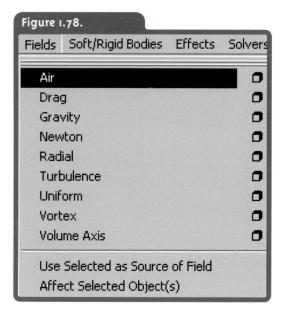

Figure 1.78.

Fields	Soft/Rigid Bodies	Effects	Solvers

Air ☐
Drag ☐
Gravity ☐
Newton ☐
Radial ☐
Turbulence ☐
Uniform ☐
Vortex ☐
Volume Axis ☐

Use Selected as Source of Field
Affect Selected Object(s)

12.) Open exercise1.3_E.mb to see the cloth with the connected field constraint. If you run the simulation now (or load E_SolveWithAir.mcc) you will see that the cloth is not really reacting to the air field yet. We need to adjust the air field before we are going to get any results. Set the magnitude of the air field to a value of 500 and the Direction Z to -1 (this will blow the air in the opposite direction he is walking).

13.) Open exercise1.3_F.mb to see the cloth with the adjusted air field. When you play the simulation now, the effect of the air field should be immediately obvious FIGURE 1.79. During the first few frames, the garment will be violently blown back. Chances are the solver will run into difficulty and will attempt to adaptively adjust the time step to achieve an accurate simulation. Eventually,

however, the solve will fail and the garment will tear through the Goblin. At first glance, it may seem that we have set the air field too high. This is an easy assumption to make given the results, but it's actually not correct. The problem is that the solver is still relaxing the garment for the first 5 frames. When the garment is relaxed, it is very stretchy and susceptible to forces outside the solver (although the solver gravity does not affect it). This illustrates a common problem that novice cloth animators will experience. Do not forget to turn off the relaxation! Set the Relax Frame Length on the solver node to 0.

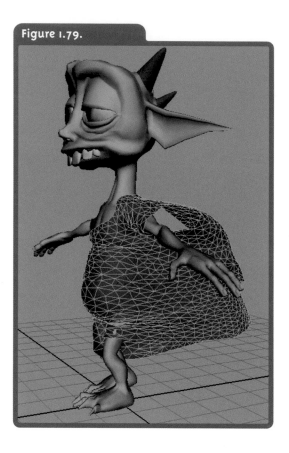

Figure 1.79.

14.) Open exercise1.3_G.mb to see the cloth with the properly adjusted solver (no relaxing) and air field. Run the simulation (or load G_SolveNoRelax. mcc from the DVD). At this point, the cloth should stay attached to the Goblin and the air field will blow the garment back. Unfortunately, because the wind is constant, it pulls the garment as though it were in a wind tunnel. Real wind is much more turbulent and varies in intensity. To simulate this, we can add an expression to the air field. Right click on the Magnitude attribute in the channel box and choose Expressions. This will open the expression editor. Now type 'airField1.magnitude = abs(noise(time)) * 200;' FIGURE 1.80. The 'noise(time)' function will return a semi-random value that oscillates between -1 and 1 as the time value changes during playback. Because we do not want the wind to blow in the opposite (negative) direction, we use the 'abs()' function to get the absolute value of the noise function.

Then we multiply this by a factor of 200 so that the magnitude is strong enough to be noticed. This simple expression should yield a nice looking, semi-random, breeze that varies in intensity over the course of the animation.

Figure 1.80.

Expression:

```
airField1.magnitude = abs(noise(time)) * 200;
```

15.) Open exercise1.3_Finished.mb to see the final cloth scene with the wind expression. If you simulate this scene (or load finalSolve_PreTweaking.mcc) you will see the effects of the expression on the air field as the garment flaps about in a light breeze. Watch the included playblasts to get a realtime view of the cloth behavior FIGURE 1.81.

Figure 1.81.

 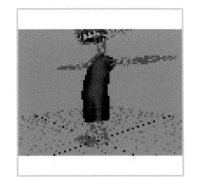 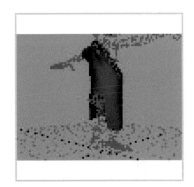

Final   finalSim_PreTweak_Front finalSim_PreTweak_Rear

16.) Finally, we are getting an effect that is looking quite realistic. When you are happy with the way the simulation is looking, you can begin adding any minor tweaks to the final simulation. Sometimes, it may be necessary to manually tweak stray vertices or soften certain areas where collisions have caused some faces to get tangled. Once you have a frame looking the way you want, select it and choose Simulation > Update Cloth State. If things get really messy, you can always increase the accuracy of the solve as this can sometimes sort-out small glitches and collision issues. For the Goblin's garment, I manually tweaked some areas where his fingers poked through the sides of the garment. This stage took me about ½ an hour.

Figure 1.82.

 D_Solve.mcc
MCC File
3,370 KB

 E_SolveWithAir.mcc
MCC File
3,370 KB

 G_SolveNoRelax.mcc
MCC File
3,370 KB

 finalSolve_PreTweaking.mcc
MCC File
3,370 KB

 exercise1.3_Finished.mcc
MCC File
3,370 KB

You can see the final simulation by loading the final cache file (exercise1.3_Finished.mcc) from the DVD. This cache file contains all of the manual edits that I made to sort-out minor collision issues and vertex glitches FIGURE 1.82.

Open GoblinWalkGarment_Final.mb to see the render garment with some basic shaders and smoothing FIGURE 1.83. This shows the final quality before rendering. Be sure to watch the included playblasts to see how the smoothed render garment looks once animated.

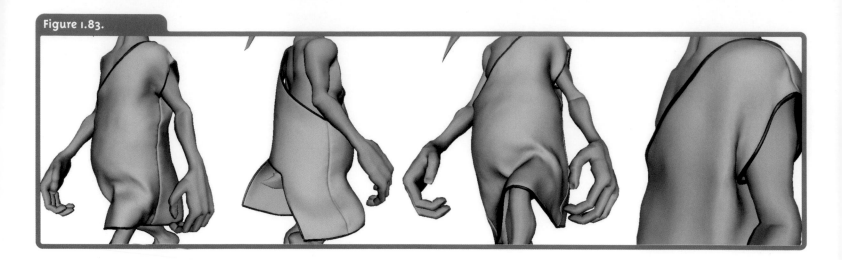

Figure 1.83.

Final Thoughts:

In chapter four, we will revisit cloth simulation where you will see some more advanced techniques for gaining absolute control over your cloth simulations. Before then, I highly recommend running through a few simulations of your own because, like most things, animating cloth takes a lot of practice.

In our continued search for the ultimate believable character animation, we must consider many different facets. With the fundamentals of cloth under our belts, the next chapter will guide you through the world of simulating long flowing hair. Chapter two is then followed by coverage of short hair (referred to as 'fur', in chapter three). With all three of these new weapons at your disposal (cloth, hair and fur), you can tackle almost any character that is thrown your way.

With any luck (and the help of this chapter), you should find that you can now create predictable and professional results with Maya Cloth. Specifically, you should be able to:.

- Model Garments for Simulation
- Drape and Fit a Garment to a Character
- Create Realistic 'Render' Garments
- Adjust a Cloth Solver for any Situation
- Adjust a Cloth Property for any Type of Cloth
- Animate Simple Garments
- Apply Constraints and Forces to Cloth
- Tweak a Cloth Cache to Fix Glitches

Chapter 2
Hair Fundamentals

Introduction:

There are a handful of natural phenomena that 3d artists have always struggled to reproduce. The most popular of which are probably fluids, cloth, subsurface scattering and hair. These struggles are nothing new. As early as 1937, artists at Disney Feature Animation toiled away countless hours trying to understand exactly how to animate and render these natural effects.

We've come a long way since the classic-Disney era of the early twentieth century. While pencils and pastels have given-way to mice and keyboards, artists still find themselves struggling to capture the raw chaotic beauty that surrounds our everyday lives. The simplest things, like pouring a glass of water, can easily become computational behemoths. So, like our pioneering pencil-pushers, modern day effects artists must resort to *simplification*. Only by breaking these effects into their primary elements can we even begin to reproduce them.

As the name implies, this chapter is all about hair. Up until recently, animated hair has been avoided like the plague. The task of modeling, designing, controlling and rendering such a complex and chaotic effect was simply too daunting to be considered for most productions. Over the years, most artists have resorted to the use of cheats and hacks (usually involving alpha masks on textured planes) to create the look of long hair. Cheating hair is no longer necessary. Long, realistic hair can now be styled, animated and rendered using off-the-shelf software. The only limitation now is actually knowing *how* to do it.

This chapter will introduce you to the powerful Maya Hair module. We will explore this extremely deep toolset to uncover the secrets to getting professional, believable results. Specifically, we will be learning:

- What 'Hair' Is
- How to Style Hair
- Animating Hair with Dynamics
- Rendering Hair with mental ray
- Non-Hair Effects

Introduction to Hair:

Since v6.0, Maya Unlimited has included the Hair module. Maya Hair is a collection of tools that allow for the realistic creation, styling, animation and rendering of long hair. It is an extremely robust system that gives users complete control over the look and feel of every strand.

Maya Hair can be used to create various styles including braids, ponytails, dreadlocks and updos FIGURE 2.1. It can be used to create frizzy, straight or curly hair. The color, thickness, opacity and translucence of the hair are completely customizable. It really is a very well thought-out system and as you will soon see, is capable of amazing results in the hands of a capable artist.

Before we dive into the details of how Maya Hair works, let's step-back and think about exactly what 'hair' is made of. The next section should give you a better understanding of real world hair.

Figure 2.1.

Real Hair:

Real hair is a very interesting phenomenon. It is a characteristic that is unique to mammals. Every hair grows from a small indentation in the skin known as a *follicle*. It is inside the follicle that new hair cells are created. As new cells are formed, they push older cells out of the follicle where they die and become a part of the hair *strand*. The strand is what we see and is completely composed of dead cells (hence the reason it doesn't hurt to get your hair cut).

A hair follicle will only produce new hair cells for a certain period of time. This is known as the *growth phase*. Once the growth phase expires, the follicle stops producing new cells and the strand will fall out. It then enters what is referred to as the *rest phase* before re-starting the entire process. Thus, the length of the growth phase determines the maximum length that the hair strand can reach. The hair found on a human head has a very long growth phase (as opposed to the hairs found on an arm or a leg). This is why humans can grow such a long mane on their heads, but not on their arms.

It's interesting to note that some animals have hair follicles with *synchronized* rest phases. This causes all of their hair to fall out at once. We call this shedding. It is important to keep in mind what type of hair you are designing. Since animal fur has a synchronized rest phase, there is very little variation in length between neighboring hairs. A human's head-hair, however, remains at a constant density because the rest phases of the individual follicles are randomized (we never shed all at once, but rather slowly and over a long period of time). This randomized rest length results in much larger variations in length between neighboring hairs.

The sheer density of hair is the main reason it is so difficult to simulate in a computer. Most of us have between 100 000 and 150 000 hairs on our heads. When is the last time you rendered a scene with even 50000 pieces? It's not difficult to see the problem with modeling such complexity. Even if we did try modeling thousands of individual polygon strands, we would still have the problem of lighting and shading all of them. It's obvious that this problem cannot be easily solved using traditional modeling and shading techniques.

To add to the problem, hair is a semi-translucent material. When light enters a thick chunk of hair, it is diffused according to the thickness and density of the individual strands. In a typical head of hair, light is almost completely blocked before it reaches the scalp. This creates deep shadows that give hair its unique texture. Rendering this effect with a computer is computationally expensive. Not to worry though, we will tackle this issue later in the chapter where we discuss how to render hair with mental ray.

Just as important as the *look* of hair, is its *behavior*. We've all seen the shampoo commercials where some beautiful actress extols the virtues of ingredients we can't even pronounce (much less understand). Inevitably, at some point during the 30 second advert, she will flip her hair in front of the camera (usually in slow motion) thus proving once and for all that we must have brand 'X' shampoo.

There's no denying it, hair looks cool. Its motion can be enticing and attractive. It can say as much about a character as clothes or facial expressions. Long, attractive hair has a magical fluidity, while stale, frizzy, hair moves with the grace of a freight train.

Knowing the look and behavior of the hair you want to create is half the battle. With this much decided, you are ready to start getting your hands dirty. Read-on to discover how Maya Hair can used to simulate this amazing natural phenomenon.

Maya Hair in a Nutshell:

At the core of the Maya Hair system is a single node, the *hairSystem* node. This node acts as a global control for the look and behavior of the hair. Think of the hair system node as the 'base of operations'. All of the follicles, curves and hair settings are piped through this node before being sent to the rendered hair FIGURE 2.2.

Each hair system node is connected to one or more *follicle* nodes. On a typical head, you may have anywhere from 25 to 300 follicles (depending on the effect). Each follicle node controls the look and behavior of a single hair curve. You can override the global settings from the hair system node to specify per-follicle attributes (like dynamic behavior or shading settings). While it is not always necessary to have per-follicle control, you may find it useful in some cases. But by default, the attributes on the follicle node are completely overridden by the hair system node.

Figure 2.2.

Each follicle node is represented in the viewport with a peg shape FIGURE 2.3. These are attached to the surface they were created on and will deform along with it. The follicle represents the attachment point for a *hair curve*. Hair curves represent the shape of the hair. While they are not actually created as DAG objects in your scene, you can see their affect on the output of the hair system. These hair curves can be made dynamic to react to physical forces and collisions.

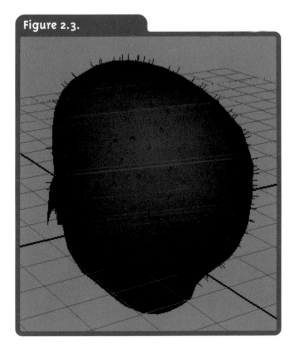

Figure 2.3.

To create the actual rendered hairs, Maya creates a single paint effects brush that is attracted to the hair curves. Each follicle has a clump of paint effects hairs that will follow the motion of their corresponding follicle. When rendered in Maya Software, these hairs are composited as a post-process (just like any other paint effects brush). This is quite limiting and makes it difficult to achieve a photorealistic look.

By rendering in mental ray, the paint effects brush is converted into mental ray's native *hair primitive* which is fully integrated into the scene. This allows hair to be rendered with effects like motion blur and depth of field or lighting techniques like global illumination and ray tracing. The performance hit is negligible (considering the increased quality) making mental ray the clear winner for rendering hair.

A typical workflow for creating digital hair goes like this:

1. Layout the UVs on the surface you want to grow hair from. Clean UV space (ranging from 0 to 1) is necessary to define the position of individual follicles.
2. Select the surface and choose `Hair > Create Hair`. The default creation options will create an array of about 64 dynamic follicles across the surface (an 8x8 grid in U and V directions) with an attached paint effects brush (default brown hair).
3. Use the Paint Hair Follicles tool to add/remove follicles where necessary. You can also adjust the length of individual follicles and control their precise placement.
4. Shape the Start Curves to style the hair. This can be done by manually moving the control vertices or by utilizing one of the many dynamic hair constraints (discussed later).
5. Adjust the shading options on the hair system node (or individual follicle nodes) to suit the style you want.
6. Light the hair and setup self-shadowing. At this point, you may wish to add passive follicles to help fill-in sparse areas (discussed later).
7. Run the animation and create a cache of the dynamic motion.
8. Light, render, and composite the hair.

As you can see, the workflow is fairly simple. It may seem confusing at first with all the strange nodes and follicles, start curves, dynamic follicles, passive follicles, static follicles, paint effects and blah blah blah... but don't be discouraged!

I guarantee that if you stick to this chapter and follow the exercises, it will all come together nicely. Maya Hair is an elegant system and its workflow, while strange at first, is actually very straightforward. To start with, let's discuss how to create and design a hairstyle. Once we have the creation and design stage covered, the chapter will move onwards to cover simulation and rendering.

Creating and Designing Hair:

Imagine, for a second, that you are a setup artist who has just started work on a brand new production. The director is extra excited about the new project because you've promised to deliver realistic hair effects! After seeing a couple tests of 'hairy' spheres, the director is convinced that the technology is ready and the green light is given.

This is the scariest (and most exciting) part of a production. The commitment has been made and there's no turning back! Now the first thing to understand about designing hair for a production is that, like most props, they must be fleshed-out on paper first. Let the concept artists do the brunt of the work. Only once a design is finalized should it be passed-on to the hair TD.

With the concept complete, the model prepared (and a copy of this book in-hand) let's open Maya and get crackin'. Obviously, before we can begin styling the hair to match the concept art, we must create it.

Creating Hair:

If you haven't already, please read the 'Maya Hair in a Nutshell' section. This will give you the big-picture and prevent you from getting lost in the details. That section introduced the four basic elements of Maya Hair:

1. **The Hair System Node** : provides global control over the look and behavior of the hair.
2. **The Follicles** : are the attachment points for hair curves that drive the rendered hair.
3. **Hair Curves**: Attached to a follicle, the hair curves drive the motion of either paint effects or output curves.
4. **A Paint Effects Brush**: This brush is attached to the hair curves and can be rendered as either paint effects or hair primitives in mental ray.

These four pieces make-up the hair puzzle and it just so happens that they can all be created with the click of a button! To create hair on a surface, select the surface and choose Hair > Create Hair. There are quite a few options here, the majority of which may not make a lot of sense at this point (not to worry, we'll get to them). With the default settings, if you hit the Create Hairs button, the following pieces are setup FIGURE 2.4:

- ı Hair System node
- About 64 Follicles
- ı Start Curve for each Follicle
- ı Paint Effects brush

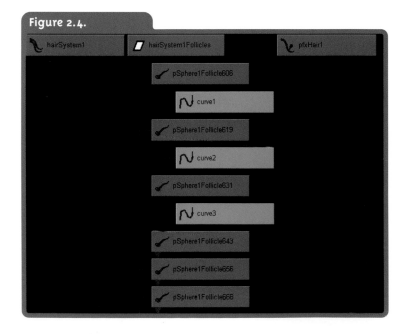
Figure 2.4.

As you can see, this tool has created all four of the basic elements needed to create hair. The default creation options may work fine, (the placement and number of follicles can always be changed after creation) however it is still useful to be aware of how the creation options affect the output.

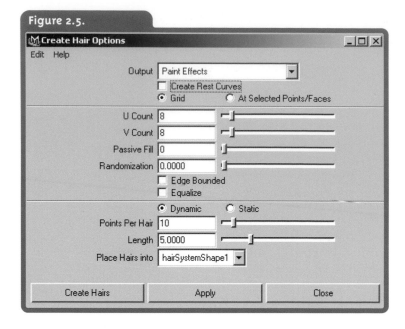
Figure 2.5.

There are *three* sections in the hair creation options that you need to be aware of FIGURE 2.5. These options must be understood to ensure that the hair is created properly:

1. The Output Method: This is where you choose what you want to attach to the hair curves. The four options are:

Paint Effects: The default option, this will create a generic brown-hair paint effects stroke and attach it to the hair curves.

NURBS Curves: This option creates a set of NURBS curves that follow the motion of the hair curves. This set of NURBS curves can then be used to visualize the hair's motion, or drive whatever else you wish. For example, they can be used to drive Maya Fur, pieces of geometry (via wire deformers) or even some other completely proprietary system.

Paint Effects and NURBS Curves: this option will attach a paint effects brush to the hairSystem. It also creates a set of output NURBS curves. This option is useful if you wish to drive paint effects hair and utilize the output curves for something else. Driving fur with output curves is covered in the next chapter.

Create Rest Curves: checking this setting will create another separate set of NURBS curves. A single rest curve is created for each follicle. Rest curves are rarely needed. They represent the position the hair will assume when at rest (discussed later).

2. The Follicle Distribution Settings: These settings control how Maya places the follicles across the selected surface. Follicle placement may be manually edited after creation, but tweaking these options will help you get there faster:

U and V Count: These attributes control the number of follicles that are placed along the U and V directions. Obviously, higher numbers will yield denser hair, but it is important to strike a balance between follicle density and paint effects thickness. A good hair setup will use fewer follicles to achieve the same look (thus making the whole setup faster and easier to work with).

Passive Fill: this attribute controls the creation of passive hair curves (discussed later). A value of 1 will place a row of passive curves after every row of dynamic curves. A value of 2 places passive curves at every second row, and so on. Passive curves are fully discussed in the next section on hair curves.

Randomization: This value ranges from 0 to 1. Non-zero values will apply a psuedo-randomness to the arrangement of follicles on the surface. As the value approaches zero, the follicles align into a perfect grid FIGURE 2.6. Small amounts of randomness can give the hair a more natural look.

Grid vs. Selected Points/Faces: If Grid is checked, the follicles are arranged across the entire surface. You may wish to add hair to a specific region of the mesh (preventing hair from being placed on the face and neck, for example) by selecting vertices or faces and checking the Selected Points/Faces box. This will create one follicle at each selected point or face.

setting-up all of the relevant nodes to give you a complete hair system with one click. That's not to say that it does all of the work for you, it simply creates a template. No amount of tweaking the hair creation options will give you a finished hairstyle; the finished look will take a fair bit of elbow grease.

At this point, you should be familiar with the basics of Maya Hair. It goes something like this: the hair system node affects everything, but primarily controls follicles, which are the anchors for hair curves, which ultimately drive the paint effects or output curves (and output curves can then drive whatever else you wish).

The task of customizing your hairstyle involves manual editing of the follicles, hair curves and shading options to create a specific look. The next section will show you how to gain absolute control over the placement and behavior of each follicle.

Working with Follicles:

After using the hair creation tool, you will be left with an array of follicles evenly distributed across your surface FIGURE 2.7. In order to create custom hair-dos, we need more precise control over each follicle.

Figure 2.6.

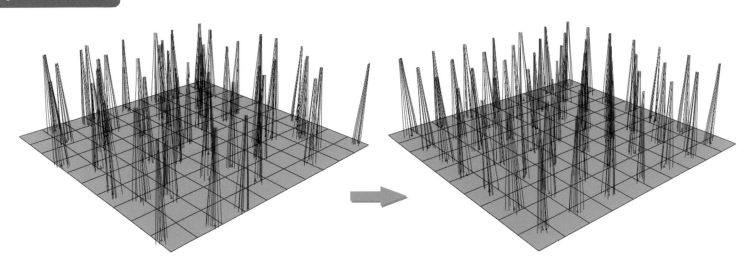

3. The Hair Curve Settings: These creation attributes control the settings of the hair curves that will be attached to each follicle.

Points Per Hair: An extremely important attribute; this specifies the number of control vertices on the hair curve. With a value of 20, the hair curve will be extremely dense. Hair curves with 5 or fewer points are less articulate, but simulate much more quickly and are easier to control.

Length: The length of the hair curve in world units. This can be adjusted afterwards with the Scale Hair Tool (Hair " Scale Hair Tool).

Place Hairs Into: By default, the newly created follicles will become children of an existing hair system (if there is one). Use this drop-down menu to specify which system you would like to control them with. You can re-assign follicles to any hair system you like, at any time. To do this, select any follicles, curves, or CVs and choose, Hair > Assign Hair System.

The hair creation options are there to help you quickly get started by

Figure 2.7.

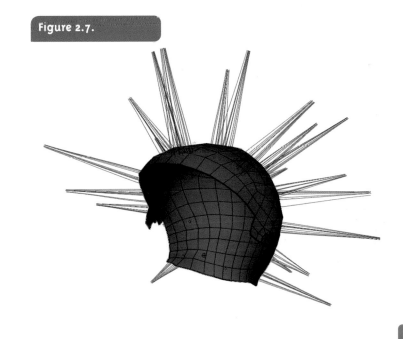

Follicles can be manually shifted across a surface by editing their Parameter U and V attributes. These two values specify the two dimensional UV coordinates of the follicle. If you middle mouse drag on this attribute, the follicle will slide across the surface to the new point FIGURE 2.8.

Working directly with UV coordinates is not always intuitive, especially if the UV space runs in odd directions. In this case, you can always add follicles at particular points or faces by selecting the components before running the create hair tool (using the 'At Selected Points/Faces' checkbox). This will create a new follicle at each selected point or face on the mesh.

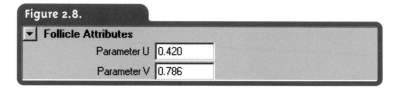

Figure 2.8.

Follicle Attributes	
Parameter U	0.420
Parameter V	0.786

Perhaps the most intuitive method of adding follicles is the Paint Hair Follicles Tool (Hair > Paint Hair Follicles). This tool uses the artisan interface to allow you to quickly and easily add or remove follicles FIGURE 2.9. In addition to adding and removing follicles, you can also paint per-follicle attributes. When the per-follicle attributes are adjusted (either via the paint tool or in the attribute editor) they override the global settings from the hair system node.

The Paint Hair Follicles tool is the only means with which the length of a hair can be changed (after creation). The Trim Hairs and Extend Hairs options allow you to changes both the hair length and number of points per hair (its resolution). Many hairstyles rely on varying lengths of hair to create a specific affect. To trim the hair, select Trim Hairs from the paint settings and use the Replace operation in the paint attributes FIGURE 2.10 (thankfully, you won't have to sit and read fashion magazines while you wait for the hair cut).

The per-follicle overrides include options for adjusting the dynamics and shading properties on a per-follicle basis FIGURE 2.11. These attributes have exact counterparts on the hair system node and are explained in the following sections on simulation and rendering. In the meantime, understand that they are there to provide additional control if needed (but by default, have no effect).

Remember that follicles act as controllers for individual hairs, which are then used to drive clumps of paint effects. There is no need to create a single follicle for every hair, and doing so is wasteful and impractical. Creating the right amount of follicles and correctly placing them requires a little bit of trial and error.

Before we move-on to styling hair, let's discuss the different 'states' that a follicle can be in. These states determine the *behavior* of the hair and have nothing to with the shape of the paint effects or shading properties.

Figure 2.9.

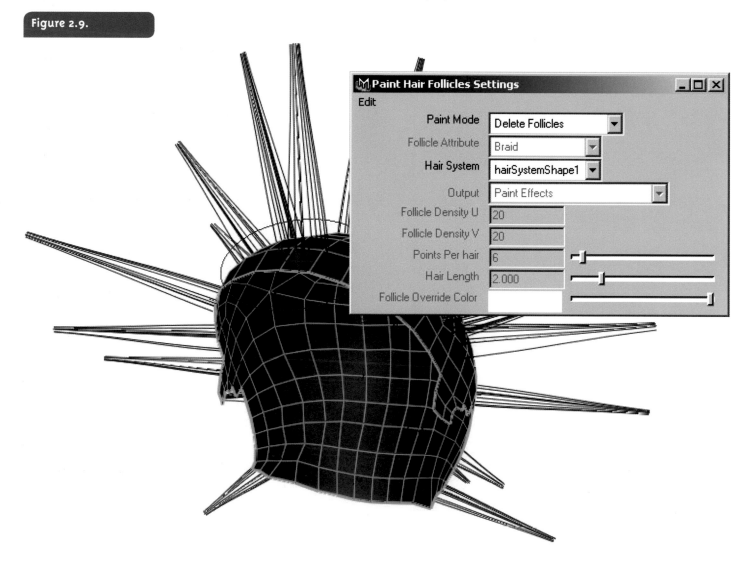

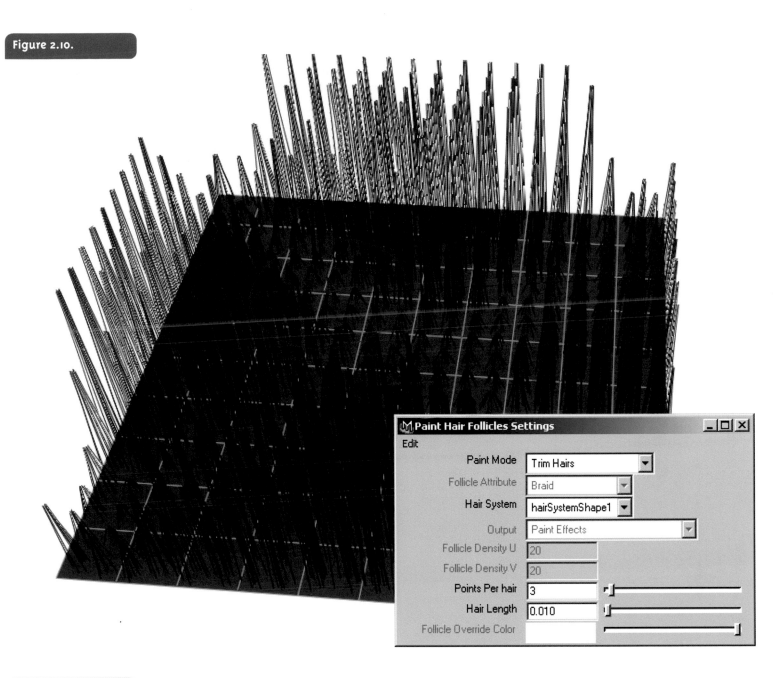

Figure 2.10.

Paint Hair Follicles Settings

Edit

Paint Mode	Trim Hairs
Follicle Attribute	Braid
Hair System	hairSystemShape1
Output	Paint Effects
Follicle Density U	20
Follicle Density V	20
Points Per hair	3
Hair Length	0.010
Follicle Override Color	

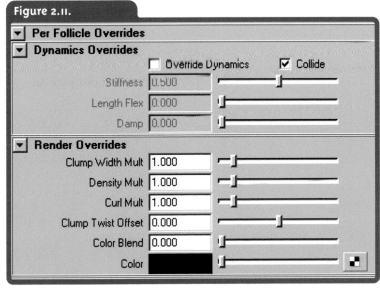

Figure 2.11.

Per Follicle Overrides

Dynamics Overrides

☐ Override Dynamics   ☑ Collide

Stiffness   0.500

Length Flex   0.000

Damp   0.000

Render Overrides

Clump Width Mult   1.000

Density Mult   1.000

Curl Mult   1.000

Clump Twist Offset   0.000

Color Blend   0.000

Color

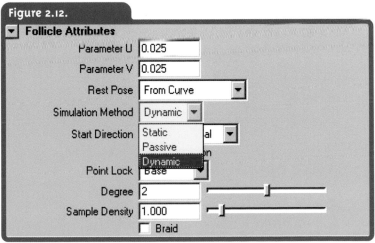

Figure 2.12.

Follicle Attributes

Parameter U   0.025

Parameter V   0.025

Rest Pose   From Curve

Simulation Method   Dynamic

Start Direction   Static
                   Passive
                   Dynamic

Point Lock   Base

Degree   2

Sample Density   1.000

☐ Braid

There are three different animation states that a follicle can be in. To switch between them, select the follicle node and find the 'Simulation Method' drop-down list FIGURE 2.12. It includes three options:

Dynamic: By default, all follicles are created as dynamic. Dynamic follicles are controlled by the Maya Hair dynamics engine. They can react to the built-in gravity, or even respond to any dynamic field you attach to them (good for creating wind effects). Dynamic curves can be set to collide with any polygonal object or with an implicitly defined box, sphere or ground plane. The details of the dynamic attributes are covered in a later section.

Static: If you set a follicle to be static, it simply remains stationary. It will follow its parent follicle, but the shape will remain stiff. Static hairs are very useful for providing *explicit control* over hair. There may be times when you have a hair positioned precisely and do not want it to be affected by surrounding hairs, or the dynamics. Making it static will cause it to assume the shape of the start curve for the duration of the animation. This can be a very useful feature.

Passive: When a follicle is set to passive, it is neither static nor dynamic. Passive follicles generate their motion by interpolating the motion of the neighboring hairs. Passive hairs provide several functions. Adding passive hairs to a finished hair style will create hairs that assume the shape of their neighbors. There is no need to remodel them to match the surrounding hairs. This provides a great way to quickly add density to the hair. While they are computationally cheaper than a dynamically animated hair, the real advantage is that they tend to create the effect of self-collision; adding volume to the hair without the cost of computing real self-collisions (which is also possible).

It can be useful to switch follicles between these three states as you work. In fact, you may switch a follicle between all three states several times throughout the styling process. For now, just recognize that a follicle has three states and that its state determines what is controlling its motion (either dynamics, nothing or neighboring follicles).

Follicles contain several other attributes, the majority of which are self-explanatory and are well covered in Maya's documentation. For the most part, the only thing you will have to adjust will be the simulation method (dynamic, static or passive), and the per-follicle dynamic/shading attributes (used to override the settings from the hair system).

Creating hair is a simple matter of adjusting the creation options and placing follicles, but *designing* hair is done by manipulating the start and rest curves (which, in-turn, affect the *shape* of the hair). The next section explains exactly what you need to know about the different hair curves to begin manipulating them into a custom design.

All About Hair Curves:

When you create a set of follicles, each follicle is (by default) given a single NURBS curve that is parented directly underneath it FIGURE 2.13. This curve represents the starting shape of that particular strand of hair. The Start Curve is the position the hair will be in at the *starting* frame. You can also create *rest* curves that represent the shape of the hair when it is at rest.

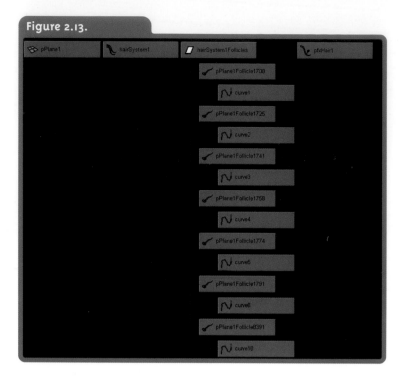

Figure 2.13.

Styling hair is the process of adjusting these curves so that they form the shape of the particular hairstyle. Combined with varied lengths, displacements and shading, these hair curves help create the 'look' of the hair:

1.**Start Curves:** A start curve is always created with a new follicle. You can see it in the hypergraph where it is parented directly under its corresponding follicle node. Start curves represent the starting shape of the hair and are used to style the hair for the beginning of an animation FIGURE 2.14. Since the addition of the Start Curve Attract feature (in Maya v7.0) Start Curves can actually replace the need for Rest Curves in most cases.

2.**Rest Curves:** These are only created if the 'Rest Curves' option is selected at creation time. A Rest Curve is created for each follicle and represents the shape the hair will assume when at rest. Rest Curves are also parented directly under their corresponding follicle node.

Figure 2.14.

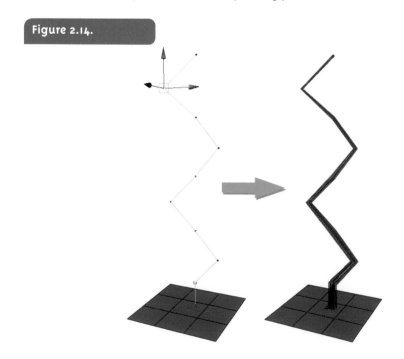

Do not confuse start and rest curves with output curves. If created, output curves display the current position of the hair FIGURE 2.15. They can be useful for getting faster feedback than the paint effects (which can be somewhat slow during animation) or by providing a means to attach the hair movement to something else (ie. fur or geometry via a wire deformer). They do not, however, affect the hair in any way (although they can add significant computational overhead to the simulation and should be deleted if not needed).

As you may have already guessed, the task of styling hair involves modeling the start and/or rest curves into the desired shape. When you are working on a hairstyle, it is common to want to constantly switch between viewing the start curves, rest curves and final paint effects. Doing so is easily done by using the Display sub-menu under the hair menu. It contains options for displaying the start, rest and current positions which correspond to the start curves, rest curves and paint effects (and/or output curves) respectively FIGURE 2.16.

With all these different curves, things tend to get confusing in the viewport. The three types of curves are color-coded to help you differentiate between them. Start curves are dark blue, rest curves are brown and output curves are bright blue.

Figure 2.16.

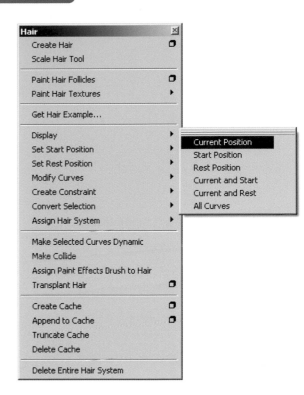

Figure 2.15.

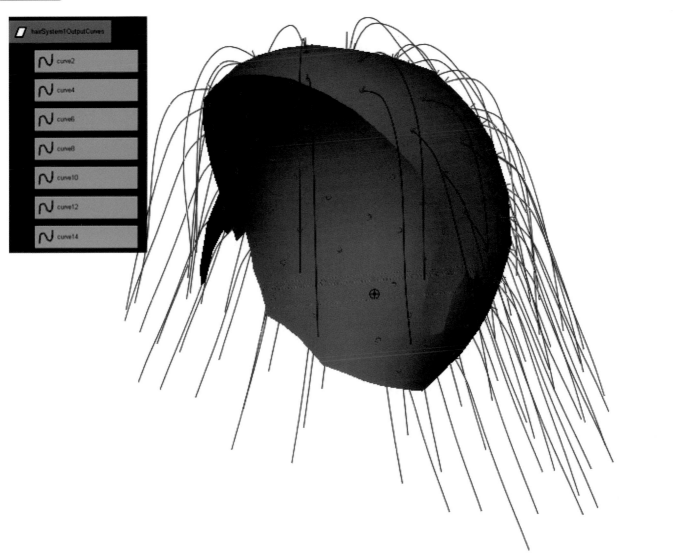

Styling with Hair Curves:

A finished hairstyle requires heavy editing of both the hair curves and the paint effects properties. It can easily take many hours of work to arrive at the final look. While much of this chapter has been presented in a linear fashion, please recognize that you will spend much of your time while styling hair going back and forth. It's not uncommon to have to add/remove follicles, re-model hair curves and tweak displacement all at the same time.

This section explains some techniques for modeling hair curves quickly and easily. Once the hair curves have been tamed, more refined control is possible by adjusting the shading and displacement properties. These properties are covered in the next section.

Once the follicles are placed and adjusted, the hair can finally begin to be styled. There are two basic controls for adjusting the style of a hair system:

1. **Modeling the Start/Rest Curves:** By changing the shape of the start and/or rest curves, you can adjust the shape of the hair clumps along their length.

2. **Tweaking the Shading and Displacement Attributes:** The hair system node contains a myriad of options for tweaking the look of the paint effects and/or hair primitives.

Recall that start curves represent the shape the hair will assume at the beginning of the animation (before the dynamics kick-in). Once a simulation begins, its initial shape can sometimes be completely lost as a result of gravity and other forces. Increasing the stiffness may help, but results in slower calculations and (at very high levels) solver instability (ie. hairs that wobble uncontrollably). Basically, the hair loses its modeled shape and flops all over the place.

In the real world, we tackle this problem with hairspray (or if you are like me, a baseball cap). In Maya, we have two options to keep hair together:

1. **The Start Curve Attract Feature:** This feature was added to Maya in v7.0 and is a huge blessing for hair animators. The attribute can be found on the hair system node FIGURE 2.17. When set to a non-zero value, all hairs in the system will try to assume the shape of their start curves during simulation. Increasing this value will make the hair very stiff. At a value of 1, the hair will remain in its start shape through even the strongest forces (like the hair gel you had in high school).

2. **Rest Curves:** Rest curves were the only solution for keeping a hair's shape before the release of Maya 7.0. For almost all intents and purposes, rest curves are no longer needed. If you happen to be working with Maya 6.0, you should know that rest curves are limited in that they are only adjustable through the Stiffness attribute. This is unfortunate because the stiffness feature causes instability when set to a very high value. Stiff hairstyles are much more controllable with the Start Curve Attract feature.

Knowing this, it's clear that rest curves are rarely needed anymore. The duration of this chapter is going to assume access to the Start Curve Attract feature. If you don't have it, just recognize that rest curves will

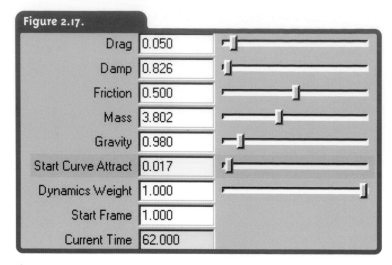

Figure 2.17.

do the trick, but will require more tweaking and longer simulation times.

The Start Curve Attract feature has changed the workflow for styling hair. Now, rather than model rest curves, we can style a single set of curves (start curves) and set the attraction to keep the hair in place.

As a side note, this feature can also be used as a method of blending between keyframe animation and dynamics. It is possible to put keyframe animation on the start curves (via deformers), and set the Start Curve Attract to a low value. This will allow for the absolute control of keyframe animation, while retaining the realism of a semi-dynamic simulation. Truly a powerful combination.

So, if styling the shape of hair is a matter of modeling the start curves, surely we don't have to resort to manually pushing hundreds of CVs on the curves into the desired shape, do we? The answer is... not always. There are quite a few shortcuts that can be used to help you model the shape of the start curves. The following tips and techniques have helped me turn this potential nightmare, into an enjoyable activity:

Customize Your Interface: While shaping the hair curves, you will want to constantly switch between viewing the start curves, and the final paint effects. Use the `Hair > Display` menu to quickly switch between viewing the start and current positions. In fact, I always tear-off the entire hair menu, drop into a single perspective view and build a custom shelf as I work. It won't take you long to figure out what operations need to be accessed over-and-over (and thus belong on a shelf).

Use the Hair Dynamics: Run the simulation. Adjust the gravity, stiffness and dampening to create hair that droops realistically. You can also apply a dynamic field to the hair to create a messy or windblown look. When the hair is in place, stop the playback and choose `Hair > Set Start Position > From Current`.

Use Hair Constraints and Interactive Playback: It won't take long before you wish you could just reach through your monitor and start grabbing the hair with your bare hands. To avoid damaging your monitor, use the Maya hair constraints in conjunction with interactive playback. Select the start curves you want to manipulate and choose `Hair > Convert Selection > to Start Curve End CVs`. With all the tip CVs selected, choose `Hair > Create Constraint > Transform`. This will create a locator in the center of the CVs. Now grab the locator and under the Dynamics menu-set choose `Solvers > Interactive Playback`. The scene will begin playing-back while you are free to manipulate the locator! Move and rotate the locator to manually tug the hairs into position. When you are happy, stop the playback and choose `Hair > Set Start Position > From Current`.

Use Passive Follicles: There is no need to manually style every single hair. Style a select few hairs and make the surrounding hairs passive. The passive hairs will move along (with a nice falloff) without the need for manual adjustment. Don't be afraid to switch a follicle between passive and dynamic as you need. Alternatively, you can style a relatively sparse set of dynamic follicles; when finished, paint additional passive follicles to thicken the hair. The additional passive follicles will automatically assume the shape of the already styled hairs.

Use the Modify Curves Tools: Sometimes it will be necessary to roll-up your sleeves and get dirty by manually moving curve CVs. While this does give you ultimate control, moving CVs can create jagged looking curves that lose their length. To fix this, lock the length of a curve before editing it (`Hair > Modify Curves > Lock Length`). There are also tools for smoothing, straightening, curling and bending the hair curve FIGURE 2.18. Use the Modify Curve tools in conjunction with manual point-pushing to achieve any specific shape.

Figure 2.18.

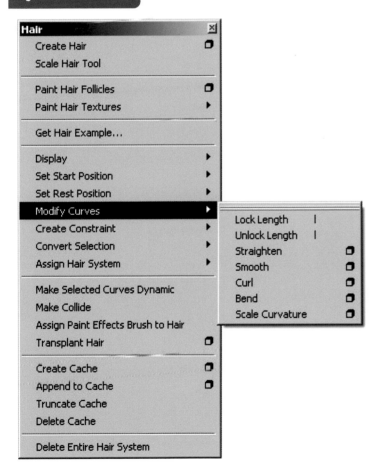

Typically, I start every styling session by making very broad changes to the hair. Just like a painting, it helps to keep your edits very general at first, and then progressively add more detail. Start by styling the hair with dynamics to get it pointed in the right direction. Then go in with hair constraints and manually pull it into position. Once the bulk of the hair is looking good, add detail by manually tweaking the curves. When styling with hair constraints, you can set half of the follicles to be passive. They will follow their neighboring dynamics follicles without the need to manually constrain them. Once they are in the correct position,

you can switch them back to dynamic before simulating the animation. This makes for a much faster workflow when styling thick hair.

With the hair almost finished, it's always a good idea to create a few stray hairs. Add some randomness by selecting a few curves and applying a few straightening/curling iterations to make them stick out (no hair is perfect). Finally, vary the length and clump width of the follicles slightly to create a more natural hairstyle.

Exercise 2.1	The 'Villainous' Hair Style

Because hair is such a newly mastered phenomenon in computer graphics, there aren't many examples of its use in commercial productions. Perhaps one of the best examples of CG hair can be seen in Pixar's *The Incredibles*. In it, the main villain sports a wild orange updo. His hair acts as a symbol of his strength. When he's at his best, the hair is stiff and majestic. Upon his ultimate defeat, the mass of hair falls limp, along with his sense of pride.

In this exercise, we will create a hairstyle much like the one seen on the villain from The Incredibles. This way, you can see exactly how to manipulate hair to achieve a specific effect. If you haven't already seen The Incredibles, promptly scold yourself and head straight to the video store before continuing.

1.) Open exercise2.1_Start.mb. This file contains a single piece of geometry in the shape of a generic head. It has had its UV's cleanly arranged within the 0-to-1 space. To get started, let's create some hair. Select the head and choose `Hair > Create Hair`. Set the hair creation options as shown in FIGURE 2.19. Notice that we are not creating rest curves. That is because we will be styling the start curves directly (and then using the Start Curve Attract feature to keep them in place). The points per hair is set to a value of 8 to provide adequate resolution. The initial length of 6 provides a good starting place. Also, note that we are creating Paint Effects as our output, even though the hair will be rendered as hair primitives in mental ray.

Figure 2.19.

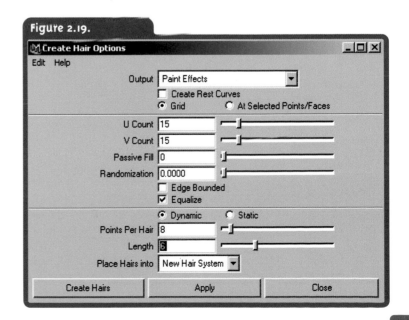

2.) Open exercise2.1_A.mb. This file contains the hair after the initial creation. As you can see in FIGURE 2.20, we have a lot of styling to do. At this point, the hair is pointing straight-out; normal to the surface. We want it to look swept upwards. To style the hair into the general shape we want, let's utilize some dynamics.

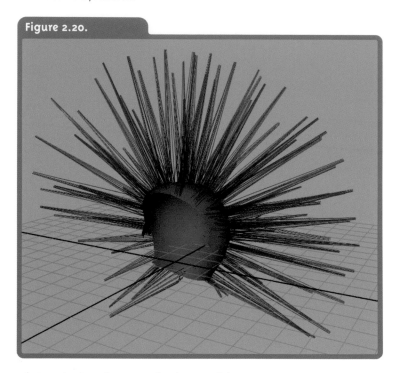
Figure 2.20.

3.) Try playing the scene (make sure 'Play Every Frame' is checked in the playback options). The hair should settle as the scene plays. At frame 100, the hair will look like FIGURE 2.21. It's an interesting look, but we want the hair pulled *up*, not dragged down. Why not reverse the gravity? Select the hair system node and put a negative sign in front of the Gravity value. Rewind, and play the scene again.

Figure 2.21.

This time, the hair should flip upwards and settle into something like FIGURE 2.22. Now select the paint effects hair and choose Hair > Set Start Position > From Current. Now when the scene is re-wound, the hair will remain pointed upwards.

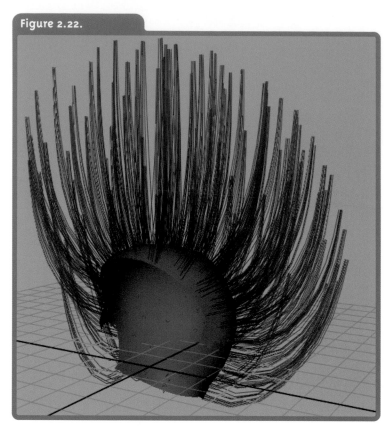
Figure 2.22.

4.) Open exercise2.1_B.mb to see the progress thus far. At this point, the hair is pointed upwards but it's far too spread-out. Notice in the finished hairdo, that the hairs are *pulled together* at the top. Let's use a constraint to manually pull the hair into the desired shape. We will be constraining and manipulating the start curves, so we must display them first. Select the paint effects and choose Hair > Display > Start Curves. The paint effects will be hidden and the start curves revealed FIGURE 2.23. Notice that they have now assumed an upwards shape as well.

5.) Rather than try and shape all of the curves at once, let's focus on the top, sides and back of the head separately. Select all of the curves on the top of the head as shown in FIGURE 2.24. Now select Hair > Convert Selection > To Start Curve End CVs. This will automatically select all of the control vertices at the tips of the start curves. Now select Hair > Create Constraint > Transform. This will create a locator in the middle of the selection. When manipulated, this locator will pull on the constrained hairs, just as though you had grabbed them with your hand.

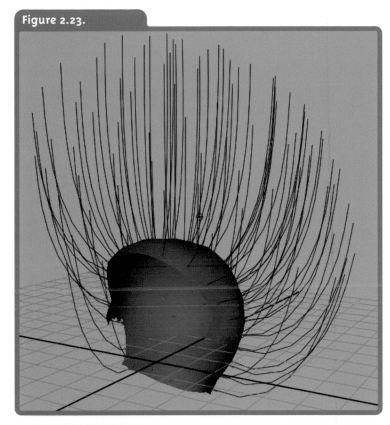

Figure 2.23.

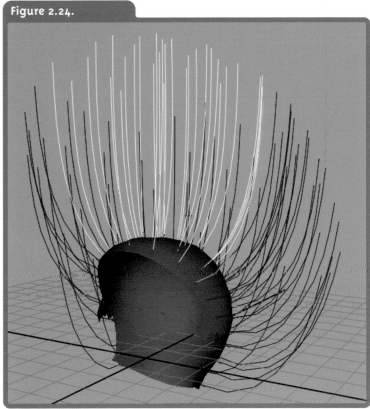

Figure 2.24.

6.) Open exercise2.1_C.mb to see the finished constraint. To actually move this constraint, you *could* simply set some keys on it, but wouldn't it be much more intuitive to simply pull it around and have the hair update in realtime? This is possible by utilizing the Interactive Playback feature. Interactive Playback works by playing back the scene and calculating the dynamics, but still allowing manipulations in the viewport

(like translation, rotation and scaling). To give ourselves adequate time to manipulate the hair, set the scene's end frame to 3000.

7.) Before we can manipulate the hair, we must display the paint effects again in order to see any effect. If we were to only watch the start curves, nothing would appear to happen as the scene played; we must display the output of the hair system (whether that be paint effects or output curves). Select any hair curve and choose `Hair > Display Current Position`. This will display the paint effects and hide the start curves (you should also see springs drawn between the locator and the affected vertices FIGURE 2.25). From now on, we will assume that you know how to switch between displaying the start and current positions (corresponding to the start curve and paint effects respectively).

Figure 2.25.

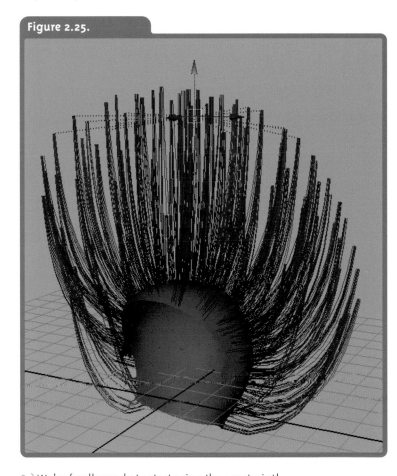

8.) We're finally ready to start using the constraint! Select the locator and choose `Simulation > Interactive Playback` (from the Dynamics menu set). While the scene is playing, pull the hair up slightly (by translating the locator) and scale the locator inwards to pull the hair together. When the top hairs are styled something like in FIGURE 2.26, stop the playback and set this to the start position (`Hair > Set Start Position > From Current`). Now you can safely rewind the scene and the new style will remain intact.

Figure 2.26.

Figure 2.27.

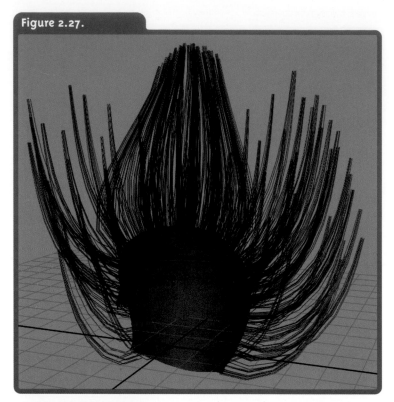

Figure 2.28.

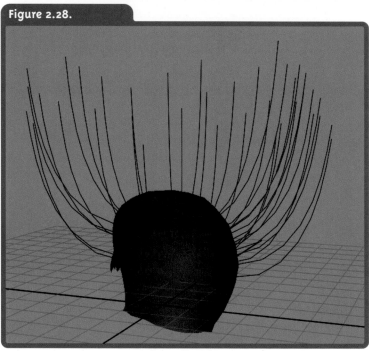

9.) Open exercise2.1_D.mb to see the hairstyle with the top hairs pulled into position. There are a couple of issues at this point. Firstly, the hair is somewhat crimped at the top where it was constrained. Secondly, if you now play the scene, the hairs will fall out of their custom shape. The Start Curve Attract feature can solve both these issues. Select the hair system node and set the Start Curve Attract attribute to a value of 0.2. Now play the scene. The hairs will remain somewhat intact (like hairspray) and the dynamics should force any kinks out of the hair curves FIGURE 2.27. Voila! Create a new start position from the dynamic simulation.

10.) Open exercise2.1_E.mb to see the hairstyle after adjusting the Start Curve Attract feature. Now that the top of the head is under control, let's tackle the hairs a little further down. Create another transform constraint to pull-in the hairs shown in FIGURE 2.28. Don't get greedy and try to style them all at once, it's much easier to work in layers, like a real hairdresser. If you notice the constraint is causing the tips of the constrained hairs to lag, set the stiffness of the constraint to a value of 1 (100%).

11.) Open exercise2.1_F.mb to see the second hair constraint for the middle hairs. Use an interactive simulation to pull these hairs inwards and blend them into the clump on top of the head. When finished, they should look like FIGURE 2.29.

Figure 2.29.

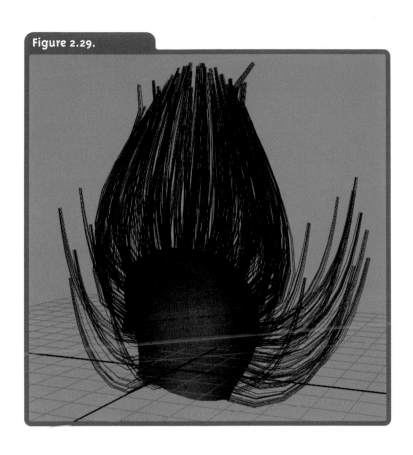

12.) Open exercise2.1_G.mb. This file contains the hairdo after using only two hair constraints. At this point, the hair on the top and sides of the head is looking good, but the hairs running down the back of the neck have yet to be tamed. Using the techniques outlined above, constrain them and pull them inwards like in FIGURE 2.30. This concludes the majority of the constraining.

Figure 2.30.

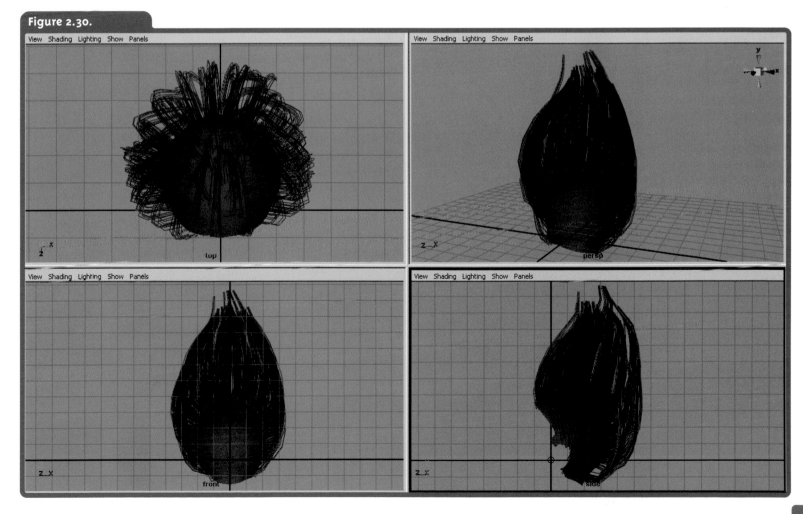

13.) Open exercise2.1_H.mb to see the hair after constraining. You may notice that the shape of the hair has appeared to diminish during the constraining phase. This is because each time you saved the start position, it was after the simulation had relaxed the hair slightly. This continued relaxation, over time, will cause the hair to lose shape. We could have lessoned this effect by reducing the gravity, or completely avoided it by setting the styled follicles to be static. But having seen the problem, you are now more likely to remember the cause.

14.) Once the bulk of the hairdo is complete, it's time to dig in there and begin tweaking. This phase will easily take 95% of your time and, due to the nature of the work, is impossible to cover in a step-by-step tutorial. Basically, you must use all of the available tools to sculpt the start curves into the proper position. Try to resist getting tunnel vision during this process. Remember, these are regular NURBS curves, and as such, they can be sculpted using many different tools. I find lattices can sometimes provide a nice way to globally affect several curves at once (other deformers may be useful too). Of course, don't forget about the `Hair > Modify Curves` menu either.

15.) Lastly, ensure that you apply some variation in the length of the hair. This can be done quite easily by selecting some start curves, activating the scale hair tool and dragging left/right in the viewport (to shrink/grow the hair). Manipulate the hair by hand if necessary, just try to add as much variation as you can to avoid an artificial look. You may wish to watch the included video lecture (on the DVD) to gain insight into the workflows that are available for sculpting hair curves.

16.) Open exercise2.1_Finished.mb to see the hairdo with the final, sculpted start curves FIGURE 2.31. At this point, the hair curves are properly styled, but the paint effects still need much work. We will pick-up from here in exercise 2.2 to discuss the shading, displacements and lighting of this hairdo.

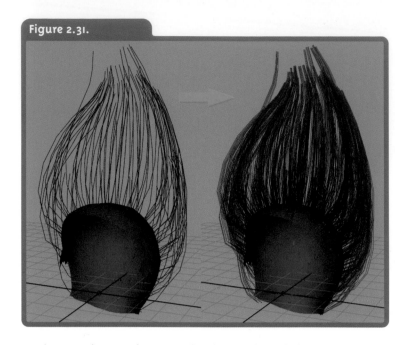

Figure 2.31.

Read-on to discover how to take this newly styled hair and apply shading with displacements to bring it closer to the final look.

Styling with Clumps, Shading and Displacements:

Recall that hair curves determine the shape of the hair along its length. Obviously, there are many other factors affecting the look of a hairstyle, beyond its shape. Attributes like thickness, color, clumping, frizziness and specularity must be customized to create the final effect.

To attach the paint effects brush to hair curves, Maya Hair creates a 'clump' of strands for each follicle. By default, these clumps are tightly knit creating a very clumpy hairstyle. Clumps must be tweaked in order to achieve a smooth density of hair across the surface.

Maya Hair combines all of these attributes (and several more) onto the hair system node FIGURE 2.32. Adjusting the various parameters on the hair system node allows the hair to assume almost any look (including both realistic and highly stylized). These properties are split into three major sections:

1. **Clump and Hair Shape:** As the name implies, these attributes control how hairs clump together. Hair thickness and clump-shape can also be adjusted.

2. **Shading**: Like a surface shader, these properties determine how light reacts to the hair.

3. **Displacements:** The displacements affect the shape of the *paint effects* hair that is attached to the hair system (not to be confused with the shape of the hair curves; which are not affected by displacements). Displacements are used to create irregularities along the hair strand (for frizziness and curling).

Figure 2.32.

▶	Clump and Hair Shape
▶	Dynamics
▶	Collisions
▶	Turbulence
▶	Shading
▶	Displacements
▶	Multi Streaks
▶	Render Stats
▶	mental ray
▶	Object Display
▶	Node Behavior
▶	Extra Attributes

The following table examines the effect of all the important attributes found under the Clump and Hair Shape tab:

Clump and Hair Shape Properties:

# Property	Use	Example
Hairs Per Clump	The hairs per clump attribute specifies the number of strands in each clump. This corresponds to the number of hairs in each follicle. Multiplying this value by the number of follicles will give you the total number of hairs in the system. Tweak this value (along with the hair thickness and number of follicles) to achieve thick or thin hair styles.	Figure 2.33. 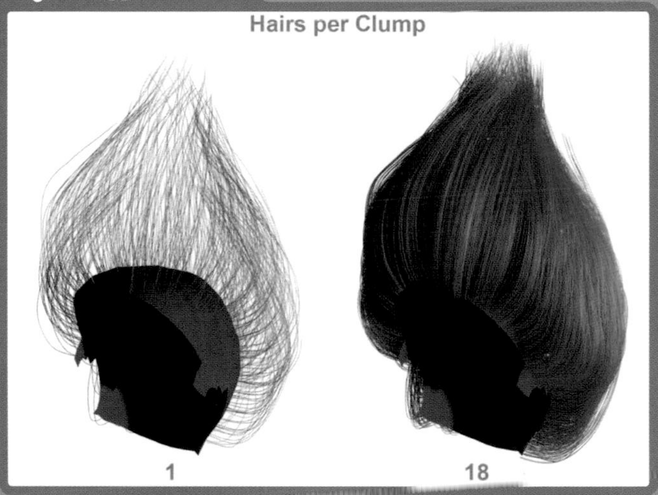 Hairs per Clump 1 18
Baldness Map	By plugging a texture into this attribute, hairs growing from a black region will be removed. This provides per-pixel control for the placement of hairs. It can be used to create a custom shape for the edge of the hair. For example, you may paint a baldness map to give a character a receding hair line. Trying to do this by manually positioning follicles would be much more difficult (and less accurate). Baldness maps can also be painted using the artisan brush (under the Hair menu).	Figure 2.34. 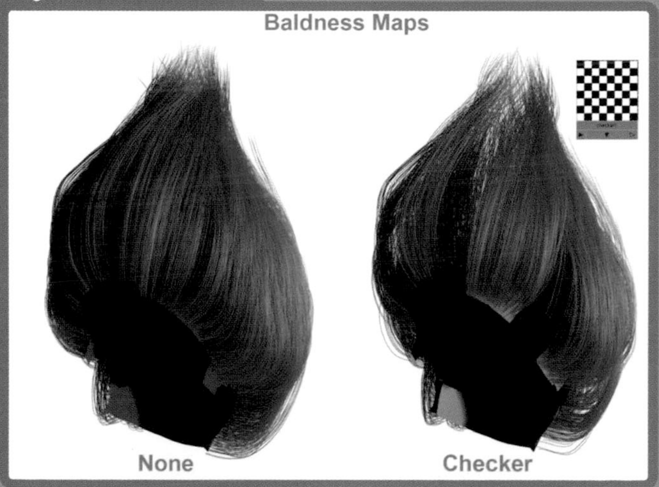 Baldness Maps None Checker

Sub Segments

This attribute specifies the number of divisions between vertices along the length of the hair curve. Lower values will give hair a very unattractive angular look. If the hair is long and curly, it will need more resolution to approximate bending. The sub segments value works in tandem with the number of points on the hair curves to create a smooth looking strand of hair. More sub segments will increase render times so raise this value in small increments until any jaggedness is gone.

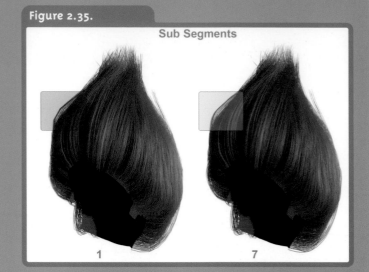

Figure 2.35.

Sub Segments

1   7

Thinning

This value ranges from 0 to 1 and controls the number of shorter hairs in each clump. At a value of 0, every hair in the clump is the same length. This can create sharp, unrealistic edges that look artificial. Increase this value until the hair tips are nicely feathered.

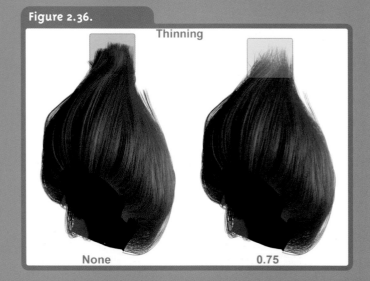

Figure 2.36.

Thinning

None   0.75

Clump Twist

The clump twist value ranges from -1 to 1 (-180 to 180 degrees respectively). This value is used to rotate a clump of hair about its base. The rotating is uniform along the length of the clump and so it does not create a twisted looking clump (contrary to the name). The only difference is that the individual strands will be rotated about their base. This value has little affect for styling hair unless the hair clumps are flattened (thus making their orientation visible).

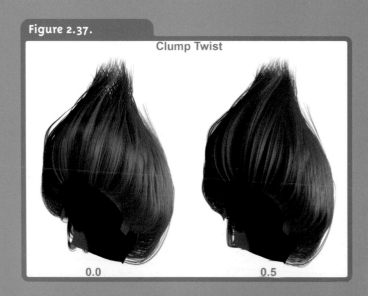

Figure 2.37.

Clump Twist

0.0   0.5

# Property	Use	Example

Clump Width

The clump width determines how far hair strands will grow from the center of the hair. Low values create very tight clumps. If this value is increased so that neighboring clumps blend into each other, the clumpy nature of the hair system can be effectively hidden. This is very useful for creating evenly distributed hair across a surface.

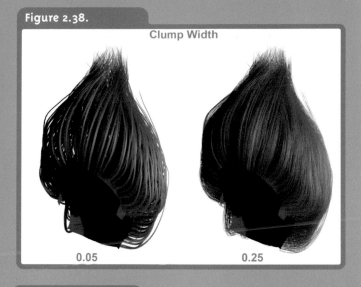

Figure 2.38.

Clump Width

0.05   0.25

Hair Width

This value controls the girth of all the hairs in the system. Obviously, this is an extremely important attribute for creating thick or thin hairstyles. It should be adjusted along with the number of hairs per clump and the follicle density to achieve the desired thickness.

Figure 2.39.

Hair Width

0.001   0.02

Clump Width Scale

This graph is used to scale the clump width along the length of the clump. The left side of the graph represents the base of the clump, and the right corresponds to the tip. Tapering a hair clump towards the tip usually creates a more realistic image. You can also taper the width of the hair strands themselves using the Hair Width Scale graph.

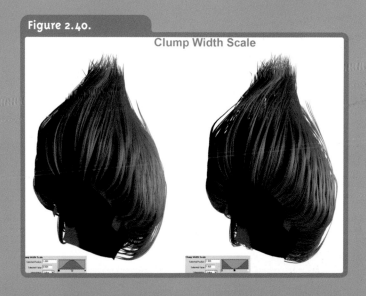

Figure 2.40.

Clump Width Scale

# Property	Use	Example

Clump Curl

Unlike the deceptively named Clump Twist attribute, this graph can actually create a twisted looking clump of hair. It does this by allowing for a varying amount of rotation along the length of the hair. Just like the other graphs, the left represents the base, while the right-side controls the tip. Values of 0.5 create no twisting, while values closer to 1 or 0 will twist the clump in opposite directions.

Clump Flatness

This graph controls how flat the clump of hair is along its length. Flattened clumps can be used to create highly stylized designs or (in less amounts) very wet hair. Once a clump has been flattened, you may need to adjust its orientation using the Clump Twist attribute.

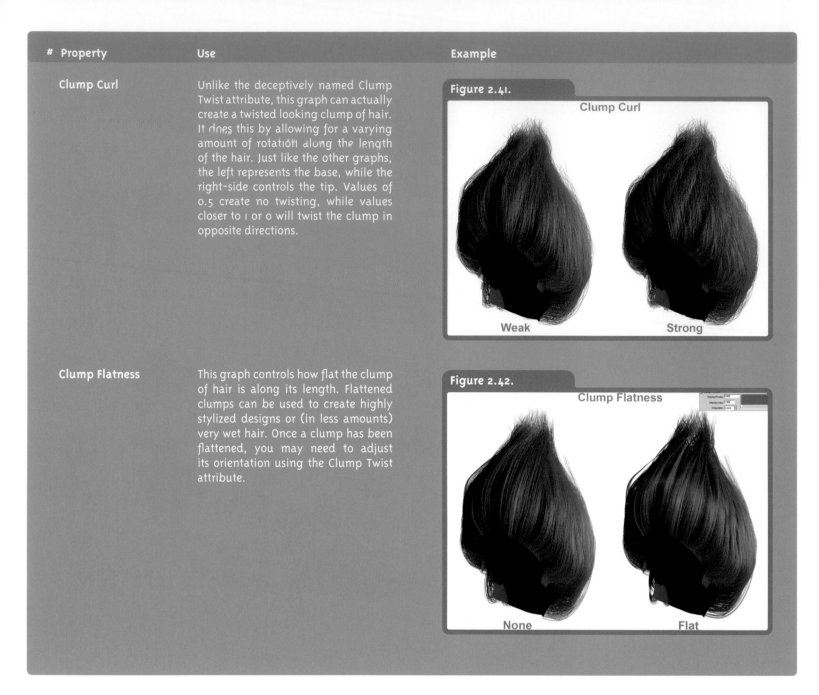

Figure 2.41.

Clump Curl

Weak   Strong

Figure 2.42.

Clump Flatness

None   Flat

The following table (opposite page) explores the various shading properties under the Shading tab on the hair system node. These properties control how light will interact with the rendered hair:

# Property	Use	Example
Hair Color	Quite simply, this is the diffuse contribution to the hair's color. The hair color can also be mapped to create really interesting effects. Hairs will inherit the color of the pixel at the UV coordinate from which they are grown. Streaks can be created by manually painting dots wherever you would like a streak to originate from. The final color of the hair is affected by this attribute plus the hair color scale and randomization parameters.	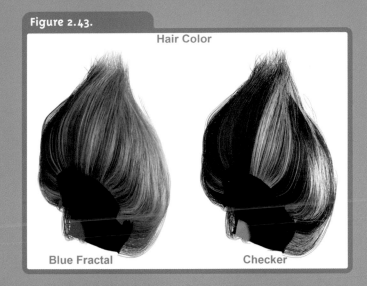 **Figure 2.43.** Hair Color — Blue Fractal — Checker
Hair Color Scale	This ramp controls the color of the hair along its length. The left side of the ramp is the color of the hair at the base of the strand, while the right side is the color at the tips. You can specify an RGB value at each key along the length of the ramp (or even a map). These values are then multiplied by the hair color value (before randomization is factored in). Typically, the hair color should lighten towards the tips to simulate a root-shadowing effect.	**Figure 2.44.** Hair Color Scale — Selected Position 0.000 — Selected Color — Interpolation Spline
Opacity	This value adjusts the opacity of the hair. A value of 0 is fully transparent and 1 is fully opaque. The default value of 1 may be fine for most cases. Lowering the value makes the hair look wispy and lite. Opaque hair tends to look much more coarse and solid (like porcupine quills).	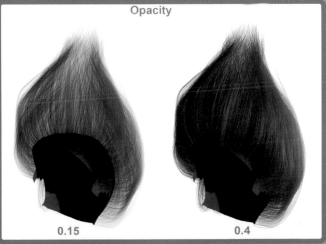 **Figure 2.45.** Opacity — 0.15 — 0.4

# Property	Use	Example

Translucence

This value adjusts the translucence of the hair; value close to 1 allows light to penetrate deeply into the hair. This parameter is especially important for achieving believable self-shadowing effects. If the translucence is too low, the hair shading will look harsh. Higher values (typically around 0.75) allow light to penetrate the hair and scatter throughout. This brightens shadows and gives the hair a more natural feel.

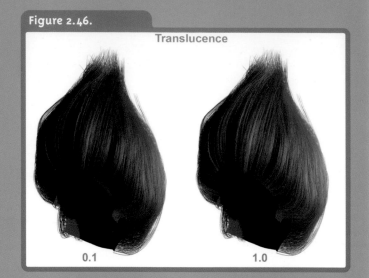

Figure 2.46.
Translucence

0.1   1.0

Specular Color

The specularity of hair is a very important aspect of its shading. Typically, specular highlights in hair are the same color as the hair itself, except lighter. If the hair is predominately brown, give the specular color a very light brownish tint. Adjusting the specular *power* affects the intensity of the specular highlights.

Figure 2.47.
Specular Color

Light Green   Light Blue

Cast Shadows

If checked on, the hair will cast shadows on both itself, and surrounding objects. If checked off, the hair is ignored in shadow map and raytrace shadow calculations. Hair shadowing is covered in the section on rendering hair.

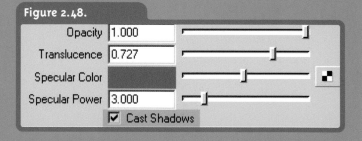

Figure 2.48.

Opacity	1.000	
Translucence	0.727	
Specular Color		
Specular Power	3.000	

☑ Cast Shadows

Color Randomization

This tab contains five parameters for randomizing the diffuse, specular, hue, saturation and value attributes. Each parameter ranges from 0 to 1. As the value approaches 1, more randomness is added. Except for perhaps extremely stylized hairdos, a small amount of randomness greatly enhances the believability of the hair.

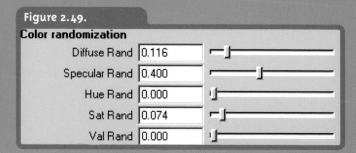

Figure 2.49.
Color randomization

Diffuse Rand	0.116	
Specular Rand	0.400	
Hue Rand	0.000	
Sat Rand	0.074	
Val Rand	0.000	

Finally, we get to displacements. Recall that these are used to vary the shape of the paint effects (or hair primitives in mental ray), not the actual hair curves. The following list covers all three of the various displacements that can be applied to Maya Hair:

Curling FIGURE 2.50 : The curling displacement attribute causes individual hairs to assume a wavy shape. To get large curls comprised of several hairs, you must style the hair curve itself; displacements will not suffice. The curl attributes are great for adding waviness to a hairstyle. To make large, soft, waves in the hair, set the Curl Frequency to a low value. Larger frequency values will create smaller waves (like crimped hair). Be aware, however, that the hair must have an adequate number of sub segments in order to fully represent high-frequency curling (it's not uncommon to set the sub segments to as high as 20). The additional displacement calculations and sub segments will increase render times significantly (use with caution).

Sub Clumping FIGURE 2.52: As the name implies, sub clumps are smaller clumps of hairs that reside within the larger, per-follicle clumps. Sub-clumping is the phenomenon seen when hair is wet or greasy (like after an all-night Maya binge). The amount that the hair is attracted into sub clumps is specified by the Sub Clumping attribute. The number of sub clumps is specified by the Num UClumps/VClumps attributes. These two values, multiplied together, will yield the approximate total number of sub clumps. There is also a randomness attribute that will scatter the clumps for a more natural look. By animating these attributes, along with the color, specularity, and dynamic weight, a dry-to-wet effect can be achieved.

These three displacements are extremely useful for fine-tuning the look of a hairstyle. Always remember a few things when using displacements (see below):

Figure 2.50.

Curling Displacement

Low Frequency

High Frequency

Noise FIGURE 2.51 : No hair strand is perfectly smooth. Noise is great for adding small imperfections (at a low level) or creating frizzy, wild hair (at larger values). There are three methods of adding noise to the hair: Random, Surface UV and Clump UV. For a typical noisy effect, the Random method will work fine. Simply jack-up the noise value and adjust the frequency to fine-tune the scale of the displacements. For additional control over the frequency, you can use the Surface UV and Clump UV methods. The Surface UV method defines the noise volumetrically with control for the noise frequency in the U,V and W directions (U and V correspond to the plane the hair is grown from, while the W axis points along the length of the hair). The Clump UV method allows for the same axial-specific control, but the frequencies are applied per-clump (rather than computed across the entire surface).

- Adequate Sub Segments are necessary in order to see the effect of high-frequency noise and curling.

- The more displacements you add, the more computations are needed to arrive at the final shape of the hair; directly translating into significantly longer render times. It's not uncommon for render times to increase by a factor of 2-5 times.

- Displacements can be previewed in the viewport by viewing the paint effects. For realtime feedback in the viewport, decrease the total number of hairs while you tweak displacements.

Figure 2.51.

Noise Displacement

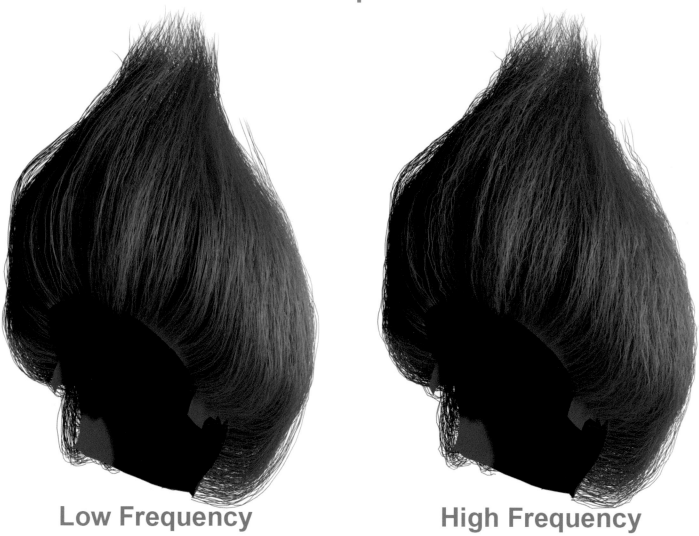

Low Frequency   High Frequency

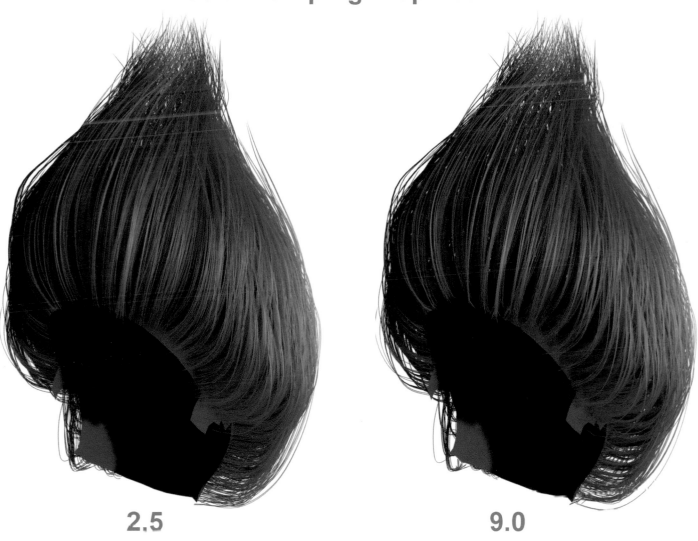

Sub Clumping Displacement

2.5   9.0

Figure 2.52.

The Displacement Scale graph provides control over the strength of the displacements along the length of the hair. Recall that real hair grows outwards from the follicle (not from within the strand, like a tree-trunk). For this reason, hair at the tips is much older than the new hair at the roots. This makes the tips of a hair strand much more fragile and thus susceptible to displacements (hence the reason for 'split-ends'). By cutting the Displacement Scale graph such that the left side is low, and the right side is high (a value approaching 1) the displacements will taper towards the roots for a much more believable effect FIGURE 2.53.

Figure 2.53.

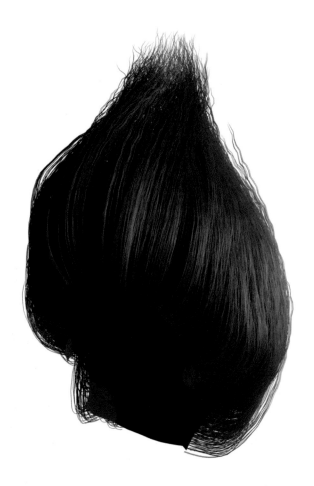

Simulating Hair:

If you have followed along (and completed exercise 2.2), you should already be familiar with the basics of hair simulation. Each follicle is attached to a hair. When the scene is played, these hairs react according to the properties on the hair system node (or the overrides on the follicle, if used). These properties affect the behavior of the hair. By tweaking these values (and employing other tricks), we can approximate a multitude of situations: windy hair, underwater hair, stiff hair, or even hair colliding with an object.

Animating Hair:

In addition to the dynamic properties on the hair system node, there are several other ways of manipulating the motion of hair. Here is a list of the available options:

1. **Hair System Node:** This node contains several dynamic properties that act as global settings for the entire system. These properties affect the motion of every follicle attached to the system unless the dynamic properties on the follicle have been overridden. The hair system node is discussed in detail later in this section.

2. **Follicle Overrides:** Each follicle contains attributes for adjusting the dampening, stiffness and length flex. These attributes are only necessary if you wish to specify a different behavior for that particular follicle. If used, these attributes override the settings from the hair system node.

3. **Hair Constraints:** These are used to gain per-vertex control over the hairs. In addition to being useful for styling, they can also be used to control the hair during animation. Constraints are particularly useful for simulating ponytails or interaction with the hair (like a hand grabbing and pulling/twisting the hair).

4. **Collisions:** Hair can collide with any polygonal geometry or even with itself. While the geometry collision calculations are certainly useful, more accurate collisions can be simulated with the use of implicitly defined spheres and boxes. These calculate faster, are more stable (fewer interpenetrations) and provide more control (the intensity of the collision can be modulated with a stiffness attribute).

5. **Dynamic Fields:** As a testament to how well Maya Hair is integrated with the rest of the software, hair may be attached to any dynamic field (gravity, air, Newton, radial or turbulence). These are especially useful for creating nature effects like windblown hair or for styling.

6. **Keyframes:** Sometimes it may be easier to simply keyframe the motion you want, rather than rely entirely on a dynamic simulation. This is made possible by animating the start curves, with the use of the Start Curve Attract feature. The start curves should have some manner of rigging for easy control (joints and lattices work great). The keyframed motion can then be blended with dynamics by setting the Start Curve Attract to a value less than 1.

The task of animating hair involves setting-up the dynamics (and/or keyframe animation), simulating the hair and then creating a cache. Once the cache is created, it is safe to batch render the hair before compositing it into the final image. The rest of this section covers the specifics of the various techniques used to animate hair, starting with the dynamic properties on the hair system node.

The Hair System Dynamics:

The hair system node contains the majority of the properties used to animate hair FIGURE 2.54. You may find that it provides all the control you will ever need. The following is a table of each attribute, and its affect on the hair (opposite page):

Figure 2.54.

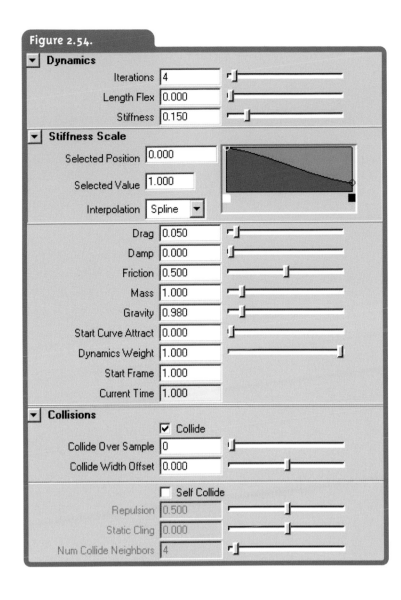

#	Dynamic Property	Effect on the Hair
	Iterations	This controls the number of calculations per time step of the hair solver. Higher numbers mean more calculations which results in slower (but more accurate) simulations. Increase this from its default value of 4 (by small increments) to fix solver instability or interpenetrating collisions.
	Length Flex	This value adjusts the hair's resistance to stretching. Increasing this value allows the hair to stretch under force. It can be used to create some nice cartoony or non-hair effects, but should be limited in realistic hair animations.

#	Dynamic Property	Effect on the Hair
	Stiffness	A hair will try to assume its rest shape (by default, this shape is perfectly straight) against outside forces. The stiffness value controls how much the hair is attracted to its rest shape. Increasing the stiffness forces the hair into a straight line (unless another rest shape is specified. This can be done with a rest curve.). Typically, it is better to use the Start Curve Attract feature to create stiff hair, while keeping this at a very low value.
	Stiffness Scale	The stiffness of the hair may be varied along its length. By default, this graph will taper the stiffness towards the tips.
	Drag	The drag feature simulates the friction between the hair, and the medium it is traveling through. Higher values can approximate the look of underwater hair. At a value of 1.0, the hair has no inertia and appears to be suspended in a thick liquid.
	Damp	As real hair settles after a movement, much of its kinetic energy is lost to self-friction . This value dampens the motion of the hair to simulate this effect. If you experience wild oscillations in your hair simulation, dampening can often alleviate the problem.
	Friction	This attribute controls the amount of friction between the hair and collision objects. At a higher value, hair will stick to collision objects rather than slide across them.
	Gravity	This force is applied to the hair in the direction of the -Y axis and simulates the gravitational pull of the earth.
	Start Curve Attract	This is much like the stiffness attribute, except the Start Curve Attract value controls the attraction of the hair to the start position, not the rest position. The strength of this attraction is also affected by the Stiffness Scale graph (allowing for a varied intensity of attraction along the length of the hair).

# Dynamic Property	Effect on the Hair
Dynamics Weight	Controls the weight of the hair. Increasing this value basically increases the effect of any forces applied to the hair.
Start Frame	The hair solver begins simulating the hair at the frame specified by this value. If you have animation on negative frames, this value must be adjusted accordingly.
Current Time	The hair solver calculates the position of each hair as the time changes. By default, this attribute is connected to the main time node in your scene, although it can be connected to whatever you want (only useful for creating custom effects).

# Dynamic Property	Effect on the Hair
Num Collide Neighbors	This value determines the number of neighboring hairs to collide with. Obviously, higher values increase simulation times.
Collide Ground / Ground Height	When Collide Ground is checked on, the hair will collide with an invisible ground plane. The height of the ground plane is specified by the Ground Height attribute. This feature is simply a convenience and could be replaced by manually configuring collision objects.
Draw Collide Width / Width Draw Skip	By turning on Draw Collide Width, Maya will draw circles around each strand of hair to show its collision width FIGURE 2.55. The Width Draw Skip value is used to specify how many segments to skip before drawing another circle. Increasing this value simply reduces the clutter in the viewport.

Maya Hair includes control for making hairs collide with geometry, implicit spheres/cubes and other hairs.

Self collision can help large hairstyles maintain volume. Use this sparingly as it tends to increase simulation times dramatically. The use of passive follicles can help maintain volume without adding much in terms of computational overhead.

The following table covers the collision attributes found on the hair system node:

# Dynamic Property	Effect on the Hair
Collide	This check box is used to enable/disable collisions for all hair in the system.
Collide Over Sample	Increase this value to create more accurate collisions. Higher values increase simulation times.
Collide With Offset	This value specifies a distance relative to the width of the hair clump to offset collisions. If dynamic hairs are colliding with neighboring passive clumps, this value can help create a buffer.
Self Collide	If turned on, this attribute will enable hair-to-hair collisions.
Static Cling	When self collisions are being computed, this value determines how much neighboring hairs are attracted to each other. At high values, it can create the look of hair with lots of static electricity.

Figure 2.55.

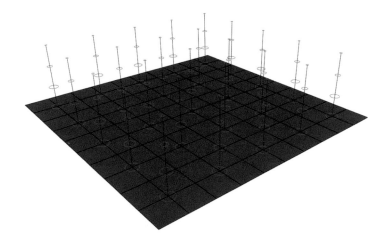

Hair Constraints:

If you followed along through exercise 2.1, you should already be familiar with the basic use of hair constraints. Hair constraints provide a means of controlling exactly how hair behaves. You can tie several strands together to create a ponytail, or simulate a character tugging on their hair.

To create a constraint, simply select the start curves for the hairs you wish to constrain and execute the constraint command from the Hair > Create Constraint menu. This will create a locator in the center of the selected curves. For some constraints, this locator must be translated, rotated or scaled to affect the hairs. When the output is displayed, Maya draws springs showing what the constraint is connecting FIGURE 2.56.

You can change the type of constraint *after creation* by adjusting the Constraint Method attribute on the constraint node.

Figure 2.56.

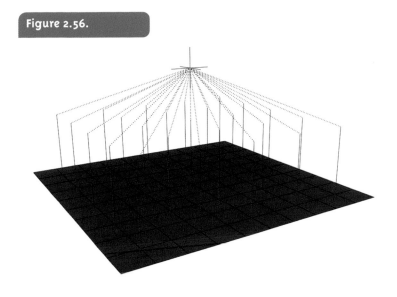

The different constraint types are well covered in Maya's documentation, but the following list should help clarify their uses. There are five types of constraints (not counting the implicit collisions):

Rubber Band: The rubber band constraint creates springs between each selected point and the constraint locator. When the locator is translated, these springs attempt to remain the same length and thus will pull the attached hairs along with them. Rotating a rubber band constraint has no effect because the springs are effectively *point constrained* to the locator (ignoring rotations).

Stick: The stick constraint creates springs, much like the rubber band, except that these springs will pull *and* push the hairs. When a stick constraint locator is translated, the hairs remain at a fixed distance from the locator. It behaves as though the hairs are pinned to the locator, or attached with solid 'sticks'.

Transform: The transform constraint behaves much like the rubber band except that its springs are effectively *parented* to the locator (rather than point constrained). So, unlike the rubber band, a transform constraint can be translated, rotated and scaled to affect the hair.

Hair to Hair: The last two constraints (hair to hair and hair bunch) are not affected by the translation, rotation or scaling of their locators. In fact, the locator does not affect these constraints at all. The Hair to Hair constraint creates springs between each of the selected hair CVs. Like a stick constraint, these springs will push and pull the hairs to keep them at the same distance from each other. But, unlike the stick constraint, the center of a Hair to Hair constraint will move freely with the hair. The best way to imagine this behavior is as being like a scrunchie. A scrunchie keeps hairs together, and yet moves freely with the hair.

Hair Bunch: The Hair Bunch constraint is used as an alternative to self-collisions. Like a Hair to Hair, this constraint creates springs between all of the selected CVs. But, unlike the Hair to Hair constraint, this constraint only pushes hair apart (it does not pull the hair together). This constraint can keep neighboring hairs from collapsing on each other, thus adding volume to the hair without the need to compute expensive self-collisions.

All hair constraints have the same set of attributes for adjusting their behavior. Some of these attributes are *not* very well explained in the Maya documentation; the following list should help you understand how to use them:

Constraint Method: this drop-down menu allows you to switch between the five main constraint types. This allows the type of hair constraint to be edited *after* creation, although it's not usually a good idea to do so (I have experienced buggy behavior from switching between constraint types).

Point Method: This drop-down menu provides three choices: Nearest, U Parameter and U Distance. This is how the constraint determines what piece of the hair (along its length) to constrain to. By default, it will constrain the sections of the selected hairs that are nearest to each other. If the point method is set to U Parameter, it will constrain the hair at the point along the curve as specified by the U Parameter attribute. Similarly, the U Distance method constrains those points that lie at the distance (along the length of the curve and measured in world units) as specified by the U Distance attribute. Recall that the point along the length of a curve is specified by the variable 'U'. At the start of the curve, U = 0. At the tip of the curve, the U value equals 1.0 (half-way along the curve, U = 0.5).

Stiffness: This defines how stiff the springs are in the constraint. This value ranges between 0 and 1. At a value of 1, the springs are completely rigid. This value is usually best left at value lower than 1 to add some softness to the constraint.

Glue Strength: The glue strength specifies how far a hair must lag before it is removed from the constraint. With a glue strength of 1, the hair will remain constrained regardless of its distance from the constraint center. At a low value (approaching zero), the hair will break away from the constraint quite easily. Hairs that break away from a constraint are no longer affected by the constraint and will not 're-join' the constraint for the duration of the animation.

U Parameter: If the point method is set to U Parameter, this attribute specifies the location (along the length of the hair) that the spring will be attached to. This value ranges from 0 to 1. At a value of 1, the spring is attached to the tip of the hair.

U Distance: If the point method is set to U Distance, this attribute specifies the distance (along the length of the hair) that the spring will be attached to. This value is measured in world units. If the hair is 5 units long, a value of 2.5 will place the spring half-way along the length of the hair.

Constraints are difficult to convey with words alone. I highly recommend watching the included video lecture (on the DVD) to gain a better understanding of how each constraint differs and how they should be used.

Collisions:

Like constraints, collisions affect the motion of the hair, but do so by limiting where the strands can move. By setting an object to collide with the hair, it will hit the object and will either slide across the surface or stick to it (depending on its friction parameter).

There are three types of collisions:

1. **Surface Collision Objects:** Hairs can collide with any polygonal or NURBS surface (subdivisions are not supported). Simply select the surface, shift select the hair system and choose `Hair > Make Collide`. A geoconnector node will be created and attached to the collision surface. This node contains a friction attribute.

2. **Implicit Collision Objects:** There are two types of implicit collision objects; spheres and cubes. The shape of these objects is defined implicitly (using simple mathematical equations). This simplified definition makes accurate and stable collision calculations much easier for the solver. Typically, implicit collision objects are much faster to calculate and do not cause hairs to get stuck (as can be witnessed in some cases with surface collisions). To create one, simply select a hair system (or individual start curves) and choose `Hair > Create Constraint > Collide Sphere / Collide Cube`. This will create a sphere or a cube. These shapes can then be manually transformed (including non-linear scaling) to approximate more complex shapes.

3. **Self-Collisions:** Hairs can also be set to collide with each other. While somewhat expensive to calculate, this feature is still quite useful in some instances (self-collision may be approximated with the clever use of passive hair curves and/or hair bunch constraints). To enable self-collision, select the hair system node and check the Self Collide box. There are several attributes for fine-tuning self-collisions. These attributes are covered in the Hair System Dynamic Properties table earlier in this chapter.

Caching the Simulation:

Once the hair animation is complete and ready for rendering, a cache may be created to store the animation data for all of the hair curves. The cache is useful for two reasons:

1. A hair cache enables you to quickly scrub-through and preview the hair animation without the need to re-simulate.

2. A cached simulation will never change. It will always look exactly the same regardless of what machine it is played on. This consistency makes distributed rendering possible.

To create a cache, select the hair system and choose `Hair > Create Cache`. The cache options allow you to specify the frame range and sampling (more samples creates a more accurate simulation). When created, the scene will playback through each frame while the shape of each curve is recorded. Once finished, you can scrub in the timeline to preview the hair animation.

It is also possible to truncate and append the cache. Truncating a cache will continue the simulation from the current frame, while overwriting the previous cache (up to the end of the previous cache). Appending will simply add the specified frame range to the cache. It can be used to extend the length of the cache, or overwrite a segment of the cache (as specified in the creation options).

Once cached, the simulation is ready to be rendered. It's always a good idea to cache a hair simulation before rendering. It ensures that the rendered images will be consistent with what you see in the viewport.

Special Note: As an added bonus, cached simulations do *not* require Maya Unlimited in order to render.

Rendering Hair:

Unfortunately, simply hitting the render button will not produce very good results with Maya Hair. Both the shading properties (on the hair system node) and the scene's lighting must be carefully tuned to produce believable results.

Maya Software vs. Mental Ray:

There are two choices for rendering Maya Hair; Maya Software, or mental ray (you may also choose to render the hair with a proprietary solution or export to Pixar's Renderman). For all intents and purposes, rendering with the Maya Software renderer is not recommended. Up until Maya v7.0, hair had to be rendered in Maya Software (unless it was first converted to polygons, but this was a terrible solution). This meant that the effect was rendered as paint effects and applied as a post-process. Paint effects cannot be included in ray-tracing (preventing hair from appearing in reflections/refractions) or 2d motion blur. On top of all that, it is simply much more difficult to get realistic results from the Maya Software renderer.

With mental ray, the paint effects hair is first converted to the native hair primitive format before transformation and lighting. Hair primitives are a special feature of the mental ray renderer that were specifically designed to represent hairs and fur (Maya Fur is also converted to hair primitives before being rendered). Other paint effects brushes cannot, therefore, be converted to hair primitives. Hair primitives work fine with features like depth of field and motion blur.

Self Shadowing and Lighting:

A large part of what makes hair look the way it does (in the real world) is the phenomenon known as *self-shadowing*. Self-shadowing (in mental ray) simulates the way light is blocked as it travels deeper into a volume of hair. In the real world, light can be almost totally blocked before it reaches the scalp. This is why the roots of the hair appear darker FIGURE 2.57. The thinner the hair is, the deeper the light will penetrate.

Figure 2.57.

Mental ray produces great hair renderings from the classic 3-point lighting technique. The key light should be set to an intensity close to 1 (or slightly under). This light provides the majority of the illumination in the scene and should definitely cast shadows. The second light (the fill light) compliments the key light and is usually positioned to illuminate the areas that the key light will miss. Lastly, the rim light is positioned behind the hair to help it contrast with the background. Combined, these lights will create a very nice effect (with proper tweaking, of course). The artistic principles of lighting are beyond the scope of this chapter, but that doesn't mean we can't discuss how its done. To setup a scene to be rendered with mental ray using self-shadowing:

1.) First set the render globals to render with mental ray. In Maya 7.0, there is a quality preset for mental ray called ProductionRapidHair FIGURE 2.58. This preset will drastically improve the quality of the hair. The mental ray presets only affect the settings in the mental ray globals. It won't change anything in the hair system itself.

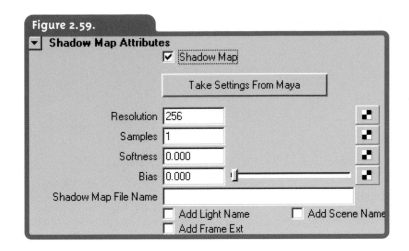

Figure 2.59.

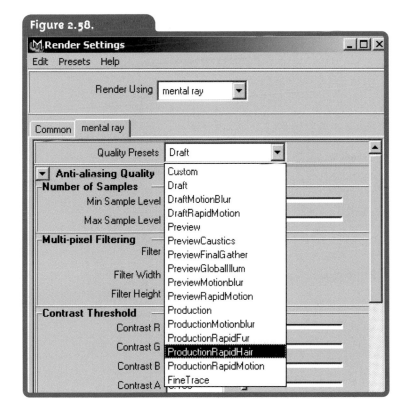

Figure 2.58.

2.) Select the light you want to cast shadows from. The key light should always cast shadows, but you may wish to cast shadows from other lights as well (this can add depth to the shading). Keep in mind that shadow map calculations greatly increase the render times, so use them sparingly.

3.) In the attribute editor, find the mental ray section and check Shadow Map on FIGURE 2.59. A shadow map is a 2d map, rendered from the point of view of the camera that uses depth information (rather than rays) to calculate the shadow data.

4.) Just like any other map, a shadow map has a size defined in pixels. This is controlled by the resolution attribute on the light. Larger resolutions (typically around 512 to 1024) will create more accurate shadows FIGURE 2.60. Be aware, however, that larger resolutions will require more samples.

5.) With the resolution properly adjusted, it may be necessary to adjust the softness of the shadow map. The greater the softness, the more blurred the shadow becomes (but also less accurate) FIGURE 2.61. Typically, extremely low values must be used to create a pleasing shadow effect. Values approaching 0.5 tend to completely wash-out the shadow and should be avoided.

6.) With softer shadows comes the problem of added grain in the image. This nuisance is the result of having too few samples on the shadow map FIGURE 2.62. The Samples attribute should usually be set to between 5 and 20 in order to alleviate this affect.

7.) With the shadows, lighting and render globals setup, you're ready to render. Remember to create a cache of the hair animation before doing a batch render.

In addition to self-shadowing, the hair must have properly tuned shading attributes. This depends largely on the look you are going for, but usually involves adjusting the color, translucence, opacity and specularity to suite the desired style. These attributes are discussed in the Styling with Clumps, Shading and Displacements section (earlier in this chapter).

Rendering hair is not difficult. Just like with any other lighting/shading endeavor, the majority of the setup time is spent tweaking the attributes to achieve a specific look. By utilizing mental ray's excellent shadow map feature, we can create believable hair with depth and volume.

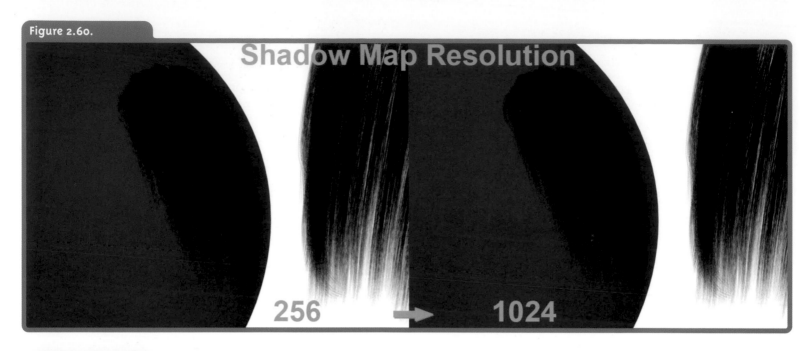

Figure 2.60.

Shadow Map Resolution

256 → 1024

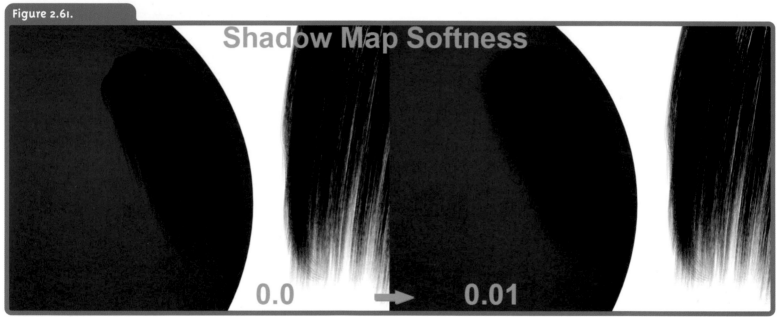

Figure 2.61.

Shadow Map Softness

0.0 → 0.01

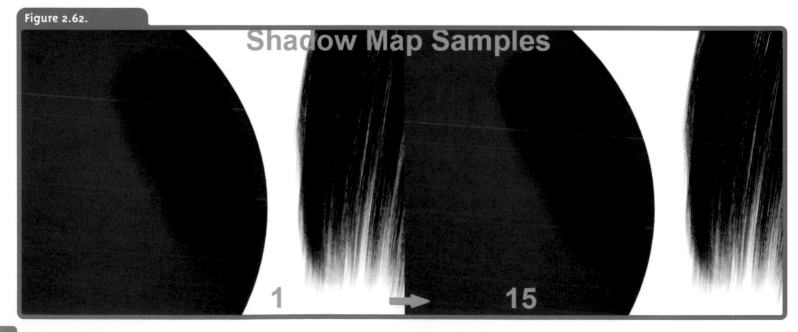

Figure 2.62.

Shadow Map Samples

1 → 15

In exercise 2.1, we created a hairstyle from scratch. This hairstyle (reminiscent of the popular villain from Pixar's The Incredibles) was created with the default brown-hair paint effects brush. This is not exactly the effect we are going for and will require some work before we approach the desired look (seen in pictures throughout this chapter).

To achieve this look, we are going to setup the shading and lighting. This exercise begins exactly where we left-off in exercise 2.1.

1.) Open exercise2.2_Start.mb. The hair in this scene has been properly styled, but it certainly doesn't look anything like how we want it, yet. This scene file is exactly the same as exercise2.1_Finished.mb, except that we have created and placed a camera in the scene to render the hair from (named, 'renderCam'). If you render at this point, you will get an image like FIGURE 2.63. Not very pretty is it? Not to worry though, we're going to fix that.

Figure 2.64.

Figure 2.63.

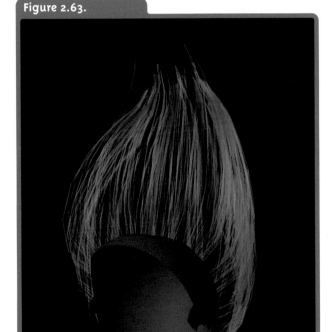

2.) By default, hair will render with the Maya Software renderer; but we want to use mental ray. Open the render globals and select mental ray from the Render Using drop-down menu. Now click on the mental ray tab and set the Quality preset to ProductionRapidHair. Now the render looks like FIGURE 2.64. Still not much better is it?

3.) Notice that in the previous renderings, the background is black. A black background is not ideal for rendering hair. It makes it difficult to distinguish between the hair and background. Let's fix this by creating a backdrop. Position a polygon plane behind the hair and apply a surface shader to the plane (it must be a surface shader, do not use a Lambert or a Blinn). Now set the color on the surface shader to a value of pure white. The render should now look like FIGURE 2.65. It's still not great, but at least we can see the hair now.

Figure 2.65.

4.) Open exercise2.2_A.mb to see the backdrop and edited render globals. Now we're ready to start lighting the hair (at this point the hair is only illuminated because of the default light). Create a spotlight. With it selected, open the Panels menu (in any viewport) and choose Look Through Selected. Now track and dolly until the spotlight is aimed directly at the left side of the head FIGURE 2.66.

Figure 2.68.

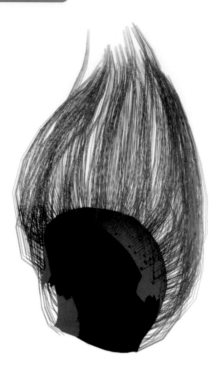

Figure 2.66.

5.) Open exercise2.2_B.mb to see the placement of the first light. At this point, the hair will render like FIGURE 2.67. Still not very pretty, is it? The reason the hair looks so flat, is because there is no shadowing in this scene. Select the spotlight, find the mental ray tab in the attribute editor and check the Shadow Map box. With shadows, the render will look like FIGURE 2.68.

6.) The hair is beginning to look a little better, but notice that the shadows are somewhat aliased. This is because the shadow map does not have a sufficient resolution to accurately represent the shadows. For a more accurate shadow, set the resolution to 512. Now the shadows are crisp as in FIGURE 2.69.

Figure 2.69.

Figure 2.67.

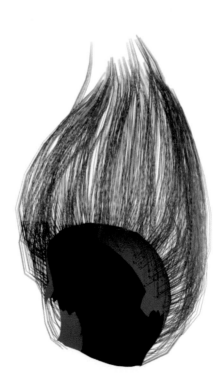

7.) With increased accuracy, the edges of the shadows are somewhat harsh. Let's soften this by setting the Softness from 0, to a very small value of 0.01. The render should now look like FIGURE 2.70.

Figure 2.70.

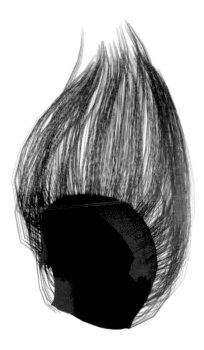

8.) The edges of the shadows are now softer, but this has introduced a new problem; the shadows are grainy. This noise is the result of insufficient sampling. Set the Samples from 1, to a value of 10. This will blur the graininess and create a much more pleasing image FIGURE 2.71.

Figure 2.71.

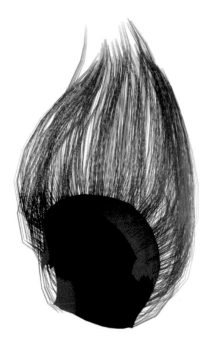

9.) Open exercise2.2_C.mb to see the final shadow settings. This is as far as we are going to go with the lighting. The lighting is now good enough that we will be able to judge the effects of any changes we make to the shading and displacements of the hair itself. The fill and rim lights can be added later. Now find the hair system node and open the Clump and Hair Shape tab FIGURE 2.72.

Figure 2.72.

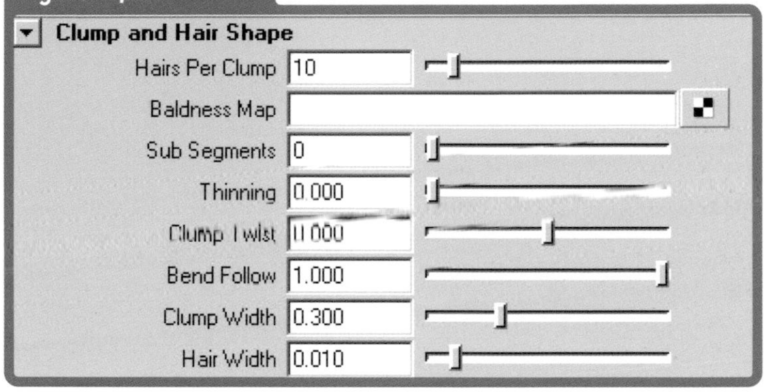

▼ Clump and Hair Shape		
Hairs Per Clump	10	
Baldness Map		▪
Sub Segments	0	
Thinning	0.000	
Clump Twist	11.000	
Bend Follow	1.000	
Clump Width	0.300	
Hair Width	0.010	

10.) Notice the tips of the hairs are very square. This looks quite artificial and must be addressed. Set the Thinning attribute to a value of 0.25. This will taper the tips of the hairs like in FIGURE 2.73.

11.) Notice that the hair has a very angular look (especially along its profile). This is due to insufficient sub segments. Set this to a value of 5 to give the hair more resolution along its length and smooth-out those nasty edges FIGURE 2.74.

Figure 2.73.

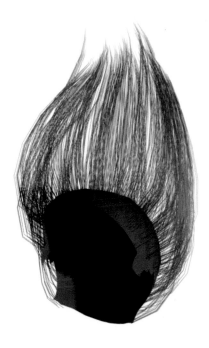

Figure 2.74.

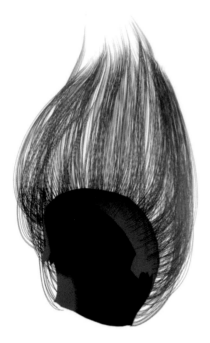

12.) The hair is looking somewhat wispy and very thin. Increasing the number of hairs per clump will not suffice. Quite simply, we need more clumps. To do this, let's add some passive hair follicles to help fill-in the hair. Select the head and choose Hair > Paint Hair Follicles. This will bring-up a floating window and activate the artisan brush. Now select Create Passive Follicles as the paint mode. Set the brush settings as specified in FIGURE 2.75 and paint across the entire head. Do not worry about overlapping strokes; the brush will only paint to the specified density.

Figure 2.75.

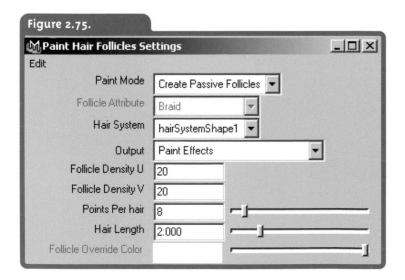

13.) Open exercise2.2_D.mb to see the newly added follicles FIGURE 2.76. Notice that the newly added hairs automatically assumed the shape of their neighbors. No extra styling was required. When rendered, the head should now look like FIGURE 2.77.

Figure 2.76.

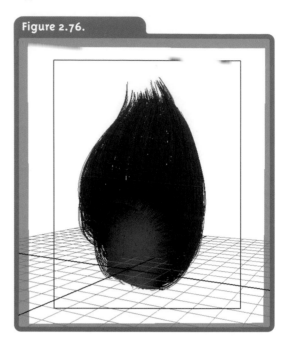

Figure 2.77.

14.) The hair is looking much better now, but some additional tweaking of the clump shapes would help give it a more natural look. Increase the number of hairs per clump from 10, to 18 and increase the hair width from 0.01 to 0.015. This will give the hair a much thicker look FIGURE 2.78.

Figure 2.78.

15.) At this point, the individual hairs are perfectly smooth. We need some per-hair displacements to help break the 'CG' look. Open the displacements section on the hair system node and find the Curl attribute. Increase this from zero to a value of 0.2. Set the frequency to a low value of about 8 to create large, subtle waves in the hair FIGURE 2.79.

Figure 2.79.

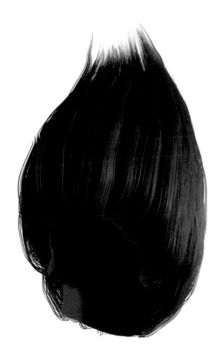

16.) The subtle waviness is helping, but the hair still looks somewhat uniform in its shape. To fix this, set the Noise from zero to a value of 0.3 with a frequency of 1.5. This will create subtle perturbations along the length of the hair FIGURE 2.80. The noise may not be consciously recognized by the audience, but its absence will be.

Figure 2.80.

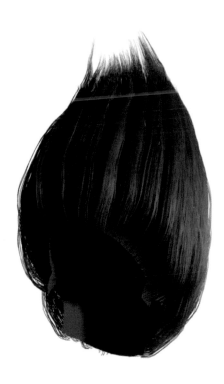

17.) As a final touch to the shape of the hair, let's add some sub clumping. This is the effect where hair pulls together to create small clumps. This is most noticeable when hair very wet, but can be observed (to a lesser degree) in dry hair as well. Set the sub clumping to a value of 8.8 (very small) with a randomness of 0.5. Set the number of clumps in the U and V directions to 20. This will create hundreds of tiny clumps that attract the hair in a subtle manner FIGURE 2.81.

Figure 2.81.

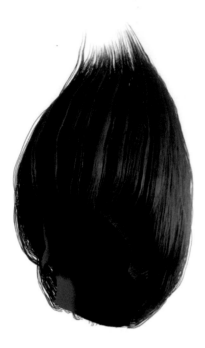

19.) We want the hair to be a dirty orange color. Open the fractal texture in the attribute editor and find the Color Balance section. Set the Color Gain to a bright orange and the Color Offset to a light orange/brownish color FIGURE 2.84.

Figure 2.84.

18.) Open exercise2.2_E.mb to see the final displacement settings. From here, all we have to do is edit the shading attributes of the hair. Open the Shading tab and find the Color attribute FIGURE 2.82. Click the map button and click the 2d fractal texture. This will create a procedural texture and link it to the color of the hair FIGURE 2.83.

Figure 2.82.

20.) To finish shading the hair, I increased the Translucence to a value of 0.9 (from 0.5), decreased the Opacity to 0.6 (from 1.0) and played with the fractal to create a more subtle variation in the color of the hair. This produced the following render: FIGURE 2.85.

Figure 2.83.

Figure 2.85.

21.) Open exercise2.2_Finished.mb to see the final hairstyle. To make a final render, be sure to add fill lights and rim lights. After adding two additional lights and increasing the shadow map quality (along with the size of the render) I was able to produce the following image: FIGURE 2.86.

Figure 2.86.

I have saved my final scene file on the DVD as villainHairFinalRender. This took approximately five minutes to render on my machine (a fairly modest workstation by todays standards). Hair is not a cheap thing to render, but the setup pains can be somewhat alleviated by only cranking-up the major culprits (large shadow maps, large numbers of hairs and hair opacity) for the final render.

Final Thoughts:

With any luck, you've come away from this chapter with a new appreciation for the Maya Hair module. I know it can be frustrating at times. Like most things that are worth learning, it takes time and practice.

It's always exciting when you learn a technique that adds a significant skill to your personal collection. That's what I love so much about animation. What other field has so much opportunity for innovation and discovery? Like the intrepid animators of the early 20th century, we are constantly breaking new grounds and creating new experiences for a worldwide audience. The specifics of the job aren't always glamorous, but the end-result is something that can spark an audience's imagination; and that's a pretty cool thing.

Please check out the videos and animations on the DVD to learn more about the Maya Hair module. The next chapter will dive into the details of Hairs best friend, Fur. In chapter three, we will learn how to create

and style realistic short fur, and even how to connect it to a hair system for dynamic animation. Thanks for following along.

In this chapter, we have covered:

- How a Hair System Works
- Styling Hair with Hair Curves
- Styling Hair with Shading and Displacements
- Animating Hair with Constraints and Collisions
- Simulating and Caching Hair Animations
- Rendering Hair with mental ray

Chapter 3
Fur Fundamentals

▶

Introduction:

The modeling and animation of *long* hair is perhaps one of the most difficult tasks in computer animation, but *short* hair presents its own set of problems. In the real world, we refer to short, thick hair as 'fur'.

The fur that is commonly found on animals consists of basically two types of hairs; ground hairs and guard hairs. Both of these are present in every coat of fur. When combined, they create a protection for the animal from nature's elements.

Most people are familiar with the soft coat of fur that is visible on young animals. This baby coat consists of ground hairs, commonly referred to as 'down'. As anyone who has seen a baby chicken can attest, down is a very soft, fluffy fur comprised of shorter, curly hairs.

As animals mature, the down is covered by a heavier coat composed of guard hairs. This top layer consists of long, straight hairs that stick out from the undercoat. In most animals, the guard hairs completely hide the underlying ground hairs. In the case of an animal like a dog or a cat, the guard hairs may be all that we ever see. Guard hairs come in many shapes and sizes and vary greatly between species. Additionally, guard hairs often have bizarre colorations including stripes (like a zebra) or spots (like a leopard).

Creating believable fur is a difficult task, but with the help of this chapter, it will become not only possible, but enjoyable. Using the Maya Fur module, we will learn how to position, style, and color fur, attach it to a creature mesh and even animate it with dynamics.

Specifically, we will cover:

■ An Introduction to Maya Fur
■ How to Create and Style Different Types of Fur
■ Attaching Fur to a Creature Mesh
■ Adding Motion to Fur with Hair-Based Attractors
■ Shading, Lighting and Rendering Fur with mental ray

Introduction to Maya Fur:

Like many of Maya's deeper tools, Fur is often lambasted for being difficult to master. Beginners often hit seemingly impenetrable roadblocks at every turn. These are usually encountered only minutes after they attempt to create anything more complex than a furry sphere.

Believe it or not, Fur is actually a fairly straightforward Maya module. With a little help, you should find that creating believable fur becomes more of an artistic challenge, than a technical one. That's not to say that there aren't any technical considerations, but rather once these are tamed, fur really is quite easy to work with.

Much of the confusion over how to effectively use fur stems from its reliance on the UV space of the surface it is applied to. Like Hair, the Fur module uses UV parameters to position the individual strands across the 3-dimensional surface. If these UV coordinates are not properly arranged, the fur will not be properly distributed (all of this is fully discussed later in this chapter).

Once the UV issue is dealt with, there are still the styling, animation and rendering issues. These are usually quite painless and with the correct workflow, shouldn't give you much trouble. In fact, I'm sure that after having read the Hair chapter, this will seem like a walk in the park!

Basic Maya Fur Overview:

Like all complicated processes, it's always best to have a solid understanding of the big picture to prevent getting lost in the details. Without having first seen the entire workflow, the individual steps may get confusing. Do not worry if it doesn't all make sense at first, the rest of the chapter will explore these techniques in detail. The following demonstrates a typical workflow that may be used to add fur to an animated character:

1.Model and Texture the Character using Polygons: Using the technique in this book, the UVs on the character may be arranged in whatever manner best suits the texturing. A fur-specific UV layout will be created separately.

2.Create Fur Surfaces: With the character in its default pose, duplicate patches of polygons wherever you wish to add fur. These patches will have their UVs manually arranged to align with the direction you wish the fur to point in.

3.Attach a New Fur Description to the Patches: This will create a *fur feedback* transform node for the fur (for translating, rotating and scaling the fur) as well as a *fur description* node which contains all of the attributes for styling the fur.

4.Adjust the Fur Description: By tweaking the attributes on the fur description node, the fur can be made to look like everything from grass to gorilla hair. At this stage, the artisan brush is often used to paint fur attributes. Fur textures may also be painted in Photoshop. While relatively straightforward, this step can easily take 95% of the total setup time.

5.Animate with Attractors: If the fur is animated, it can be set to 'attract' to hair curves. By using hair dynamics, the fur can react to forces and collisions. If the character is animated, the fur patches must be attached to the character at this point.

6.Light and Render with mental ray: Just like hair, fur needs self-shadowing in order to look believable. Fur is often rendered in a separate pass that is then composited for additional control (although single-pass renderings are perfectly reasonable in some situations).

As you can see, the workflow is pretty straightforward. With an understanding of the reasons behind each step, you should find fur to be a very plausible addition to your next production.

Other Fur Solutions:

You may be wondering why there are two separate modules for hair and fur. The truth is that these modules could easily be combined and, in many ways, they are indistinguishable. Perhaps the only reason they are *not* combined is because their developments were separated by many years. The Fur module was released in Maya's infancy, long before Hair (which was only released in May, 2004).

For whatever reason, when Hair was released in Maya 6.0, it was kept as a completely separate module. With the release of Maya 7.0, we have seen Fur adopt the Hair dynamics engine to replace the old joint-chain attractor system (more on this later). In short, Hair and Fur are complimentary, not competing. In fact, when rendered with mental ray or Renderman, both are internally converted to hair primitives and rendered in exactly the same manner.

Since the release of Maya 7.0 (and the support of Hair dynamics on Fur) there are no major differences between the modules. The only important distinction to make is that one is better for styling long hair, while the other is better for short hair or fur. In fact, it's not uncommon to combine fur with hair to create the look of a short undercoat of fur covered with long guard hairs.

When discussing the different fur and hair solutions for Maya, it is also important to note the work of a talented third-party developer by the name of Joe Alter. Many of the major Hollywood visual effects shots involving hair and fur were done using a piece of software developed by Alter called *Shave and a Haircut*. This software is available as a Maya plugin (also available for XSI and 3ds Max).

At less than $400 USD for a copy, Shave and a Haircut is a very viable alternative to Maya Hair/Fur. Shave includes many additional tools that are very helpful for combing/texturing long fur and hair. It even includes a completely separate OpenGL-based window with a custom-designed artisan-esque brush for styling FIGURE 3.1. It also includes Maya Hair-esque dynamics and a very nice proprietary renderer (with support for export to RIB, the Renderman file format).

Shave and a Haircut is a total package that has found it's way into many major productions including the exceptionally astounding King Kong film (arguably the best showcase of computer generated fur effects to date). That being said, Maya Hair/Fur have been used in many feature films as well. This book is solely focused on Maya's native toolset, but it should be noted that learning Maya Hair/Fur will prepare you for Shave and a Haircut (and indeed any other hair/fur software). The concepts are exactly the same; even many of the attributes are strikingly similar FIGURE 3.2.

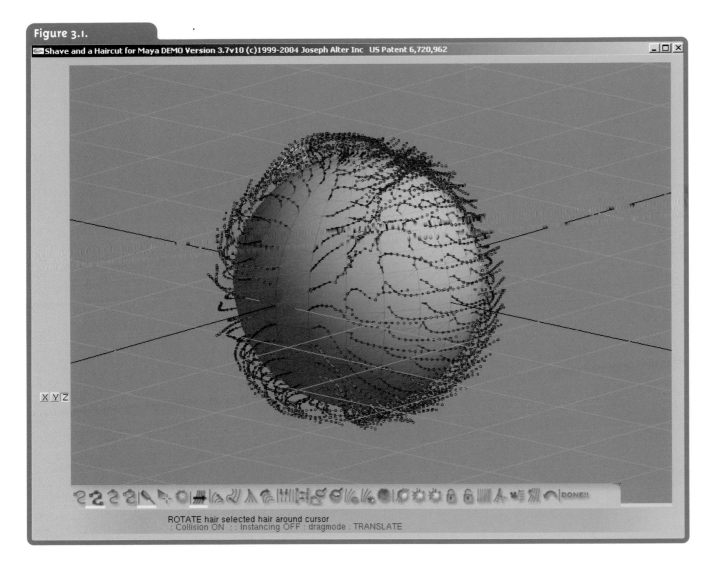

Figure 3.1.

Shave and a Haircut for Maya DEMO Version 3.7v10 (c)1999-2004 Joseph Alter Inc US Patent 6,720,962

ROTATE hair selected hair around cursor
: Collision ON : : Instancing OFF : dragmode : TRANSLATE

I want to stress that Maya Hair and Fur are complete and production proven packages on their own. Shave and a Haircut is a brilliant plugin with some great additional features, but unless your particular project requires massive amounts of fur and hair, it may be extraneous (especially if copies of Maya Unlimited 7.0 are readily available). Before the release of Maya 7.0, I would have highly recommended Shave to everyone for it's superior dynamics; with the new Maya Hair dynamics, it no longer has that edge. Fortunately, you can decide for yourself whether or not Shave will be a worthy addition to your pipeline by downloading the free demo from **www.joealter.com.**

Remember, Shave and a Haircut is a great package, but Maya Fur is definitely no slouch (as you are about to witness). Regardless, learning Fur will prepare you for any software you are likely to encounter now, or in the future. Knowing this, let's continue by learning exactly how fur is created...

Figure 3.2.

shaveNode1
time1

Hair Color Texture R	0
Hair Color Texture G	0
Hair Color Texture B	0
Mutant Hair Color Texture R	0
Mutant Hair Color Texture G	0
Mutant Hair Color Texture B	0
Root Hair Color Texture R	0
Root Hair Color Texture G	0
Root Hair Color Texture B	0
Amb/diff	0.59504
Frizz Anim	0
Anim Dir X	0
Anim Dir Y	1
Anim Dir Z	0
Anim Speed	0
Displacement	0
Frizz XFrequency	138.209
Frizz YFrequency	131.117996
Frizz ZFrequency	138.209
Root Frizz	1.7935
Tip Frizz	42.002998
Gloss	0.085124
Hair Red	0.964507
Hair Green	1
Hair Blue	0.78
Hue Variation	18.181999
Kink XFrequency	155
Kink YFrequency	155
Kink ZFrequency	155
Root Kink	0
Tip Kink	0
Mutant Hair Red	0.470588
Mutant Hair Green	0.470588
Mutant Hair Blue	0.470588
Percent Mutant Hairs	0
Rand Scale	0.4
Root Red	0.70248
Root Green	0.665963
Root Blue	0.396901

Creating Fur:

Obviously, before we can begin to style fur, we must create it. Creating fur is done by creating a Fur Description and then attaching it to a surface. This can be done in a single step by simply selecting any NURBS or polygon surface and choosing `Fur > Attach Fur Description > New` FIGURE 3.3.

Figure 3.3.

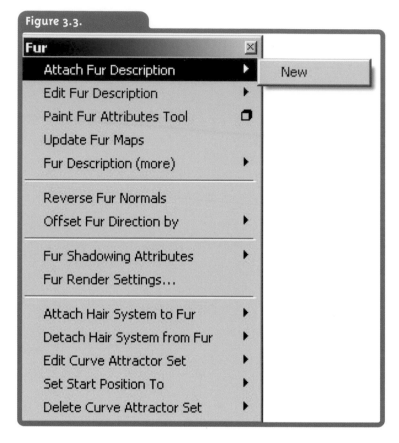

Note: Do not try to work with Fur on subdivision surfaces. They are not fully supported and will provide guaranteed and completely unnecessary headaches.

After creating and applying a new fur description, the surface will be covered with an array of small white hairs FIGURE 3.4. These are the

Figure 3.4.

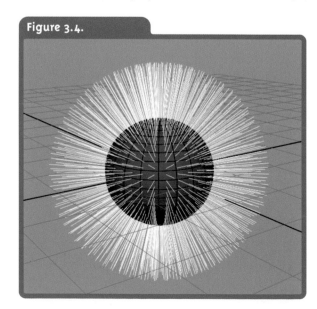

OpenGL approximations of the final hairs. When the fur description node is tweaked, these hairs will update to provide a quick and basic representation of the fur. That being said, the viewport will never provide a *perfect* representation of the fur. For that, the fur must be rendered using either Maya Software or mental ray.

With the fur created and applied, its time to start tweaking the fur description node. Think of the fur description as the mother node for the entire fur system (similar to the hair system node). It includes all of the controls for styling and coloring the fur FIGURE 3.5.

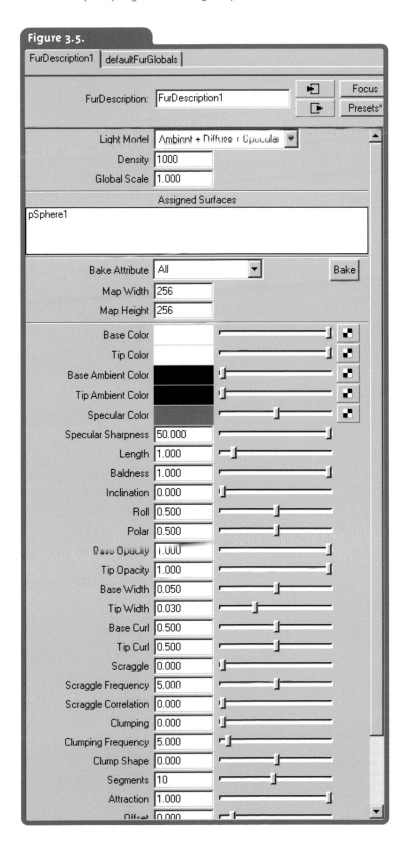

Figure 3.5.

A single fur description node may be applied to multiple surfaces. Simply select the surface and choose Fur > Attach Fur Description > NameOfFur (where 'NameOfFur' is the name of the description you wish to attach). By using a single fur description across multiple surfaces, you can maintain a consistent style and save a considerable amount of setup time.

Preparing a Polygonal Surface for Fur:

If you haven't already tried applying fur directly to a creature mesh, this may surprise you:

■ **Fur is extremely picky about UV layout.**

This is probably the biggest source of confusion for novice fur users. After applying a fur description to a creature mesh, they are left with a tangled mess of sparsely placed hairs that seem to point in odd directions FIGURE 3.6. If the model doesn't have UVs, fur won't even work at all!

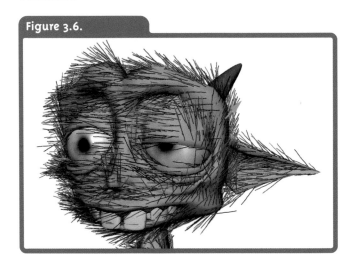

Figure 3.6.

In order to vanquish this confusion once and for all, let me explain exactly what happens when a fur description is applied to a surface. Firstly, Maya Fur decides where each hair should be placed across the surface (makes sense, right?). To do this, it looks at the arrangement of UV coordinates that reside within the 0 to 1 space. If a polygon face does not have corresponding UVs that reside within this square, it simply will *not* be given any fur. In FIGURE 3.7 we see a half-bald surface. Looking at the UV layout, it becomes apparent why half of the faces were seemingly ignored.

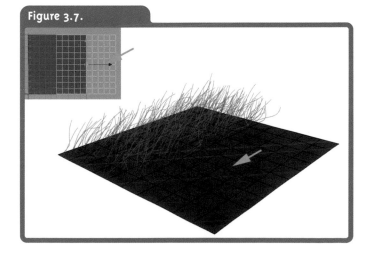

Figure 3.7.

Maya then places the number of hairs as specified by the density attribute across the entire 0-to-1 UV space. To ensure that the hairs are evenly distributed across the surface, an equalizer map is automatically generated. This map is computed by comparing the distance in 3d space between neighboring vertices and comparing that to the distance between the UVs. By accounting for uneven parameterization, the equalizer map ensures that even warped or stretched UV layouts will create an even distribution of fur across the surface.

As if the dependency on UVs residing within the unit square wasn't bothersome enough, Maya Fur is also heavily dependent on the *direction* of the UVs. The direction is used to determine how the fur inclines across the surface. By default, the fur will tilt towards the *top* of the UV square FIGURE 3.8. Even if the surface UVs are properly arranged within the 0-to-1 space, they may not necessarily point in the proper direction. This is why a UV arrangement designed for texturing may not be adequate for placing fur.

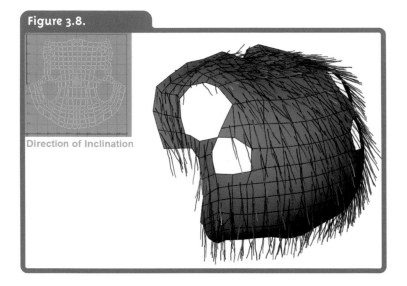

Figure 3.8.

Direction of Inclination

To counter these apparent limitations, you have four options:

1. Create a Separate UV Set: You can create a completely separate UV set specifically designed for the fur. By default, fur will be placed using the 'map1' UV set. You can specify a different UV set in the UV Linking editor (Window > Relationship Editors > UV Linking > Fur/UV). This UV set should contain UV shells that are arranged within the unit square and point in the proper direction. The UVs must change direction wherever the fur flows.

2. Use NURBS: Because NURBS surfaces have implicitly defined UV space, they are great for defining the distribution and direction of fur. NURBS patches can be wrap deformed to a creature mesh to create small patches of fur like eyebrows or mustaches. To change the direction the fur points in, simply reverse the direction of the NURBS surface (Edit NURBS > Reverse Surface Direction).

3. Create Polygon Fur Patches: For reasons explained below, this is my favorite solution. Basically, smaller portions of the character mesh must be duplicated. These separate polygon surfaces then have their UVs manually arranged to flow with the direction of the fur. Once finished, these patches are then wrap deformed to the creature mesh. Because the patches are generated directly from the creature mesh itself, the fur will follow the contours of the mesh perfectly (no visible offset). When rendered, the patch is hidden. This method also provides absolute control over the direction of the inclination of the fur. It should

be noted that this technique requires attention and care in order to work correctly. That being said, it's the easiest way to gain absolute, predictable control over the orientation and placement of the fur.

4. Use Shave and a Haircut: The Shave plugin was designed to work independently of the surface UVs. When Shave fur is applied to a polygonal surface, the UVs are not used to define distribution and/or inclination. For character work involving full-body fur, Shave is faster to work with.

All four of these solutions are perfectly reasonable and well suited to different tasks. To help you determine what technique you should use for any particular situation, let's discuss the four basic scenarios you may encounter in any production:

1. Full-Body Fur (ie. dog or cow): In these cases, the character is completely covered in fur from head to toe. This situation would necessitate a great deal of planning with regards to the UV layout in order to ensure a proper inclination of the fur across the body. Ideally, you will have access to a plugin, like Shave and a Haircut, for such work. If not, I highly recommend using the polygon patch method as it provides the most control for accurate placement of Maya Fur.

2. Partial-Body Fur (ie. back hair on a pig or a spider leg): This situation is probably the most common as many creatures and mammals (humans included) have fur distributed in different parts of their body. For this type of work, it is best to create localized patches of fur on separated polygon pieces. This is the type of fur we will tackle in chapter four with the Minx character.

3. Patchy Fur (ie. mustache or eyebrow): With patchy fur there is usually a very specific region that requires some hair. For these cases, it is best to use either a simple NURBS surface or a polygon patch to place the fur.

4. Non Fur Effects (ie. grass or wheat field): Non-hair/fur effects are very common. While Maya Fur can simulate a simple looking grass, it is not well suited for much else. In order to create, for example, a field of wheat or corn, one would need to replace the hair primitive with a completely different object. This is called 'instancing' and is not supported in Maya Hair or Fur. Shave and a Haircut, on the other hand, does support instancing. That being said, Maya Hair's output curves may be connected (with the help of a clever script and a wire deformer) to whatever you like. These types of effects typically require a lot of R&D and a well organized MEL-based pipeline to help you deal with the placement and control of such a large number of objects.

It should be noted that working with full-body fur can present a nightmarish logistical challenge. When fur is applied to an entire creature mesh, viewport feedback can be brought to a screeching halt. Even on a typical medium-resolution mesh, seemingly simple tasks like painting attributes and tweaking the fur description attributes can bog-down the entire system. The bottom line is this:

■ **Just like with all rigging tasks, fur *requires* a modular approach.**

So what does that actually mean? It means that in order to be successful with applying fur in a production environment, you must split things up accordingly. Rather than trying to work with the entire body of fur at once, work on one piece at a time!

In chapter five, we will tackle the entire body of the Minx character. In that chapter, you will see exactly how we split the body into manageable chunks, only bringing it all together when before rendering.

Styling Fur:

With a new fur description created and applied to a surface, you are ready to begin styling. This is where you take the generic fur description and turn it into whatever you want. Fur can be made to assume many different shapes and styles. There are basically three tools available for styling fur:

1.**The Fur Description Node:** This node contains a list of attributes for controlling every facet of the fur. There are controls for color, clumping, scraggle, curling and much more.

2.**The Paint Fur Attributes Tool / Photoshop:** Using the artisan interface, this tool allows a setup artist to paint attribute maps for many of the controls found on the fur description node. Maps may also be painted in an external image editor, like Photoshop.

3.**Maya Hair Curves:** By attaching a hair system to the fur, we can style the shape of the fur along it's length by modeling the start curves.

Combined, these three techniques provide a great deal of control for achieving any effect. The rest of this section will dive into both the fur description node and the paint attributes tool. Styling with Hair curves is covered in the next section of this chapter where we explore the options for adding motion to Maya Fur.

The Fur Description:

Recall that the fur description node is the center of operations. It controls the styling of the fur and can be applied to multiple surfaces. An entire character with over twenty patches of fur may only require a single fur description.

The default settings for a new fur description node will yield very bland looking fur. By default, the fur doesn't really look like fur at all. By adjusting the myriad of attributes, adding randomization with noise and painting custom attribute maps, we can begin to create many different effects ranging from a soft young chicken, to a sharp prickly porcupine FIGURE 3.9.

There are about thirty different attributes and each includes several controls for adding noise. In total, there are well over a hundred different sliders for adjusting the exact look of the fur. Fortunately, Maya has included about twenty presets that will help you get started. These presets include animals like bears, bison, ducklings and gorillas. The presets may never give you a finished look, but they can provide a great starting place from which further customization may be added. Presets may even be blended with each other to create new and strange effects.

For example, you can mix 10% gorilla, with 90% duckling for a completely new effect. To use a preset, create a new fur description and click the 'Preset' button at the top of the attribute editor. This will expand a list of available presets from which you can choose to either replace or blend-with the current description FIGURE 3.10. Additionally, you may wish to save presets for use in a different scene. This can be done by choosing the 'Save FurDescription Preset' option from the Presets menu (the same menu used to access the presets).

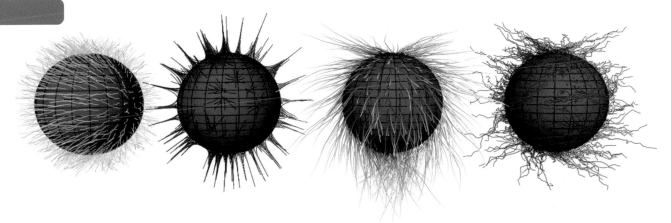

Figure 3.10.

| Save FurDescription Preset... |
| Edit Presets... |

Bear	▶
Bison	▶
CalicoCat	▶
Dreadlocks	▶
Duckling	▶
Gorilla	▶
Grass	▶
LionMane	▶
Llama	▶
Mouse	▶
PolarBear	▶
Porcupine	▶
Punk	▶
Raccoon	▶
Sheep	▶
Squirrel	▶
WetLabrador	▶
WetOtter	▶

replace
blend 90%
blend 75%
blend 50%
blend 25%
blend 10%

Figure 3.9.

While presets are a great way to get started, ultimately, you will need to understand how each attribute affects the fur in order to create a specific look. The following table illustrates the various attributes on the fur description node that affect the look of the fur:

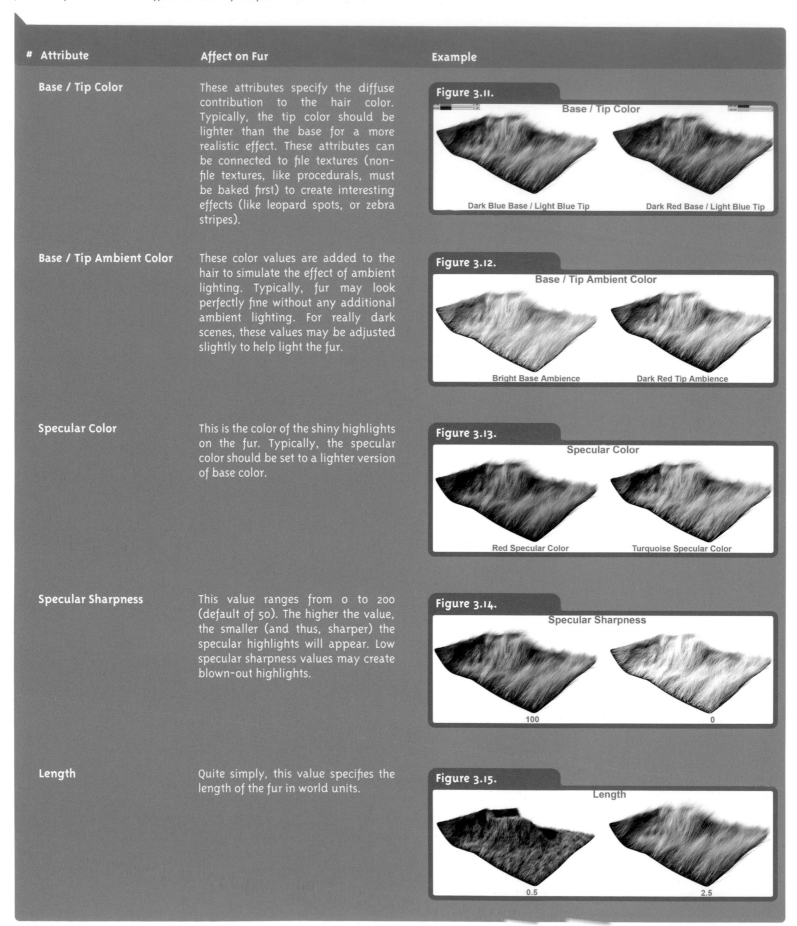

#	Attribute	Affect on Fur	Example
	Base / Tip Color	These attributes specify the diffuse contribution to the hair color. Typically, the tip color should be lighter than the base for a more realistic effect. These attributes can be connected to file textures (non-file textures, like procedurals, must be baked first) to create interesting effects (like leopard spots, or zebra stripes).	**Figure 3.11.** Base / Tip Color — Dark Blue Base / Light Blue Tip — Dark Red Base / Light Blue Tip
	Base / Tip Ambient Color	These color values are added to the hair to simulate the effect of ambient lighting. Typically, fur may look perfectly fine without any additional ambient lighting. For really dark scenes, these values may be adjusted slightly to help light the fur.	**Figure 3.12.** Base / Tip Ambient Color — Bright Base Ambience — Dark Red Tip Ambience
	Specular Color	This is the color of the shiny highlights on the fur. Typically, the specular color should be set to a lighter version of base color.	**Figure 3.13.** Specular Color — Red Specular Color — Turquoise Specular Color
	Specular Sharpness	This value ranges from 0 to 200 (default of 50). The higher the value, the smaller (and thus, sharper) the specular highlights will appear. Low specular sharpness values may create blown-out highlights.	**Figure 3.14.** Specular Sharpness — 100 — 0
	Length	Quite simply, this value specifies the length of the fur in world units.	**Figure 3.15.** Length — 0.5 — 2.5

# Attribute	Affect on Fur	Example
Baldness	The baldness attribute is used to add/remove fur from a specific region. This attribute enables the painting of the density of the fur. Unless you paint a map for this attribute, it is better to simply use the density attribute itself to thin/thicken the hair. A value of 0 removes all hairs (complete baldness).	**Figure 3.16.** 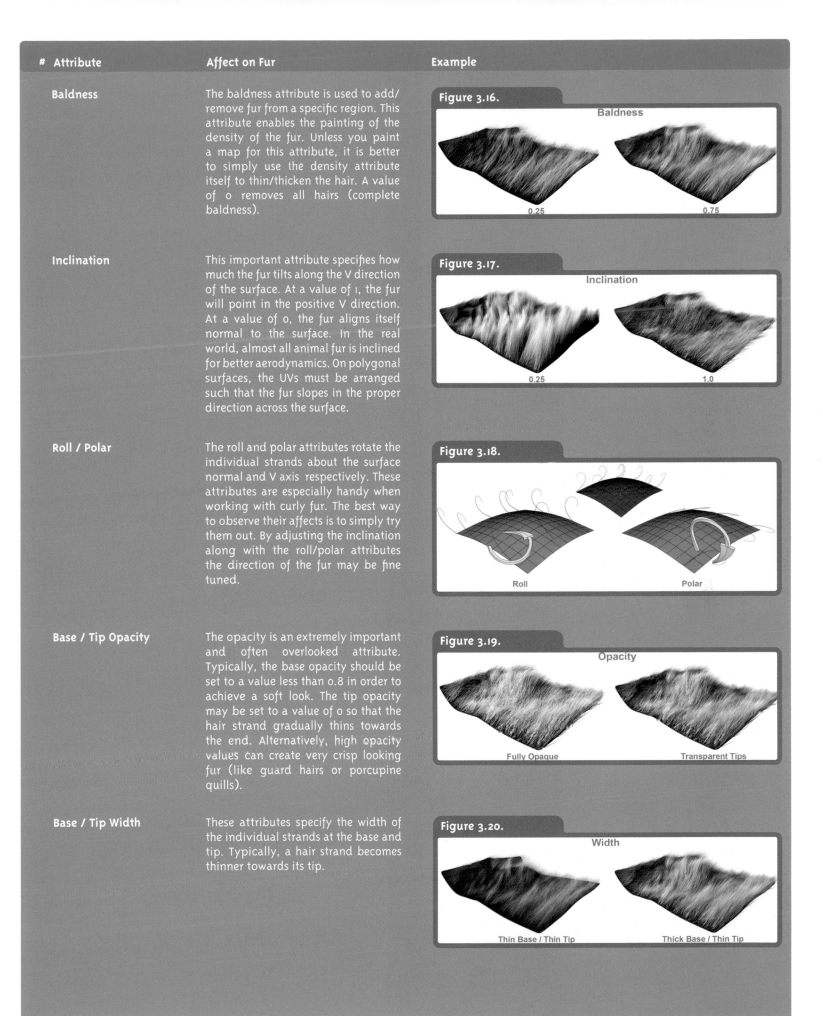
Inclination	This important attribute specifies how much the fur tilts along the V direction of the surface. At a value of 1, the fur will point in the positive V direction. At a value of 0, the fur aligns itself normal to the surface. In the real world, almost all animal fur is inclined for better aerodynamics. On polygonal surfaces, the UVs must be arranged such that the fur slopes in the proper direction across the surface.	**Figure 3.17.**
Roll / Polar	The roll and polar attributes rotate the individual strands about the surface normal and V axis respectively. These attributes are especially handy when working with curly fur. The best way to observe their affects is to simply try them out. By adjusting the inclination along with the roll/polar attributes the direction of the fur may be fine tuned.	**Figure 3.18.**
Base / Tip Opacity	The opacity is an extremely important and often overlooked attribute. Typically, the base opacity should be set to a value less than 0.8 in order to achieve a soft look. The tip opacity may be set to a value of 0 so that the hair strand gradually thins towards the end. Alternatively, high opacity values can create very crisp looking fur (like guard hairs or porcupine quills).	**Figure 3.19.**
Base / Tip Width	These attributes specify the width of the individual strands at the base and tip. Typically, a hair strand becomes thinner towards its tip.	**Figure 3.20.**

# Attribute	Affect on Fur	Example
Base / Tip Curl	These values range from 0 to 1 with 0.5 being the default (no curl). At either extreme, the hair strand will curl in opposite directions. At a value of 1 or 0, the strand will curl into a half-circle.	
Scraggle	Scraggle gives the fur a noisy, crooked shape. At a value of 1 (full scraggle), the hair will twist wildly. Typically, small amounts of scraggle are beneficial to even the straightest of styles. This attribute works in conjunction with a frequency attribute that controls the 'size' of the deformations. Higher frequency values make smaller kinks along the length of the hair strand.	
Clumping	This attribute pulls the hairs together into clumps. At higher values, clumping can approximate a 'wet' look. This attribute works in conjunction with a frequency and shape attribute. The frequency controls the size of the clumps (higher values yield smaller clumps). The shape attribute ranges from -10 to 10 and defines the contour of each clump. At a value of -10, each clump is 'sucked' inwards (higher values bow the clump outwards).	
Segments	Determines the resolution of the individual strands. Short, straight hairs require fewer segments. As a strand becomes longer or more deformed, additional resolution may be required in order to accurately assume the desired shape.	

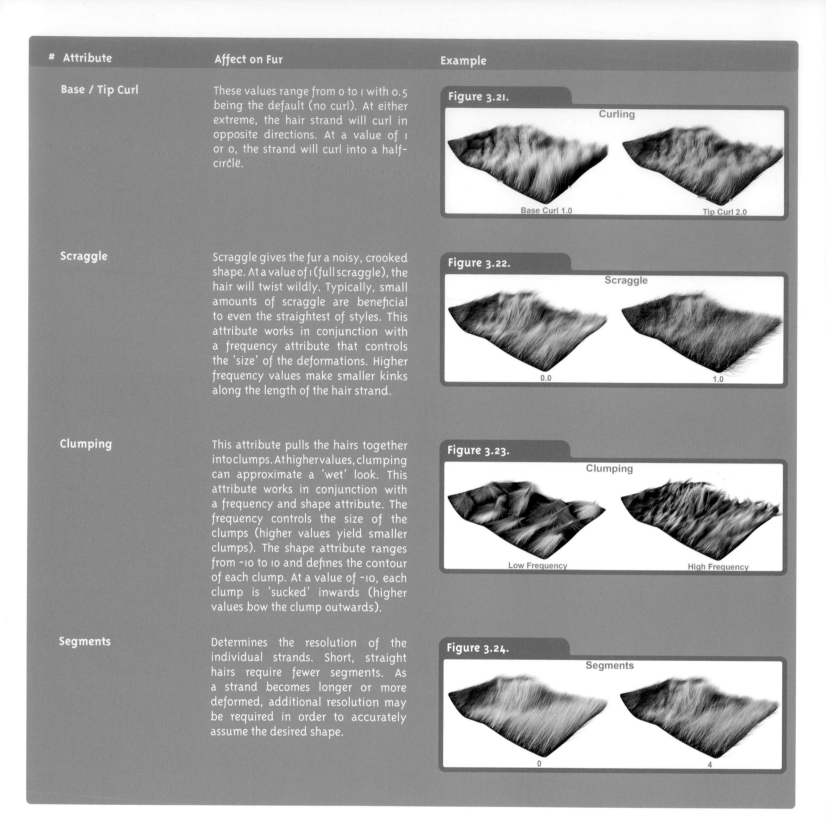

Figure 3.21.
Curling
Base Curl 1.0   Tip Curl 2.0

Figure 3.22.
Scraggle
0.0   1.0

Figure 3.23.
Clumping
Low Frequency   High Frequency

Figure 3.24.
Segments
0   4

Each of these attributes includes additional control in the form of noise parameters. Expanding the Details tab in the attribute editor will reveal a long list of tabs, one for each fur attribute FIGURE 3.25. These sub-tabs includes additional controls for adding randomness to the fur. This is a great way to help break the look of artificiality.

The following attributes may be found in the Details section for each attribute:

Noise Amplitude: This attribute controls the strength of the noise. At a value of 0 (default) no noise is applied. Higher values (usually around 0.5 to 2.0) will add an element of randomization to the attribute. For

example, adding noise to the Clumping attribute causes some hairs to clump more than others. This enhances the believability of the fur making for a much more pleasing image.

Noise Frequency: This attribute controls the frequency of the noise (not the frequency of the attribute itself). Small values (0.5 to 5.0) create larger areas of randomness. For example, high frequency Clumping noise will create small 'pockets' of hairs that vary in 'clumpiness'. If the Clumping noise frequency is set to a lower value, the pockets of randomness are fewer and larger.

Figure 3.25.

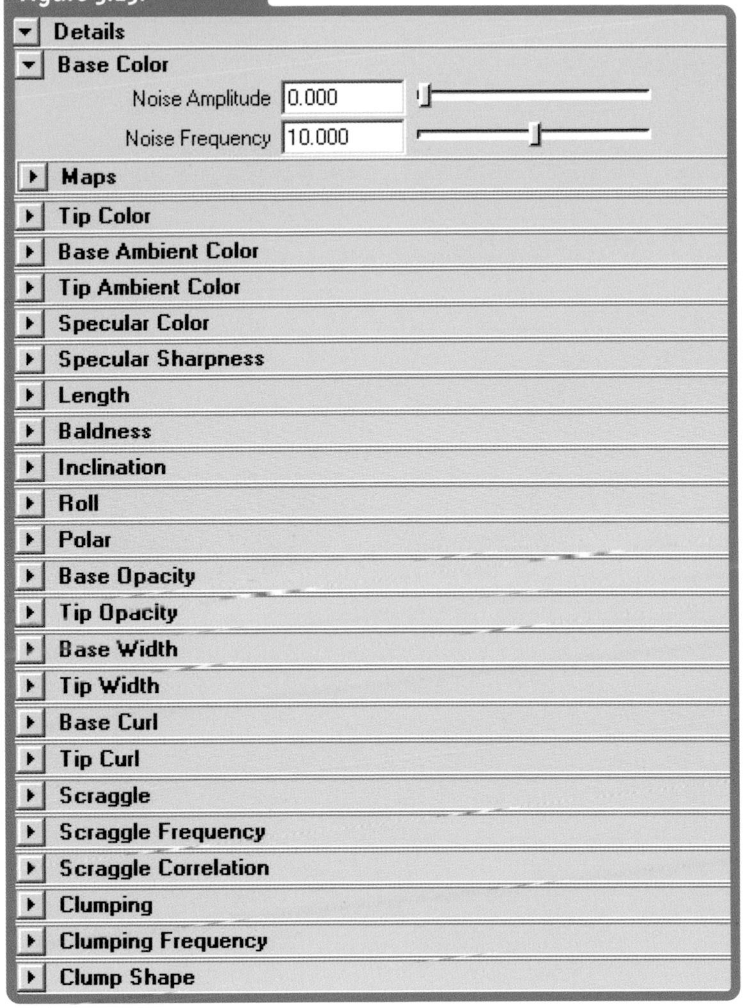

▼ **Details**
▼ **Base Color**
    Noise Amplitude   `0.000`
    Noise Frequency   `10.000`
▶ **Maps**
▶ **Tip Color**
▶ **Base Ambient Color**
▶ **Tip Ambient Color**
▶ **Specular Color**
▶ **Specular Sharpness**
▶ **Length**
▶ **Baldness**
▶ **Inclination**
▶ **Roll**
▶ **Polar**
▶ **Base Opacity**
▶ **Tip Opacity**
▶ **Base Width**
▶ **Tip Width**
▶ **Base Curl**
▶ **Tip Curl**
▶ **Scraggle**
▶ **Scraggle Frequency**
▶ **Scraggle Correlation**
▶ **Clumping**
▶ **Clumping Frequency**
▶ **Clump Shape**

It must be noted that the included fur presets are perhaps the best way to learn exactly what attribute combinations may be used to achieve any specific effect. In addition to the obvious head-start, they also provide useful notes for each effect FIGURE 3.26. Be sure to do some test renders of the available presets rather than relying solely on the OpenGL feedback FIGURE 3.27 .

In addition to the Noise Amplitude / Frequency attributes, some fur attributes may include the Map Offset and Map Multiplier attributes. These are only used when the attribute has been mapped to a file texture. The Offset attribute simply adds the specified value to the value from the map (effectively offsetting the map value) while the multiplier specifies a factor that is multiplied by the map value.

For example, if the length of the fur is mapped to a file texture, a Map Multiplier value of 2 will double the length of the fur. The specifics of mapping fur attributes are covered in the next section.

Figure 3.26.

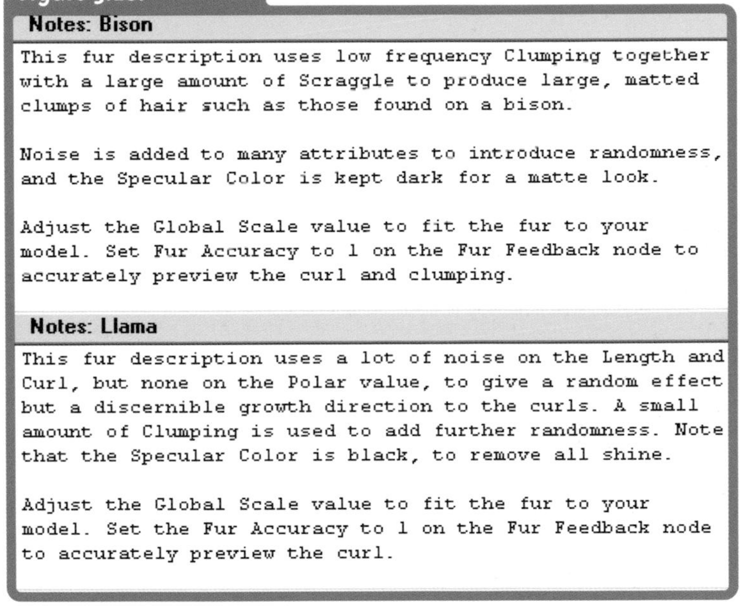

Notes: Bison

This fur description uses low frequency Clumping together with a large amount of Scraggle to produce large, matted clumps of hair such as those found on a bison.

Noise is added to many attributes to introduce randomness, and the Specular Color is kept dark for a matte look.

Adjust the Global Scale value to fit the fur to your model. Set Fur Accuracy to 1 on the Fur Feedback node to accurately preview the curl and clumping.

Notes: Llama

This fur description uses a lot of noise on the Length and Curl, but none on the Polar value, to give a random effect but a discernible growth direction to the curls. A small amount of Clumping is used to add further randomness. Note that the Specular Color is black, to remove all shine.

Adjust the Global Scale value to fit the fur to your model. Set the Fur Accuracy to 1 on the Fur Feedback node to accurately preview the curl.

Figure 3.27.

Presets

Bison

Llama

Creating Fur Maps:

The fur description node contains plenty of control for achieving almost any furry effect. Although the attribute list is quite comprehensive, it does not provide the type of control needed to create localized and specific effects. What if the production calls for a patch of fur in the shape of a crop circle? For this level of detail, you must map the attribute to a file texture.

Fur textures are either color or greyscale maps (depending on the attribute they are affecting). There are basically two methods of creating textures for a fur attribute:

1.The Paint Fur Attributes Tool: Using the artisan brush, fur textures may be painted directly on the fur surface.

2.Photoshop: Like any other texture map, fur attribute maps may be painted in Photoshop. Aside from the color attributes, these maps must be greyscale with black representing the value 0 and white representing the value 1.0.

To use the artisan tool, select the surface you wish to paint-on and choose `Fur > Paint Fur Attributes Tool`. This will bring-up a floating window with a drop-down list of available attributes to paint FIGURE 3.28. In addition to the fur attributes found on the fur description node, there is an additional 'direction' attribute. When painted, this attribute effectively combs the fur in the direction the brush is moving.

Figure 3.28.

Because the direction attribute adjusts the actual rotation of the individual strands, no effect will be noticed unless the strands are first *inclined*. Be sure to set the inclination to a non-zero value before painting this attribute. Do not make the mistake of trying to use the direction feature to comb fur that is messy due to improperly adjusted UVs. This is a sure way to give yourself a headache. Combing fur with the artisan brush can be clumsy and difficult to control in a precise fashion. Use it to nudge the fur in specific places, but do not become dependent on it as a means of flattening the whole coat; it simply won't suffice.

When an attribute is painted with the artisan tool, Maya creates a texture map of a size specified by the Attribute Map Width/Height controls on the tool settings. The default resolution of 256 x 256 will likely not suffice for anything but the smallest of patches. Increasing the texture resolution enables more accurate definition of the fur attributes. For example, if the baldness attribute is being used to define the edge of a neatly trimmed mustache, its resolution must be sufficiently dense in order to avoid noticeable pixelation along the edges.

The resultant texture map itself resides within the /furAttrMap directory in the project folder FIGURE 3.29. When painting attributes, Maya automatically creates these texture files and names them according to a strict convention:

`nameOfScene_nameOfSurface_nameOfFurDescrition_AttributeName.iff`

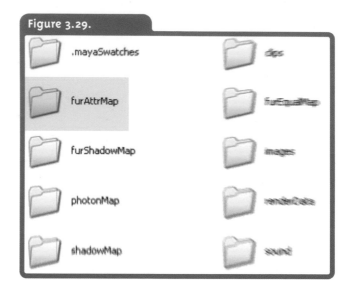
Figure 3.29.

If additional changes are made to an attribute map, these files are overwritten. All of this happens 'behind-the-scenes' but can be taken advantage of to help in the texturing process. Knowing that the attribute maps are written to disk, we can take these into Photoshop for further manipulation. The following workflow has proven extremely helpful when working with fur textures:

1. Use the Paint Fur Attribute Tool to paint a general attribute map. Because the artisan brush resides within 3d space, it is well suited to defining boundaries and larges areas that need attention (like a hairline, for example). These areas can be difficult to distinguish when looking at a blank UV layout in a 2d paint program.

2. Now that the general texture has been created in 3d, we can perform the finer manipulations using a more competent image editor (the 3d paint tool lacks the refinement of a full image editor). Open the resultant .iff texture file (located in the /furAttrMaps folder) with FCheck and save a bitmap file for use in Photoshop FIGURE 3.30.

3. Open the bitmap in Photoshop and make any necessary manipulations. For example, if you are painting the base color attribute for a zebra, you may use Photoshop to paint high resolution stripes across the canvas using the strokes from the 3d brush as a guide.

4. When the texture is finished, save a copy with FCheck and replace the original texture in the /furAttrMaps directory (being sure to save in the native .iff format and with the same name).

Using the 3d paint tool in conjunction with a fully featured image editor enables complete control over the look and placement of every hair. Of course, you may find that either Photoshop or the 3d paint tool will suffice on their own; but using both is sometimes easiest.

There is one last caveat to be aware of when creating textures for Maya Fur. Maya Fur is only capable of reading texture map files; it will not

Figure 3.30.

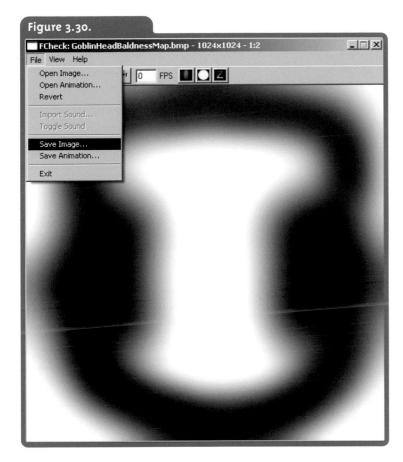

recognize procedural textures. Any non-file attribute map will be ignored until it is baked. If you attach a procedural to one of the fur attributes, you must select it from the drop-down menu at the top of the attribute and click the Bake button FIGURE 3.31. This will write an .iff texture file to the /furAttrMaps directory. Hence, removing the procedural texture will not remove the baked texture. To do this, you must either delete the texture itself, or disconnect the procedural and re-bake the attribute.

Figure 3.31.

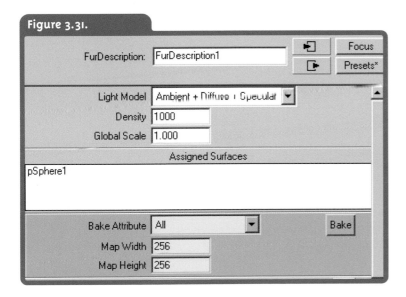

Applying Fur Maps:

The workflow for texturing fur is slightly awkward and definitely requires some explanation. Painting a single fur attribute map is simple enough, but the task of applying multiple textures across multiple surfaces sharing the same fur description can be somewhat confusing.

It is important to note that you will often find yourself needing to apply multiple textures on multiple surfaces. For example, for the Minx character (coming-up in chapter four) we must have a way of applying unique fur attribute maps to multiple surfaces sharing the same fur description node. Doing so enables a greater degree of control with regards to the placement of fur (baldness maps) and the varying length and color of the fur (length, base color and tip color attributes).

Control of the per-surface attribute maps is found on the fur description node itself. Each mappable attribute contains a tab under it's Detail section for adding and removing maps FIGURE 3.32. To add a custom map to a fur attribute on a *specific surface*, do the following:

1. Select the fur description node and locate the Assigned Surfaces list at the top of the attribute editor. As you may have guessed, this contains a list of all surfaces that are currently attached to the fur description node FIGURE 3.33. Before you can assign/remove attribute maps, you must select the surface from this list.

Figure 3.32.

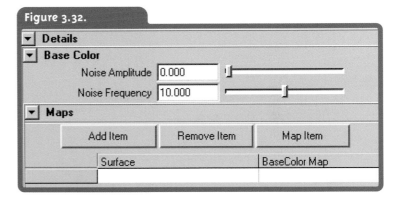

Figure 3.33.

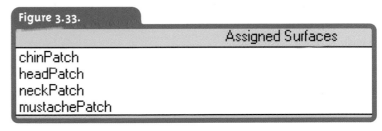

2. With the surface selected, open the Details tab for the attribute you wish to map and find the 'maps' tab. This will display a full list of attribute maps currently being used FIGURE 3.34. It is from this section that you can add/remove or edit the mapping of surface-specific attribute maps.

3. To assign a new map, click the Add Item button. This will bring up a file browser where you can choose the texture map you wish to link to the attribute for the currently selected surface.

4. To remove an attribute map, select it in the list and choose Remove Item.

5. To change an attribute map, select it in the list and hit the Map Item button. This will provide a file browser for you to choose a different map.

Figure 3.34.

Working with multiple maps across multiple surfaces is definitely somewhat clunky (and the archaic interface that Maya Fur uses doesn't help). Regardless, once you get the hang of it, this will enable ultimate control over every facet of the fur description on every surface it is applied to; truly a powerful feature. I encourage you to watch the included DVD video for a better understanding of how to work with multiple textures on multiple surfaces.

Exercise 3.1   Giving the Goblin a Mohawk

At this point in the chapter, we have covered enough of Maya Fur to begin putting it to use. In this exercise, we will create a patch of fur for the Goblin's head. To do this, we must create a patch to grow the fur from and layout the UVs appropriately. We will then create a new fur description, adjust its settings and paint some custom attribute maps to tweak the fur style.

This exercise covers the creation of a fur patch and the use of the fur description node. The second exercise will take this fur and apply some dynamic motion using what we know from Maya Hair. Once the dynamics are applied, we can light and shade it to prepare for rendering.

1. Open exercise3.1_Start.mb. This scene file contains the Goblin creature in his default pose, ready to be setup with fur FIGURE 3.35. If you play the scene, you will see that the Goblin blends from his setup pose into the beginning of a walk cycle at frame 0 and continues walking until frame 120. It is important to setup both hair and fur on a character that is in their default pose. Before we start the fur setup, we must setup the project. Do this by selecting File > Project > Set and locate the project folder on the DVD. This project directory will contain the sub-folders necessary to store the custom fur attribute maps and eventually some dynamics caches (in the next exercise). You may wish to copy this project to your hard drive.

2. With the project set, save a start scene file and grab a cup of coffee; this is where we get going. We want to create a Mohawk hairstyle for the Goblin. To do this, we must grow some fur from his head. Because growing fur from a large mesh is cumbersome and impossibly unwieldy, we must create a 'patch'. To do this, select all of the faces on the top of the Goblin's head (being sure to avoid the horns FIGURE 3.36) and execute Polygons > Duplicate Face. This will create a separate polygon object to grow the fur from. Export this piece and save it as 'headPatch.mb'. For consistency, please use the head patch provided on the DVD.

3. Now re-open exercise3.1_Start.mb and import the head patch (headPatch.mb from the DVD). Place it in a separate layer and template the Goblin mesh.

4. Open exercise3.1_A.mb to see the Goblin with the new head patch. Before we can use this piece to grow fur from, we must adjust its UV layout. To do so, we will start with a planar camera projection (sounds nasty, but it's dead simple). Simply place the camera as though it were a light shining on the head patch; the UVs will be projected from this angle FIGURE 3.37. Now select all of the faces and choose Polygon UVs > Planar Mapping (open the options). Reset the options and check the Camera radio button under Mapping Direction. Hit Project. Now open the UV Texture Editor (Window > UV Texture Editor) and take a look at the UVs FIGURE 3.38. Not bad, but we can easily improve them further.

5. In the UV Texture Editor, select all of the UVs and choose (from the UV Editor menu) Polygons > Unfold UVs (open the options). Reset the options and set Solver Weighting to a value of 1.0. Now hit Apply and watch as the UVs almost magically arrange themselves into a much more accurate layout FIGURE 3.39. While the UVs are now cleanly mapped with very little distortion, we still need to lay them out properly. Recall that fur inclines towards the top of the UV square. Select the UVs and rotate them such that the neck region is closest to the top. Translate and scale them to fit inside the square FIGURE 3.40. Now delete the history on the head patch and save the scene.

6. Open exercise3.1_B.mb to see the head patch with the properly adjusted UV layout. We're finally ready to create some fur! Select the surface and choose Fur > Attach Fur Description > New. This will create the default fur description and attach it to the head patch. As you can see, the default settings create a spiky white fur FIGURE 3.41.

7. With the fur created, it's time to begin tweaking. The quickest way to get started adjusting a fur description is to assign a preset. Find the 'preset' button on the fur description node and replace the fur with the Gorilla preset FIGURE 3.42. Now it's starting to look like fur, but it still doesn't look like a Mohawk.

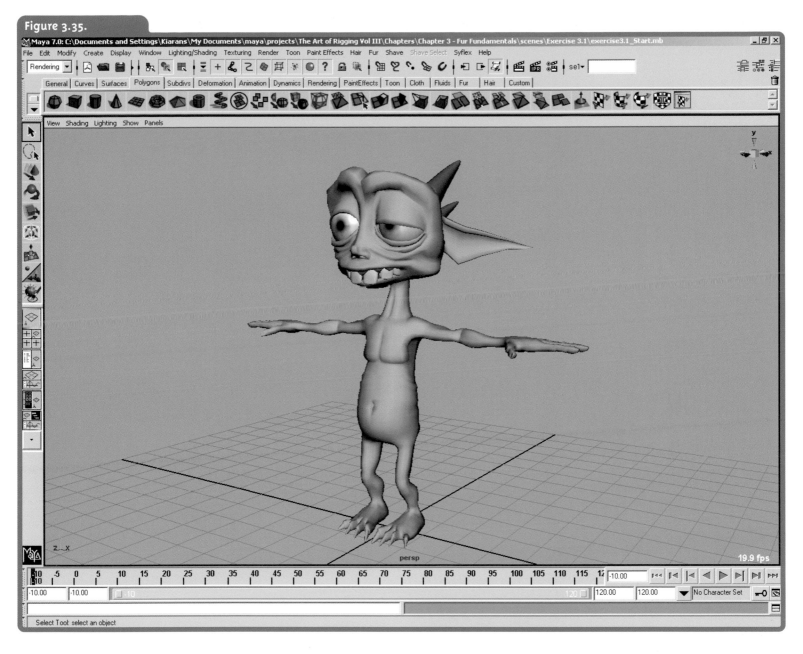

Figure 3.35.

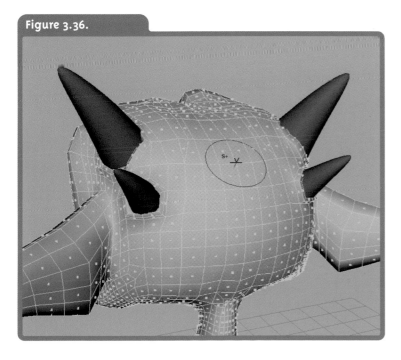

Figure 3.36.

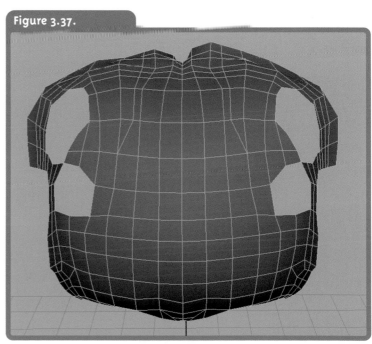

Figure 3.37.

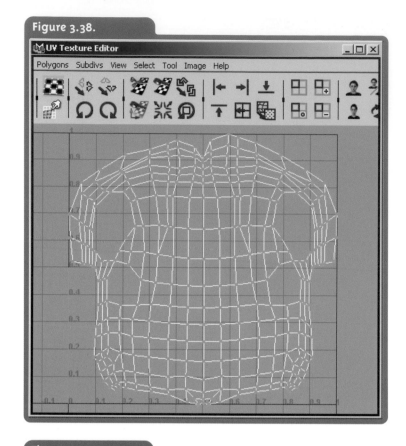

Figure 3.38.

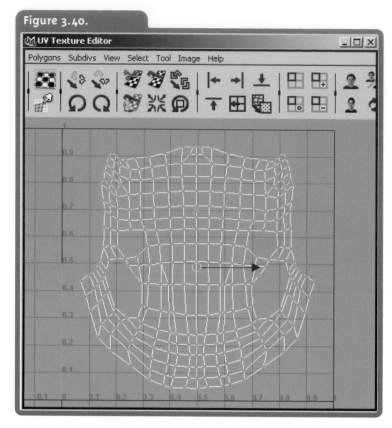

Figure 3.40.

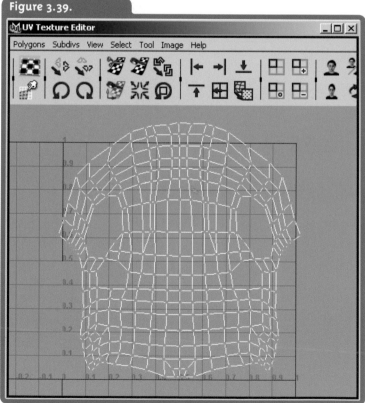

Figure 3.39.

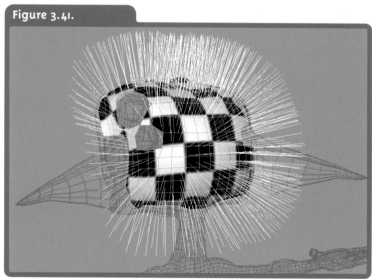

Figure 3.41.

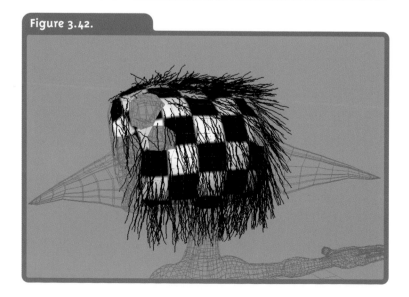

Figure 3.42.

8. Open exercise3.1_C.mb to see the Goblin hair style with the Gorilla preset. Now let's create a length map to define the length of the fur to create a Mohawk. Select the surface and choose Fur > Paint Fur Attributes Tool. This will activate the artisan brush. Open the tool options and set the paint operation to 'replace' with a value of 0.05.

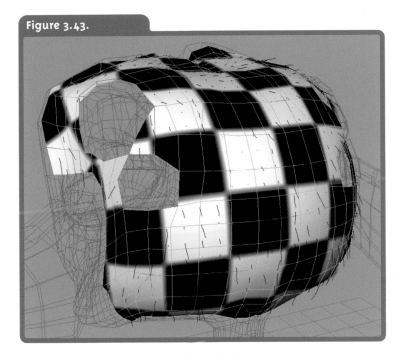

Figure 3.43.

Then hit the Flood button. This will set the fur across the entire scalp to a very short length FIGURE 3.43.

9. At this point, the fur has been effectively buzz cut. With the paint tool, select the Replace operation with a value of 1.0. Paint a stripe down the center of the head to create the Mohawk FIGURE 3.44. This part is a matter of taste, but I decided to taper the Mohawk so that it gets shorter across the back of the head. I also blended it slightly with the Smooth paint operation. Experiment with the paint tool to create different styles.

10. Open exercise3.1_D.mb to see the finished length map (you may need to adjust the inclination to notice the affect on the fur). I also painted a baldness map that trims the fur around the edges of the patch. By smoothing the edges, the fur will gradually taper into the surrounding skin.

11. Now to make the fur more interesting, set the Inclination to 0.15 to make the Mohawk point straight-up. Also adjust the Base/Tip Color attributes to dark brown and red respectively. Try experimenting with the other attributes (like curling) to create whatever effect you like FIGURE 3.45.

12. You may notice that the length attribute slider no longer has any affect on the fur. This is because that attribute has been mapped. To adjust the length of the fur, we now have to adjust the Map

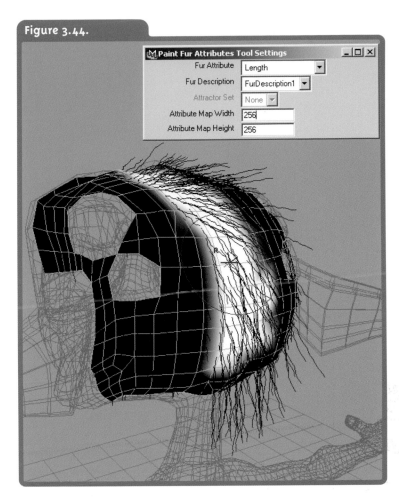

Figure 3.44.

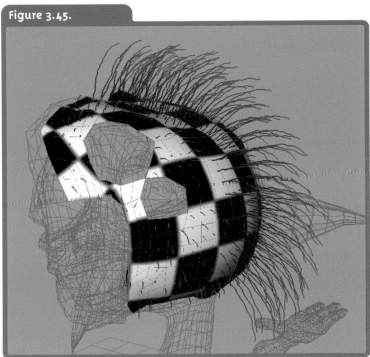

Figure 3.45.

Multiplier attribute under the details section of the fur description node. Setting this to a value of 1.5 should produce a nice long Mohawk for our Goblin (the envy of every street punk) FIGURE 3.46.

13. Open exercise3.1_E.mb to see the final fur style. At this point, it hasn't been adjusted for rendering, but the placement, baldness and length of the hair

Figure 3.46.

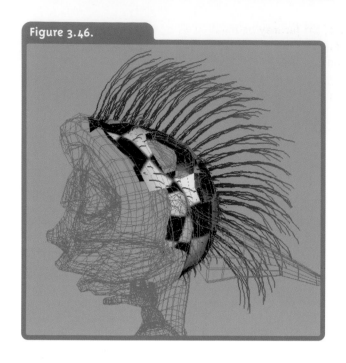

have been adjusted to my liking. The only thing left to do now is attach it! Select the head patch surface, shift select the Goblin mesh and choose `Deform > Create Wrap` (with default settings). This will wrap deform the fur patch to the Goblin mesh.

14. Open exercise3.1_Finished.mb to see the final fur patch. If you play the scene now, the fur will follow the Goblin as he walks around FIGURE 3.47. To learn about finishing the Goblin's Mohawk with custom attribute maps, lighting and dynamics, please continue with the next exercise.

This exercise has introduced you to a complete workflow for adding fur to a character. By utilizing a fur patch, we were able to gain complete control over the placement of the fur and easily work with attribute maps without hindrance. For additional control, these fur maps could be copied from the /furAttrMaps folder and tweaked in Photoshop (this is covered in the next exercise).

Before we finish this chapter, there are two more issues to deal with: adding motion to fur (animating) and shading/lighting the fur (rendering).

Figure 3.47.

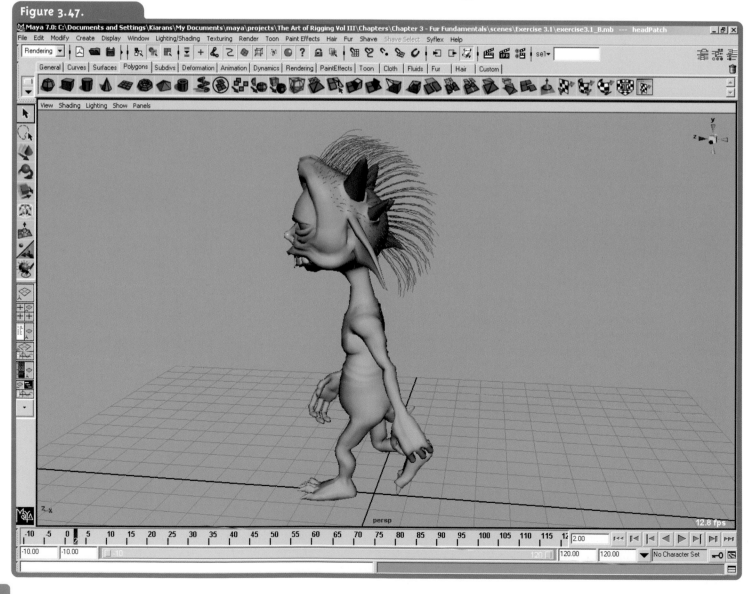

Adding Motion to Fur:

Before the release of Maya 7.0, the only method of adding motion to fur was through the use of an extremely convoluted method involving 'attractors'. These were nothing more than small joint chains setup with spline IK FIGURE 3.48. The spline IK curves were then made soft-bodies and the particle goal weights were the only means of adjusting the dynamic behavior.

Figure 3.48.

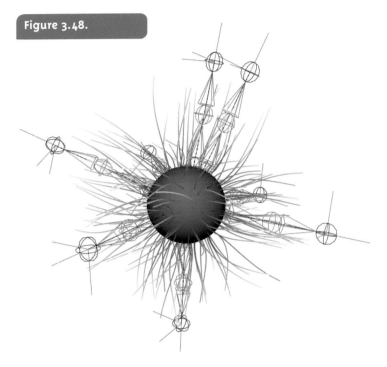

Not surprisingly, this method was Maya Fur's biggest weakness. Many productions resorted to proprietary solutions rather than battling with the dreaded fur attractors. Since the release of Maya 7.0, joint-based fur attractors have been eclipsed by the ability to now drive the motion of fur using Hair curves.

Making fur dynamic is now a very simple matter of connecting the output curves from a hair system to a fur description. The process works like this:

1.) With the fur finished, create a hair system with output curves. Position the follicles wherever you wish to add movement to the fur. Fur located within a close proximity to a hair curve will inherit its motion.

2.) Select any part of the hair system (ie. a curve, or a follicle) and choose Fur > Attach Hair System to Fur, then choose the fur description you want to connect. This will create a FurCurveAttractors node that houses some controls for adjusting the affect of the hair curves.

3.) Play the scene and adjust the dynamics. The fur will now follow the motion of the dynamic hair curves with fully adjustable influence and a nice falloff.

4.) Finally, cache the hair dynamics before rendering the fur.

In addition to being able to animate the fur with dynamics, the Hair curves may also be used to manually animate/style the fur. To do so, simply select the follicle and set its Simulation Method to 'static'. Now the shape of the fur may be modeled by modeling the corresponding start curves. Additionally, these start curves may be rigged with controls for keyframe animation. This technique provides a great interface for gaining complete control over the shape of the fur.

Animating fur with hair dynamics really is quite simple. In order to blast away any doubt of its usefulness, we will explore this technique in exercise 3.2 where we add dynamic behavior to the Goblin's Mohawk.

But before we tackle that, let's discuss the final step in creating believable fur...

Rendering Fur:

When rendering with mental ray, both hair and fur are first converted to hair primitives. But what is a hair primitive you ask? Well, back in 2003, rendering gurus decided that trying to render the tens of thousands of strands typically associated with a head of hair required a special sort of surface primitive (primitives, in this context, are the basic surface types that a rendering program will recognize). Originally, very thin NURBS patches or polygon strip was used. Unfortunately, managing and rendering that many objects was simply too difficult. It was clear, regular surface types would not suffice.

The development of the hair primitive coincided with the pre-production for The Matrix Reloaded film. Because Esc Entertainment needed a better solution for rendering photorealistic hair on their digital doubles, they collaborated with mental images (the creators of mental ray) to implement the new faster and more memory efficient hair primitive into the mental ray renderer. This allowed for the accurate rendering of thousands of hairs without the need for a million-dollar render farm.

Fast forward to today and the hair primitive is finally getting the recognition it deserves. Alias have fully implemented a converter for both Maya Hair and Maya Fur so that they both now render as hair primitives in mental ray.

So why do you care about the hair primitive? Well, apart from the nice history lesson, it should now be abundantly clear that hair and fur abide by the same rules when it comes to rendering. In fact, you can use the exact same lighting/shadow and render global setups for both. All of the rendering techniques discussed in the hair chapter are, quite thankfully, applicable to fur as well.

Perhaps the only distinction to be made between rendering fur and hair is the addition of the 'light model' control (found at the top of the fur description node). This allows fur to be rendered in discrete passes for additional control during the compositing stage. You may choose to render the fur in any of the following models:

- Only Ambient
- Ambient + Diffuse
- Ambient + Diffuse + Specular
- Only Specular

By separating the different contributions to the fur, additional tweaking may be done during the compositing process. Typically, the best workflow involves two passes; ambient plus diffuse, and only specular.

It should also be noted that fur is well suited for rendering with Pixar's Renderman. The Maya-To-Renderman (MTOR) converter handles fur wonderfully; allowing full access to Renderman's amazing deep shadow technology (the same technology that shaded Sully's fur in Monsters Inc). For those looking for a robust yet simple solution, Pixar also offers Renderman for Maya (a Maya plugin) with full support for fur and hair rendering. Renderman for Maya is relatively cheap compared to the full-blown PRMan package while being only moderately limited and very easy to use FIGURE 3.49.

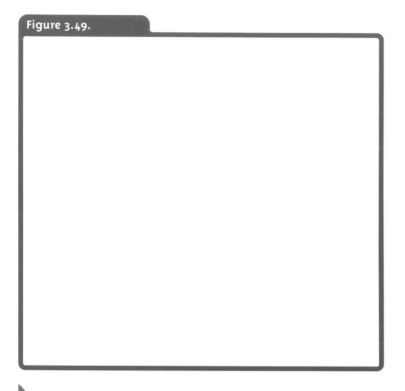

Figure 3.49.

| Exercise 3.2 | Finishing the Goblin's Mohawk |

This exercise picks-up where exercise 3.1 finished. The Goblin's Mohawk has been created, but it needs some additional work to up the 'cool factor'. We will be adding some custom fur attribute maps, 3-point lighting and dynamic motion via Hair curves.

Because the fur attribute maps are dependent on the project directory structure, please ensure that the current project is set to the 'Exercise 3.2' folder from the DVD. When working through this exercise, you should copy the entire project folder to your hard drive. If at any time the Goblin's fur is not in the shape of a Mohawk, it is likely because the attribute maps were not found due to an improperly set project.

1. Open exercise3.2_Start.mb. This file contains the Goblin as we left him at the end of exercise 3.1. He's got a patch of fur growing from his head that has been shaped into a rough-looking Mohawk FIGURE 3.50. You may notice a large white sphere encompassing the entire scene (unhide the background layer to see it). This sphere provides a white backdrop to help us see the fur in test renderings.

2. If you render the fur at this point, you aren't going to get a very pleasing image FIGURE 3.51.

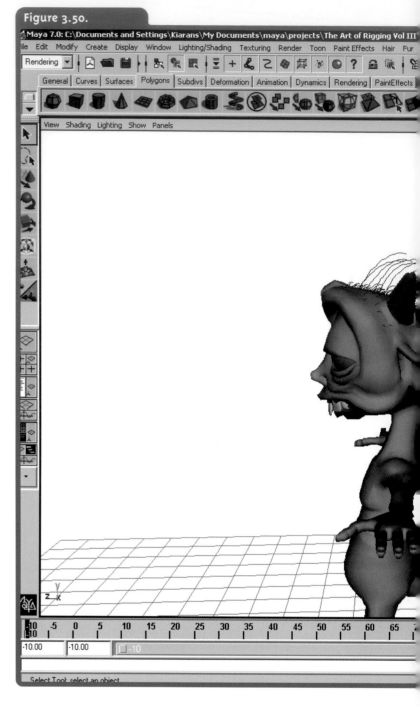

Figure 3.50.

Change the current renderer to mental ray and choose the ProductionRapidFur quality preset in the mental ray render globals.

3. Using mental ray won't magically create nice fur renders on its own. For that, we need soft self-shadowing and carefully adjusted lighting. Open exercise3.2_A.mb to see the lighting rig I used for the Goblin's fur. It contains a basic 3-point lighting setup. The key and fill lights are spotlights aimed at opposite sides of the head, while a point light (with a bluish tinge) is hovering in front of the Goblin FIGURE 3.52. Each light has had it's intensity adjusted to prevent the image from blowing-out or looking too dark. The lighting setup is nothing fancy, but it gets the job done. You can use my lights or create your own for practice.

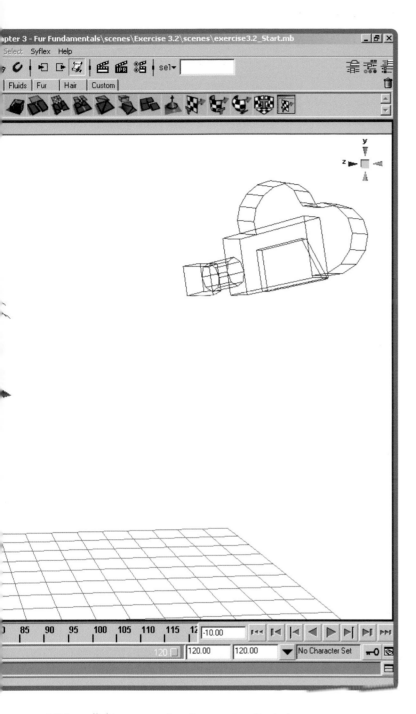

Figure 3.51.

Notice the head patch is already connected to an attribute map (if the project directory is properly setup). This is the map created from the paint tool. I have prepared custom baldness and length maps that can be found in the fur/furAttrMaps directory of the exercise 3.2 project folder FIGURE 3.54. Attach these custom maps by first selecting the head patch from Assigned Surfaces list on the fur description node and then hitting the Map Item button. Attach the GoblinHeadBaldnessMap.bmp and GoblinHeadLengthMap.bmp textures to the appropriate fur attributes.

6. Open exercise3.2_B.mb to see the fur with the properly connected custom attribute maps FIGURE 3.55. By painting the maps in Photoshop, I was able to gain more control over the maps than what is available with the 3d paint tool alone.

7. With the Mohawk looking better styled, let's fiddle with the fur description to tweak it further. To makes the haircut sharper, try lowering the Noise Amplitude on the length map to a value of about 0.1. Less noise will make the Mohawk sharper. To make the Mohawk really stand out, let's stretch It out. Set the length Map Multiplier to a value of 1.5 FIGURE 3.56 . This multiplies each value on the length map by a value of 1.5 which effectively increases the length of the fur.

8. To soften the fur, set the Base Width and Tip Width to a value of 0.01. Lowering the opacity will reduce the harshness of the fur strands. I set the base and tip opacity to 0.5 and 0.3 respectively FIGURE 3.57.

9. With the fur looking much better, let's finish it off with some nice dynamically driven motion. Unhide the head patch layer and select the head patch. Now choose Hair > Create Hair and set the options like in FIGURE 3.58 . This will create a few hair curves across the head surface, but *no paint*

4. With our lights arranged and properly adjusted, we will get an image like FIGURE 3.53. Still not great. To really give the fur a sense of volume, it must have self-shadows. Open the attribute editor for the key and fill lights and check the Shadow Map box under the mental ray tab. Set the resolutions to 1024 and give them a very mild softness (0.001). To alleviate the graininess, set the samples to a value of about 10. The samples and resolution may be increased for the final render, but these values will be adequate for testing purposes.

5. Although the Goblin's head has already been styled into a Mohawk using the Paint Fur Attribute tool, we can create more accurate and interesting maps. Open the fur description node and under the details tab find the map section under length.

Figure 3.52.

Figure 3.53.

effects FIGURE 3.59. We are going to attach these hair curves to the fur, and don't want to actually create any hair.

10. Because we only need the Mohawk to flop around (and not the other short hairs), remove the follicles that are not running down the center of the head. This can be done by simply deleting them or through the Paint Hair Follicles Tool (`Hair > Paint Hair Follicles`). By only using about

Figure 3.54.

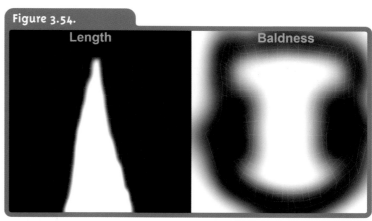

4 or 5 follicles running down the length of the Mohawk, we will help keep the rig computationally efficient.

11. Open exercise3.2_C.mb to see the properly adjusted Mohawk with the carefully placed hair follicles FIGURE 3.60 . Before these follicles will affect the fur, we must attach them. Select one of the hair curves and choose `Fur > Attach Hair System to Fur > FurDescription1`.

12. Playing the scene will show the fur flopping around with the hair curves. Dead simple isn't it? By default, the hair curves are way too floppy for a stiff, punk hairstyle like our Mohawk. Grab the hair system node and open the Dynamics section

Figure 3.55.

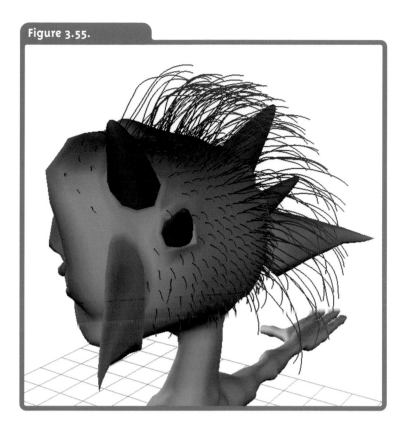

Figure 3.56.

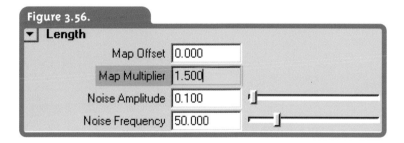

Figure 3.57.

Figure 3.58.

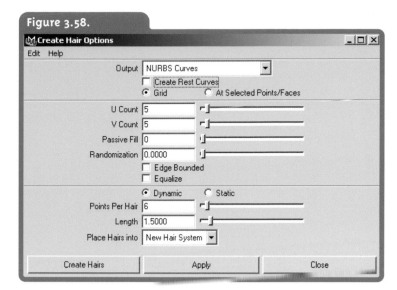

in the attribute editor. Find the Start Curve Attract attribute and set it to a value of about 0.7. Now play the scene and notice that the hairs bounce in a much more controllable manner (we just gave the Goblin a hefty dose of hairspray). While you are in the hairsystem node, set the Start Frame to -10 so that the dynamics can settle before the animation begins.

13. Open exercise3.2_D.mb to see the properly setup hair system driving the motion of the fur. It's astonishingly easy to get great behavior from Maya Hair if you know what you are doing. Hit play to watch the Mohawk bounce around with the motion of the walk cycle. When you are happy, select a piece of the hair system (any follicle will suffice) and choose `Hair > Create Cache`. Cache the entire animation to prepare the scene for rendering.

14. Open exercise3.2_Finished.mb to see the final Goblin Mohawk complete with custom attribute maps, lighting and dynamic animation.

Following through a written tutorial, regardless of how thorough it may be, will never replicate the experience of actually watching somebody. Even if you feel confident with the concepts presented in this exercise, I highly recommend watching the included video lectures. Also be sure to check out the video on the DVD showing a test render of the Goblin Mohawk in action.

Figure 3.59.

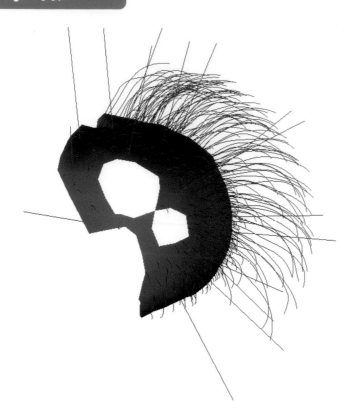

Figure 3.60.

Final Thoughts:

If you are reading this book in a linear fashion, the end of this chapter concludes the part of the book dedicated to teaching fundamentals. With the raw technical hurdles out of the way, the ability to produce believable cloth, hair and fur animation now hinges on basically two key factors:

1. Smooth / Dependable / Cost-Efficient Integration into a Production Pipeline

2. Practical Experience

Only through mastering both of these 'secondary' issues will these advanced effects truly come into the realm of possibility. Indeed, knowing how to create such finishing touches is of little value if they prove too unwieldy or difficult to integrate into a real production.

For this reason, I have tried to point-out potential pitfalls wherever possible. You may have noticed a lot of discussion on such topics as reducing the 'computational overhead' or creating 'efficient' and 'sustainable' workflows. In the next two chapters, these issues will become paramount as we explore a real production scenario involving the Minx character. Without further ado, please read-on to discover how the Minx character was effectively brought-to-life thanks to diligent attention to detail and constant consideration of the issues related to a stable pipeline.

Before continuing, it is worth checking to ensure that you are familiar with the concepts we explored in this chapter, specifically:

- What 'Maya Fur' Is
- How to Create Fur on Any Creature Mesh
- Creating Fur Patches
- Customizing the Fur Description Node
- Using the Paint Fur Attribute Tool
- Attaching Custom Fur Attribute Maps
- Adding Motion to Fur with Hair-Based Attractors
- Shading, Lighting and Rendering Fur with mental ray

Chapter 4
Applied Character Effects

Introduction:

There is no doubt that the future of digital animation revolves around increasing complexity, while driving-down production times. This increased complexity will manifest itself in the form of crowds of highly detailed, personalized digital characters. These massive jumps in detail and complexity are quickly becoming expected by modern audiences. Their insatiable thirst for improved visuals in both the real-time and pre-rendered mediums is what drives computer animators to keep raising the bar. But in this constant struggle to keep-up, many animators are finding it difficult to integrate all of the various layers of detail into a single scene. Indeed, the management of such complex assets has become a central issue.

It isn't sufficient to know simply how to create fur, or model clothing. Many of the issues faced today are related to the application of these effects in a production. This chapter will guide you through the various techniques used to successfully combine advanced character effects (fur/hair and cloth). By guiding you through the technical hurdles involved with outfitting a complete character with full-body fur and clothing.

Having already discussed the specifics of fur/hair and cloth effects, this chapter focuses on bringing everything together using an interesting character. While we will also discuss the specifics of the effects themselves, emphasis will be on integration and workflow. In the following chapter, we will take this character and simulate the fur and clothing for a particular shot. Before we can do that, let's discuss the creation of these advanced character effects.

Specifically, we will be covering:

- The Origins of the Minx Character
- Advanced Character Pipelines
- Rigging Overview for Animation Rig
- Rigging Overview for High-Res Rig
- Creating the Minx's Fur
- Creating the Minx's Clothing
- A Cloth Workflow MEL Script
- A Case Study in MEL GUI Design

The Minx:

The character we will be following throughout this chapter is called the 'Minx'. The Minx started life, like most digital characters, as a drawing. The concept, created by Mike McCarthy, shows a character covered in long shaggy fur and strips of cloth FIGURE 4.1. Characters like these were once so prohibitive, only world-class facilities with teams of research PhDs would even attempt to create them. In fact, the Minx would have been extremely difficult to realize as little as five years ago. Fortunately for us, modern software and hardware advances have continued reflecting Moore's Law (halving price/performance ratios every two years).

Figure 4.1.

With the concept finished, the next step was turning the drawing into a polygonal mesh. For that, we hired the brilliant talents of a sculptor by the name of Glen Southern (www.southerngfx.co.uk). Glen used the popular (and budget priced) polygon modeler, Silo, to construct the polygonal mesh FIGURE 4.2. The Minx's unsmoothed mesh is comprised of approximately 7k vertices. In order to provide the extra resolution for sculpting subtle deformations, the mesh was smoothed once to produce 31k vertices. Additional smoothing can be applied at render time as necessary.

Figure 4.2.

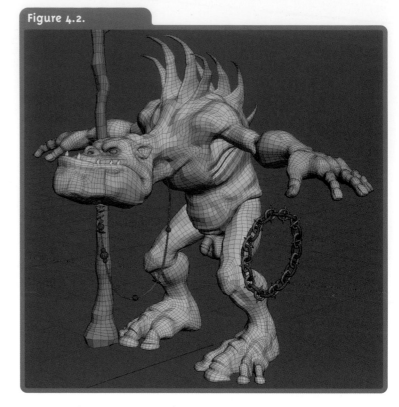

In addition to a fully-quadrilateral, cleanly constructed base mesh, the Minx takes advantage of the latest surfacing technologies to provide additional detail. Cleanly unwrapped UVs were created along with a displacement map that was generated in Pixologic's Zbrush FIGURE 4.3. By sculpting the finer pieces in a program like Zbrush, extremely large amounts of detail can be added to the mesh with no regard for interrupting the skinning process. Displacement maps hold small forms and skin textures that are difficult (nigh impossible) to capture into the mesh itself. In fact, many details that would previously have been added to the mesh itself would have created uneven topology and exacerbated weighting issues in those areas. In short, Zbrush displacement maps are to a weight painter what a nail gun is to a carpenter; not absolutely necessary, but greatly appreciated.

In addition to the displacement map, a hand-painted color map has been included for use in the diffuse channel of the material shader. This map was hand-painted in Photoshop to give the Minx a nice, vibrant skin tone FIGURE 4.4. All of the maps and the mesh itself are included on the DVD (along with the finished scene files). If you are a student, or a professional looking to sharpen their skills on the weekend, I highly recommend following along through this chapter to get a good sense of what it takes to rig a character like this. Even if you don't follow along, this chapter chronicles the journey well enough that you should be able to successfully apply the techniques to your own characters. Just remember, we went to great lengths to include a professional quality asset with this chapter, so have fun with it!

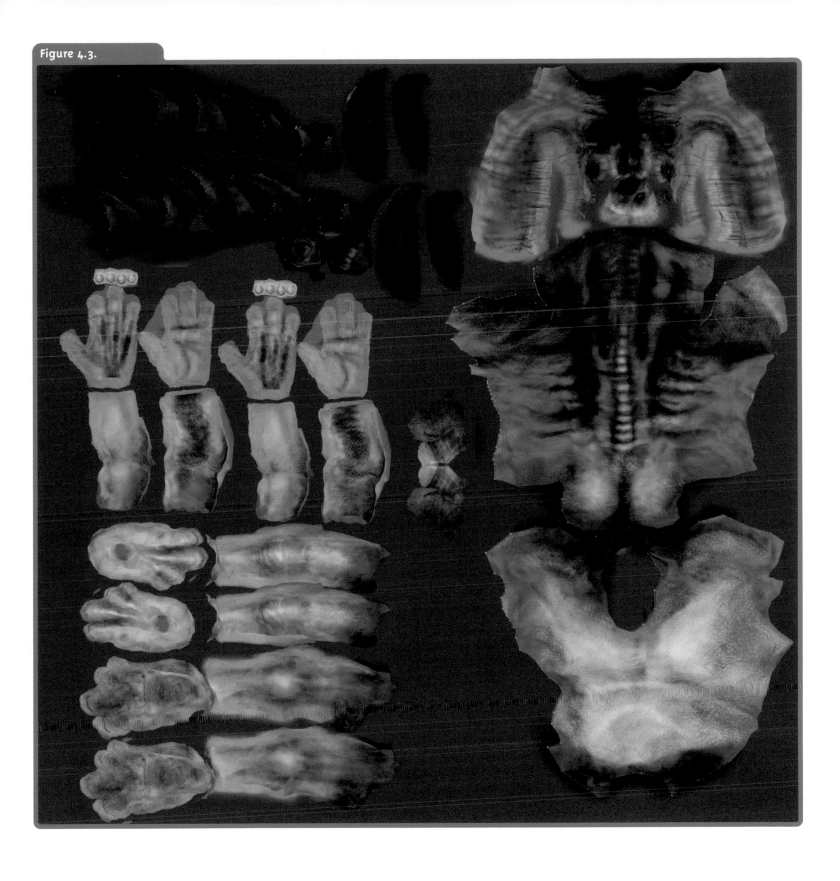

Figure 4.3.

Figure 4.4.

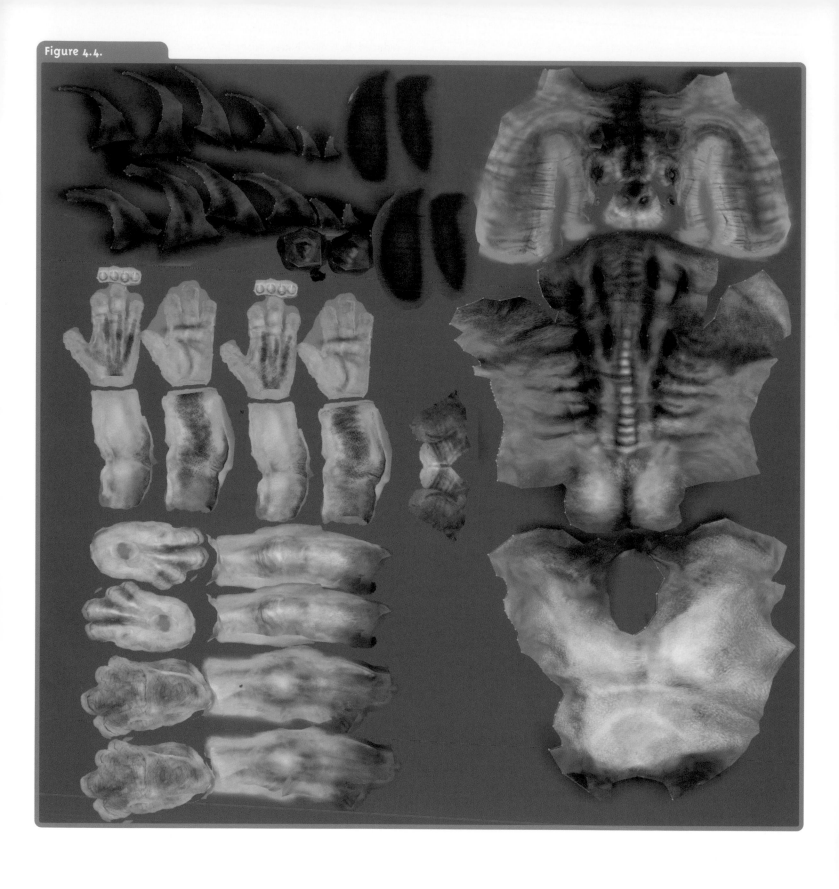

Advanced Rigging Pipelines:

When a character moves beyond being a simple weighted mesh to become a complex dynamically simulated combination of effects, the importance of having a smooth pipeline becomes paramount. What may have worked on your last production is not necessarily sufficient for characters of this complexity. Many of these issues were touched upon in The Art of Rigging Vol II where we tackled the problem of animating an extremely dense model. In that case, we were tackling a static, non-deforming mesh (the SP-23 robot), as you will see, things change when deformations are added to the mix. To quickly revisit the issue, let's discuss some of the popular methods of moving an animated character through a pipeline:

1.One Scene File, One Layer: This is where the animator works on the rig that will eventually be rendered. There is no separation between animation and deformation. For all but the simplest of characters, this technique can lead to serious issues. That being said, sometimes this can work just fine and is actually the preferable method.

2.High / Low Layers: Probably the most obvious solution is to include two versions of the model (high resolution and low resolution) in the same scene file. The low-res layer contains a skeleton with animation controls and either a simple bound mesh or parent-constrained pieces. These calculate in realtime allowing the animator to adjust their timing without hindrance. When the scene is to be playblasted or rendered, the high resolution layer is unhidden and the low-res layer is toggled off.

3.Animation Transfer: Just like before, there are two versions of the rig except this time they are kept in completely separate scene files. Once the animation is finished, it may be exported to disk (using a proprietary script or custom technique). This animation data may then be copied onto the duplicate skeleton in the high-res scene file. This method keeps the animation rig completely separate from the deformation rig.

4.Even More Modularized: Many productions push this idea even further by separating almost every significant element of a character into its own scene file. This can lead to characters with perhaps four or more scene files; one for animation, deformation, cloth simulation and secondary simulations. The scene files contain individual elements that are eventually animated and integrated into a final scene file before being rendered.

You may have noticed these pipeline methods are basically varying degrees of modularity. The question you have to ask yourself is: How much do I want to split things up? On one end of the spectrum (option #1) the pipeline is completely integrated, the opposite side is completely modularized FIGURE 4.5.

Figure 4.5.

| Modular | Balanced | Fully Integrated |

As your pipeline tends towards integration, scene file complexity increases. This increases loading times, introduces chances for naming conflicts (especially when using scripted solutions) and generally makes the hypergraph much more difficult to traverse and de-bug.

As the pipeline tends towards modularity, scene file complexity is reduced but new issues arise. In a completely modular approach, bugs can arise where separate elements do not interact properly. For example, the cloth must respect the position of the fur to avoid penetrations. If they are in separate scene files, it can be difficult to detect such a problem. Modularized pipelines also require an initial time investment to ensure that the animation data flows properly and connects precisely.

An overly modularized pipeline creates more problems than it solves. Similarly, too much integration creates issues of complexity. This is the balance between integration and modularization. Finding the right middle-ground takes time and practice, but is instrumental in creating a successful animation pipeline.

The Minx's Pipeline:

So what type of animation pipeline will we be using for the Minx? After some careful consideration, we decided to use the animation transfer pipeline. Basically, the Minx will be split into two scene files:

Figure 4.6.

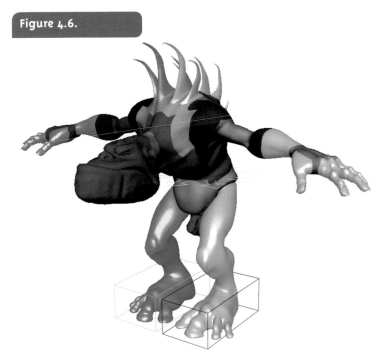

1.Animation Scene: This scene file contains the animation rig and a simple deformation rig. One layer contains a proxy version of the Minx that has been sliced-up and parent constrained to the skeleton. This is the layer with all of the animation controls FIGURE 4.6. There is another layer containing only the Minx's smooth bound mesh. This layer can be toggled on to give the animator a better idea of how their pose is looking, although it will be too slow to animate directly.

2.High-Res Scene: This scene contains a skeleton (with no constraints or controls of any kind). This skeleton is connected to the mesh with a skinCluster. The mesh also includes a blendshape node with several corrective shapes for fixing deformations at specific poses. In addition to the more detailed deformations, this scene file includes all of the fur, cloth and dynamically animated spikes.

In the next chapter, we will step through the complete simulation of an entire shot. But before we get to that, it is important that you know exactly what sort of workflow we will be using to animate the Minx.

Getting the animation from start to finish will involve these steps:

1. Keyframe animation is done on the animation scene file. Once completed, this file is handed to a TD for processing. The animator needn't worry about the rest of the process.

2. The MEL utility jcAnimCS.mel is used to copy the keyframe animation from the skeleton itself (not the controllers). This is stored on the hard drive as a .jca file.

3. The high-res scene is opened. The MEL utility is used to copy the animation from the .jca file to the new scene file. Once this is completed, the deformation skeleton will contain the exact animation from the animation scene.

4. With the animation copied, the TD can now begin working through the various reactionary elements. The spikes, cloth and fur all require dynamic simulation.

5. Working on one piece at a time, the TD simulates the piece, tweaks the necessary parameters and bakes the animation. Baking is done with the help of two custom scripts (discussed later).

6. With the simulated pieces baked, the TD has one last opportunity to tweak the deformations in a process know as shot sculpting or 'finalizing'. Techniques for this stage are discussed later in the final chapter.

7. Last checks are made to ensure the animation is perfect and the scene file is clean before being sent to be lit and rendered.

One of the great things about keeping the animation rig separate is that it can be worked-on and updated as needed without interfering with the render scene file. In fact, the animation and deformation rigs may be worked on simultaneously by different people. The only real consistency between the two files is the skeleton itself (or any other animated attributes). As long as the joint layouts match precisely (including naming conventions, and orientations), the animation will copy over accurately. The copying process can be facilitated by several techniques. We will be using a proprietary script from The Art of Rigging Vol I (jcAnimCS.mel, included on the DVD).

It is not always the case that all of the animation curves on a character will ultimately affect joints. In these cases, we must find a way to ensure that all of the animated attributes are consistent across the animation and deformation rigs. It's not uncommon to have custom facial rigs where the animation curves affect a number of different things (blendshape weights, squash deformer weights or clusters).

To copy the animation from these odd pieces of your rig (anything that doesn't indirectly affect a joint), you should create a 'global animation node'. This can be whatever you want, but it should be a node (an empty group or character set node will suffice) with custom attributes that are hooked-up to all of the disparate attributes on the rig. With all of the attributes flowing into a single node, the task of copying all of the 'extra' animation becomes a piece of cake. The chance of missing an attribute during the copying stage is greatly diminished. Think of the global animation node as the brains of the rig. Everything flows into it and is safely stored there.

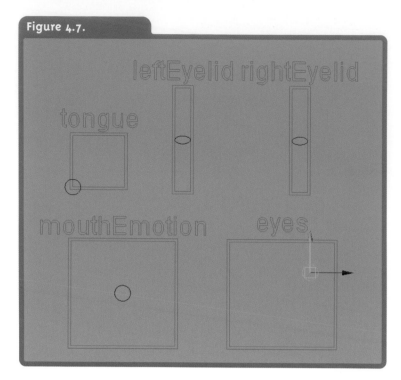

Figure 4.7.

Creating your 'global animation node' is a straightforward process, but it does require some planning. Deciding exactly what attributes to copy to the deformation rig requires that you reduce the rig to it's simplest components. To understand what that means, consider the now famous Osipa facial controller scheme. When using an Osipa-style animation controller, the animator is directly animating the translation of curve objects, nothing more FIGURE 4.7. These curve objects, however, are hooked-up via a complex web of expressions, set-driven keys or direct connections to a single node, the blendshape node. In the end, the only thing these fancy interfaces are doing is providing a level of abstraction from an underlying mechanism (in this case, blendshapes). If all they are doing is affecting blendshape attributes, then why not cut-out the middleman? There is no need to copy the animation from a gazillion controller curves. It is cleaner/easier/better to pipe the blendshape attributes into a global animation node and be done with it.

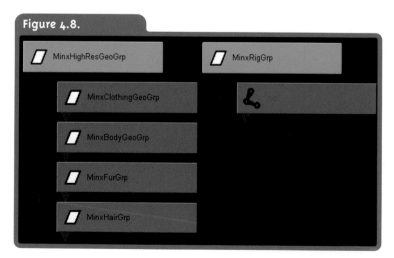

Figure 4.8.

By using this technique, not only have we simplified the animation copying process, but we have simplified the deformation rig as well. Now there is no need to have the interface in the deformation rig since the animation data can be plugged directly into the blendshapes themselves. This keeps the deformation rig clean from extraneous nodes FIGURE 4.8 .

Once you start thinking of animation rigs in terms of data, whole new possibilities for simplification will open up. When your pipeline has been simplified in this manner, you will find changes to the deformation/animation rig become much easier. By stripping the animation itself to its most basic attributes, minor changes can be made to either the animation or deformation rigs without needing to propagate those changes across every scene file. For example, one person can work on adjusting the facial interface while another person can tweak skin weights. They can work independently while knowing with confidence that, within obvious limitations, their changes won't affect each other.

With a general understanding of the pipeline method we will be using, let's continue our journey by taking a closer look at the strategy used to rig the animation puppet for the Minx character.

(Quick) Overview of Animation Rig:

The animation rig for the Minx uses a few tricks you may not be aware of. The purpose of this section is not to describe animation rigging techniques (this has been done to a great extent in the two previous volumes) but rather provide a quick overview for those who are curious about the entire process.

Because we are using an animation transfer pipeline, the animation rig itself does not need to abide by any particular rules. Keep in mind that it's sole purpose is to provide an abstraction from the joints themselves to make the animator's life easier.

In case you haven't already noticed, rigging is a very idea-centric art form. Some ideas are better than others and so they propagate through the Internet and other mediums until they become commonplace. As new technologies arise (like full-body IK, for example) older techniques may be augmented or replaced with new ones. There are as many different styles of animation rigs as there are riggers. It seems like every new rig I come across has some sort of unique style or feature. In fact, looking at other's rigs is a great way to 'steal' ideas for your own rigs.

Because of the very diverse and disorderly nature of rigging concepts, it is impossible to provide a definitive 'best solution'. To make matters worse, animators can be a picky bunch (and rightly so). They will often have conflicting views about what features are necessary or even useful. This doesn't mean that their views are wrong, just that what is 'correct' for one person may not hold true for others. This is another reason why keeping animation rigs separate from deformation rigs is especially useful in a production environment. It's not uncommon for multiple versions of a rig to be built for specific animators and even for specific shots. With a separated animation rig, this can be done without any complications.

With all of this in mind, we set out to create an animation rig that would suit our needs. The Minx's animation rig provides us with enough control to create some nifty animation to show-off the dynamic simulations. The following is a quick overview of what techniques were used in the creation of the animation puppet.

1. Joint Layout:

The very first thing we did upon receiving the Minx mesh was create the joint layout. Because the joint layout must be identical between the animation and deformation rigs, this is a critical phase that must be finalized before moving on. The Minx uses a fairly standard skeleton. The legs use the common hip, knee, ankle, ball and toe arrangement (with each toe also containing a 3-joint chain for curling the toes) FIGURE 4.9. The spine consists of a root and four spine joints placed between his spikes FIGURE 4.10. The neck is given two joints that lead to a single head joint. From the head joint, we placed a joint for the jaw and three joints for each eye (top/bottom eyelid and one for the eyeball) FIGURE 4.11. The arms use the clavicle, shoulder, elbow, forearm, wrist arrangement FIGURE 4.12. We actually added two forearm joints to smooth-out deformations in this trouble spot. The hands were rigged with four joints for each finger, with the exception of the pinky which is given an extra joint located near the wrist to give it the ability to form a ball shape FIGURE 4.13. The finger joints are parented to a palm joint. This joint is not absolutely necessary (it isn't animated), but is useful if you wish to apply IK to the arm. With an IK handle going from the shoulder to the wrist, the hand will still slide around when the parent of the IK is moved. By creating a second IK handle from the wrist to the palm joint, the hand can be stabilized (useful for planting the hand on a surface). The spikes on the Minx's back are rigged with chains of 3-5 joints each FIGURE 4.14. These will be animated dynamically and are not 'touchable' in the animation rig.

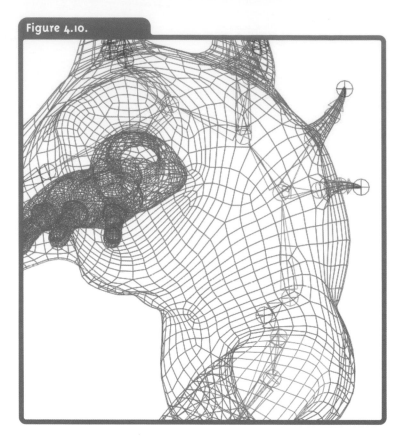

Figure 4.10.

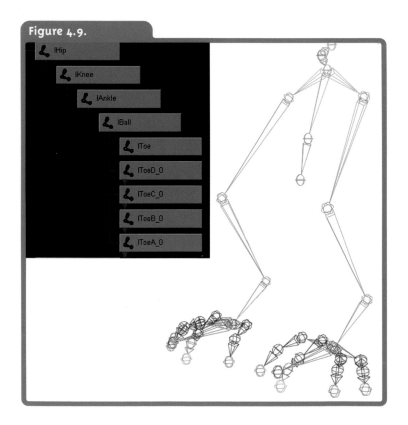

Figure 4.9.

lHip
lKnee
lAnkle
lBall
lToe
lToeD_0
lToeC_0
lToeB_0
lToeA_0

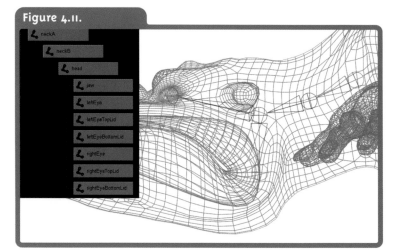

Figure 4.11.

neckA
neckB
head
jaw
leftEye
leftEyeTopLid
leftEyeBottomLid
rightEye
rightEysTopLid
rightEyeBottomLid

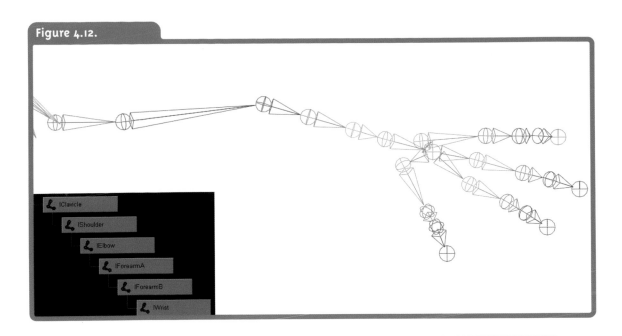

Figure 4.12.

- IClavicle
  - IShoulder
    - IElbow
      - IForearmA
        - IForearmB
          - IWrist

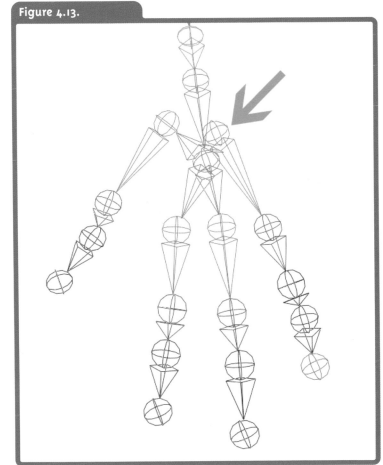

Figure 4.13.

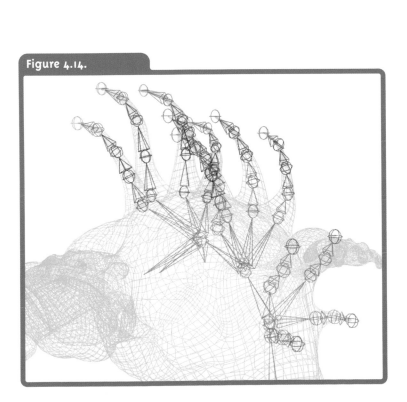

Figure 4.14.

2. Proxy Geometry:

Unless the character mesh that is being animated is extremely simple, it likely won't update in real-time. This leads to a familiar annoyance where the animator is left to constantly playblast the scene in order to get a realtime look at the timing of the animation. Obviously, this represents a significant bottleneck in the animation workflow. To counter this, many productions utilize a proxy mesh that, rather than being smooth bound, is simply parent constrained to the skeleton FIGURE 4.15. This updates in realtime and provides a good indication of the pose the character is in. A proxy mesh can be created by chopping the character mesh into pieces. Start at the extremities, selecting the faces that 'belong' to a single joint, and extract them (`Edit Polygons > Extract`). Work your way through half of the body, slicing as you go. When the limbs on half of the body are sliced, you can mirror-copy them to the other side. Be sure to delete all the unnecessary history before attaching these pieces to the skeleton.

Figure 4.15.

3. Controllers:

Curve-based controls are easily the most common. These are usually built to represent the part of the body they are intended to control. Like an icon, the hand controller may resemble the shape of a hand. When all of the controllers are curves, you can easily hide/unhide them by using the NURBS curve filter under the viewport's show menu FIGURE 4.16. There is nothing wrong with these types of controllers (in fact, they can be very useful), but we chose to use a less-common technique whereby the controllers are the actual proxy pieces of geometry. Using this technique, the animator simply selects the shoulder (or any other piece) and rotates it directly FIGURE 4.17. This type of hands-on interaction is very intuitive, but is not without its drawbacks. For parts of the body using IK, a curve controller actually makes more sense because the animator is meant to be animating a point in space (the goal for the joint chain), not the rotation of a specific bone. Also, if you want to use hands-on controllers with an IK/FK switch, you must setup an elaborate set driven key system where the FK pieces are hidden when the switch is in IK mode (and vice versa). Regardless, we used the hands-on system because IK/FK switches were not particularly necessary and they demonstrate something you may not have seen before.

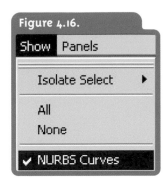

Figure 4.16.

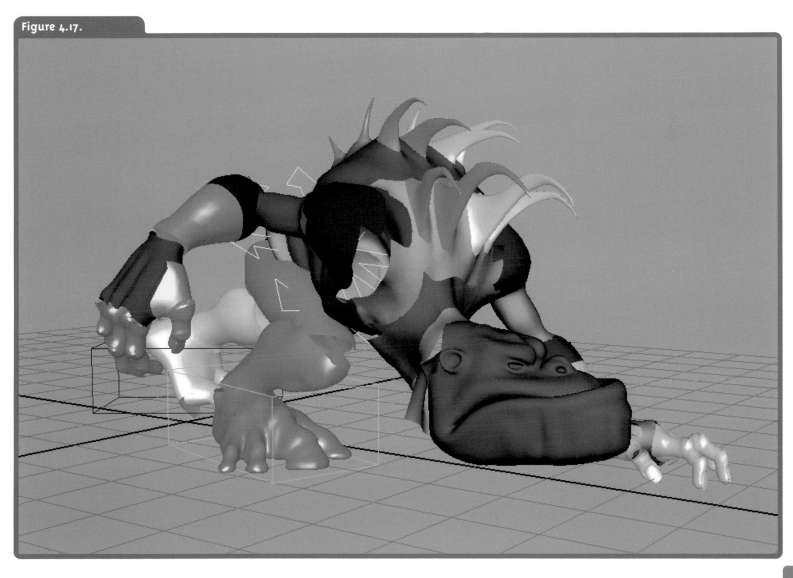

Figure 4.17.

4. Inverse Kinematics:

The legs are the only part of the body with IK. There is a rotate-plane IK solver going from the hip to the knee. This solver is rigged using the 'no-flip' knee technique from chapter one of The Art of Rigging Vol I. This technique uses utility nodes to keep the knee from flipping when the foot IK is moved FIGURE 4.18. The foot is also rigged with single chain IK handles running from the ankle to the ball and the ball to the toe. These are arranged into a group-based reverse foot setup (chapter one, The Art of Rigging Vol 1). The attributes for controlling the foot are neatly arranged on the box-shaped foot controller FIGURE 4.19. All-in-all, it is a pretty standard leg setup.

Figure 4.18.

rightFootCtrl
rightIKPlusMinusNode
rLegIK

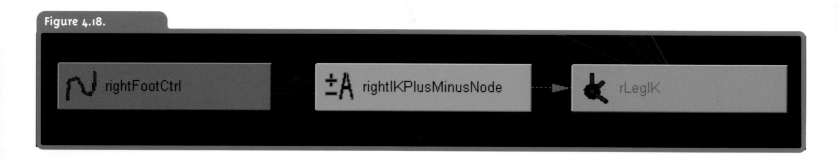

Figure 4.19.

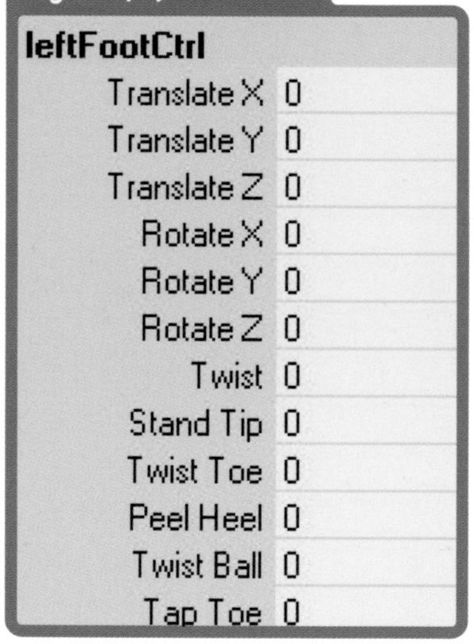

leftFootCtrl
Translate X 0
Translate Y 0
Translate Z 0
Rotate X 0
Rotate Y 0
Rotate Z 0
Twist 0
Stand Tip 0
Twist Toe 0
Peel Heel 0
Twist Ball 0
Tap Toe 0

5. Head Constraint:

The head of the Minx is rigged in such a way so that it does not behave in a purely FK manner. The animator can blend the head into a constrained state where it will remain pointing in its current direction. This may be blended off so that it behaves like an FK chain FIGURE 4.20. The head behaves as though its parent/child relationship with the neck joint can be blended on/off, even though the head joint remains parented under the neck joint in the skeletal hierarchy. This is done by orient constraining (while maintaining offsets) the head control itself to two intermediary group nodes. One of these null groups is oriented like the neck joint, the other remains in default world orientation. After the head control is orient constrained to both of these nulls, a switch is made with set driven keys to blend between them. Biological heads have a means of steadying themselves apart from the movements of the body FIGURE 4.21. This type of constraint simulates this effect by breaking the rigid FK behavior of the neck/head relationship.

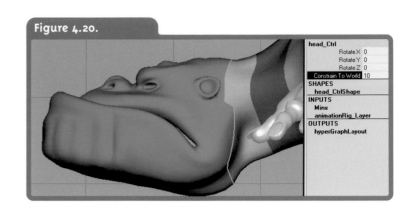

Figure 4.20.

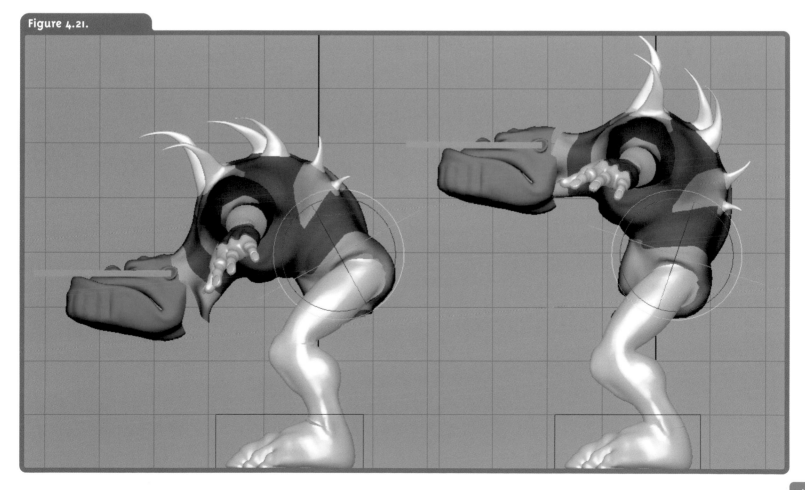

Figure 4.21.

6. The Fingers:

Rather than force the animator to position each joint in the hand individually, we opted to setup some high-level controls to bend, and spread the fingers automatically. This technique is covered in chapter one of The Art of Rigging Vol I. Using SDK's on fingers is a common technique. With it, the finger joint rotations are connected to custom attributes on the hand controllers FIGURE 4.22. One of these attributes may control the rotation of 3 or more joints. Animators enjoy automation as long as it doesn't restrict them. For this reason, the finger curling was separated into base and tip attributes. The base attribute drives the first knuckle, and the tip drives the other two. In the real world, it is difficult to bend your third knuckle apart from the second (go ahead and try, but don't hurt yourself). Additional attributes were created to spread the fingers and pose the hand into a ball shape (utilizing the extra pinky joint) FIGURE 4.23. The idea with this kind of hand rig is that the hand may be posed quickly using virtual sliders. You may ask yourself, is this as accurate as animating directly on the joints? The answer is, definitely not. But, that kind of precision posing may never be needed in a typical production.

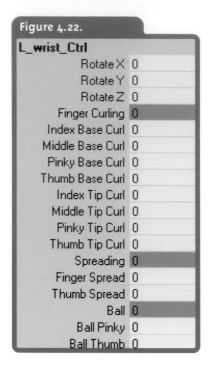

Figure 4.22.

L_wrist_Ctrl

Rotate X	0
Rotate Y	0
Rotate Z	0
Finger Curling	0
Index Base Curl	0
Middle Base Curl	0
Pinky Base Curl	0
Thumb Base Curl	0
Index Tip Curl	0
Middle Tip Curl	0
Pinky Tip Curl	0
Thumb Tip Curl	0
Spreading	0
Finger Spread	0
Thumb Spread	0
Ball	0
Ball Pinky	0
Ball Thumb	0

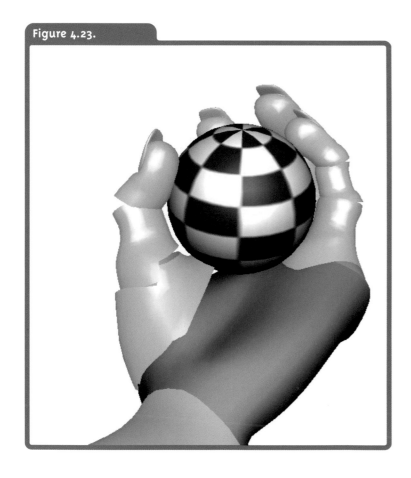

Figure 4.23.

7. Automated Pieces:

Everything about the animation rig represents some varying degree of automation, but some pieces are completely automated and are not controlled by the animator at all. The animation rig utilizes a convention whereby any piece that is shaded with specular highlights (ie. really shiny looking) is not touchable. These pieces have a phong shader applied to them to let the animator know that they aren't to be manipulated. These pieces have their overrides set to display as references. This prevents them from being selected in the viewport FIGURE 4.24. This is done on the forearm joints which are automatically driven by the rotation of the wrist. This is done with a MEL expression. Basically, instead of constraining the forearm and wrist joints to the hand controller, the rotation values of the hand controllers are fed into an expression that splits them up and distributes them across the arm. So twisting the wrist results in twisting both of the forearm joints and the wrist. The rotations are designed to falloff towards the elbow. This is a rough approximation of the interaction between the radius and ulna bones found in a real human arm. Looking at the expression itself, it is easy to see how this works:

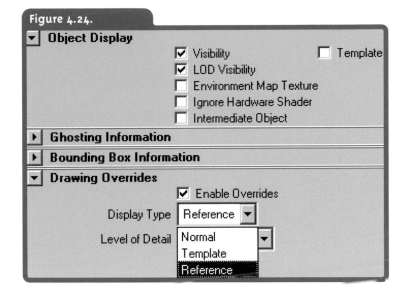

Figure 4.24.

Code

```
//Left Wrist
lWrist.rotateX = L_wrist_Ctrl.rotateX * 0.5;
lWrist.rotateY = L_wrist_Ctrl.rotateY;
lWrist.rotateZ = L_wrist_Ctrl.rotateZ;
lForearmB.rotateX = L_wrist_Ctrl.rotateX * 0.3;
lForearmA.rotateX = L_wrist_Ctrl.rotateX * 0.2;
```

It is important to note that the twisting rotations (rotateX) still add up to 1 (.5 +.3 +.2 = 1.0). If they did not, the arm would not rotate the same amount as the wrist controller which (for obvious reasons) would not work very well. Other 'untouchable' pieces include the legs (because they are controlled via IK) and the spikes on his back (because they will be simulated with dynamics to flop around) FIGURE 4.25.

Figure 4.25.

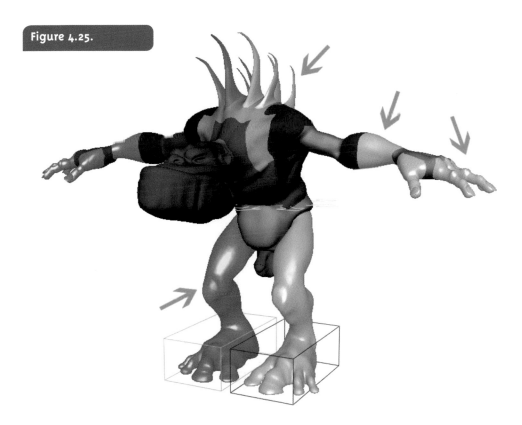

8. Cleanliness:

Recall that the animation rig scene file is used only to interact with the animator. Once the animation is done, the relevant data from this scene file (joint rotations, custom attributes etc...) will be exported and copied into the deformation scene. Even though this file is only an intermediary, it is still important to keep it extremely clean. The hypergraph is meticulously organized to be easy to traverse FIGURE 4.26. I've never made an animation rig that didn't need to be tweaked or adapted at some point. Keeping everything tidy makes it much easier to fix, edit or debug. This is especially important since you may be coming back to the scene weeks or even months later. Cleanliness doesn't stop there. The rig itself is double checked to ensure that the animator doesn't have access to channels that could potentially break the rig. As a general rule, if the animator shouldn't touch it, make it so they can't. Lock and hide unused attributes, turn the visibility of unused nodes off and put any extras into a hidden layer.

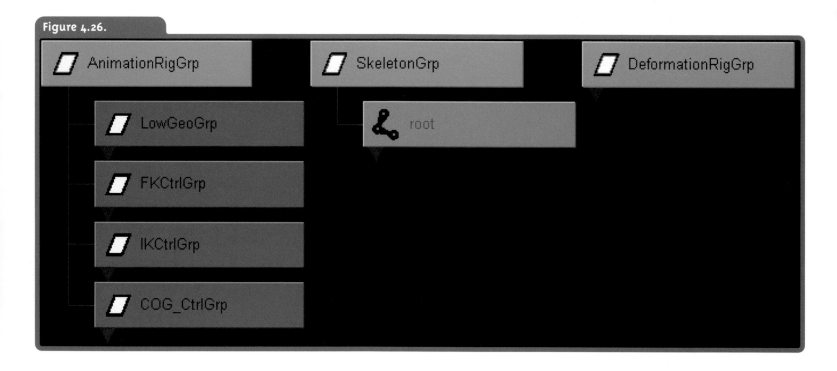

Figure 4.26.

Overview of High-Res Rig:

This section demonstrates the various features and techniques used in the Minx's deformation rig. Many of these ideas have been covered in previous volumes of The Art Of Rigging series, but we are quickly revisiting them to demonstrate how they all fit together. The last two features of the deformation rig (fur and cloth) are covered in detail later in this chapter.

Remember, this rig file is prepared to receive the animation from the animation rig. It doesn't have any controllers or interfaces of any kind (FIGURE 4.27), nor should it. The animation data that will be exported from the animation rig will be copied directly to the skeleton. The skeleton then drives the skincluster deformer and pose-based deformations (blendshapes) which affect the mesh. Once the mesh is deformed, we use these deformations to affect the cloth simulation (as a collision object) and the fur (through hair curves). So the animation flows from skeleton, to skin, to extras (cloth and fur) FIGURE 4.28. Hence, the cloth and fur are referred to as the *reactionary* pieces because they 'react' to the underlying motion of the skeleton.

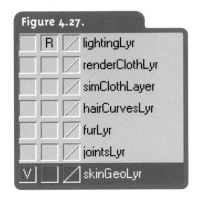

Figure 4.27.

	R		lightingLyr
			renderClothLyr
			simClothLayer
			hairCurvesLyr
			furLyr
			jointsLyr
V			skinGeoLyr

Figure 4.28.

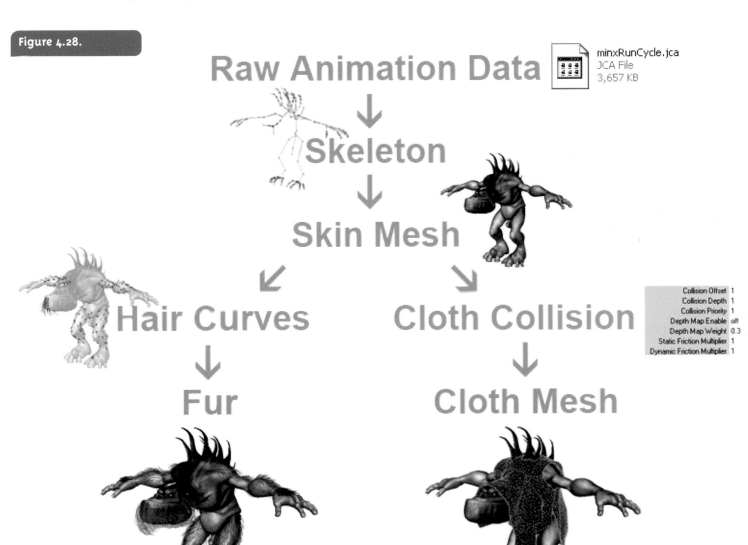

Raw Animation Data minxRunCycle.jca JCA File 3,657 KB
↓
Skeleton
↓
Skin Mesh
↓ ↓
Hair Curves   Cloth Collision
↓ ↓
Fur   Cloth Mesh

Collision Offset 1
Collision Depth 1
Collision Priority 1
Depth Map Enable off
Depth Map Weight 0.3
Static Friction Multiplier 1
Dynamic Friction Multiplier 1

1.Smooth Skin Deformations: The first step in creating the deformation rig involves importing the skeleton and base mesh into a new scene file. It's always best to start a new scene file whenever possible to avoid stray construction nodes being accidentally propagated. With the mesh properly prepared, it may can be attached to the skeleton. In this case, we are using smooth skinning in conjunction with pose-based corrective blendshapes to deform the skin. Regardless of what skinning method you use (muscle systems are no exception), creating good skin weights is essential. For an in-depth guide to painting creature weights, I will refer you to Appendix B in The Art of Rigging Vol II. To help with the Minx character's weights, I utilized a common technique for distributing weights. I started by flooding the root joint with a value of 1.0; adding all of the weighting to a single joint. From there, I worked outwards with the add brush FIGURE 4.29. By working up the spine and out to the extremities, I was able to avoid the most common pitfall with painting weights, working in circles. I took several passes over the entire body, always working on the left side and mirroring (Skin > Edit Smooth Skin > Mirror Skin Weights) as I went. In the final pass, you may wish to make use of the smooth brush to help soften the gradients between joints FIGURE 4.30. That being said, most of the smoothing should be done explicitly with the add brush to avoid pesky and random weight redistribution due to normalization.

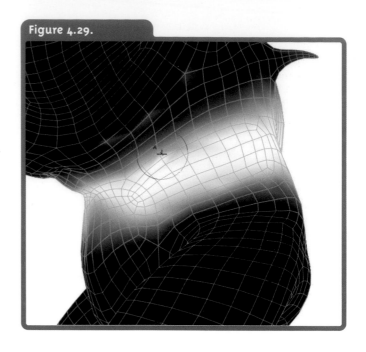

Figure 4.29.

Figure 4.30.

2.Pose-Based Deformations: Only once the smooth binding is complete should you begin creating pose-based deformations, or any other layered deformations for that matter. Pose-based deformations are deformations that are enacted when the character strikes a certain pose. Usually this involves a blendshape that is hooked-up via set driven keys to the rotation of a joint (but they may be driven by anything) FIGURE 4.31. These are covered in great deal in chapter six of The Art of Rigging Vol I. The great thing about pose-based deformations is that they can be added as they are needed, on a shot-by-shot basis. There is no need to create an all encompassing set of corrective blendshapes (which could easily take weeks) unless the character is sure to strike every extreme pose. That being said, there are a few trouble spots that are almost guaranteed to cause problems. The elbows and knees are especially susceptible to a severe loss of volume when undergoing regular posing. You may also wish to preemptively tackle the belly and love handle region to make sure they deform as needed. In the case of the Minx, more attention was paid to the limbs than his core simply because the majority of his body is covered in a robe. Why bother spending hours sculpting corrective shapes that won't even be seen?

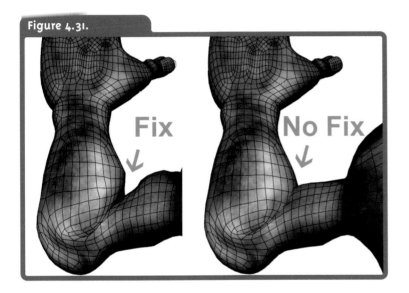

Figure 4.31.

3.Dynamic Floppy Spikes: For seasoned readers of The Art of Rigging series, it should be no surprise that we will be using the dynamic chain script to animate pieces of the Minx (cgTkDynChain.mel). For the uninitiated, the dynamic chain script was introduced in The Art of Rigging Vol I as a means of applying controllable dynamic motion to a chain of joints FIGURE 4.32. Basically, the script applies a spline IK solver to the joint chain. The spline curve controls the orientation of the joints. This curve is made a dynamic hair curve (this requires Maya Unlimited).

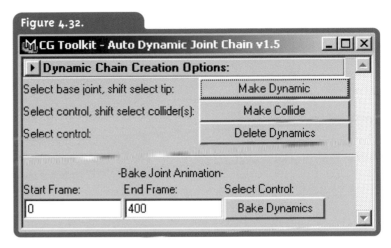

Figure 4.32.

By adjusting the dynamic properties of the hair curve, we can control the way the joint chain flops around and reacts to forces (like gravity or wind). This entire process, once scripted, only takes a few mouse clicks. When the animation is looking good, everything can be baked into keyframes on the joints themselves (a process that is also facilitated by the script) FIGURE 4.33. With the animation baked, the user is free to remove the extra hair nodes and pass-on a clean scene file, ready for rendering (without the need for any further simulation).

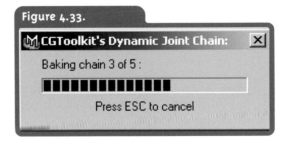

Figure 4.33.

4.Hair-Driven Fur: If you followed through the previous chapters on hair and fur, you should be familiar with the techniques used to create the Minx's furry coat. Basically, the fur is attached to various polygonal 'patches' that are strategically placed across the Minx's body FIGURE 4.34. These patches are then wrap deformed to the skin mesh so that when it deforms, they come along for the ride. To give the fur some dynamic motion, hair curves are attached to the patches and connected to the fur. By carefully hand-placing hair curves across the patches, we can add dynamic motion wherever it is required FIGURE 4.35. The fur itself can significantly slow-down the scene, so it is placed in a separate layer that can be accessed when needed or simply turned on before being rendered.

Figure 4.34.

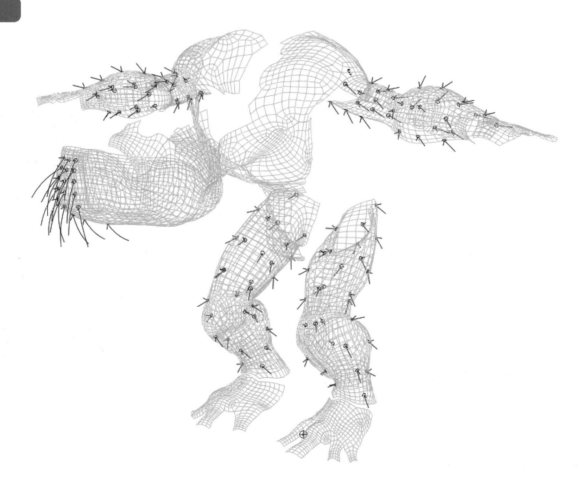

Figure 4.35.

5.Cloth Simulation: The technique used to animate the Minx's robe is the same as that taught in chapter one. The Minx's garment was built using Maya Cloth's panels and stitching paradigm. The robe is a single polygon mesh constructed from eleven panels with seventeen separate seams FIGURE 4.36. The final robe has about 3k vertices. Using the techniques borrowed from chapter one, a render garment was constructed by quadrangulating and extruding the garment. This thicker garment has it's UVs carefully arranged to allow for texturing FIGURE 4.37. A wrap deformer is used so that the thick garment deforms along with the simulation garment. The wrap and simulation garments are kept in separate layers. Once the simulation is done, the TD can bake the cloth animation using a technique covered in the last chapter.

Figure 4.36.

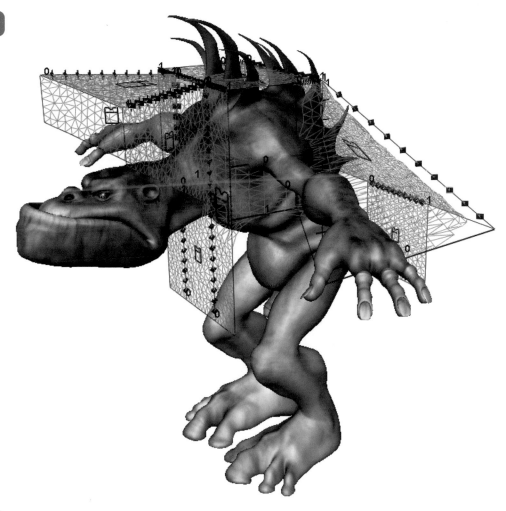

Figure 4.37.

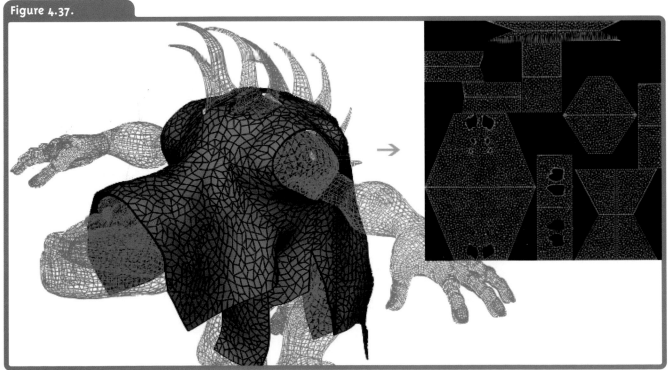

The Minx's Fur:

The task of applying fur to a polygonal creature was tackled in chapter three when we discussed the fundamentals of Maya Fur. In that chapter, we also discovered how to add dynamic motion to the fur using Maya Hair curves. Because we are using both modules, I recommend reading through chapters two and three before you continue with this section. This section will dive into the issues that arise from adding fur to a production-level character. We will *not* be reiterating the fundamentals.

Preparing the Patches:

Recall that fur is very dependent on the direction of the UVs on the surface it is attached to. The UV direction determines how the fur will tilt across the surface. The Minx's UVs were not arranged with this in mind. They were prepared so that they could be painted on in Photoshop and Zbrush. The UVs were laid out with no regard for what direction they were pointing in FIGURE 4.38. This is how all 3d models are usually unwrapped. Why would a texture artist care what direction his UVs are pointing in, except perhaps to make them easier to paint-on in a 2d program?

Figure 4.38.

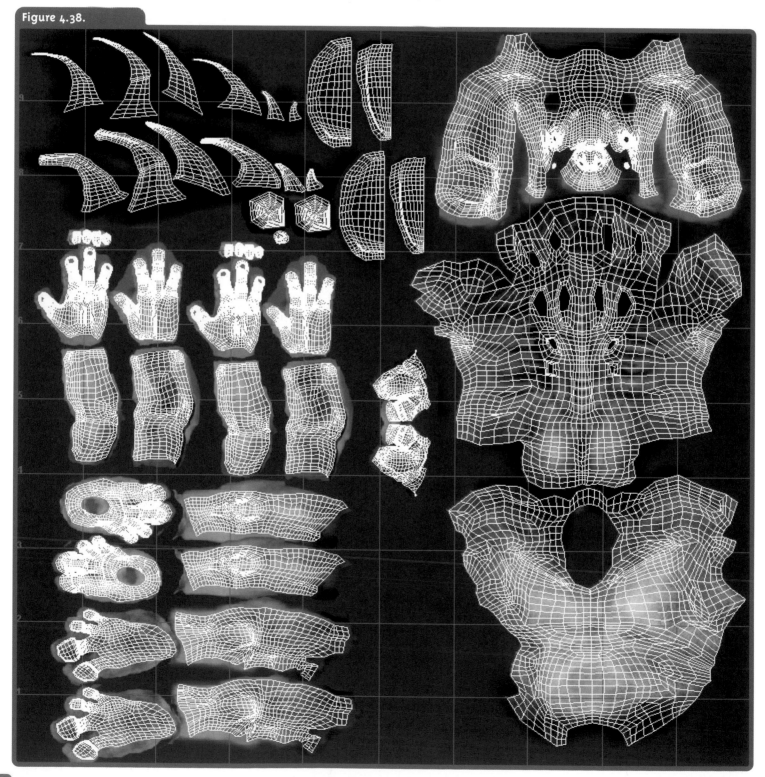

So, does this mean we have to start unwrapping models such that the UVs are distortion free, efficiently laid-out and pointing in the correct direction? The short answer is, no. In fact, doing so would be extremely prohibitive because efficient, distortion-free UVs will, by nature, point in odd directions. In other words, the direction of the UVs is not something that texture artists should be worried about. As anyone who as ever unwrapped a character can attest, there are enough difficulties in the process already. Worrying about direction would only exacerbate the already difficult task of creating nice UV layouts.

But wouldn't it be nice to simply apply a single fur description to an entire body and be done with it? Why would you split it up into patches? Can't you create a separate UV set purely for the purposes of adding fur? This is the obvious solution, and, in some cases, probably the best. The reason we chose to split the Minx into small patches was two fold:

1. We only want fur in specific areas. By creating patches, we are also defining areas of baldness. The same could be done with a large baldness map, but it is easier to simply pick the faces you want to grow fur from and create a patch.

2. The fur on his toes must be different than the fur on his chin. By using patches, we are able to apply different (but similar) fur descriptions to the different parts of his body. Again, the same thing could be done by painting custom attribute maps for all of the various attributes (length, scraggle, color etc...) but it is much easier to simple apply a different description and tweak the parameters as needed for any particular part of the body.

When you strip it all down, one could make the argument that the patch method involves more work than is necessary. This is true *only* if the character is relatively simple and uniform in their fur coverage (ie. the fur does not change much across the surface, like a rabbit). In these cases, it may be better to create a separate set of UVs specifically arranged for the fur. Remember that fur descriptions may be linked to any UV set you wish. In the end, you will have to decide what technique is going to work best for your particular case. In the case of the Minx, patches were the clear winner.

Actually creating the patches is a fairly straightforward process, but I do have some workflow tips that will help you alleviate the guesswork. Firstly, make sure that you start-off with a good understanding of how the fur should be distributed across the surface. The Minx's body hair is loosely based on that of a human. Do a Google image search for fur reference. You might be surprised to see how the direction of fur changes across the body of an animal.

The Minx's fur is spread across his entire body. It is not as uniform as the coat of a sheep, but more sporadic and patchy, like a human. I started by importing the Minx mesh into a new scene file and preparing a new shelf with buttons for the paint selection tool, extracting polygons and deleting history FIGURE 4.39.

The process of creating a patch involves first determining what faces should be included. When doing this, always make the patch larger than the area you want to apply fur to. You can create much more natural-looking hairlines using a baldness map, rather than relying on the square edges of a polygon face. For example, the knee cap does not have any fur on it (hairy knees are rare because the skin is tough and loose hairs rub-off easily). Rather than leave the knee out of the thigh patch, I included it so that a baldness map could be used to gradually thin the hair into that region FIGURE 4.40. Remember that areas where the fur thins-out should be simulated with a baldness map, not by excluding the region completely. We will revisit this concept when we talk more about baldness maps.

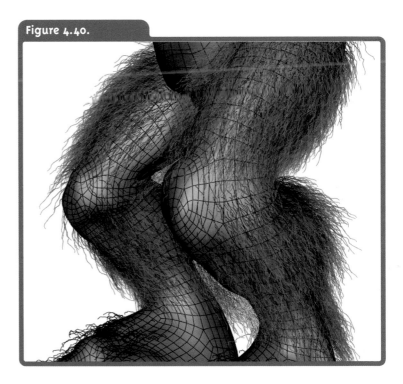

Figure 4.40.

Also remember that these patches must be split-up wherever the fur should be pointing in a different direction. For example, the Minx's side burns are separate patches from his chin because I wanted the fur in their respective areas to run in different directions FIGURE 4.41. Even though these regions border each other, they were created as separate patches. Real world reference will help you determine where fur changes direction across a body.

Figure 4.39.

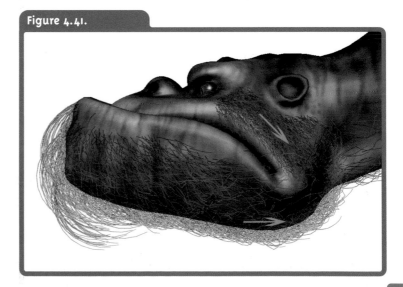

Figure 4.41.

With the polygon faces for the patch selected, execute the `Edit Polygons > Extract` command. This will create a new polygon object. With the patch created, you need to layout the UVs so that they point in the desired direction before attaching the fur and wrap deforming the patch to the creature's skin. This process is covered in detail in exercise 4.1.

You will want to prevent the patches themselves from rendering. Oddly enough, they must *not* have their visibility turned off, or else the attached fur will not render. To get around this, turn off all of the options in the render stats of the shape node FIGURE 4.42. This will prevent the patch from rendering, while still allowing the attached fur to render.

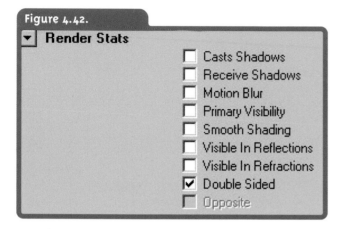

Figure 4.42.

It can definitely take some practice to become proficient with the patch technique. The following exercise demonstrates the creation of the Minx's chin patch from start to finish. As is the case with almost any artistic technique, it can really help to watch somebody do this to help solidify the concepts in your own mind. Be sure to check out the included video lecture on the DVD to watch the author complete the same exercise.

| Exercise 4.1 | Creating the Minx's Fur Patches |

Many novice animators have a tendency to want to do everything in a single scene file. When doing modeling work of any kind, it is always a good idea to work in a completely separate scene from the animation file. This may be common sense to experienced artists, but I still see people who's work suffers from a lack of simple organization.

Regardless, the task of creating fur patches should be done in a completely new scene file. To that end, we will start this exercise from scratch. The Minx's mesh will be imported into a fresh scene file before we get to work slicing it up.

1. Open a new scene file in Maya and save it as exercise4.1_Start.mb. The only thing we need to start creating fur patches is the Minx's mesh itself. Choose `File > Import` and browse to the exercise 4.1 folder on the DVD. Find MinxSkin.obj and import this file. This is the Minx's skin geometry FIGURE 4.43.

2. Open exercise4.1_A.mb to see the imported skin mesh. With our scene prepared, let's get started. For this exercise, we will be concentrating on the chin region. This is a potentially tricky area but, as you will soon see, it won't present any difficulties when tackled in the proper manner. We want to give the Minx a thick beard that wraps across his large chin and down under his neck. The fur must change direction in this single patch. Around his lips, it must be pointed downwards, while under his neck, the fur will point towards his back FIGURE 4.44.

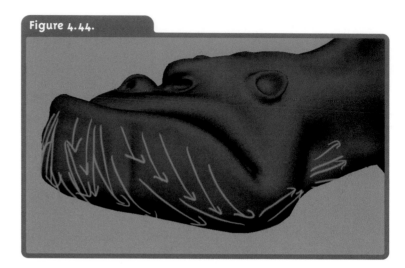

Figure 4.44.

3. Before we worry anymore about the direction of the fur, let's first create the patch. Select the mesh and activate the Paint Selection Tool (`Edit > Paint Selection Tool`). Now go into face mode and paint across the chin area to select all of the faces like in FIGURE 4.45. To ensure consistency, you may use the exact selection set from this exercise by choosing `Edit > Quick Select Sets > ChinFaces`. This will automatically select all of the faces in the chin region for you.

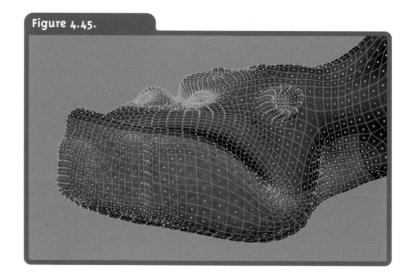

Figure 4.45.

4. Notice that the selection covers his entire chin and spreads into his neck. We will taper the fur in this direction and do not want to add more fur further up his neck. The reason being that when his robe is added, it will cover this area completely FIGURE 4.46. Not only would it be a waste of time to

add fur to this region, but then we would have to worry about the cloth mesh penetrating the fur as well. Be mindful of where you place the fur!

Figure 4.46.

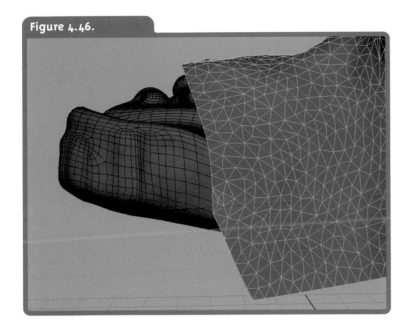

5. With the proper area around the chin selected, choose `Edit Polygons > Extract` (with default settings). This will create a separate polygon object by slicing it off of the main mesh FIGURE 4.47. Rename the mesh 'chinPatch' and delete the history on it.

Figure 4.48.

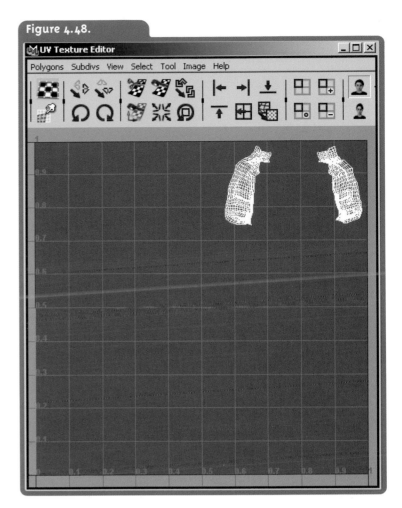

Figure 4.47.

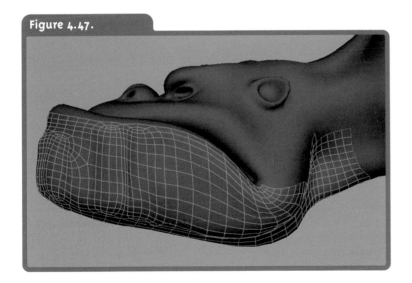

6. Open exercise4.1_B.mb to see the sliced chin patch. Now open the UV texture editor and take a look at its UV arrangement FIGURE 4.48. These are the UVs left over from when it was attached to the rest of the mesh. If you apply fur to the patch at this point, you will notice it pointing in odd directions, especially along the bottom of the chin where there is a seam FIGURE 4.49. Let's fix this by completely unwrapping the chin and rearranging the UVs.

Figure 4.49.

7. Select the chinPatch object and drop into a perspective viewport. We are going to project the UVs with a camera. To do this, position the perspective camera under the chin, looking up at it FIGURE 4.50. The position of the camera will be used to determine the plane that the UVs will be projected in.

Figure 4.50.

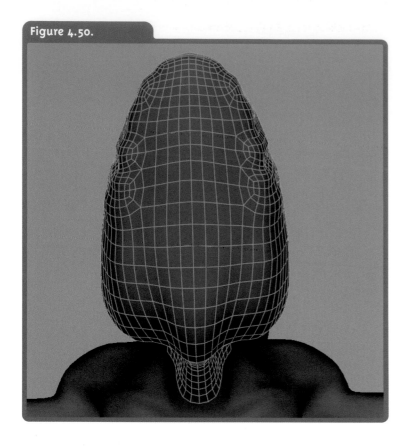

8. With the camera placed, choose `Polygon UVs > Planar Mapping` and open the options box. In the options box, select 'Camera' as the mapping direction and hit Apply. This will create the following UV arrangement, FIGURE 4.51.

Figure 4.51.

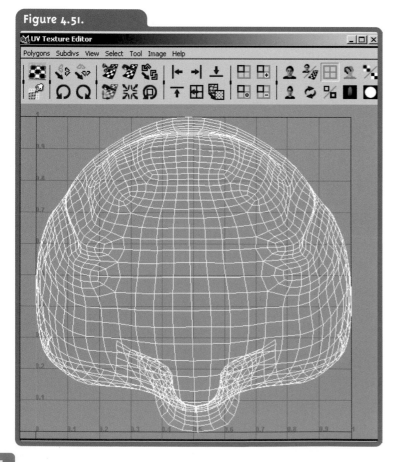

9. Open exercise4.1_C.mb to see the initial UV layout. As you can tell, this layout is not exactly perfect. There are overlapping pieces pointing in odd directions that would cause real problems with fur. It is clear that we need to fix this.

10. To unwrap the UVs and arrange them a little better, let's use a new feature in Maya 7.0, Unfold UVs. This feature uses a complex algorithm to unfold a UV arrangement and reduce distortion. It is extremely useful for both texturing and fur UVs. Select the chinPatch mesh and choose `Polygon UVs > Unfold UVs`. Open the options box and set the Solver Weighting to a value of about 0.5. Hitting Apply will bring-up a progress indicator in the help line. After a few moments, the solver should finish leaving you with a nice unwrapped chin, FIGURE 4.52.

Figure 4.52.

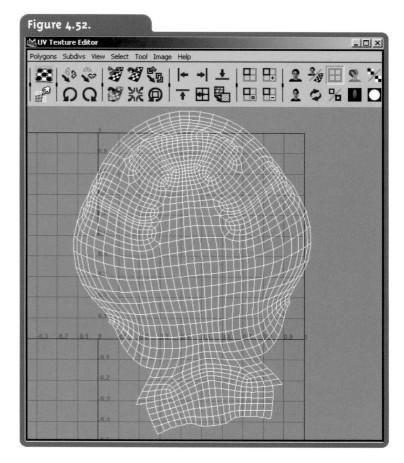

11. Open exercise4.1_D.mb to see the unfolded UV arrangement. At this point, you will have to manually reposition the UV shell to fit inside the unit square. Select the shell in the UV texture editor and use the scale, and translate tools to push it inside the 0-1 UV space FIGURE 4.53.

12. Now we can worry about the direction the UVs are pointing in. Recall that Fur points towards the positive V direction (the top of the unit square). Rotate the UVs so that they point in this direction FIGURE 4.54.

Figure 4.53.

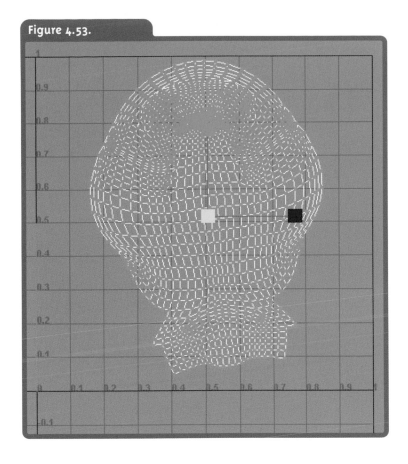

Figure 4.54.

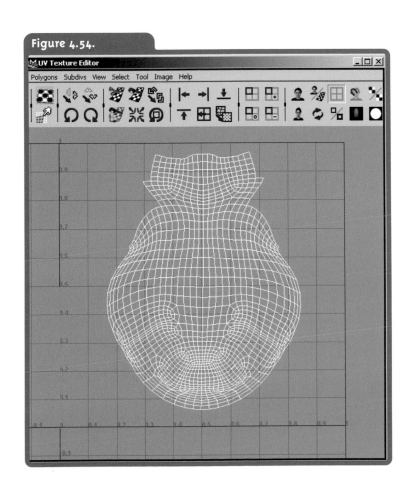

13. Open exercise4.1_E.mb to see the chin with some sample fur on it. By applying the 'mouse' fur preset (the mouse is easiest to see), we can test the UV arrangement to ensure that everything is pointing in the correct direction. To get a better look at the fur direction, be sure to adjust the number of U and V samples on the fur feedback shape node. As you can see, the fur is indeed pointing the right direction FIGURE 4.55.

Figure 4.55.

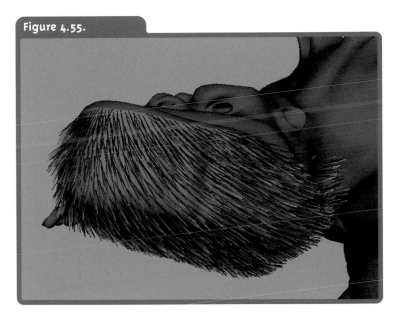

14. That concludes the creation of the Minx's chin fur patch. Now select the patch and export it as an obj file. You can find the finished patch on the DVD, titled MinxChinPatch.obj. As you work on creating fur patches, constantly export them to their own obj files. When you are ready to integrate the fur into the final scene file, you can import these patches without worrying about bringing-in any garbage nodes that may be kicking around from the creation process.

This exercise demonstrated the most difficult patch to create on the Minx (believe it or not). The other areas of the body present no significant challenges. The process is exactly the same, the only thing that changes is the direction the fur must point in.

For the sake of being thorough, the following is a list of patches used in the Minx character:

1. Chin FIGURE 4.56: As discussed in the previous exercise, this patch covers the Minx's beard and into the neck.

2. Top of Neck FIGURE 4.57: There is a patch created for the top of the Minx's neck. This is only used if the robe is flipped back, revealing that area of his body, otherwise, it will remain hidden.

3. Cheeks FIGURE 4.58: Small patches in his cheeks were created for his sideburns.

4. Chest FIGURE 4.59: A patch was created across the from of his chest and down the middle of his stomach area. This allows the placement of chest hair.

Figure 4.56.

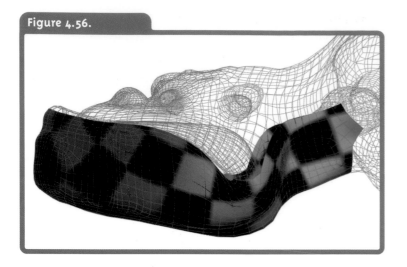

Figure 4.57.

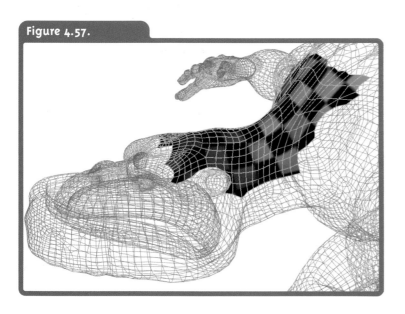

Figure 4.58.

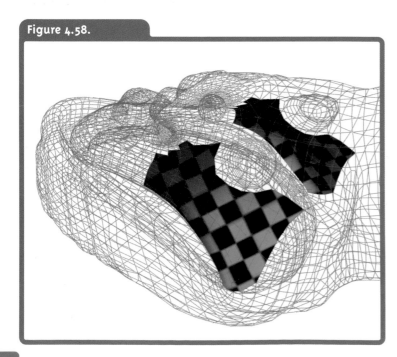

Figure 4.59.

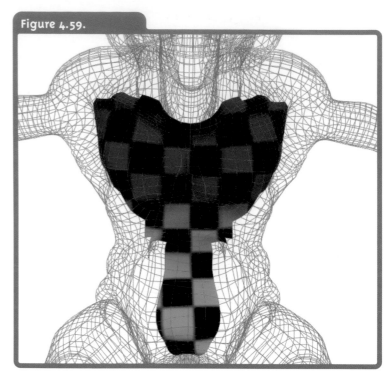

5. Back FIGURE 4.60: A large patch was created across his entire back. Once again, this patch of fur is hidden when the Minx is wearing his robe.

Figure 4.60.

6. Thigh FIGURE 4.61: Covering his entire leg from his hips to his knee, this patch houses the thick fur along the leg.

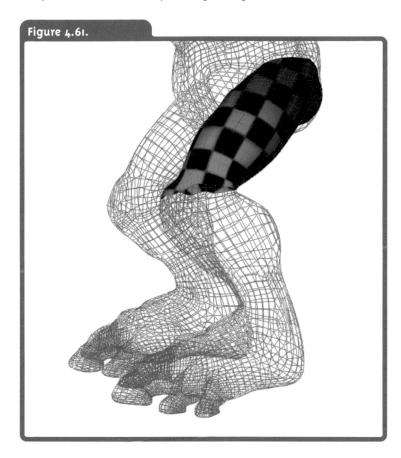

Figure 4.61.

7. Lower Leg FIGURE 4.62: This patch connects with the thigh patch and covers the entire lower leg.

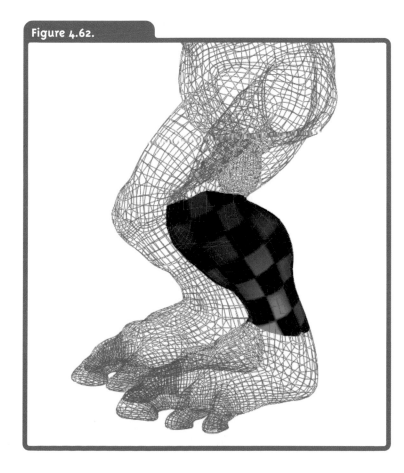

Figure 4.62.

8. Shoulder FIGURE 4.63: This patch hosts some fur that pokes-out from the sleeves of his robe.

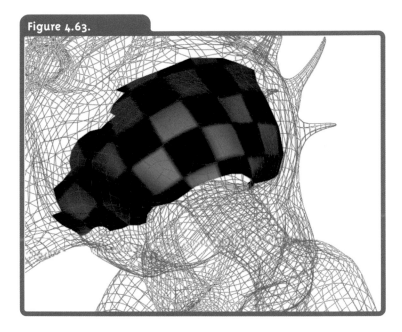

Figure 4.63.

9. Tricep FIGURE 4.64: The tricep patch covers most of the arm from the shoulder joint to the elbow. This allows for furry arms. The bicep, however, is bald. This is a phenomena caused by friction and can be observed on many people in the real world.

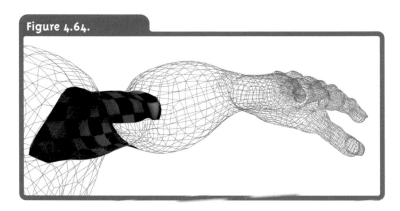

Figure 4.64.

10. Forearm FIGURE 4.65: The top of the forearm is very furry. This patch connects with the tricep patch on the back of the arm.

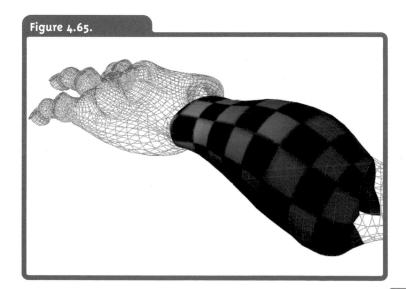

Figure 4.65.

II. Top of Hand FIGURE 4.66: This patch extends across the back of the hand and slightly into the fingers. The palm of the hand, however, is not included in this patch and remains bald.

12. Top of the Foot FIGURE 4.67: This patch extends across the top of the foot and into the toes.

Figure 4.66.

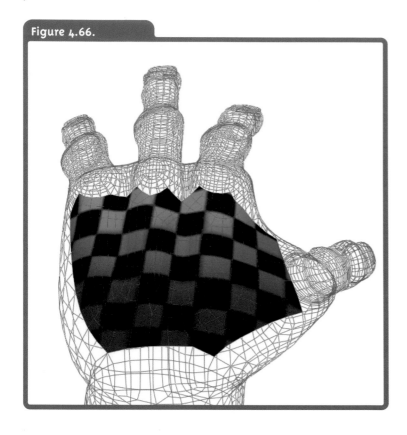

Figure 4.67.

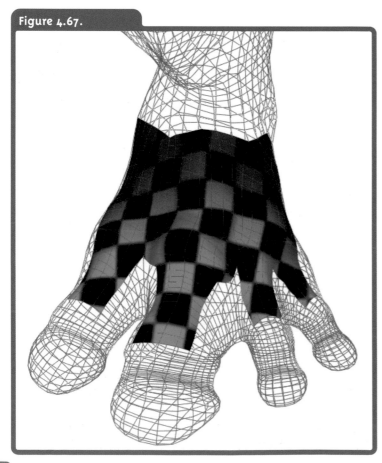

When creating these patches, I used the exact same techniques discussed in this chapter. I can assure you, there are no hidden tricks here. Just a bit of hard work and planning will get the job done. Once the patches are finished, we can move on to adding the fur.

Creating the Fur Descriptions:

Designing the 'look' of the fur is likely to consume 80-90% of the total time spent adding fur to a creature. It involves a lot of trial and error, testing, rendering and re-rendering. Like all worthy artistic tasks, it mustn't be rushed.

To get started, setup the scene with a white background and at least a basic 3-point lighting rig. At this point, we aren't trying to create a mood or an atmosphere, we just want the fur to be clearly visible. Be sure to add some rough shadowing and only do your test render with the final renderer that will be used (discrepancies between rendering software can be quite alarming, especially for fur/hair renderings). For a detailed discussion of fur/hair rendering techniques, please refer to the two previous chapters.

Getting back to the Minx, we started by creating a fur description for his chin. Once we were happy with the general look of this fur, the description node was then copied and applied to other fur patches. To lend a sense of realism, the fur description was adjusted for each part of the body. This way, the fur on the feet may be styled differently than the fur on his face. Variation enhances believability.

Exercise 4.2	Creating the Minx's Fur Description

This exercise begins with a scene file that includes all of the Minx's fur patches, each of which will eventually have it's own fur description. We will guide you through the creation of a single fur description (for the chin area). Subsequent fur descriptions (for the rest of the body) will be derived from this 'master' description. By creating a 'master' fur description (that all other descriptions will be copies of), we are able to maintain a consistency, while avoiding the kind of uniformity that would be glaringly indicative of artificial fur.

Look development can be a time-consuming process; it's full of trial and error. Rather than bore you with a two-hour exercise, we will fast-forward the creation of the fur description and concentrate on what matters.

I. Open **exercise4.2_Start.mb.** This file contains the Minx along with all of his fur patches. These show up with the green and red checkerboard shader FIGURE 4.68. This is done to show the direction each patch points in. When fur is applied to any one of the patches, it will always point towards the green side of the patch. This coloring technique was done by creating a V ramp texture and plugging it into the color attribute of a Lambert shader.

Figure 4.68.

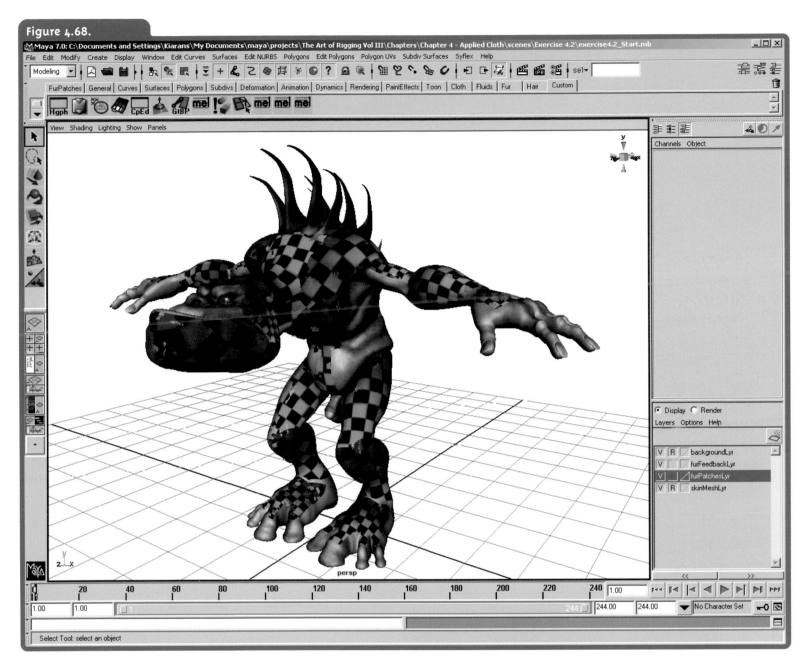

Maya 7.0: C:\Documents and Settings\Kiarans\My Documents\maya\projects\The Art of Rigging Vol III\Chapters\Chapter 4 - Applied Cloth\scenes\Exercise 4.2\exercise4.2_Start.mb

2. Take a look at the layer editor and notice how the scene is neatly organized. The 'backgroundLyr' layer contains a white sphere that encompasses the entire scene FIGURE 4.69. This provides a backdrop for our fur renderings. The default black background hides the profile of the fur.

Figure 4.69.

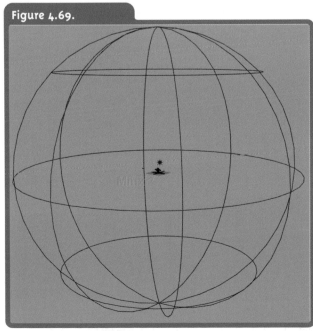

3. Look through the 'renderCam' camera FIGURE 4.70. This camera has been placed to point directly at the Minx's chin. It has had it's transforms locked so that you can't accidentally move it. This ensures that comparative renderings will be from the same perspective. When making minute adjustments to the fur, it can be difficult to ascertain their exact effects without a consistent viewpoint. Locking the camera in place simply helps us create consistent renderings.

Figure 4.70.

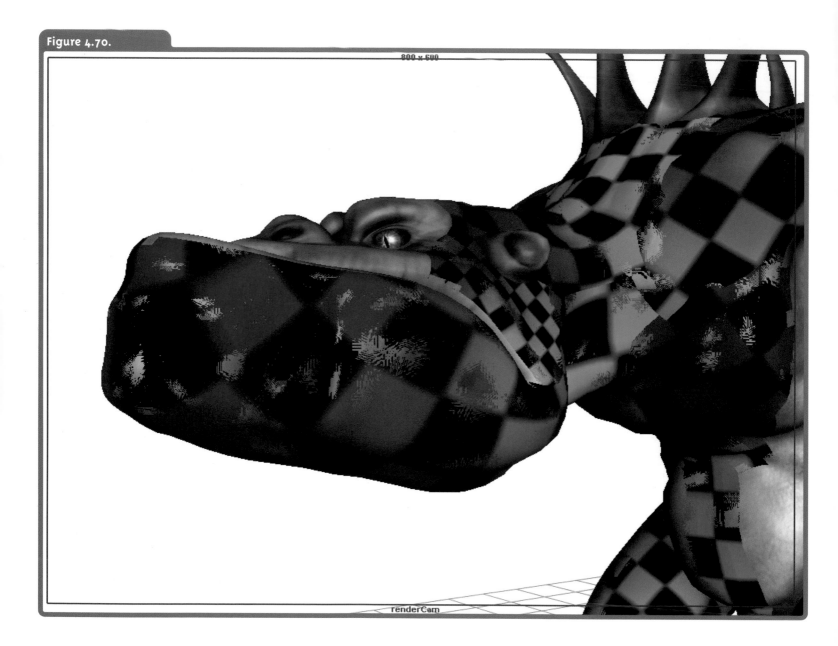

4. While looking through the renderCam, go ahead and hit the render button. After a few seconds, you should get something like FIGURE 4.71. Notice that the fur patches are not showing-up, even though they are visible in the viewport. This is because they have had their render stats adjusted on their respective shape nodes. This is a quirk of the Maya Fur system. The transform node the fur is attached to must be visible in order for the fur to render. Hence, we use the render stats on the shape node to keep the patches themselves from rendering.

Figure 4.71.

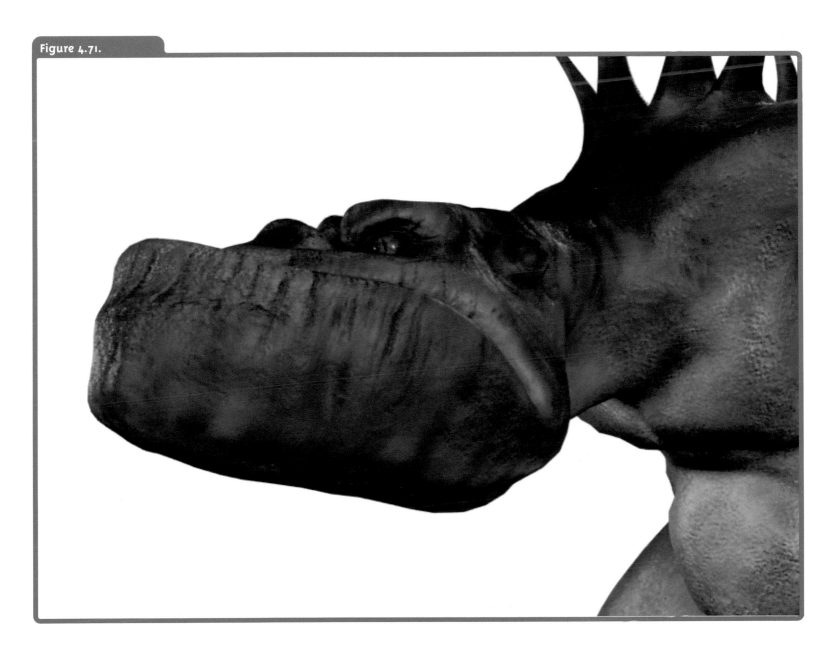

5. In addition to the background, fur patches and render camera, we also prepared a simple lighting rig. There are two spotlights acting as key and fill lights, plus a single point light with a bluish tinge for rim lighting FIGURE 4.72. Nothing fancy, but basic lighting is necessary for creating a fur description.

Figure 4.72.

7. Open **exercise4.2_A.mb** to see the initial fur description applied to the chin. Go ahead and render the scene now. You should see something like FIGURE 4.74. Obviously, this is not the look we are going for! Choose Fur > Edit Fur Description1 > FurDescription1. This will open the attribute editor and load the fur description for us.

6. Without fur ado, let's create some fur! Select the chin patch (called 'chinAndNeck_FurPatch') and choose Fur > Attach Fur Description > New. This will create a new fur description node, attach it to the surface and create a fur feedback node FIGURE 4.73. The feedback node is used to give a visual representation of the fur in the viewport.

Figure 4.73.

8. Let's take care of the obvious problems first. The individual hairs are too long, too wide, too sparse and much too white. Set the length to a value of 0.3, base width to 0.02 and tip width to 0.002. Give the base and tip color attributes a dark and light brown color respectively. Set the Density to 5000. This attribute will be increased later. By keeping the Density low at this point, we can make faster test renderings. After making these adjustments, you should get something like FIGURE 4.75.

9. Still not very convincing, is it? Hang in there please! Notice the hairs are pointing straight out. The Minx's chin looks like a pin cushion. Set the inclination to 0.7 to lay the fur down. Because the UVs of the chin surface were properly arranged ahead of time (see exercise4.1), the fur will 'magically' point in the right direction. This will produce the following render, FIGURE 4.76.

Figure 4.74.

10. Open **exercise4.2_B.mb** to see the progress thus far. The fur is still looking very harsh. More like slivers of metal than soft strands of protein. Part of this is due to the fact that real hair exhibits a translucent quality. Set the base and tip opacity to 0.4 and 0.01 respectively. This produces the following image, FIGURE 4.77.

11. It is starting to look a little bit more like fur now. Before we continue editing the fur description, let's add some shadows to the fur. This will give us much more realistic shading. Grab the spotlight named 'keyLight' and open the attribute editor. Find the Shadow Map settings under the mental ray tab. Check the Shadow Map box and set the resolution to 1024. To soften the shadows, set the Samples to 20 and the Softness to 0.005. This will significantly improve the sense of depth in the fur, FIGURE 4.78.

Figure 4.75.

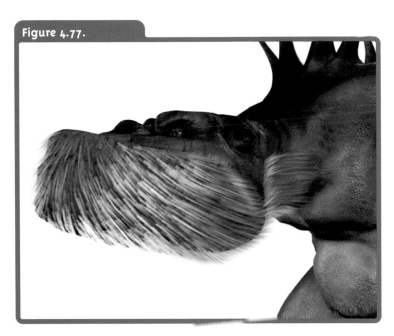

Figure 4.77.

Figure 4.76.

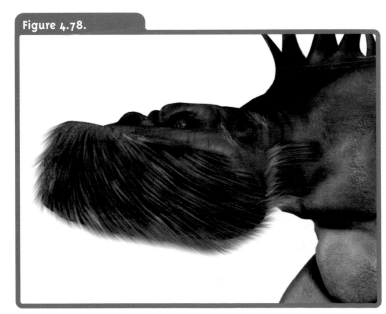

Figure 4.78.

12. Open **exercise4.2_C.mb** to see the progress thus far. Finally, we are starting to get something that resembles fur. In all honesty, we could have gotten to this point much faster by utilizing one of the fur presets. That being said, starting from fresh has the advantage of solidifying the effect of each attribute in your own mind. This takes the guesswork out of future adjustments. Before continuing, reflect on the fact that what you have done up to this point could be accomplished in a split second with a fur preset. If that hasn't made you too angry, then please keep reading.

13. Individual strands are still looking rather straight. Recall that we are creating a beard, and as such, the hair should be much more tangled and chaotic. Set the following: Sraggle/Frequency to 0.4/2.5 and Clumping/Frequency to 0.05/50. This will produce the following image, FIGURE 4.79.

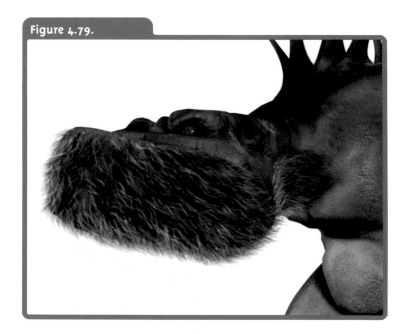

Figure 4.79.

14. Open **exercise4.2_D.mb** to see the progress thus far. The fur is looking much better, but it could still use some tweaking. To get closer to the final look, I took the red out of the base color, increased the length (to counter the loss of length from the scraggle) and curled the base of the fur slightly. This resulted in FIGURE 4.80.

15. Recall that in step 8 we increased the initial density value from 1000 to 5000 (for testing purposes). Before we can call this fur description final, we need to work on the density of the fur. At a density of 5000, the current width of the fur does a good job of creating even coverage across the Minx's face. It's certainly not vital, but real fur does tend to be thinner and denser (a larger number of hairs per surface area, each of which is thinner in circumference). Always consider the distance the fur is going to be viewed from because increasing density increases render time.

16. From a distance, the current density would suffice, but let's kick it up a notch for those close-up shots. Cut the Base Width in half, from 0.02 to 0.01. You should get a render like FIGURE 4.81.

Figure 4.80.

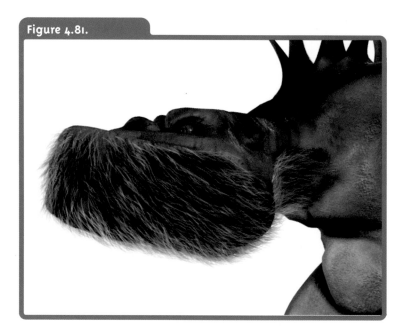

Figure 4.81.

17. Open **exercise4.2_E.mb** to see the fur before we increase the density. Notice that the render from the previous step shows the individual strands looking much more realistic (because they are thinner). This has created bald patches where previously the 'fat' fur was covering everything. Let's remedy this by cranking the density up from 5000 to 10 000. We cut the width in half, so let's double the density to compensate. Makes sense right? This will yield the following image, FIGURE 4.82.

18. Open **exercise4.2_F.mb.** Now we're getting somewhere! The increased density has added a depth and richness to the fur that is pushing it into

the sacred realm of believability. Consequently, it has also pushed the render time from about 30 seconds to over a minute. Not much, but when this is applied over the entire body, the increased density will make a significant difference on render times. Always keep this in mind and adjust the fur descriptions accordingly.

19. Open **exercise4.2_Finished.mb.** Before calling this fur description finished, I opened the details section and went a little wild adding bits of noise to the length, scraggle, inclination and color of the fur. With only a few minutes of adjustment and a couple test renderings I arrived at the following image, FIGURE 4.83.

As you can see, look development is a very artistic process. It's always a good idea to start with the general attributes like length and color, and then layer-in refinements as needed. Like every artistic piece, it is best to keep things general at first to avoid working in circles. More specifically, don't begin by adding noise and scraggle as that will only complicate the entire process. Save the details for last. If you follow these steps, you will find fur development becomes a rather enjoyable exercise.

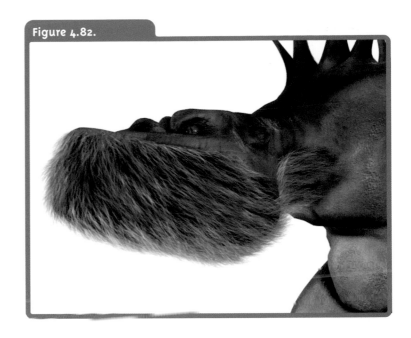

Figure 4.82.

Figure 4.83.

Adding Fur to the Entire Body:

In the previous exercise (4.2), we created a single fur description to be used on the Minx's chin. With the general look created, we can use this 'master' fur description as a template for the rest of his body. You can begin by simply applying the fur description to all of the patches on the body (Fur " Attach Fur Description " FurDescription1).

With all of the fur patches attached to a single fur description, the fur on the feet will look identical to the fur on his forearm. Obviously, there is some variation across the body in the real world. Even though it may look quite good, adjusting the descriptions will break the curse of perfect uniformity and heighten the believability of the entire effect. Do

this by duplicating the original fur description (Fur > Fur Description (more) > Duplicate > NameOfFurDescription) and then re-applying it to specific patches. The duplicate fur description will perfectly mirror the original. To mix things up, adjust the new fur description to suite the particular part of the body it belongs to.

When re-applying a fur description, be sure to first remove the old fur description or else you will have two fur descriptions growing from a single patch. Interestingly, this idea can actually be useful in some instances. For example, you may wish to have one description with large thick, sparse guard hairs, while another description takes care of the soft under hairs (like on a porcupine).

For the Minx character, we ended-up using five different fur descriptions for his entire body. The following table shows the various fur descriptions and how they were used:

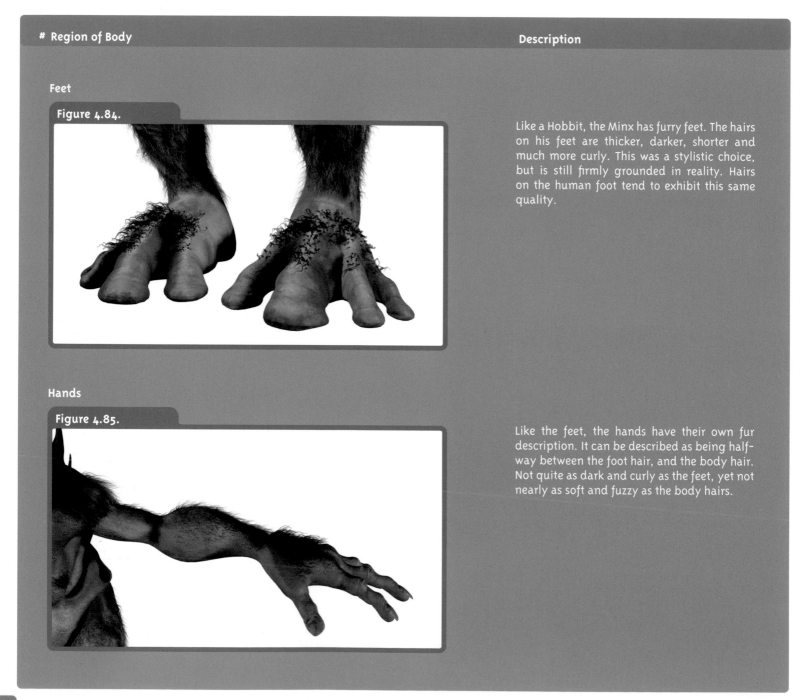

# Region of Body	Description
Feet **Figure 4.84.**	Like a Hobbit, the Minx has furry feet. The hairs on his feet are thicker, darker, shorter and much more curly. This was a stylistic choice, but is still firmly grounded in reality. Hairs on the human foot tend to exhibit this same quality.
Hands **Figure 4.85.**	Like the feet, the hands have their own fur description. It can be described as being half-way between the foot hair, and the body hair. Not quite as dark and curly as the feet, yet not nearly as soft and fuzzy as the body hairs.

Face

Figure 4.86.

After copying the fur description from the face to the surrounding body parts, I created another separate description for the face itself. This description is slightly more curly and thicker, like a beard ought to be. The longer, smoother hairs in his goatee were designed using fur maps (more about his later).

Sideburns

Figure 4.87.

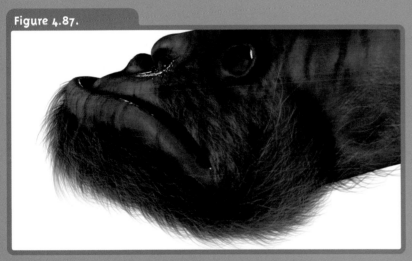

The sideburns fur description was copied from the face fur description. The only real difference here is that the sideburns are shorter and slightly more chaotic than the beard.

Other (ie. everything else)

The 'master' fur description is still used for pretty much everything else. The arms, legs, chest and back all use the same description. This could have been split-up further, but the uniformity amongst the larger areas of his body make the Minx look more like an animal. Balancing uniformity with variation creates a pleasing effect.

Creating Further Variation with Fur Maps:

The fur description node, comprehensive as it is, will never provide all of the necessary control on it's own. The fur description node can describe the general look of the fur across an entire surface, but for more localized control, we must turn to maps.

A fur map, like a bump map, is a greyscale image that may be mapped to almost any attribute on the fur description node FIGURE 4.88. This allows a fur attribute to be defined on a per-pixel basis. For a full discussion of creating and applying fur maps, please see the 'Creating Fur Maps' section of chapter three.

For the Minx character, fur maps were created for each patch. Some patches utilize only baldness maps, while others have baldness, length and even scraggle maps. Basically, you can create as many fur maps as you have time for. Of course, the time involved in creating those maps must be carefully weighed against the benefit of doing so. In the vast majority of cases, attribute maps aren't necessary.

Arguably the most beneficial attribute map (and one that every patch on the Minx uses) is the baldness map. Baldness maps may be used to smooth the transition between furry and non-furry portions of the creature. Nothing looks more artificial than a patch of fur that stops abruptly along the edge of a polygon. To combat this problem on the Minx, a map was hand-painted in Photoshop to gradually blend each fur patch into the surrounding skin. These same textures may be mapped to the length attribute as well.

Figure 4.88.

▼	Details
▶	Base Color
▶	Tip Color
▶	Base Ambient Color
▶	Tip Ambient Color
▶	Specular Color
▶	Specular Sharpness
▶	Length
▶	Baldness
▶	Inclination
▶	Roll
▶	Polar
▶	Base Opacity
▶	Tip Opacity
▶	Base Width
▶	Tip Width
▶	Base Curl
▶	Tip Curl
▶	Scraggle
▶	Scraggle Frequency
▶	Scraggle Correlation
▶	Clumping
▶	Clumping Frequency
▶	Clump Shape
▶	Segments
▶	Attraction
▶	Offset
▶	Custom Equalizer

There are a lot of maps used to fine-tune the Minx's fur. The following table shows a few before/after comparisons. These comparisons demonstrate the successful use of attribute maps in different parts of a humanoid body. After seeing this, the benefit and proper use of fur attribute maps should be plainly obvious:

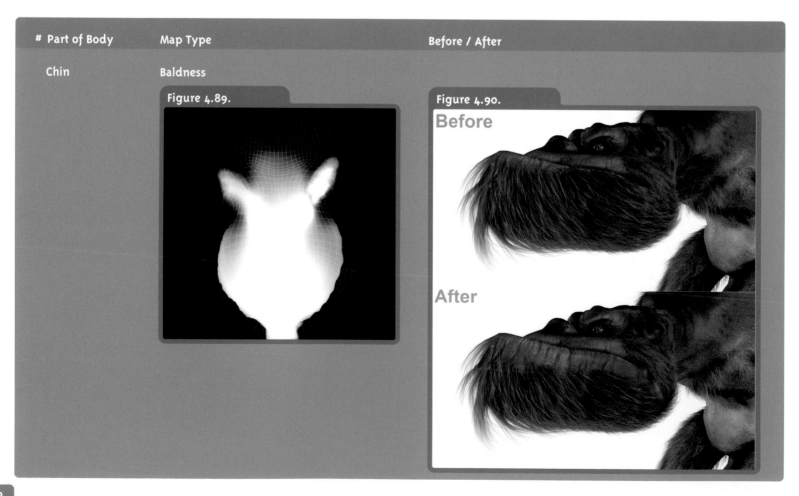

# Part of Body	Map Type	Before / After
Chin	Baldness	

Figure 4.89.

Figure 4.90.

Before

After

149

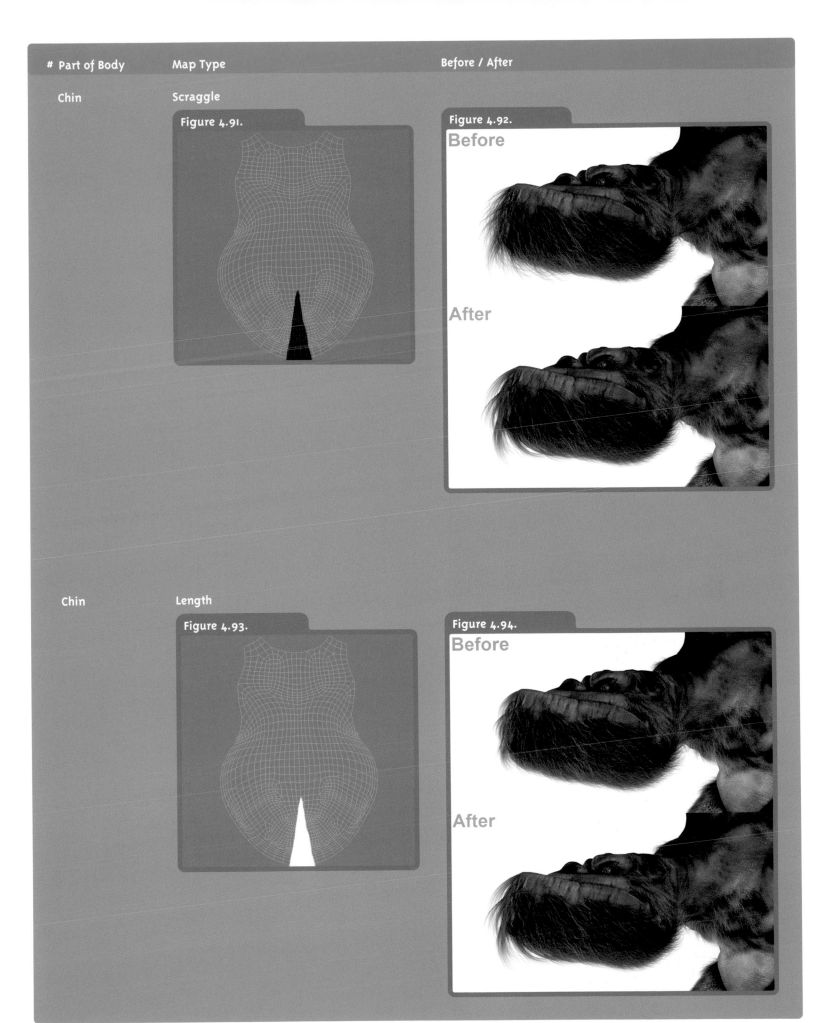

Chin

Scraggle

Figure 4.91.

Figure 4.92.

Before

After

Chin

Length

Figure 4.93.

Figure 4.94.

Before

After

Foot · Baldness

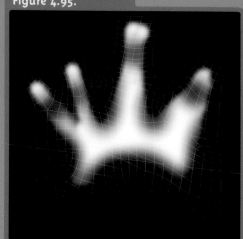

Figure 4.95.

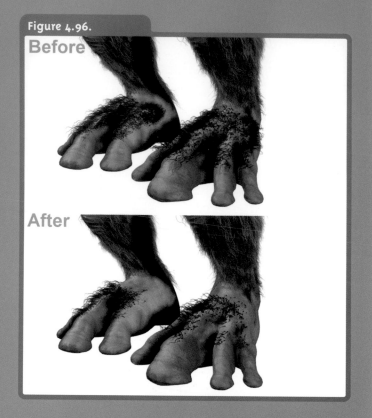

Figure 4.96.
Before
After

Chest · Baldness

Figure 4.97.

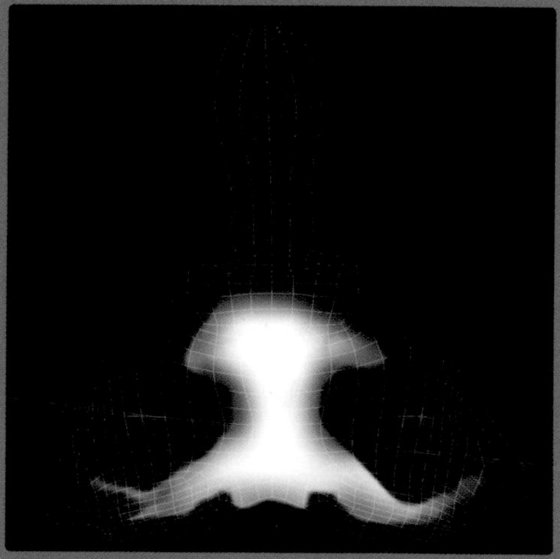

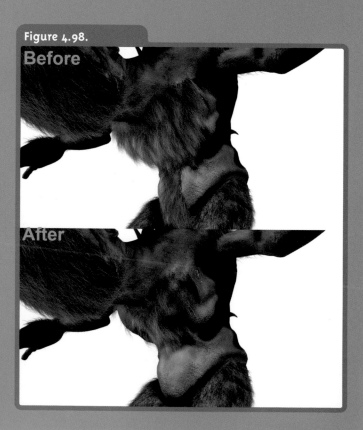

Figure 4.98.
Before
After

You may have noticed that the chin's scraggle map is simply the invert of the length map. By using the same map (but inverted), I created a style where the longer hairs (as defined in the length map) also have less scraggle. This is an effect you can notice in human beards. The longer a beard is allowed to grow, the less tangled and curly it becomes. When styling fur with attribute maps, you will often find that a single map can be used for several different attributes.

If you want to explore the Minx's attribute maps further, please check out the Minx project folder on the DVD where you will find all of the attribute maps, the final scene file and the Photoshop files with UV layouts for reference.

Making the Fur Move:

If you haven't already read the section in chapter three called 'Adding Motion to Fur', please do so before continuing. In that section, we covered the use of hair curves for adding dynamic motion to fur. We will utilize this same technique to get the Minx's coat flopping around.

When adding dynamic attractors to a coat of fur, the character must be assessed to determine what parts require motion and what parts

do not. It is not simply a matter of adding hair curves to the entire body. Indeed, being sloppy at this point will guarantee disaster. When assessing the Minx's face, I determined that I did not want to have the entire beard flop around. Only the longer fur at the tip of his chin needs any dynamic motion.

Looking at the rest of his body, it is clear that the short fur on his hands, feet and chest will not need to move either FIGURE 4.99. The only hairs that are setup to be animated are the arm, leg and chin hairs. It will greatly heighten the sense of realism if the long shaggy hairs covering his appendages displays a subtle overlapping action. Everything else is short enough to remain static without looking artificial. Indeed, adding motion to these shorter hairs could detract from the believability of the scene.

Knowing what parts need attention, it was a simple matter to begin adding dynamic hair curves and attaching them to the appropriate fur descriptions. The following overview demonstrates how this was done:

1. Using the Paint Hair Follicles tool, a dense array of follicles were painted across the middle of the chin, covering the entire goatee FIGURE 4.100. The follicles were created with output curves. These are what will be attached to the fur. To prevent the curves from flailing chaotically during animation, a value of three was used in the Points per Hair attribute FIGURE 4.101. Fewer points result in more predictable behavior and faster computation. Also be sure to set the length of the hair curves

Figure 4.99.

Figure 4.100.

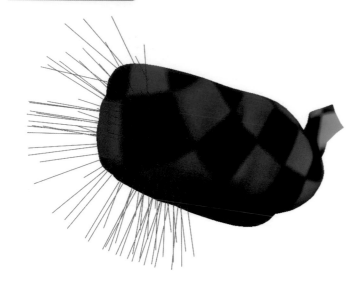

Figure 4.102.

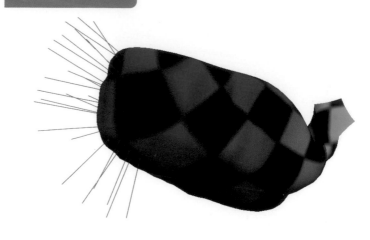

Figure 4.101.

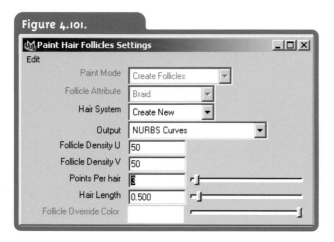

Figure 4.103.

Figure 4.104.

so that they are long enough to affect the full length of the fur (but no longer).

2. With a mass of about thirty follicles covering the chin, I then began reducing the total number of follicles. This may also be done with the Paint Hair Follicles tool (set to Delete Follicles). Removing extra follicles is done to reduce the complexity of the simulation. A hair curve becomes redundant when it is closely surrounded by several other hair curves. Fewer hair curves will result in a more manageable simulation and a better end result FIGURE 4.102.

3. Now that all of the hair curves have been carefully placed, we can attach the hair system to the fur. Select an output curve and choose `Fur > Attach Hair System to Fur > MinxChinFurDescription`. To position the hair curves to follow the direction of the fur, choose `Fur > Set Start Position To > MinxChinFurDescription` FIGURE 4.103.

4. This results in the creation of a FurCurveAttractor node FIGURE 4.104. This node acts as a conduit between the hair output curves and the fur itself. At this point, the behavior of the hair system may be adjusted as needed and the resulting motion will be seen on the fur.
As you can see, the process was extremely simple. Provided you have a

good understanding of the Maya Hair system, attaching output curves to a fur description is dead easy. However, it must be noted that when a hair system is attached to fur, the entire hair system (and all of the follicles in it) will affect the *entire* fur description. This is an important fact to keep in mind.

It's not hard to imagine how this can lead to some obvious problems. How does one prevent hair curves from affecting fur from the same description, but on a different patch? For example, the hair curves placed on the Minx's goatee are intended only for that immediate area. How can we prevent them from affecting the rest of the beard? The answer is found in the FurCurveAttractor node.

Recall that whenever hair curves are connected to a fur description, a FurCurveAttractor node is created. This node contains several attributes, the most important of which is the Radius. The Radius specifies, in world units, the distance a hair curve will look for fur to affect. Knowing this, we can adjust the Radius to a reasonable value to prevent the goatee curves from affecting the rest of the beard.

When using the Radius attribute, the influence appears to gradually decline towards its outer reaches. This creates a smooth falloff and prevents any fake looking 'edges' in the movement of the fur. Additionally, one could utilize the Threshold Length attribute to specify a length of fur that will remain unaffected by the hair curves. Either method will work fine.

The FurCurveAttractor node is the only control provided between an output curve and a fur description. At the top of its attribute editor, there is an Attractor Model drop down menu FIGURE 4.105. This allows the user to choose between the Local and Global attraction methods (default is local). Using Local attraction, the fur will reflect only *changes* from the output curves. In other words, as the output curves bend and sway, the fur will follow along. With global attraction, the fur will actively *pull towards* the nearest hair curve, like a magnet. The Global attraction method is obviously quite different and results in clumps of fur around each hair curve FIGURE 4.106. In the vast majority of cases, local attraction is what you will want.

The following list covers the various attributes used to tweak both local and global attraction:

Curves Per Fur (default 1): This value specifies the number of hair curves that can attract a single fur-hair. At a value of 3, each fur-hair will be attracted to its three closest hair curves.

Global Scale (default 1): This is a multiplier for the radius, power, influence and length parameters.

Radius (default 10): The distance, in world units, that will limit the range of a hair curve's influence.

Start/End Length (default 0/5): These two values specify a range, in world units, to limit the influence of a hair curve along its *length*. At a value of 0 for Start Length, the base of the fur will be fully influenced. Ensure that the End Length attribute is set to a suitable value to ensure that the tips of the fur are fully influenced. Setting this value to be lower than the length of the fur will result in tips that are not affected by the hair curves.

Threshold Length (default 0.33): This value is basically a filter. Any fur-hair with a length shorter than this value will remain completely unaffected by the hair curves. This is a boolean relationship (on or off) and does not allow varying degrees of influence.

Influence (default 1): Controls how much influence the hair curves have over the fur. A value of 0 removes the influence completely, while a value of 1 is standard influence. For really fast motion, this value may be increased, although typically, it should be left alone.

Power (default 1): With global attraction, this value allows you to specify the strength of influence *along the length* of the fur. The name is misleading, Power is used to vary the strength of the influence along the fur-hair. At a value of 0, the entire length of the fur is attracted equally. As the Power value approaches 1.0, the influence is pushed towards the tip, causing the base to lag behind.

It should also be noted that the FurCurveAttractor node provides an interface for hooking-up attribute maps and adding noise to the following parameters: radius, power, influence, start/end length and threshold length FIGURE 4.107. This interface works in exactly the same manner as the fur description node. Attributes may be mapped to file textures to allow local control over each hair follicle. Noise may be added to any of the attributes for an additional sense of variation.

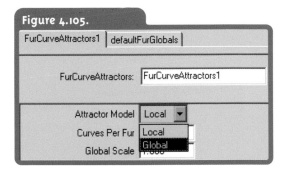

Figure 4.105.

Figure 4.106.

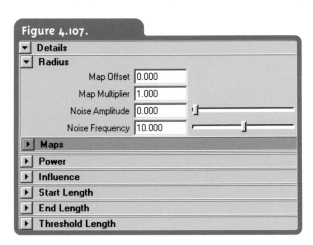

Figure 4.107.

True to Maya's 'open' style, the FurCurveAttractor node provides full access to everything. The majority of these attributes may be left alone for most applications. However, like most things in Maya, having the knowledge of its full capabilities gives you additional tools for solving the various problems that can arise in a production. Personally, I try to learn as much as possible about every node that I encounter in Maya. One never knows when that extra tidbit of trivia may lead you to a long sought after solution (and it often does).

Before we wrap-up our coverage of the Minx's fur, let's take a quick tour of how hair curves were created for the rest of his body (having already discussed his chin):

1. Because we required local precision for the Minx's chin area, recall that we utilized the Paint Hair Follicles tool. This was used to paint follicles where we needed them, and weed out extra follicles where necessary. In the case of the arms and legs, this type of local control was not necessary. Instead, we were able to use the `Hair > Create Hair` method.

2. To give the legs and arms a nice, even distribution of hair curves, the Create Hair U/V Count options were set to a value of 5. The length of the hairs were also reduced, but the number of Points per Hair remains at 3. These settings allowed the creation of a nice distribution of short hair curves across each of the Minx's eight fur patches in the arms and legs FIGURE 4.108. Since these were all created automatically, the entire process took only a few minutes.

3. Recall that the fur on the arms and legs all share a single fur description (MinxFurDescription). So that all of the hair curves could be attached at once, we made sure to create them all into a single hair system (as defined in the Create Hair option box). This results in a total of two hair systems, one for the face, and one for the body.

4. Finally, the hair curves were set to align with the direction of the fur (`Fur > Set Start Position`). With the curves properly aligned, they may be attached to the fur (`Fur > Attach Hair System to Fur`). As a general rule, it is best to adjust the dynamic properties to a reasonable behavior, even if the final behavior will be adjusted on a shot-by-shot basis. To keep the influence of each hair curve relatively localized, the radius attribute on the FurCurveAttractor node was set to a value of 0.5. The Start Curve Attract on the hair system node was set to 0.5 to give the fur some firmness.

That concludes our coverage of the Minx's fur. By applying the principles discussed in chapter three, our goal was to take all of the guesswork out of fur creation. I know that, personally, a large part of the difficulty in getting started with a new tool involves actually knowing where to start.

Knowing how to effectively use a particular technique in the context of a production can present a serious challenge, even if that particular technique is relatively simple on its own. Having successfully used one of Maya's features (like fur) in a simple test, one often forgets that taking those ideas into a production means that additional techniques and solutions must be devised to facilitate a seamless integration. Having finished our discussion of the Minx's fur, let's now turn our attention over to the creation of his robe, and using Maya Cloth.

Figure 4.108.

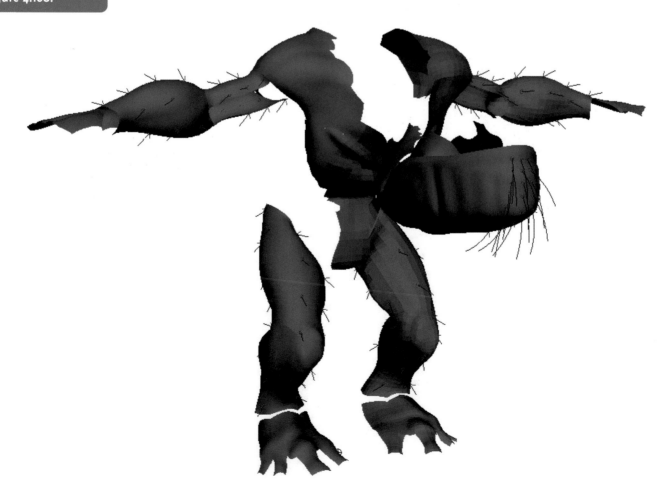

The Minx's Cloth:

In this section, we will guide you through the techniques used to model and animate the Minx's robe garment. If you haven't already read chapter one, please do so before continuing with this section. Many of the techniques discussed here are based on those from the cloth chapter. We will not be revisiting basic cloth topics during this case study.

As we discussed in the cloth chapter, the first step in creating a garment for any digital character is establishing the design of the garment. Just as a real-world fashion designer works from a pattern, so too must we create the design of the garment before opening Maya. For this step, I simply created some quick sketches in Photoshop to establish the basic layout of the panels, how it will look after draping and how it should fit the character.

My first sketch came out looking quite different from the original concept art. The Minx's garment was split into two pieces, a loincloth and a vest FIGURE 4.109. The vest featured two long panels running down the front of the body, reminiscent of a priest's Stole (the long thin pieces of cloth commonly seen draped over a priest's shoulders).

This design was turned into a set of panels that were then sewn together with Maya Cloth and prepared for animation FIGURE 4.110. After all this experimentation, it was decided that the garment was too far from the original concept and needed some readjustments. By taking another glance at the concept art, it is clear that the monk's robe-type garment suites this character better. With that in mind, it was back to the drawing board…

My second sketch tried to capture the look of the original concept, while serving to flesh out the individual panels that would make it happen. In this concept, the vest and loincloth were replaced with a single robe that covers most of his body FIGURE 4.111. The robe has holes cut into it for the spikes to fit through. The garment also includes a hood that extends from the body to cover the majority of the Minx's head. This sketch is much closer to the original concept and suites the character better than the vest/loincloth combination.

Figure 4.109.

Figure 4.110.

Figure 4.111.

The Art of Rigging III
Minx Garment Design

With this concept in mind, a cage of eleven separate panels were constructed around the Minx FIGURE 4.112. Starting at the top of his back, I placed a large square panel to cover his shoulders and first row of spikes. From this rectangular panel, I used the curve-snap tool to draw edges for the other surrounding panels. In order to keep the panels planar (something that is necessary for the curves to be turned into panels), all of the curves were drawn first in orthographic viewports, then grouped before being moved into place. It definitely takes some practice to create sets of planar curves for cloth panels, but with time it becomes second nature.

The process of creating panels, stitching them together, draping, adjusting and re-draping can take a long time. To help reduce the amount of back/forth button clicking during this phase (creating panels, testing, editing curves, re-making panels...) you can use a technique I call *instanced panels*. Basically, when you are fairly certain that the general shape and placement of the panels is finalized, create duplicate instances (check 'Instance' in the duplicate options box) of

Figure 4.112.

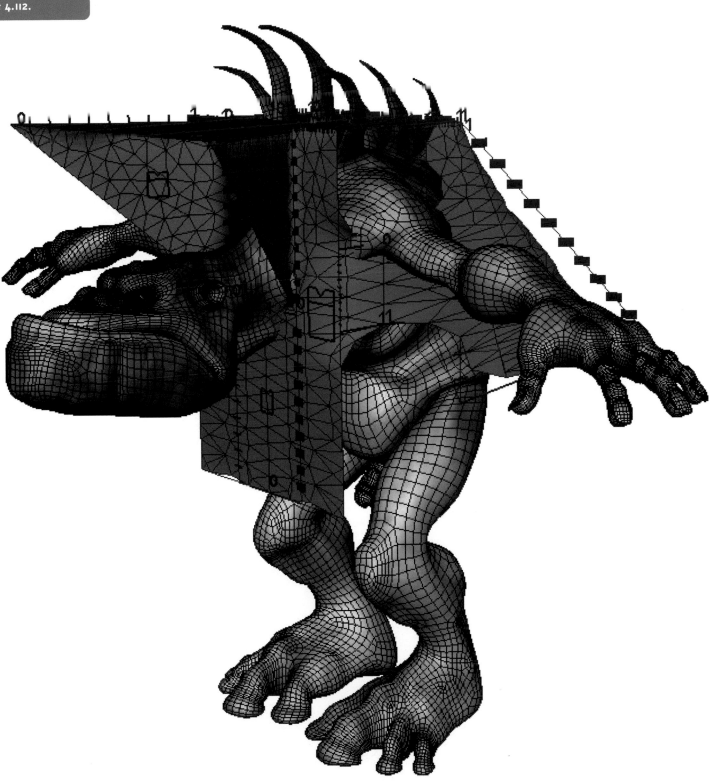

the curves FIGURE 4.113. Move the original curves to the side and create a garment from the instances. Now you can make slight adjustments to the original curves and the changes will propagate through the garment FIGURE 4.114. In fact, the garment mesh will recreate itself in real time as you pull on the CVs! If any of the panels need more or less fabric in order to drape properly, small changes may be made directly to the curves without the need to reconstruct the garment.

In the case of the Minx, we also needed to create small openings for the spikes on his back. There were basically two options here:

A. Model the holes by adjusting the panels appropriately.

B. Ignore the spikes and simply cut the holes directly into the finished garment mesh.

Due to the extremely convoluted panel work that would be necessary to slice twelve holes into the garment, we chose option B. But this presents its own problem. How are we supposed to drape the garment properly if it gets hung-up on the spikes? We needed a method of draping the garment onto the Minx while ignoring the spikes. The simplest method was to simply select all of the faces on the spikes and delete them FIGURE 4.115. This modified collision mesh could be used for the draping phase and then simply discarded. Alternatively, a collision set could be created to tell the solver to ignore the set of faces that comprise the spikes. This is the technique we ended up using. Creating a collision set is simple. Select the faces (in this case, all of the spikes) and choose `Cloth > Collision Cloth Sets > Create`. This will create a cpClothSet node with a single checkbox for enable/disabling the collisions on the specified faces FIGURE 4.116.

Figure 4.113.

Figure 4.114.

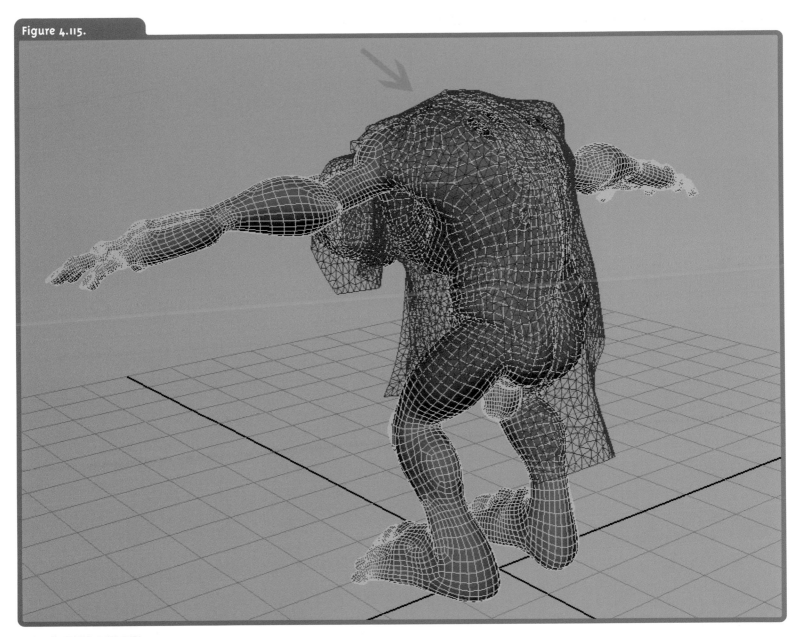

Figure 4.115.

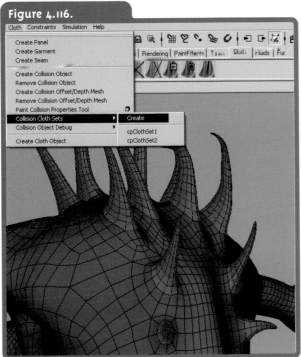

Figure 4.116.

Recall from chapter two that the technique we are using in this book involves the creation of two garments, a simulation garment and a render garment. With the Minx's robe draped and fitted, we duplicated the cloth garment to begin constructing our 'sim' and 'render' garments. The simulation garment has holes sliced into it to allow the spikes to pass through. These were created by drawing the hole with the split polygon tool and then deleting the interior faces FIGURE 4.117.

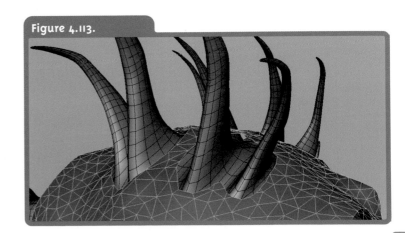

Figure 4.113.

With the simulation garment finished, another duplicate is made from which the render garment was constructed. The render garment is thickened (with an extrusion) and quadrangulated FIGURE 4.118. It is deformed along with the simulation garment via a wrap deformer. While the render garment will definitely look better *after* smoothing, this is only done after the wrap deformer to ensure that the wrap deformer is not forced to calculate the thousands of extra vertices created by the smoothing. The UVs of the render garment are also carefully arranged to allow texturing FIGURE 4.119.

That concludes the creation of the Minx's robe. Along with the robe itself, a MEL script was developed at this stage to help streamline the simulation workflow. The constant switching between nodes can become a major bottleneck during simulation (having to adjust parameters on the solver, collision objects, cloth properties etc…). The following case study shows a typical solution to such a problem.

Figure 4.118.

Figure 4.119.

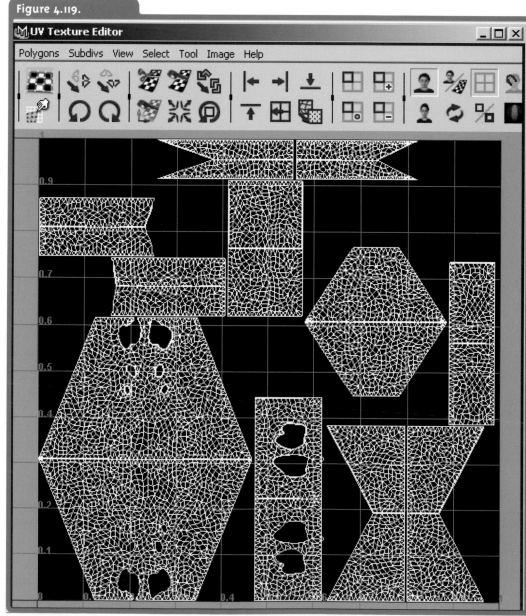

A Case Study in MEL Interface Design:

This chapter is going to swing into a different direction for a moment to concentrate on something novice MEL programmers always complain about: MEL GUIs. The Art of Rigging series has covered many examples (throughout Volumes I and II) of fully functional MEL scripts, but we have always glossed over the interface code to concentrate on the guts of the program.

For a novice, it is no surprise that MEL interfaces are frightening. They use cryptic commands and generally behave in strange ways. In other words, they aren't entirely straightforward. It may surprise you to know that the process of creating a GUI can be just as strange, even for an experienced user.

The thing with GUI's is that you often don't know exactly what is going to work until you try it. This means lots of trial and error type work. If even experienced users are forced to adopt a rather non-linear workflow for creating GUIs, it is no wonder why novices become instantly frustrated with them. The point I'm trying to make is this: There is no 'easy' way to make a nice GUI, it *requires* experimentation. Hence, the reason why there is so much frustration and why we are giving it more attention in this section.

Before we dive into the interface, let's discuss the script itself. Because the reasoning behind the layout in a MEL GUI is so dependent on the features it must facilitate, we will explore what the script is all about before we begin work on its UI.

The Creation of cgTkClothTools. mel:

This section is going to cover the creation of a MEL-based workflow tool. The sole purpose of this tool is to increase the productivity of a TD who is setting-up cloth simulations on a shot-by-shot basis. This task can quickly become a bottleneck due to the large number of nodes that must be worked with (solvers, collision objects, cloth properties, caches etc...).

To help us, we are going to create an interface that stores lists of all the relevant nodes so that they may be quickly selected and modified. In addition, we will add a solver scale calculator to automatically measure a cloth mesh and calculate the appropriate scale (based on a real-world size specified by the user).

Additionally, the script will also incorporate a method of caching simulations. It does this by automatically creating the command string to cache the simulation (for the current scene file and over a specified frame range). It then opens the Windows shell so you can paste the command and immediately start the simulation.

This is not a difficult feature to implement, but it can save a significant amount of time by freeing the finishing TD from the hassle of typing long, error-prone commands. The command to cache a simulation requires typing the precise system path to the scene file; something that can get extremely tedious after the twentieth time. A typical command string could look like this:

```
Code
mayabatch.exe -batch -file "C:/Documents and Settings/User/My Documents/
maya/projects/NameOfProject/scenes/MinxRunCycle.mb" -command "cpRunBatch
1 250"
```

Additionally, the script acts as a launching pad for another script called cgTkShotSculpt.mel. If you are not familiar with shot sculpting, just hang in there, we will cover it in the last chapter. Basically, shot sculpting is the final step in cloth simulation where the finishing TD may work-out any kinks in the mesh. It may also be used for tweaking character deformations. The specifics of this script are covered in the next chapter.

The Overview:

This script is organized into five procedures. The interface procedure contains all of the code to create the UI elements FIGURE 4.120. It also contains buttons that directly call the other four procedures to perform various tasks. To seasoned readers of The Art of Rigging series, this format should be nothing new.

Figure 4.120.

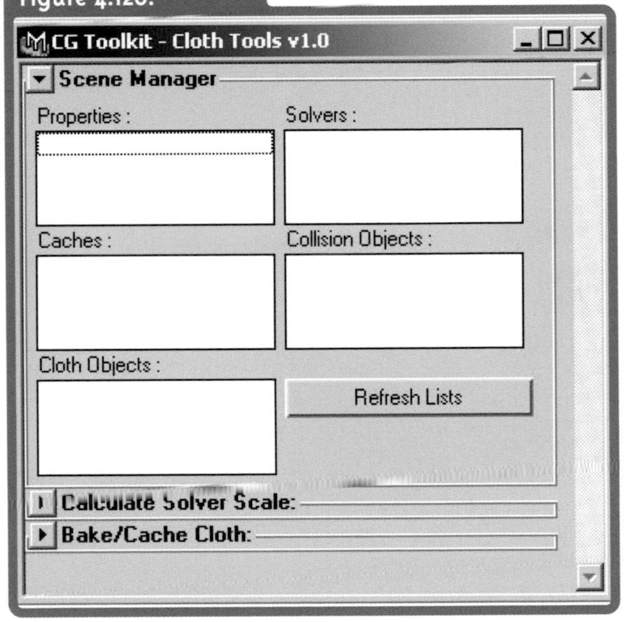

The procedures house the implementations of the various features of the program. They are:

1. **cgTkClothTools:** This is the procedure that is called to start the script; it is the entry point. This is the largest procedure, but it provides no actual functionality. It contains only the MEL commands needed to create the window and all of the interface elements. These elements include the buttons that call the other four procedures to perform various tasks.

2. **cgTkRefreshClothSceneManager:** This procedure searches through the scene to find any cloth objects, solvers, collision objects, caches or cloth properties. It then places any nodes it finds into the scripts interface. This is the only functionality of the 'scene manager' section of the script. It simply collects all of the cloth nodes in the scene and creates links to them so that they may be easily selected and modified.

3. cgTkMeshSize: The 'Load Mesh' button under the 'Calculate Solver Scale' section calls this procedure. It takes the currently selected mesh (it returns a warning if the user did not select a mesh) and calculates its scene size using the object's bounding box. It then places this value in the 'Scene Size' field on the GUI.

4. cgTkCalculateSolverScale: Like cgTkMeshSize, this procedure is called from a button (the 'Calculate' button). It takes the 'Real World Size' and the 'Scene Size' and calculates the appropriate cloth solver scale. It then pastes this into the interface for the user.

5. cgTkGenerateBatchCmd: The last procedure is called from the 'Generate Maya Cloth Batch Command' button. No surprises here, all it does is generate the batch command for the current scene file and frame range and print it out to the script editor. It also opens the command prompt so the user may quickly execute the command to start the simulation.

The actual code for the last four procedures should be largely self explanatory (assuming you have a good understanding of basic MEL scripting techniques). There are no new concepts, and so for this section, we will concentrate only on the interface procedure itself (cgTkClothTools). If you are interested in the implementation of the last four procedures, you will find ample comments in the script file itself (included on the DVD).

Elements of a MEL GUI:

If you have The Art of Rigging Vol I, you may recall that we briefly touched on the the theory behind the MEL interface paradigm, ELF (Extension Layer Framework). ELF commands are an extension of the MEL language. But what does that actually mean? It means that there are fundamentally two different types of commands known to Maya; ELF commands and non-ELF commands.

So what sort of distinction can be made between the two? ELF commands are used only in the creation/query/editing of an interface, while non-elf commands interact with the Maya scene by creating/querying/editing nodes or data. Think of the ELF commands as a subset of the grander collection of regular MEL commands.

Among this subset, we have three main categories of commands. It is extremely important to maintain a distinction between these different ELF commands:

1. Windows: There are several commands that are used specifically for the creation/editing of windows. A window may contain several layouts and controls, but *not* another window. The windows created through MEL are children of the main Maya window (user created windows do not have their own icon in the OS's taskbar).

2. Layouts: There are over ten different layouts available (each with their own command). A layout is used to specify the placement of a control (such as a button, or a slider). Common layouts are used to arrange elements into a column, a grid, or within a scroll bar. Layouts may be nested within each other, but the ultimate parent must always be a window.

3. Controls: Also called UI *elements*, a control can be anything you place into a UI. There are tons of different control types which provide ways to store, display and access information inside a window. Common elements include buttons, sliders, check boxes and radio buttons. All controls must reside within a parent layout for placement inside a window.

As you can see, ELF commands form a hierarchy. At the top of the GUI tree is a single window. The window contains a layout (which may itself contain another layout). But layouts are useless unless they are filled with controls. So the general GUI structure is like this: `window > layout(s) > element(s)`. Elements require layouts, and layouts require a window. With this in mind, let's discuss the specifics of how a GUI hierarchy is created.

Understanding GUI Hierarchies:

Like all MEL commands, it is best if ELF commands are placed inside their own procedure. That way, the GUI may be displayed by simply calling a procedure. In the case of cgTkClothTools.mel, the user calls the script by typing 'cgTkClothTools' into the command line. This is calling a global procedure of the same name. This procedure contains a series of ELF commands that build the GUI, one step at a time. You don't *need* to build a GUI inside a procedure, but it is the easiest way to encapsulate the whole process into a single call.

Assuming you are completely new to MEL GUI creation, you may be wondering how the commands should be used to create an interface. Even seasoned MEL programmers who are new to GUI creation find this process strange (and rightly so). Basically, the order that commands are encountered determines how the GUI is created. There are methods of explicitly defining what elements belong to what layouts (with the -parent flag), but as you will soon see, this is not normally needed.

Getting back to the idea of a GUI being like a hierarchy, this is how a typical GUI might look:

```
Code
Window (Base Level)
        Main Layout (Level 0)
                Sub Layout A (Level 1)
                        Control 1 (Level 2)
                        Control 2 (Level 2)
                        Sub Layout B (Level 2)
                                Control 3 (Level 3)
                                Control 4 (Level 3)
```

Let's dissect this hierarchy. Control 1, 2 and Sub Layout B are direct children of Sub Layout A. Control 3 and 4 are children of Sub Layout B. This should be no surprise, we know that elements of a user interface are arranged into hierarchies according to the *order* in which they are placed in the script.

Each new layout creates a new level in the hierarchy. We have three *layouts* in this example, hence the same number of *levels*. Each new layout places subsequent elements (control or layouts) under itself. So if this is how interfaces are organized, how would you place Sub Layout B under the Main Layout? This is a common problem; you may want to create another layout, not as a child of the previous layout, but rather as a child of the layout two or three levels back. Multiple layouts can exist at the same level.

This is done with the use of the setParent MEL command. The following example shows (in pseudo-code) how setParent would be used to place Sub Layout B, under the Main Layout:

```
Code
Window (Base Level)
        Main Layout (Level 0)
                Sub Layout A (Level 1)
                        Control 1 (Level 2)
                        Control 2 (Level 2)
                setParent..;
                Sub Layout B (Level 1)
                        Control 3 (Level 2)
                        Control 4 (Level 2)
```

Now we have both of the Sub Layout's as children of the Main Layout. Also notice that Control 3 and 4 are now in the same level as 1 and 2 (level 2). This was done with the use of the setParent command in 'upLevel' mode as specified by two periods (..) following the command name. To traverse backwards in the hierarchy by a single level, use 'setParent..'. Hopefully this is starting to make sense. Let's solidify that concept by taking a look at a real example using MEL instead of pseudo code:

```
Code
global proc testWindow()
{
        window -title "Test Window" testWindow; //Base Level
                columnLayout; // Level 0
                        rowColumnLayout -nc 2;          // Level 1
                                button;                // Level 2
                                button;                // Level 2
                                button;                // Level 2
                        setParent..;
                        columnLayout;                  // Level 1
                                button;                // Level 2
                                button;                // Level 2
                showWindow testWindow;
}
```

Firstly, we have declared a new global procedure called testWindow. When called, this procedure will create and then display a window with some buttons. The first columnLayout command creates a layout for the *entire* window. This means that the other two layouts will be arranged one on top of the other (such is the nature of the columnLayout) in the order they are created (which is the order they are encountered in the script file).

The second layout we encounter is a rowColumnLayout. This places children UI elements into a grid of rows and columns. The flag attached to this command (-nc 2) specifies the number of columns in the layout. In this case, we have two columns that will fill-up with elements from left to right. To demonstrate this, we have placed three buttons into the layout. The first two buttons will fill-up the entire first row and the third will start the second row in the leftmost column FIGURE 4.121.

Finally, we encounter the setParent..; command which sets the hierarchy back to Level 1. Now we can create another columnLayout as a child of the first columnLayout (Level 0). The last two buttons are children of this new layout and reside at the second level of the hierarchy. Because

these buttons reside within a columnLayout, they are placed one on top of the other.

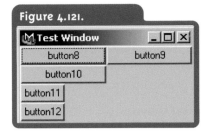

Figure 4.121.

All of the commands up to this point have created the interface in Maya's memory. To actually draw the window on the screen, we use the showWindow command and specify the name of the window (testWindow). When this code is executed, a window will be created in Maya's memory and displayed as soon as the program execution arrives at the last line.

It should be noted that it is poor programming style to omit the tabbing in interface code. Ideally, the programmer should be able to tell where a particular element resides within the hierarchy just by looking at it. Without tabbing, programming interfaces can quickly become a nightmare. Look at how difficult it is to decipher even a simple hierarchy without tabbing:

```
Code
window -title "Test Window" testWindow;
columnLayout;
columnLayout;
button;
columnLayout;
button;
setParent..;
setParent..;
columnLayout;
button;
showWindow testWindow;
```

Now look at the same code after being properly formatted:

```
Code
window -title "Test Window" testWindow;
        columnLayout; //New Level
                columnLayout; //New Level
                        button;
                        columnLayout; //New Level
                                button;
                        setParent..; //Back a Level
                setParent..; //Back a Level
                columnLayout;  //New Level
                        button;
showWindow testWindow;
```

Obviously, formatting makes a huge difference in the clarity of the code. Notice the use of two setParent commands right beside each other. It is not uncommon to use multiple setParent commands to jump back several levels. By aligning the setParent command with the level it belongs to, the intention becomes that much clearer.

Once you understand how UI hierarchies work, it's time to learn how to use them *effectively*. This means building a hierarchy that makes sense in the context of an application. For that, let's return to our case study of the cgTkClothTools.mel script.

The Cloth Tools Interface:

Like the test window we created earlier, the cloth tools script uses a single global procedure to create and display the entire GUI. This procedure is called cgTkClothTools. We are going to build the script one layout at a time and discuss it along the way in the hopes of showing *exactly* how a MEL interface is created. Let's start with the declaration of the procedure:

```
Code
global proc cgTkClothTools ()
{
        //GUI Code Goes Here...

}
```

All of the code we are going to cover in this section resides within this procedure. For clarity sake, we will eventually stop showing it, but always remember we are working within a single procedure. When called, this procedure will create and display the window for us. Typically the user calls the script by typing the name of the procedure that houses its UI. The interface includes elements that provide access to the additional functionality of the program. The rest of the procedures are of no concern to the end user.

```
Code
global proc cgTkClothTools ()
{
        if (`window -q -ex clothToolsWindow`)
                deleteUI clothToolsWindow;

        //Main Window
        window    -title "CG Toolkit - Cloth Tools v1.0"
                        -w 340 -h 330
                        -iconName "Cloth Tools"
                        clothToolsWindow;

        //Show Main Window Command
        showWindow clothToolsWindow;

}
```

The first line of our new procedure is a necessity of almost every interface. This if statement checks for the existence of a window named 'clothToolsWindow' (-ex flag returns true if the window exists). If it does exist, we delete it before creating another instance (with the deleteUI command). This simply prevents multiple copies of the same window. Without this line, Maya will display an error when trying to create a new window that is already open. This is an easy bug to avoid, so make a point of including this check in all of your windows.

With the existence check out of the way, we can begin creating the interface. It should be no surprise that the first element to create is the window itself. We've attached a title to the window to specify the name that will appear in the window's title bar. Also included is an explicit width, height and iconName (the name that appears in the title bar when the window is minimized).

Finally, we pass the name of the window to the showWindow command. This actually draws the window on the screen. At this point, we get an

interface like FIGURE 4.122. For clarity sake, let's continue building the script from the window command and assume that the procedure and showWindow commands are still there (hidden, for now). The next step is creating your main layout for the window:

Figure 4.122.

```
Code
//Main Window
window    -title "CG Toolkit - Cloth Tools v1.0"
                -w 340 -h 330
                -iconName "Cloth Tools"
                clothToolsWindow;

        //Scroll Layout
        scrollLayout -hst 0;

                //Main Column Layout
                columnLayout;
```

The effect of the scrollLayout is actually quite simple to visualize. When a scroll layout is created, it immediately requires a child layout (in this case, we used a columnLayout). The entire scope of its child layout will be scrollable. By default it creates horizontal and vertical scrollbars. For this script, we only want vertical scrollbars, so we hide the horizontal ones with the -hst flag set to 0. For more details on the individual layouts, please check out the MEL command reference that comes with Maya.

At this point, we have a columnLayout that encompasses the entire window and it is scrollable FIGURE 4.123. If you look at the finished interface (FIGURE 4.120), you will see three collapsible frames. These correspond to the three main features of the program: the scene manager, solver calculator and cache command creator. Let's add these now:

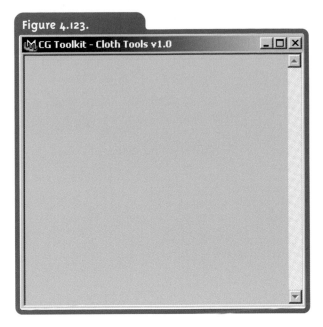

Figure 4.123.

CG Toolkit - Cloth Tools v1.0

```
Code
//Main Window
window    -title "CG Toolkit - Cloth Tools v1.0"
              -w 340 -h 330
              -iconName "Cloth Tools"
              clothToolsWindow;

    //Scroll Layout
    scrollLayout -hst 0;

        //Main Column Layout
        columnLayout;

        //Scene Manager
        frameLayout -w 300 -label "Scene Manager"
                      -labelAlign "center"
                      -collapsable 1 -collapse 0
                      -marginHeight 5 -marginWidth 5
                      -borderStyle etchedIn;
        setParent..;

        //Solver Scale Calculator
        frameLayout -w 300 -label "Calculate Solver Scale:"
                      -labelAlign "center"
                      -collapsable 1 -collapse 1
                      -borderStyle etchedIn
                      -marginHeight 5 -marginWidth 5;
        setParent..;

        //Bake/Cache Cloth
        frameLayout -w 300 -label "Bake/Cache Cloth:"
                      -labelAlign "center"
                      -collapsable 1 -collapse 1
                      -borderStyle etchedIn
                      -marginHeight 5  -marginWidth 5;
        setParent..;
```

We have added three new frame layouts to be children of the main column layout. A frame layout creates a framed region that has the option of being collapsible. We have deliberately used the long names for each of the flags for clarity's sake. If you require further explanation of what each flag is doing, look it up in the MEL command reference.

Notice the use of the setParent commands to ensure that each subsequent frame layout is placed under the main column layout (and not under the previous layout). Executing the code at this point gives us three empty frames inside the scroll layout. Notice that if the frames are expanded beyond the length of the window, the scroll bar becomes de-grayed and allows you to scroll down to see the contents of each frame layout FIGURE 4.124.

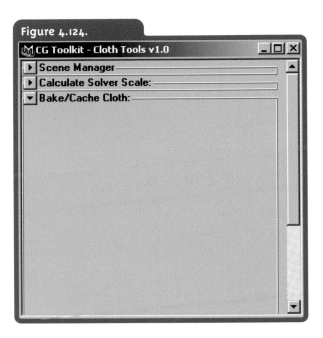

Figure 4.124.

CG Toolkit - Cloth Tools v1.0
Scene Manager
Calculate Solver Scale:
Bake/Cache Cloth:

Like scroll layouts, frame layouts require an immediate child layout to aid in the placement of elements. Let's build-up the last frame layout (Bake/Cache Cloth) since it is the simplest. The following code builds the last frame layout and its children elements (see next page):

```
//Bake Cloth
frameLayout -w 300 -label "Bake/Cache Cloth:"
        -labelAlign "center"
        -collapsable 1 -collapse 1
        -borderStyle etchedIn
        -marginHeight 5  -marginWidth 5;

    columnLayout -adj 1;
            radioButtonGrp     -numberOfRadioButtons 2
                               -label "Frames: "
                               -labelArray2 "Start/End" "Time Slider"
                               -ad3 true
                               -cl3 "center" "left" "left"
                               -sl 2
                               -cc1 ("intFieldGrp -e -enable 1 clothFrameField")
                               -cc2 ("intFieldGrp -e -enable 0 clothFrameField")
                               clothFramesRadioButtonGrp;
            intFieldGrp        -numberOfFields 2
                               -label "Start   "
                               -extraLabel "End"
                               -ad4 true
                               -cl4 "right" "left" "left" "left"
                               -enable 0
                               clothFrameField;
            separator -h 20;
            button -label "Generate Maya Cloth Batch Command" -c ("cgTkGenerateBatchCmd") ;
            button -label "Use Shot Sculpt..." -c ("cgTkShotSculpt") ;
```

Notice that directly below the frame layout we have a columnLayout command. This creates a layout that places child elements on top of each other (in a single column). In this case, we have five child elements: the radioButtonGrp, intFieldGrp, separator, and two buttons. When executed, this will create the following layout, FIGURE 4.125.

Figure 4.124.

The radio button and integer field groups are of particular interest. As you might expect, they create radio buttons and int fields respectively, but because they are groups, they have other attributes. The integer field group creates a user specified number of int fields and up to two text labels. The radio button group is even more interesting because it creates a group of radio buttons that behave in a mutually exclusive manner. Only one radio button may be selected at a time. If a new radio button is selected, the old button will be deselected. This same behavior could be accomplished with regular radio buttons (through a '-onCommand' flag) but the groups give it to you for free.

It must also be pointed out that the buttons at the bottom of the layout have some functionality. Notice the -label flag specifies the name that appears on the button. The -c flag is how a button is able to execute a task. The -c ('-command' in long form) flag specifies a command to be executed when the button is pressed. In the case of the second button, we are calling the cgTkShotSculpt procedure which is located in an entirely different script file. As long as that script was sourced, Maya will 'know' about the procedure and the call is valid. When the cgTkShotSculpt procedure is called, an entirely new window is created and displayed for shot sculpting (see the next chapter for more about this).

Now that we've got the hang of creating UI elements under a columnLayout, let's tackle something a little harder. Notice in the final GUI that the scene manager frame contains several scroll lists. What we have here is a rowColumnLayout creating a grid of 'cells'. Each cell is filled with its own columnLayout which houses a text scroll list. Sound complicated? Let's take a look at the code and figure it all out:

```
//Scene Manager
frameLayout -w 300 -label "Scene Manager"
        -labelAlign "center"
        -collapsable 1 -collapse 0
        -marginHeight 5 -marginWidth 5
        -borderStyle etchedIn;

        //Scene Manager 'Grid' Layout
        rowColumnLayout -nc 2 -cw 1 140 -cw 2 140;

                //First 'Cell'
                columnLayout;
                        text "Properties :";
                        textScrollList    -w 135 -numberOfRows 4
                                          -allowMultiSelection 1
                                          -selectCommand ("select `textScrollList -q -selectItem clothPropertiesScrollList`")
                                          clothPropertiesScrollList;
                setParent..;

                //Second 'Cell'
                columnLayout;
                        text "Solvers :";
                        textScrollList    -w 135 -numberOfRows 4
                                          -allowMultiSelection 1
                                          -selectCommand ("select `textScrollList -q -selectItem clothSolverScrollList`")
                                          clothSolverScrollList;
                setParent..;

                //Third 'Cell'
                columnLayout;
                        text "Caches :";
                        textScrollList    -w 135 -numberOfRows 4
                                          -allowMultiSelection 1
                                          -selectCommand ("select `textScrollList -q -selectItem clothCachesScrollList`")
                                          clothCachesScrollList;
                setParent..;

                //Fourth 'Cell'
                columnLayout;
                        text "Collision Objects :";
                        textScrollList -w 135 -numberOfRows 4
                                          -allowMultiSelection 1
                                          -selectCommand ("select `textScrollList -q -selectItem collisionObjScrollList`")
                                          collisionObjScrollList;
                setParent..;

                //Fifth 'Cell'
                columnLayout;
                        text "Cloth Objects :";
                        textScrollList -w 135 -numberOfRows 4
                                          -allowMultiSelection 1
                                          -selectCommand ("select `textScrollList -q -selectItem clothObjScrollList`")
                                          clothObjScrollList;
                setParent..;

                //Sixth 'Cell'
                columnLayout -adj true;

                        text " ";
                        button -label "Refresh Lists" -c ("cgTkRefreshClothSceneManager");

        setParent..; // Back to Scene Manager rowColumn Layout
        setParent..; // Back to Scene Manager Frame Layout
setParent..; // Back to Main Column Layout for Entire Window

//These last three setParent commands take the hierarchy back so that we can add more frame layouts.
```

Try not to get lost in the details here. Essentially what we have is a rowColumnLayout creating a grid of cells with two columns. Each cell contains its own columnLayout with a bit of text acting as a label for the various scrollable lists. We filled-up five of the cells with textScrollLists and the last cell is holding a button. This button calls the procedure that searches through the scene file and fills-up each textScrollList with the names of any cloth-related nodes that it finds.

The reason we had to use columnLayouts in each cell is because we want multiple elements in each cell. If the columnLayouts were removed, both the 'text' and 'textScrollList' elements would take their own cell (thus using twice as many cells as we want) FIGURE 4.126.

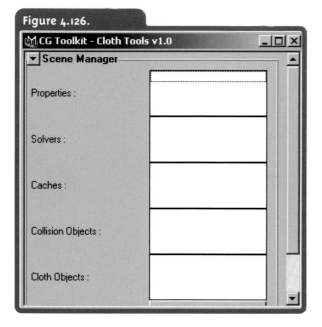

Figure 4.126.

Notice that the text scroll lists have a -selectCommand flag attached to them. This flag allows you to specify a command that is executed when the user selects one of the items in the list. In this case, we want the node itself to be selected. To do this, we pass it the 'select' MEL command. To find the name of the object the user selected, we query the textScrollList using the same MEL command used to create it (this time with the query flag). Because we want to query the currently selected item, we attach the -selectItem flag. The entire command looks like this:

```
Code
"select `textScrollList -q -selectItem nameOfScrollList`"
```

Notice the command is enclosed within quotation marks (""). This is because the -selectCommand flag requires a command in the form of a string. Just remember that any interface executed commands (buttons included) won't work unless they are in *string format*.

That concludes our coverage of the cloth tools interface. We skipped the second frame (solver scale calculator) in the interest of brevity. I know that many people find UI development to be the most difficult part of creating a working MEL tool. Hopefully having been guided through this relatively complex interface, you have been exposed to some new ideas about how interface design works.

If I could pass one piece of wisdom to future MEL GUI designers, it would be this: have patience. GUI design can be a weird concept to grasp, no doubt, but with practice you should find it demystifies itself quite

quickly. The hardest part is knowing where to start. This guide has given you that. Now its up to you. I will guarantee headaches, but also promise that, over time, they will become fewer and less painful.

Final Thoughts:

This chapter has guided you through the creation of some truly production-level advanced creature effects. Building on the concepts presented in the first three chapters, we have taken the Minx from a naked model to a fully clothed and furry beast!

The process of setting-up these effects takes care of the majority of the work involved in bringing a character like this to life. The final task involves the process of actually finishing the effects on a shot-by-shot basis. This requires understanding of a few new concepts and a bit of practice. The next chapter will supply you with the techniques needed during the finishing stage.

This chapter has covered the creation of the Minx character's fur and cloth. Along the way, we covered some new concepts. Specifically, we have covered:

- How the Minx Character was Created
- The Balance Between Integration and Modularity
- Rigging Overview for Animation Rig
- Rigging Overview for High-Res Rig
- The Creation of the Minx's Fur
- The Creation of the Minx's Clothing
- An Overview of a Cloth Tool
- Case Study: MEL GUIs Explained

Chapter 5
Rigging the face for Motion Capture

▶

Introduction to Rigging the Face for Motion Capture:

What is facial motion capture? You know, it's when they put those little white dots all over an actor's face. The 3D position of the little white dots is captured by roughly a dozen special cameras (each camera costing more than some most of us make in a year), and what the rigger ends up with is a bunch of locators, representing the little white dots. We get a bunch of points wiggling around in 3D space.

Of course, the above blurb is a huge oversimplification of the painstaking motion capture process. Admittedly, my own understanding of this process is vague at best. However, what concerns the rigger is not how to capture motion, but what to do with all those wiggling locators! How do you rig a face so that the locators drive the deformations of the mesh? What if the topology of the mesh is not even human? How would you rig the face for a game as opposed to a film? These are the questions we will tackle in this exciting chapter!

Specifically you will learn:

- The 'Perfect' Mesh Topology for Facial Animation
- Modeling the Facial Muscles Directly from the Mocap Data
- Reshaping the Muscles for a Non-Human Face
- Connecting the Mocap Data to the Muscles
- Adding the Muscles as Influence Objects to the Face
- Dealing with the Eyes, Teeth, and Tongue
- Using Sculpt Deformers
- Exaggerating the Mocap Data
- Incorporating Keyframe Animation
- Alternative Setup for Games
- Mesh Baking and Shot Sculpting
- Incorporating the Head into the Body Rig
- MEL Scripting: The Creation of cgTkFacialMocapConnect.mel

The "Perfect" Mesh Topology for Facial Animation:

I take this matter very seriously, so try not to laugh. About a year ago, I bought a baby doll in a thrift store and gessoed it over. With a Sharpie, I drew lines on it representing a spline cage. Thus began my search for the "perfect" humanoid mesh. I must have gessoed this thing over a hundred times. Every time I thought I had it, a week later I would realize that I had it all wrong. So I would gesso the doll and start fresh. This obsession did not end with the doll, but also extended itself to magazines, Victoria's Secret catalogs, and of course, my own body.

Note: If you're going to try this at home, I would not recommend using a Sharpie on your own body. Gesso is good, or Hershey's chocolate syrup (if you're into that...).

What exactly was I looking for? What qualities would the perfect mesh have? The following list is my 'Perfect Mesh Manifesto'. The 'perfect' animatable mesh...

- Is geared towards good deformation.
- Is mostly quads. A few triangles are okay. No n-gons.
- 'Brushes by' the musculature.
- Has more geometry in areas that will deform more, like the shoulder.
- Has enough detail to achieve all possible deformations.
- Has only enough detail to achieve all possible deformations.
- Remember, the mesh is only a shell for your displacement maps and bump maps.
- Should be easy to memorize.
- Flows. Flow is the most important quality of a good mesh.

While I figured out the mesh for the body quickly enough, it was the face that was giving me trouble. Over and over, I was making the mistake of trying to describe facial musculature with geometry. (A task best left up to a displacement map.) Finally, I asked myself, "What is it you are trying to describe?". The answer: Skin! Skin, not muscles, is what a mesh is supposed to be about. Skin is the outer shell—the shell that will *deform* during animation.

This realization has led me to research human wrinkle patterns. From there, the answers came quickly, until finally, my work was complete—the perfect humanoid face mesh. (You can laugh now if you want.) Here it is: FIGURE 5.1.

These lines represent a base cage. Each square is meant to be a surface of at least 2 x 2 spans. More lines can be added where necessary, especially around the eye and mouth edge loops. This base cage is only meant to be used as a starting point to establish the general flow of the mesh; add additional detail where appropriate.

Let's analyze the flow of this mesh for a moment. You'll notice that the lines follow the wrinkle patterns of the face. We are not born with wrinkles. Wrinkles form gradually over many years of habitual skin folding. Luckily, for humans, the wrinkle patterns are always the same.

FIGURE 5.2 shows the longitudinal sections of this mesh, while FIGURE 5.3 shows the latitudinal.

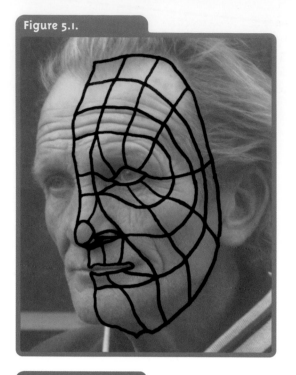

Figure 5.1.

Figure 5.2.

Figure 5.3.

FIGURE 5.4 shows the radial eye, nose, and mouth sections. Notice that the nostril is radial, too. FIGURE 5.5 shows the star-junctions (areas where five or more quad faces come together).

Figure 5.4.

Figure 5.5.

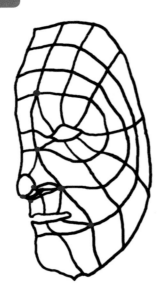

Now for the really cool part. As anyone who has ever sculpted a 'smile' blendshape knows—smiles are *the hardest shapes to sculpt*. The reason is that a smile is the most extreme deformation the face can go through. All other deformations are nil in comparison. FIGURE 5.6 shows the main area affected by a smile, ex`cluding the mouth. Notice that it takes up roughly 50% of the face area! With this topology, envision how the lines will gracefully pull up into a smile, creating the proper smile wrinkle, cheek bulge, and crow's feet.

Remember, never attempt to sculpt musculature or any actual wrinkles with geometry. These things should be described with (preferably animated) displacement maps and bump maps. Only the deepest of wrinkles, such as the smile wrinkle, should be sculpted with geometry.

Figure 5.6.

I have always approached modeling from a rigger's point of view. The above topology has consistently given me the best results, even under the most extreme deformations. I hope you will use it in your own work and pass it on to the modeling department!

Modeling the Facial Muscles Directly from the Mocap Data:

As mentioned in the introduction, when the rigger receives the mocap data, it will most likely be in the form of wiggling locators FIGURE 5.7.

Figure 5.7.

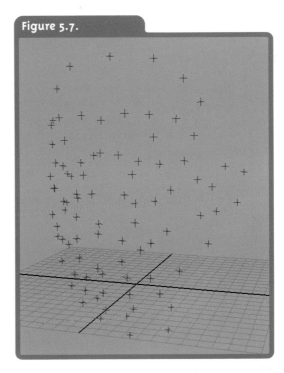

The question becomes how to make all these locators drive the face mesh. There are several ways to do this. One way to connect the mocap data to the deformations of the face is through set driven keys; with the translations of the locators driving a blendshape node. Another way is to parent a joint under every locator and bind the face mesh to the joints. Yet another way is to use clusters instead of joints. Finally, we could use influence objects or influence curves to drive the mesh. This last method is the one we will be using in this chapter. Because the influence object setup is currently unattainable in games, I will devote a separate section to a joint setup later in the chapter.

Meet Bobo FIGURE 5.8, a friendly chimpanzee with a thing for Jack Nicholson. We will be using Bobo for the duration of this chapter.

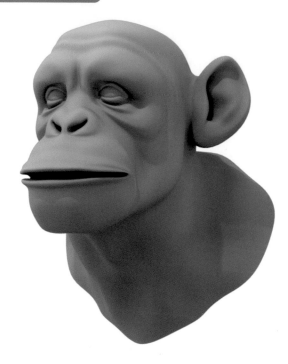

Had Bobo been a human character, the setup would have been easier. The relationship between the human actor (Eric Aten) and the human mesh would have been almost 1 to 1. However, I deliberately chose a chimpanzee, because I wanted to demonstrate that it is possible to drive not only human meshes, but non-human meshes as well.

The first thing we must do to make this setup work is create the facial muscles (influence objects) that will drive the mesh. Because every mocap data locator must be taken into account, it is best to create the facial muscles directly from the locators themselves. Thankfully, in Maya, this is a fairly straightforward process.

I would like to draw your attention to FIGURE 5.9. This is the facial marker layout prepared by Remington Scott, the mocap session director.

During a facial mocap session, markers (tiny reflective spheres) are glued onto the actor's face. Throughout the actor's performance, the motion of the markers is captured by dozens of high-end mocap cameras. Finally, through some magical process (triangulation), we end up with the mocap data—locators (representing the markers) with a keyframe on every frame, wiggling around in 3D space. So, because every dot on the marker layout represents a marker, and every marker represents a mocap data locator, it would make sense to closely follow this marker layout when creating the facial muscle's geometry.

Open mocapExercise1A.ma. Let's create the forehead region first. Go to frame 1. It is very important to be in the neutral pose when creating the facial muscles. Now, with the Create Polygon Tool, snap to the following locators using the V key in this order: 1, 2, 3, 4, 5, 6, 7, 16, 15, 14, 13, 12, 11, 10, 9, and 8. You should have a polygon similar to FIGURE 5.10.

In order to create the connecting edges, use the following trick: Triangulate the polygon first and then immediately Quadrangulate it. Create the following shelf button to help you do this:

```
polyTriangulate;
polyQuad;
```

Your forehead muscle should now look like FIGURE 5.11.

Figure 5.9.

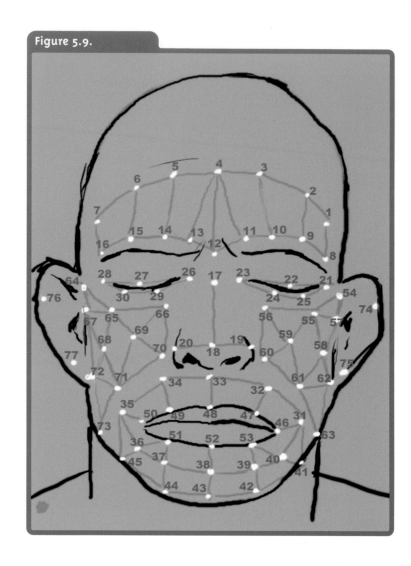

Figure 5.10.

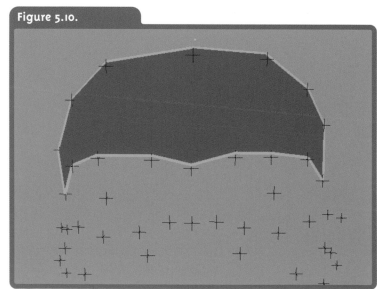

Figure 5.11.

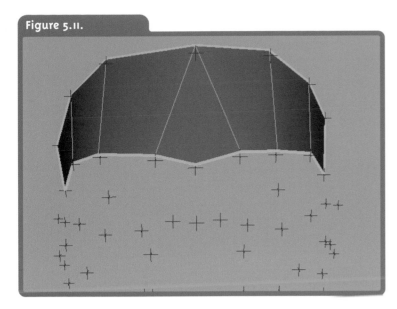

Make sure the Normals are facing out by using the `ToggleFaceNormals` command. If they are not facing out, use `ReversePolygonNormals`.

Now that you have the idea, continue creating other muscles, such as eyes, cheeks, top lip, bottom lip, chin, neck, and ears. Open **mocapExercise1B.ma** to see what the final muscles should look like FIGURE 5.12.

Figure 5.12.

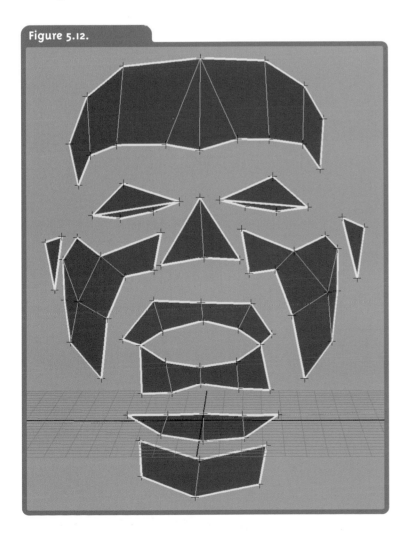

Name all the muscles appropriately, delete all history, and group them so that they are ready to be exported FIGURE 5.13.

Figure 5.13.

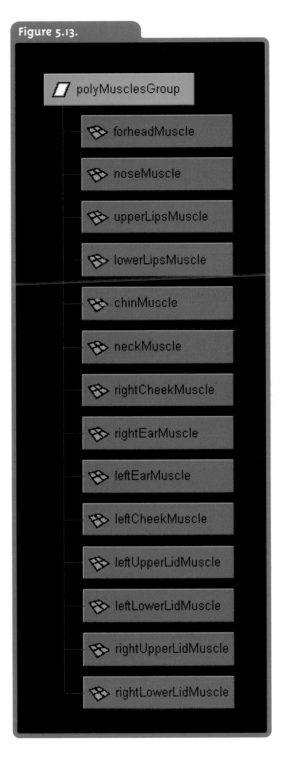

Reshaping the Muscles for a Non-Human Face:

The next step is also straightforward. We must reshape these muscles so that they better fit Bobo's face. Open **mocapExercise2A.ma** FIGURE 5.14.

As you can see, the muscles don't fit Bobo's mesh at all. So, we'll make them fit! Let's start with the forehead muscle again. Reshape the vertices of the forehead muscle to better fit Bobo's forehead. It really helps to use the V key to snap to vertices on Bobo's actual mesh. FIGURE 5.15 shows the forehead muscle after it has been reshaped.

Continue reshaping all the muscles until you are satisfied. Open **mocapExercise2B.ma** to see what the final reshaped muscles should look like FIGURE 5.16. Much better.

Figure 5.14.

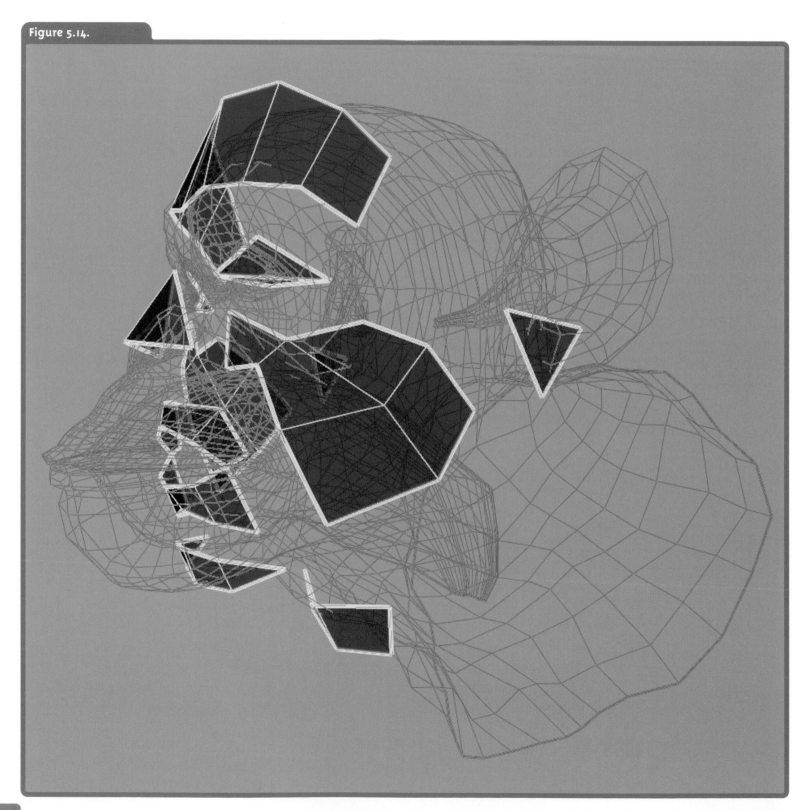

Figure 5.15.

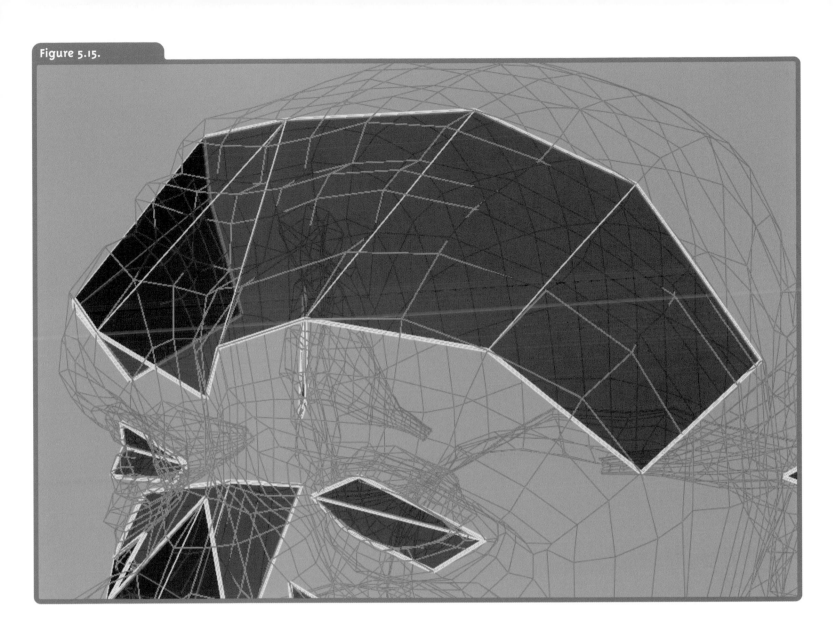

Figure 5.16.

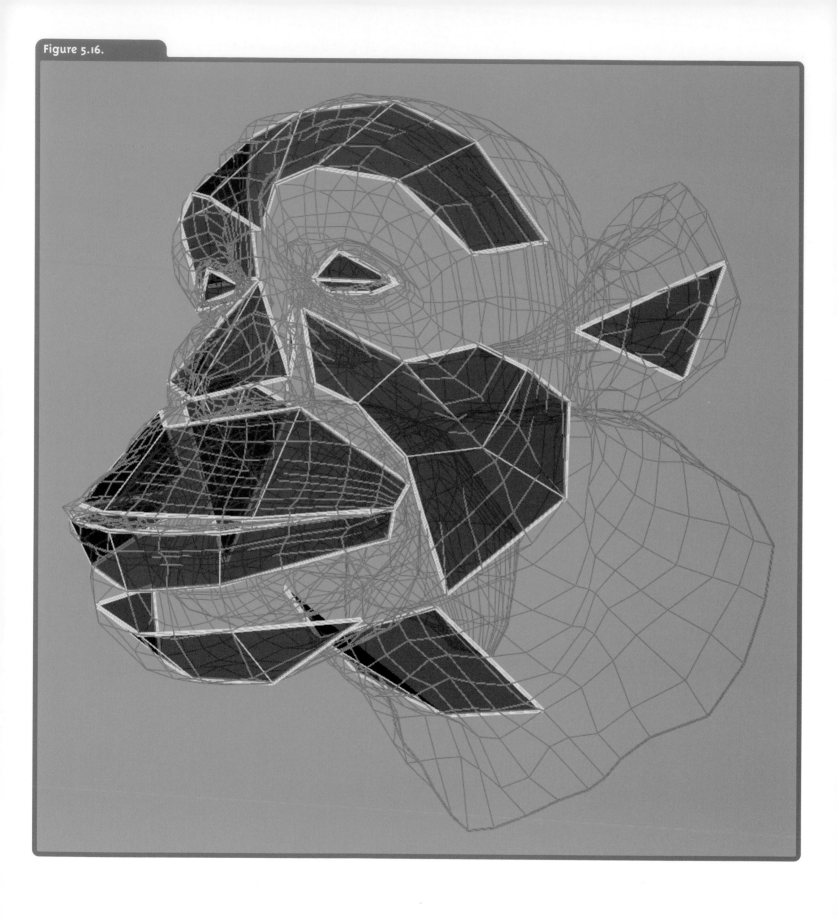

Connecting the Mocap Data to the Muscles:

Now comes the fun part: connecting our muscles to the mocap data locators. To assist us with this and most subsequent steps, I have written a few MEL scripts called cgTk Facial Mocap Tools FIGURE 5.17.

Figure 5.17.

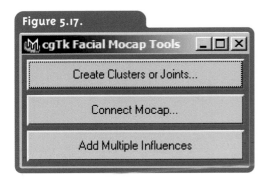

These tools will make the rest of the steps in this setup as painless as humanly possible. While it is possible to achieve this setup without using MEL, it would be impractical. As we go through the steps, you will notice the amount of repetitive tasks we must do. Setting up a single character like Bobo without MEL is painful but doable. But what if you had to set up several different characters? Without some kind of MEL solution, you will quickly go insane trying to manage all the data. With this (or a similar) MEL toolkit under our belts, the entire setup process will be a pleasure instead of a pain.

The tools are arranged from top to bottom, and are, in fact, the steps that we will follow to create our rig, in that order. First, make sure the tools are installed by copying all the cgTkFacialMocap MEL scripts to your scripts directory and restarting Maya. Execute cgTkFacialMocapTools to bring up the main UI.

Open **mocapExercise3A.ma** FIGURE 5.18.

You will see Bobo's muscles on the left and the mocap data locators on the right. I have also lined up the original "human" muscles with the mocap data locators, so that it will be easier to discern which locator is which.

Next, we'll use MEL to create the clusters that will deform Bobo's muscles. In the Facial Mocap Tools UI, click on 'Create Clusters or Joints'. FIGURE 5.19 shows the UI that pops up.

Figure 5.19.

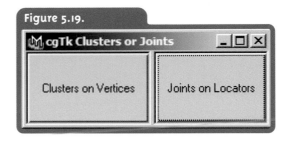

There are only two buttons: "Clusters on Vertices" and "Joints on Locators". We will use the first button now. We'll touch the "Joints on Locators" button later, when we discuss an alternative joint-based setup for games.

Select all of Bobo's muscle geometry and press "Clusters on Vertices". In a matter of seconds, a cluster is created at each vertex. Every cluster has been parented to a locator. Pulling on the muscle locators is the equivalent of pulling on the vertices of the muscles.

I like to make my locators a bit smaller so they are easier to tell apart. Use this command to select all locators in the scene:

```
select `ls -type locator`;
```

Then, using the Channel Box, set the Local Scale X, Y, and Z to about 0.1. Your scene should look like FIGURE 5.20.

Figure 5.18.

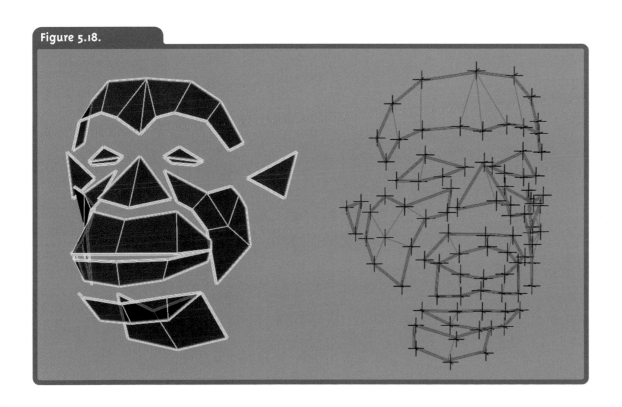

Figure 5.20.

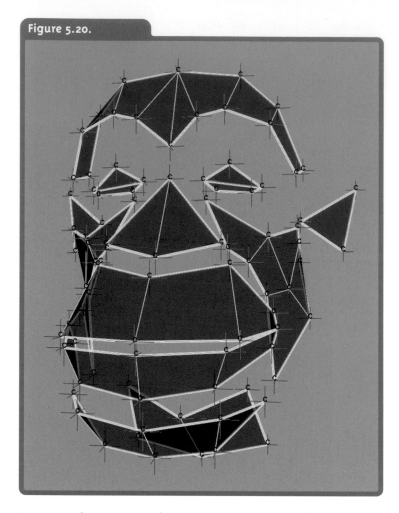

selection to every even selection. It will also create an optional shelf button with a long list of commands similar to the following:

```
Code
//DELETE CONSTRAINTS START
//Frame check
if (`currentTime -q` != 1) error "You must be at frame 1.";
catch(`delete -cn forheadMuscleLocator2`);
catch(`delete -cn forheadMuscleLocator3`);
catch(`delete -cn forheadMuscleLocator4`);
catch(`delete -cn forheadMuscleLocator5`);
catch(`delete -cn forheadMuscleLocator6`);
…
//DELETE CONSTRAINTS END
```

With these two shelf buttons, Connect and Disconnect, it is now possible to quickly connect or disconnect the muscles to or from the mocap data. Say you don't like a particular take. Just select the mocap data locator group and delete it, import new mocap data, and reconnect it to the rig with the press of a button. Again, I want to emphasize that it is very important to do all connections and disconnections at frame 1 in the neutral pose. Otherwise, the face may look lopsided when it deforms.

Open **mocapExercise3B.ma** to play with Bobo's connected muscles.

Adding the Muscles as Influence Objects to the Face:

In order to make the muscles drive Bobo's face mesh, we will add them as influence objects. Open mocapExercise4A.ma. To add any influence objects, we must first bind Bobo's mesh to a skinCluster. Go to the side view and create a single joint right in the middle of Bobo's head FIGURE 5.23. Name it "boboBindJoint".

We are ready to connect the mocap data locators to the locators on Bobo's muscles. Invoke the cgTk Facial Mocap Tools and click on "Connect Mocap" FIGURE 5.21.

Figure 5.21.

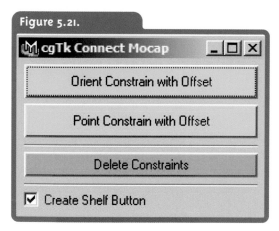

Traditionally, motion capture data is hooked up to rigs with constraints. For skeletons, it is usually Orient Constraints, but for facial rigs, Point Constraints are used. The idea is to Point Constrain with Offset every mocap data locator to every corresponding locator on Bobo's muscles. Creating these constraints one by one would be tedious, but with MEL—it's fun!

One by one, shift-select a mocap data locator on the right and the corresponding rig locator on the left. It helps to turn off the visibility of the clusters, so that you don't accidentally select them. This step will take a few minutes. When you are finished shift-selecting all the locator pairs, make sure you are at frame 1 and press the 'Point Constrain with Offset' button. The Connect Mocap script will constrain every odd

Figure 5.23.

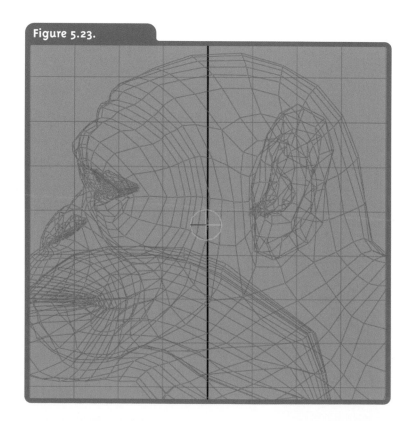

Untemplate Bobo's head and smooth bind it to this joint with the default options. We are now ready to add the muscles as influence objects.

Bring up cgTk Facial Mocap Tools. Make the polyMuscles display layer visible. Select Bobo's mesh first, then shift-select all the muscles. Finally, press the 'Add Multiple Influences' button. All of the muscles will be added to the skinCluster as influences.

In order for the muscles to actually deform the mesh, we must turn on an attribute in the skinCluster that is normally off by default. Select Bobo's mesh. In the Channel Box, in the skinCluster node, turn on 'Use Components' FIGURE 5.24. Now the vertices of the muscles will actually deform Bobo's mesh.

If you play the timeline now, Bobo's mesh will not deform with the muscles. So, the next step is, you guessed it—painting skin weights! Select Bobo's mesh and open the Paint Skin Weights Tool. You will notice that all of the muscles in the influence list are on 'Hold'. This is because the Add Multiple Influences script adds objects with an initial weight of 0. It is up to us to paint skin weights on the muscles exactly where we want it. Turn off 'Hold' for all the muscles in the list by using 'Toggle Hold Weights on Selected'.

Let's add weight to the forehead muscle. Select it in the influence list. Then, using the Add brush with a weight of 1, paint the area of influence on Bobo's forehead and eyebrows. Use the Smooth brush around the edges of the influence. Do not use Flood Smooth. Using Flood Smooth adds tiny amounts of weight to all influences (bad idea). The influence of the forehead should look like FIGURE 5.25.

Play the timeline to see Bobo's forehead wiggle! Now, it's simply a matter of painting weights on the rest of influence muscles. As you paint the weights, please refer to FIGURE 5.26, a color coded diagram of all the influence weights in one convenient image. The mouth is usually the hardest area to paint. The best way to approach it is to scrub the timeline until Bobo opens his mouth. Then you can get in there and separate the lips by painting weights for the top and bottom lips individually.

Figure 5.24.

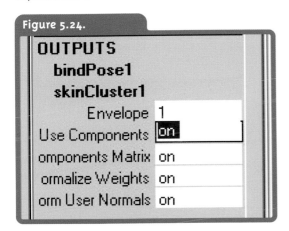

```
OUTPUTS
  bindPose1
  skinCluster1
       Envelope  1
  Use Components  on
  omponents Matrix  on
  ormalize Weights  on
  orm User Normals  on
```

Figure 5.25.

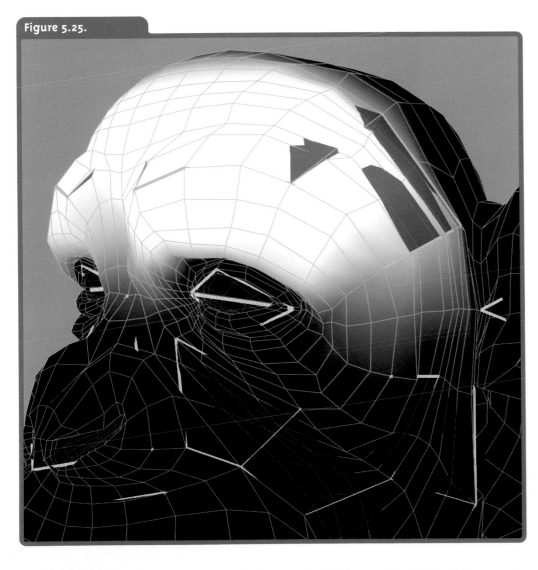

Figure 5.26.

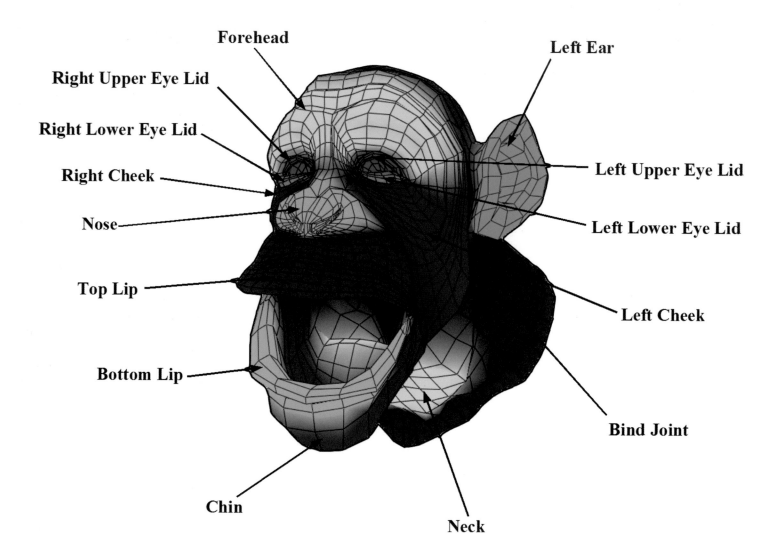

Bobo's Skin Weights

When you are done painting weights, play the timeline to see Bobo's face deform FIGURE 5.27! Open **mocapExercise4B.ma** to see Bobo's finished weights.

Figure 5.27.

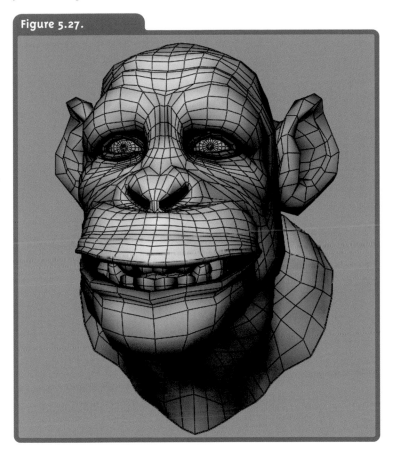

Although it may seem like we are finished with the rig, there are still a few important areas that need our attention. But don't worry, the hard part is over. Please read on!

Dealing with the Eyes, Teeth, and Tongue:

The face parts, such as the eyes, teeth, and tongue, are rigged as usual. The only difference from a normal setup is that all the face parts are smooth bound to joints, not parented or constrained. The reason for smooth binding instead of parenting or constraining is because the entire head, face parts included, will later be piped through a blendshape to the *actual* head on the body rig. (More on this later.)

Rigging the face parts is absolutely necessary, because they cannot be motion captured. The eyes and tongue must be animated by hand. The lower teeth are an exception, however—they can be constrained with an IK handle to follow one of the chin locators.

Rigging the face parts is beyond the scope of this chapter and is well covered in Chapter 4 in *The Art of Rigging, Volume I*. However, I would like to briefly go over how I handled Bobo's face parts.

FIGURE 5.28 shows Bobo's face parts.

Figure 5.28.

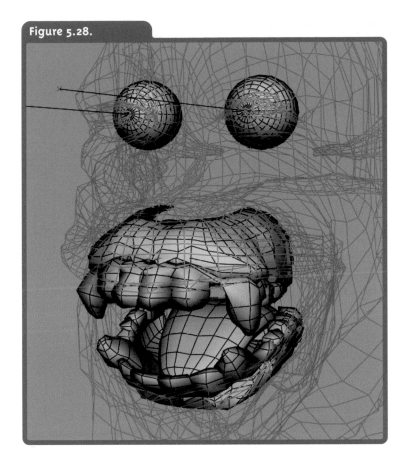

FIGURE 5.29 shows the skeleton for the face parts. The root is Bobo's bind joint, of course (see the section on Adding the Muscles as Influence Objects to the Face for more information about the bind joint). The eyes are smooth bound to their respective eye joints. The upper teeth are bound to the root bind joint. The lower teeth are bound to the jaw joint. Notice the smaller joint chain for the tongue. The tongue geometry is bound to this joint chain. The tongue joint chain is parented to the jaw joint. Finally, notice the IK handle for the jaw joint. This IK handle controls the rotation of the jaw and is parent constrained to one of the chin locators on Bobo's muscles. In fact, this parent constraint should be a part of the shelf button we created earlier for hooking up Bobo's muscles to the mocap data locators. Simply append something like the following to this shelf button:

```
//Connect Jaw Ik
catch(`parentConstraint -mo chinMuscleLocator4 jawIK`);
```

The eyes and tongue have been rigged in the popular fashion with NURBS control boxes. These controls have been hooked up with set driven keys to drive the eyes and tongue joints. Also, these controls have been parented to a new camera called faceCam. This way, the controls are always in the view, like a videogame HUD FIGURE 5.30.

You may choose to rig the face parts differently, but the main thing to remember about this section is that the face parts are smooth bound and not parented or constrained. Open **mocapExercise5A.ma** to play with Bobo's face parts rig.

Figure 5.29.

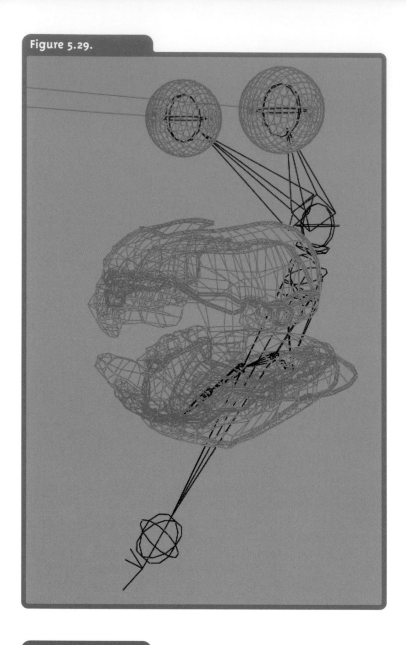

Figure 5.30.

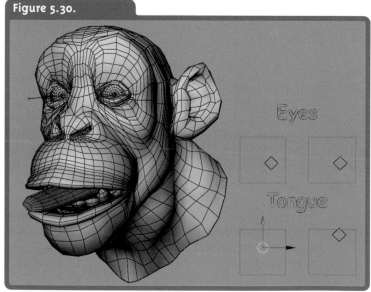

Using Sculpt Deformers:

If you're with me so far, you'll notice that when you play the timeline, there are times when Bobo's upper lip penetrates the upper teeth. This problem could be solved by placing a sculpt deformer inside Bobo's mouth. Sculpt deformers are great for creating the effect of skin sliding over bone, or a mouse scurrying under a carpet. One thing to keep in mind about sculpt deformers, is that they are computationally expensive, especially when used with the NURBS object feature. Therefore, it is a good idea to keep sculpt deformers to a minimum in your rigs.

Open **mocapExercise6A.ma.** Go to frame 365. At this frame, Bobo's upper lip is seriously penetrating the upper gums and teeth FIGURE 5.31.

Figure 5.31.

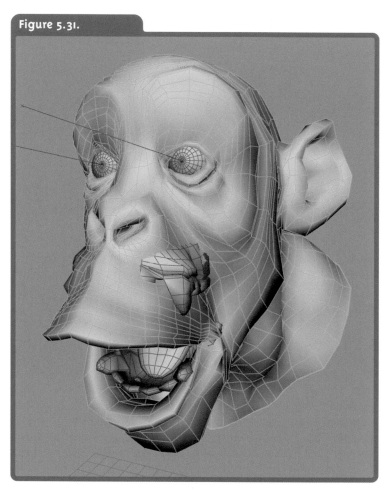

Select Bobo's mesh. Choose Deform > Create Sculpt Deformer > Options. Create a sculpt deformer with the options in FIGURE 5.32.

A sculptGroup consisting of a sculptor and sculptStretchOrigin will be created in the middle of Bobo's head FIGURE 5.33.

Select the sculptGroup, center its pivot, and position it inside Bobo's upper lip. Scale the sculptGroup to completely encompass the upper gums and teeth FIGURE 5.34.

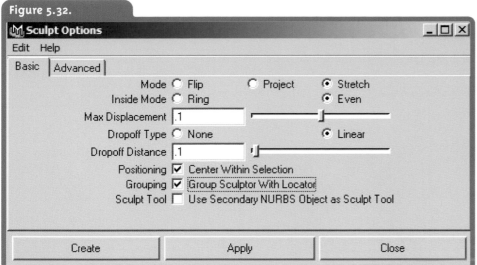

Figure 5.32.

Sculpt Options

Edit Help

Basic | Advanced |

Mode	○ Flip	○ Project	● Stretch
Inside Mode	○ Ring		● Even

Max Displacement [.1] ————————|————

Dropoff Type ○ None   ● Linear

Dropoff Distance [.1] —|—————————————

Positioning ☑ Center Within Selection

Grouping ☑ Group Sculptor With Locator

Sculpt Tool ☐ Use Secondary NURBS Object as Sculpt Tool

Create	Apply	Close

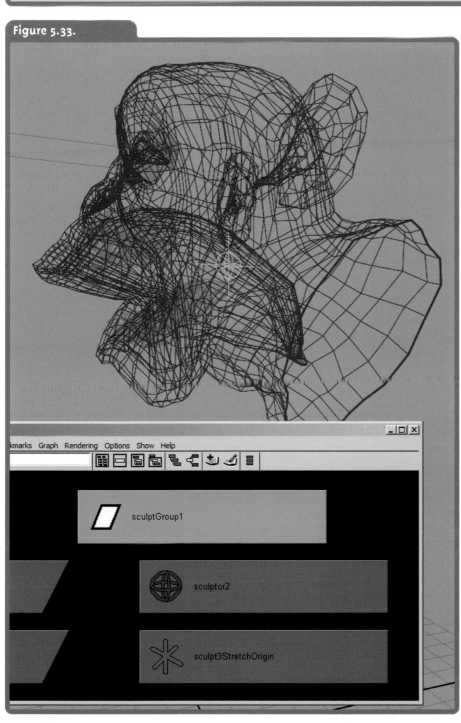

Figure 5.33.

kmarks Graph Rendering Options Show Help

sculptGroup1

sculptor2

sculpt3StretchOrigin

Figure 5.34.

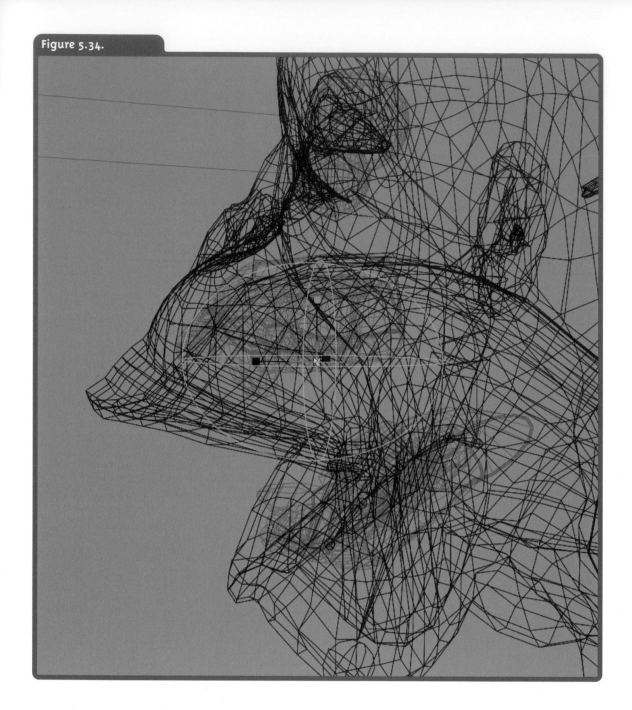

The teeth should no longer penetrate the upper lip. However, there is still a problem, because now the sculpt deformer is pushing the inside of the mouth bag to be on the same level as the outside of the upper lip. The solution is remove the vertices of the mouth bag from the sculpt deformer's membership set. Select Bobo's head and choose `Deform > Paint Set Membership Tool`. Under Paint Operations, choose Remove. Under Select Set to Modify, choose sculptiSet. You should see all of Bobo's vertices light up yellow. Then, simply paint inside the mouth bag until all mouth bag vertices are dimmed FIGURE 5.35.

That's it. The mouth bag no longer touches the upper lip and the teeth no longer penetrate the upper lip FIGURE 5.36. Not only that, but now it actually looks like Bobo's upper lip is sliding over the teeth and gums! Open **mocapExercise6B** to see how the sculpt deformer has been placed. You'll also notice, that in this file I have placed another sculpt deformer inside Bobo's forehead. This makes his eyebrows slide over his frontal bone.

One last note on this section is that the deformation order is important. If you had a polySmooth node, for example, and added the sculpt deformer after it, the polySmooth node will no longer give the correct results. To fix this, right-click Bobo's mesh and choose `Inputs > All Inputs`. Middle-mouse drag the Sculpt nodes to be above the skinCluster, but below the polySmooth node FIGURE 5.37. Now the polySmooth should work properly.

Figure 5.35.

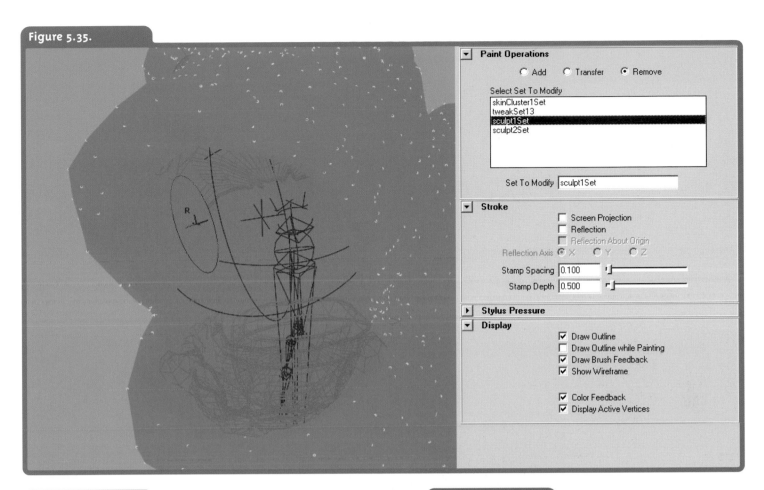

Paint Operations

- ☐ Add ☐ Transfer ☑ Remove

Select Set To Modify

skinCluster1Set
tweakSet13
sculpt1Set
sculpt2Set

Set To Modify sculpt1Set

Stroke

- ☐ Screen Projection
- ☐ Reflection
- ☐ Reflection About Origin

Reflection Axis ☑ X ☐ Y ☐ Z

Stamp Spacing 0.100

Stamp Depth 0.500

Stylus Pressure

Display

- ☑ Draw Outline
- ☐ Draw Outline while Painting
- ☑ Draw Brush Feedback
- ☑ Show Wireframe

- ☑ Color Feedback
- ☑ Display Active Vertices

Figure 5.36.

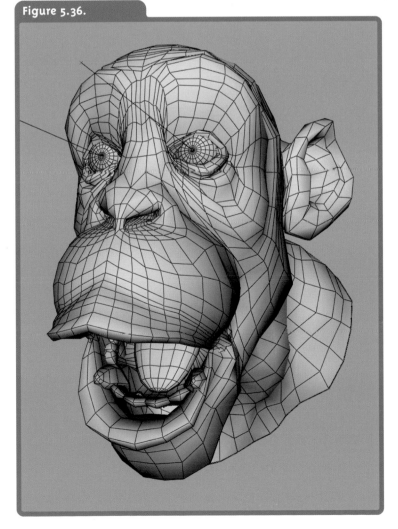

Figure 5.37.

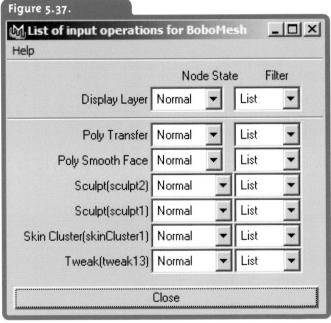

List of input operations for BoboMesh

Help

	Node State	Filter
Display Layer	Normal	List
Poly Transfer	Normal	List
Poly Smooth Face	Normal	List
Sculpt(sculpt2)	Normal	List
Sculpt(sculpt1)	Normal	List
Skin Cluster(skinCluster1)	Normal	List
Tweak(tweak13)	Normal	List

Close

Exaggerating the Motion Capture Data:

The following is a cool, simple trick to breathe even more life into your mocap face rig. You would think that the relationship between the mocap data locators and the muscles should be 1 to 1, as in FIGURE 5.38. Notice that the mocap locators group is roughly the same size as Bobo's head.

Connecting the data at frame 1 with this 1 to 1 ratio will give Bobo the range of motion of a normal human face. But who said that this relationship has to be 1:1? Imagine what would happen if you scaled the mocap locators group to be 1 ½ times bigger than Bobo's head. That would mean that the relationship between the motion of the mocap locators and the motion of the muscles will be 1.5 to 1. This would amplify the motion of the muscles by 50%!

Open **mocapExercise7A.ma** and try it out. First connect the mocap data with the mocap locators group scaled at 1 (x,y, and z, respectively). Make sure you do all connections and disconnections at frame 1. Play the timeline to see Bobo's face deform. Then, go back to frame 1, disconnect the mocap, scale the mocap locators group to 1.5 (x,y, and z, respectively), and reconnect the mocap. Play the timeline again to see Bobo's face exaggerate the motion.

Play with different scales. At really high scales, Bobo's face will be completely torn apart. Try to find a happy medium. Of course, if for some reason you wanted to lessen the motion, scale the mocap locators group to be less than 1. Also, try non-proportionally scaling the group and see what happens!

FIGURE 5.39 shows the difference between a 1 to 1 relationship and a 1.5 to 1 relationship.

Figure 5.38.

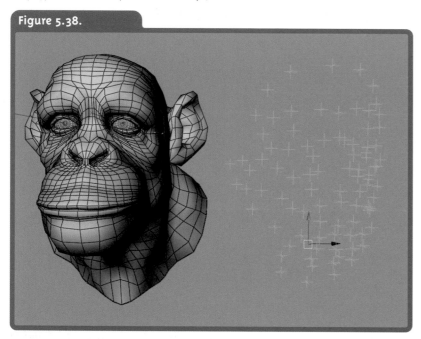

Figure 5.39.

1 to 1

1.5 to 1

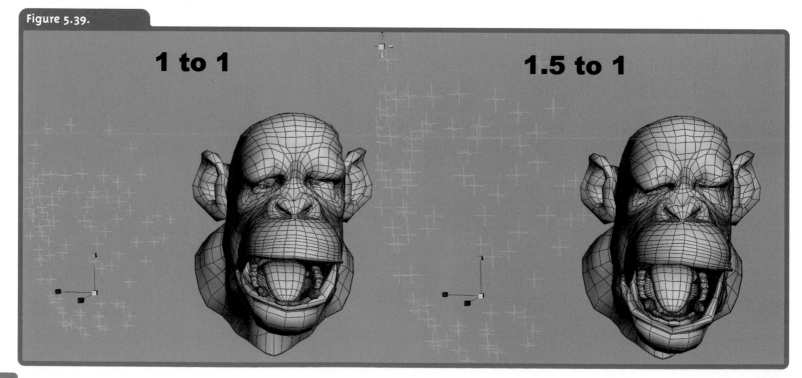

Incorporating Keyframe Animation:

Oftentimes, a mocap performance needs to be tweaked or enhanced by an animator. Rigging a full facial animation rig is beyond the scope of this chapter. However, let me briefly go over how it would be possible to blend between the animation rig and the mocap rig.

If you've been reading the *Art of Rigging* series religiously, then you should already know how to do this—constraints. The setup would be very similar to an IK/FK switch, only Point Constraints would be used instead of Orient Constraints. There would be three sets of locators sitting on top of each other:

- The locators constrained to the mocap data locators—the mocap rig
- The locators rigged with set driven keys to create facial expressions and phonemes—the animation rig
- The muscle locators driving the deformations of the muscles—the muscle rig

Each muscle locator would be Point Constrained between its corresponding mocap rig locator and animation rig locator.

Finally, a control could be rigged up with set driven keys that will allow the animator to blend the weight of the point constraints between the mocap rig and animation rig on a muscle-by-muscle basis. So, for example, if the animator is happy with the overall mocap performance, but wants to change the animation of the left eyelid only, he can. Similarly, if he wants to continue animating the face after a mocap take is over, he can simply blend all the muscles to follow the animation rig after a certain point.

Alternative Setup for Games:

Up to this point, Bobo has been rigged with a combination of influence object muscles and sculpt deformers—none of which are currently available in a game engine. Joints and blendshapes are the only deformers currently available in games. Therefore, a slightly different approach must be used to rig a face for a game.

There are two popular methods for rigging faces for games: joint-based and blendshape based. In the joint-based setup, the face is bound to around 50-100 joints that deform the face. In the blendshape setup, the face interpolates between many target shapes, as in a normal blendshape setup. So which approach should we take when rigging a face for motion capture for games? The answer is *both*.

While it is possible to create a blendshape setup that is driven through set driven keys by the positions of the mocap locators, this kind of setup defeats the purpose of having mocap data. A joint-based setup, with a joint corresponding to every mocap locator, makes more sense. However, a pure joint based setup driven by mocap data will have problems, such as collapsing of the mesh and interpenetration of geometry. Therefore, corrective blendshapes must be used to fix these problems. So, a combination of joints and blendshapes will give us the best results when rigging a face for motion capture for games.

Open **mocapExercise8A.ma.** In this file, you will see that I have placed locators around Bobo's mesh. Each locator corresponds to a mocap data locator FIGURE 5.40. The locators are hooked up to the mocap data in the same way as before (if you haven't already, please read the section on Connecting the Mocap Data to the Muscles). You may also notice that there are only 62 locators around Bobo's mesh as opposed to the 90 mocap locators used previously. Some locators were omitted because I wanted to keep the amount of joints at an efficient number for a game engine. However, if your game engine can handle 90 joints in the face without slowing down the game, use all 90 locators!

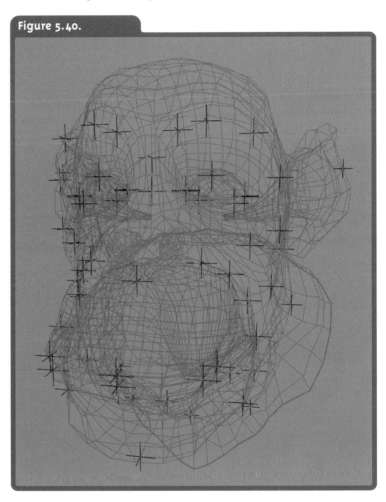

Figure 5.40.

Invoke cgTk Facial Mocap Tools and press Create Clusters or Joints. Then select all the locators around Bobo's mesh and press Joints on Locators. A joint will be created and parented under each locator. Select all the created joints and change their radius to around 0.2, so they are easier to see FIGURE 5.41.

Now, select all the joints, including Bobo's Bind Joint (located in the joint_displayLayer), then shift-select Bobo's mesh and smooth bind the mesh to the joints with the Selected Joints option.

The next step, painting skin weights on 63 individual joints, is my idea of a rigger's hell. Hand this part over to your trusty intern. If you don't have an intern (or if he isn't trusty), I'm sorry—you'll have to do this yourself. Each joint should cover a small area of influence, except the bind joint, which should affect the upper scull and back of the neck. The mouth will be the hardest to paint weights on. Painting weights on individual joints is not as intuitive as painting weights on influence muscles, but is necessary for this setup.

When you are finished, play the timeline to test out your rig. Even if you painted weights well, there is still the problem of the upper teeth penetrating through the upper lip. This is where a corrective blendshape can help.

Duplicate Bobo's mesh, unlock all the channels, and move it to the side. Call this mesh something like teethInterpenetrationFix. Create a blendshape from teethInterpenetrationFix to Bobo's mesh. Make sure the blendshape node sits below the skinCluster in the inputs (see the section on Using Sculpt Deformers on how to change the deformation order). Turn the teethInterpenetrationFix blendshape to 1. Then go to a frame in the animation where the teeth are interpenetrating with the upper lip. Using the Sculpt Geometry Tool, pull the upper lip of the teethInterpenetrationFix mesh up until the problem is solved. Your blendshape target should look something like FIGURE 5.42.

Finally, use set driven keys to connect the value of the teethInterpenetrationFix blendshape to the chin locator. When the chin locator is in the default position at frame 1, the value of the teethInterpenetrationFix blendshape should be 0. When the chin locator is all the way down, when the mouth is fully open, the value of the teethInterpenetrationFix blendshape should be 1. This should fix the interpenetration of the upper teeth FIGURE 5.43. (Corrective blendshapes are covered in much more detail In Chapter 6 of The Art of Rigging, Volume 1.)

This just about covers rigging a face for motion capture for games. Open **mocapExercise8B.ma** to play with the finished 'games' rig.

Figure 5.41.

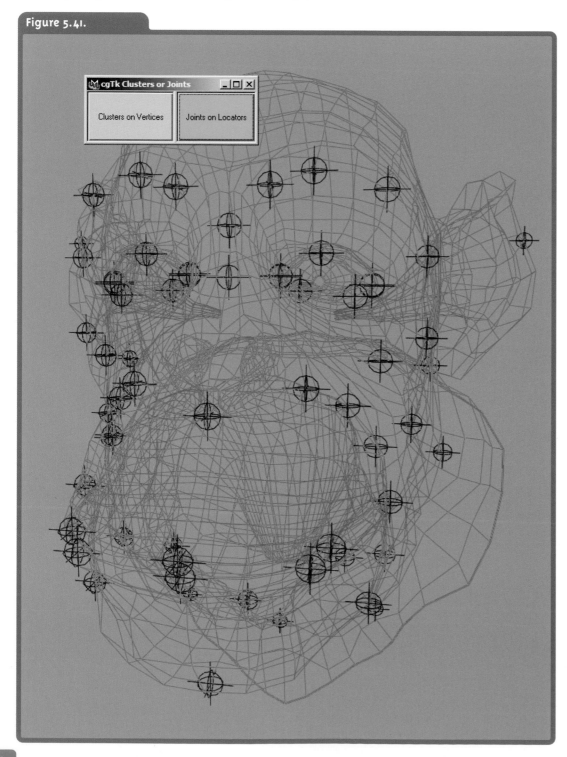

Figure 5.42.

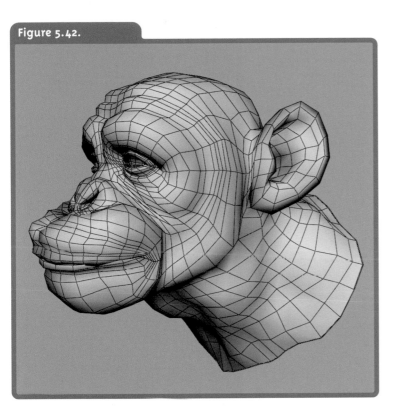

Figure 5.43.

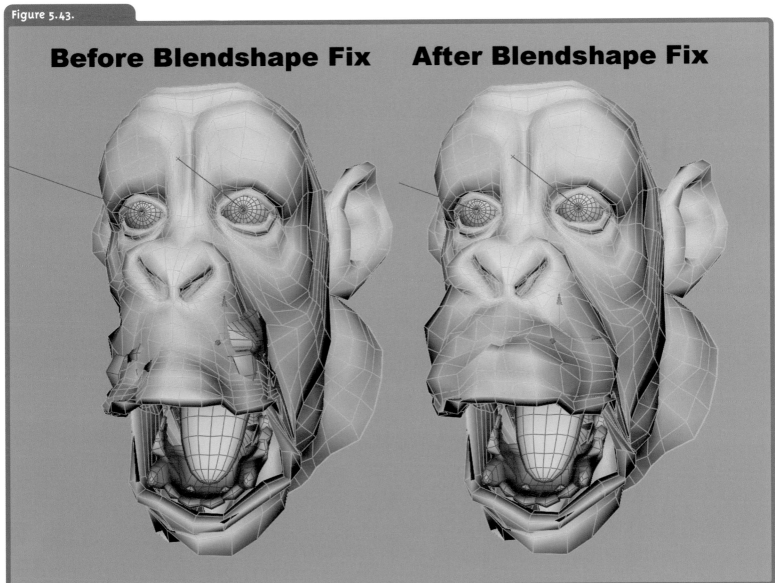

Before Blendshape Fix   **After Blendshape Fix**

Mesh Baking and Shot Sculpting:

When you are happy with the facial deformations during animation, it is a good idea to *bake the mesh*. A mesh may have a dozen different deformers operating on it at the same time. Baking the mesh ensures that the calculations for the deformers only have to be performed once. Baking is especially useful in distributed rendering settings, where custom deformers may not be available on every machine. Baking is also extremely beneficial when using Maya's Cloth module. See the next chapter for more discussion on baking cloth.

Shot sculpting is the ability to edit the mesh after it has been baked. The most common use of shot sculpting is the fixing of kinks in the deformations. It can also be used to enhance a particular deformation.

Maya provides several methods of baking the mesh:

Open **mocapExercise9B.ma.** Here you will find Bobo's baked exported mesh. Now we can concentrate on shot sculpting the deformations without having to worry about the rest of the rig.

However, before we even begin, let's clean up the animation curves. Cleaning up the curves will significantly reduce the size of the file. There are two things we can do to clean up the curves: Delete all static channels (dead curves) and Simplify the curves. To delete all static channels, for example, the curves for the immobile vertices at the back of Bobo's head, choose Edit > Delete All by Type > Static Channels. To Simplify the curves, use the following MEL command:

```
//Simplify all animation curves with the Dense Data option
filterCurve-f simplify-timeTolerance .05 `ls -type animCurve`;
```

Mesk Baking Methods:

#	Method	How It Works	Shot Sculpting Control	File Size
	Bake Simulation with the Control Points option.	Creates translation animation curves for every vertex.	Ability to edit the animation curves of the vertices. Ultimate deformation control.	Large file sizes.
	Bake to Blendshape	Creates an in-between blendshape for every frame.	Ability to edit individual blendshape targets and blend them into the rest of the animation. Only useful for a handful of frames at a time. No per-vertex control. See the Cloth chapter for more information about this shot sculpting technique.	Large file sizes.
	Soft Body Particle Cache.	Creates a particle cache of the mesh, once it has been converted to a soft body.	None.	Smaller file sizes. Creates a separate cache file for every frame. Inefficient.
	Jiggle Cache	Creates a jiggle cache of a mesh with a jiggle deformer applied.	None.	Smallest file sizes. Creates a single cache file. Most efficient.

As you can see, the more shot sculpting control you have with a baking method, the higher the file size will be.

Open **mocapExercise9A.ma.** Here you will find Bobo rig with some mocap hooked up. We are going to bake 100 frames, 1250-1350, with the Bake Simulation with Control Points method. Select Bobo's top group, Bobo_Group. Then go to Edit > Keys > Bake Simulation > Options. Set the options to what they are in FIGURE 5.44 and press Bake.

Bobo's mesh will now be baked for those 100 frames. Animation curves will be created for every vertex for every frame. The next step would be to export Bobo_Group into a separate file, but I have already done this for you.

Once you have done these two things, the next step would be to save the file, but I have already done this for you.

Open **mocapExercise9C.ma.** This is the file with the cleaned up curves. Notice that this file is only 11 MB, while the previous file was 35 MB!

Play the timeline. Around frame 1300 you will notice a serious kink in both corners of Bobo's mouth as he smiles FIGURE 5.45.

Because this kink lasts for about 100 frames (no coincidence), it must be fixed at the vertex level so that our edits do not affect the rest of the mesh during animation. Basically, this means we will be setting keys on the problem vertices themselves.

Figure 5.44.

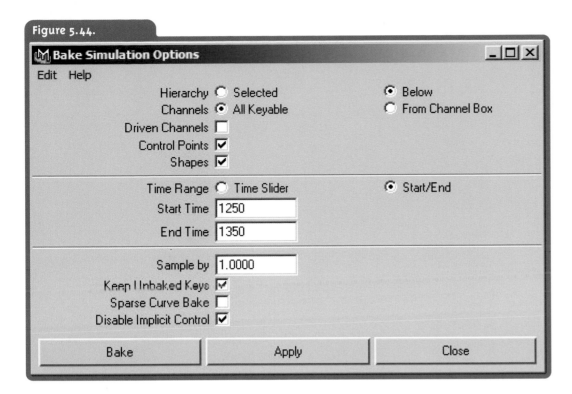

Bake Simulation Options

Edit   Help

Hierarchy ○ Selected   ● Below
Channels   ● All Keyable   ○ From Channel Box
Driven Channels ☐
Control Points ☑
Shapes ☑

Time Range ○ Time Slider   ● Start/End
Start Time 1250
End Time   1350

Sample by   1.0000
Keep Unbaked Keys ☑
Sparse Curve Bake ☐
Disable Implicit Control ☑

| Bake | Apply | Close |

Figure 5.45.

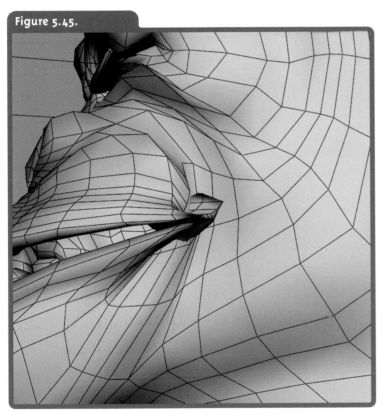

Select some vertices around Bobo's left mouth corner. Your selection should entirely encompass the kink. Create a Quick Select Set or shelf button so that you can reselect these exact vertices later. Open the Graph Editor. The curves for the selected vertices should look like FIGURE 5.46.

Do not be intimidated by all these keyframes. As you will see, the shot sculpting process is actually very straightforward.

Go to frame 1301. With the Sculpt Geometry Tool, smooth out the kink in the left corner of Bobo's mouth. When you have smoothed out the

kink, reselect the vertices that you have created a Quick Selection Set for previously and hit S to set a key. The Graph Editor should now look like FIGURE 5.47.

Now go to frame 1275 and do the same thing—smooth out the kink and set a key on those vertices. Do the same on frames 1271 and 1265.

Finally, simply delete all the keyframes that fall in-between the frames you've shot sculpted. Specifically, delete all keyframes between frame 1265 and 1271; 1271 and 1275; 1275 and 1301; 1301 and 1350. The new curves should look like FIGURE 5.48.

Play the animation. You will see that the kink in the left corner of Bobo's mouth is gone FIGURE 5.49.

This is a basic shot sculpting process. As mentioned previously, there are plenty of other methods of shot sculpting. Unfortunately, the best method of baking a mesh involves the use of a Maya plugin. We were unable to show you a plugin-based shot sculpting solution, but I can assure you, the principle is the same. Other methods are covered in more detail in the next chapter.

Open **mocapExercise9D.ma.** This file contains Bobo with the left corner of his mouth shot sculpted. See if you can shot sculpt the kink in the right corner of his mouth by yourself!

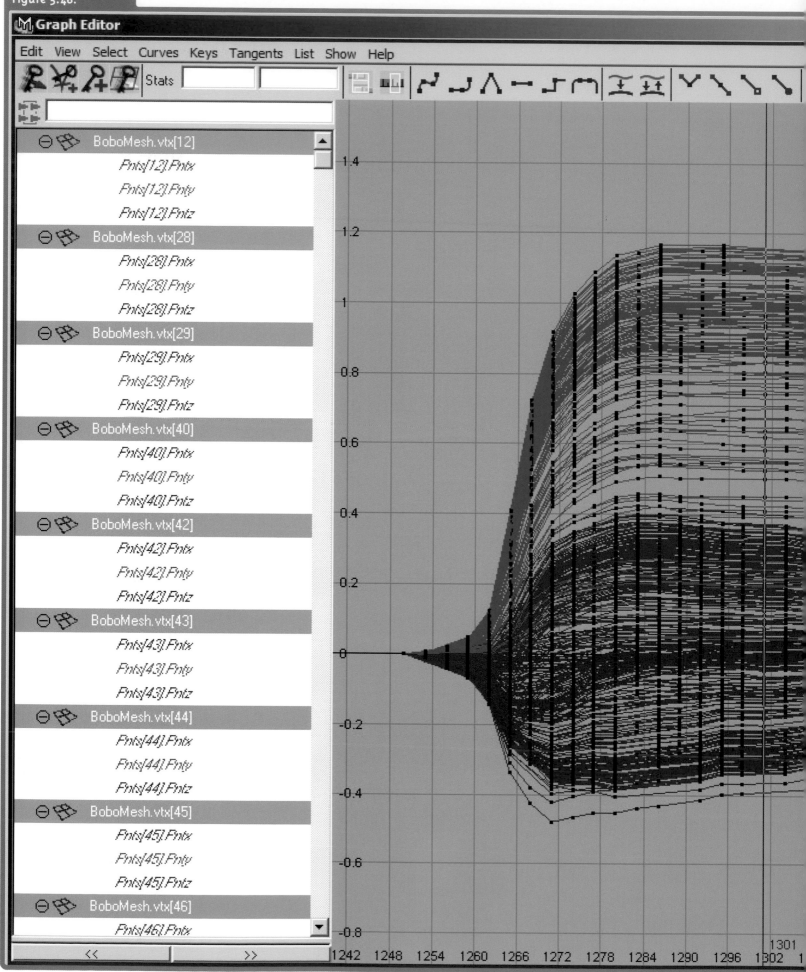

Figure 5.46.

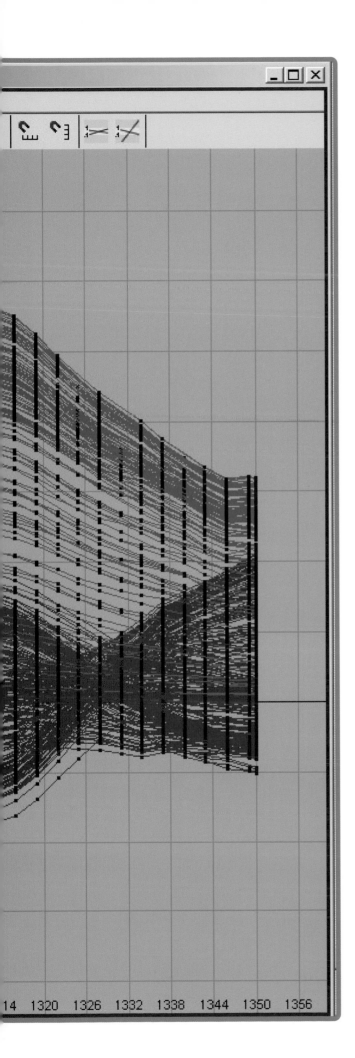

Figure 5.47.

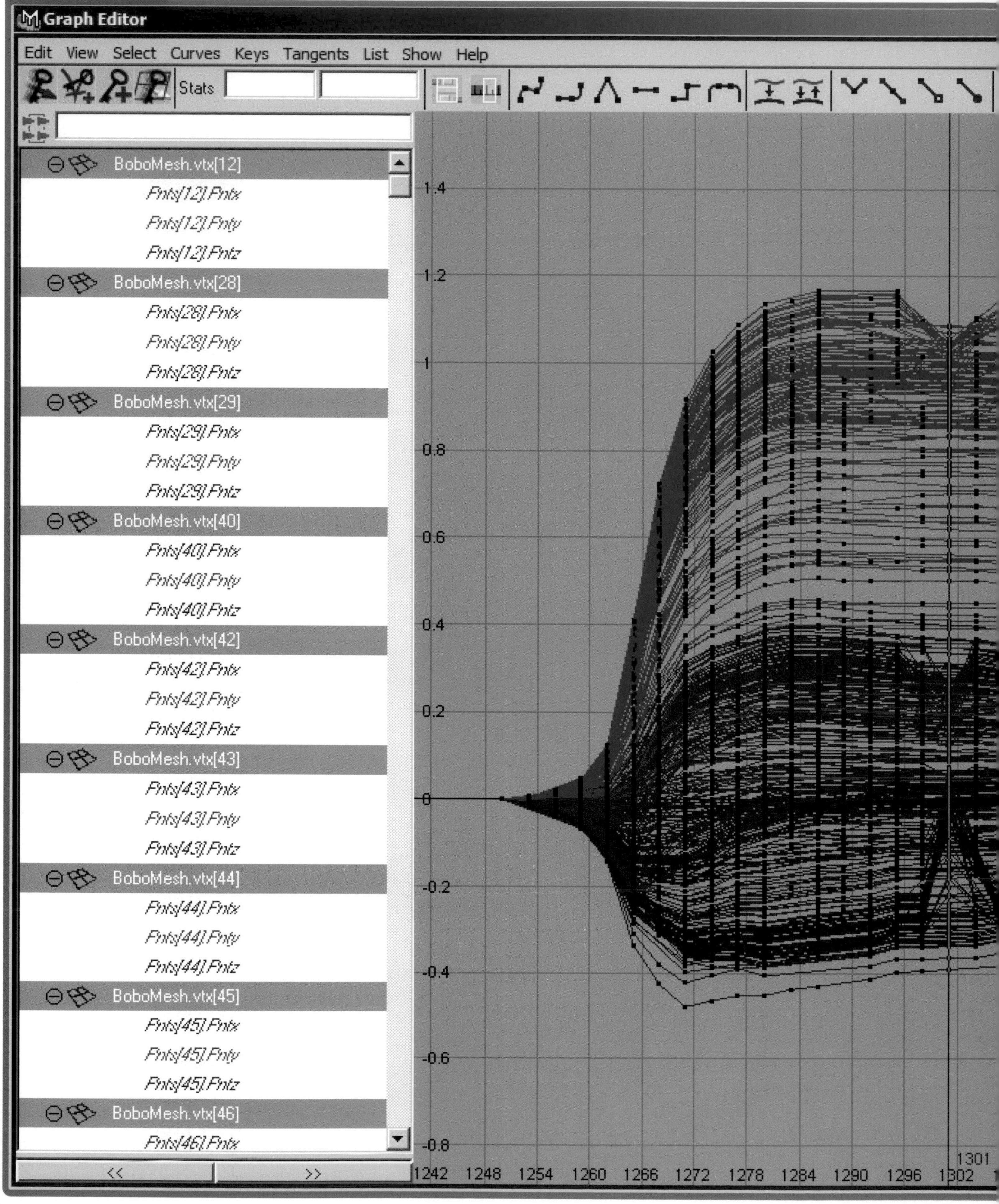
Graph Editor
Edit View Select Curves Keys Tangents List Show Help
Stats
BoboMesh.vtx[12]
Pnts[12].Pntx
Pnts[12].Pnty
Pnts[12].Pntz
BoboMesh.vtx[28]
Pnts[28].Pntx
Pnts[28].Pnty
Pnts[28].Pntz
BoboMesh.vtx[29]
Pnts[29].Pntx
Pnts[29].Pnty
Pnts[29].Pntz
BoboMesh.vtx[40]
Pnts[40].Pntx
Pnts[40].Pnty
Pnts[40].Pntz
BoboMesh.vtx[42]
Pnts[42].Pntx
Pnts[42].Pnty
Pnts[42].Pntz
BoboMesh.vtx[43]
Pnts[43].Pntx
Pnts[43].Pnty
Pnts[43].Pntz
BoboMesh.vtx[44]
Pnts[44].Pntx
Pnts[44].Pnty
Pnts[44].Pntz
BoboMesh.vtx[45]
Pnts[45].Pntx
Pnts[45].Pnty
Pnts[45].Pntz
BoboMesh.vtx[46]
Pnts[46].Pntx
1.4
1.2
1
0.8
0.6
0.4
0.2
0
-0.2
-0.4
-0.6
-0.8
1242 1248 1254 1260 1266 1272 1278 1284 1290 1296 1302
1301

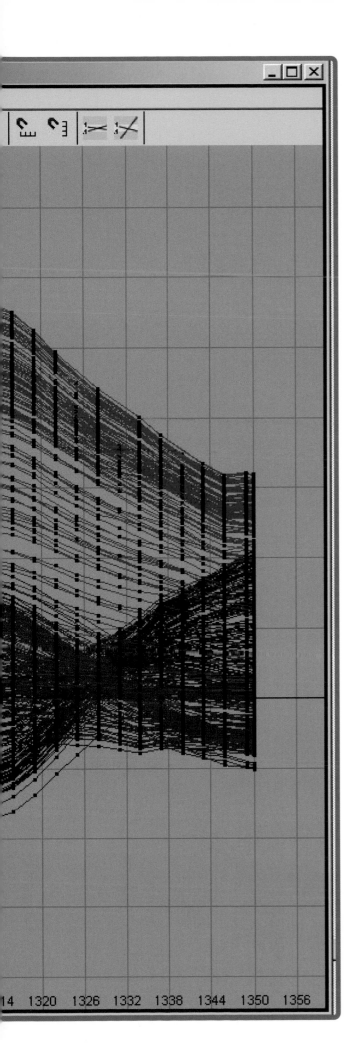

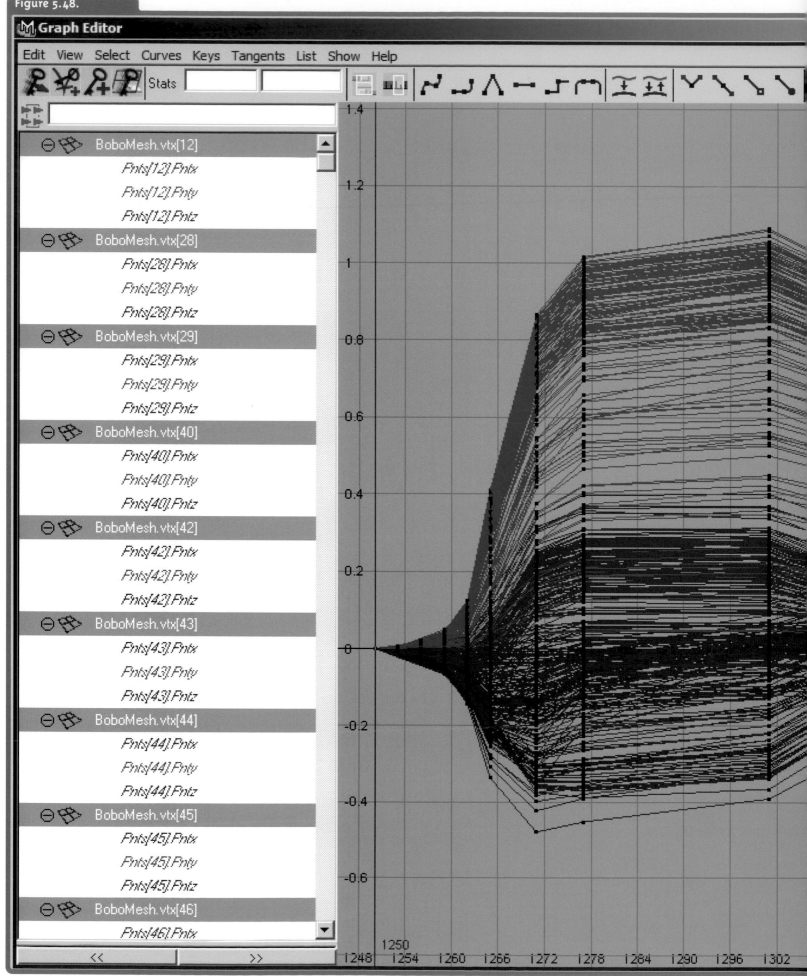

Figure 5.48.

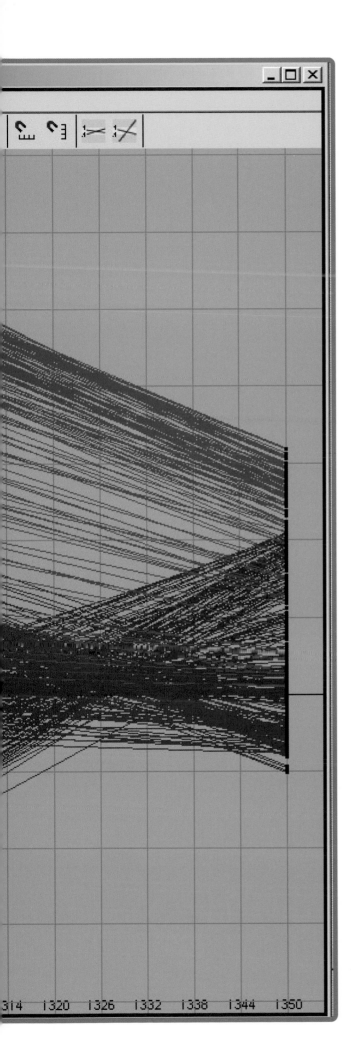

Figure 5.49.

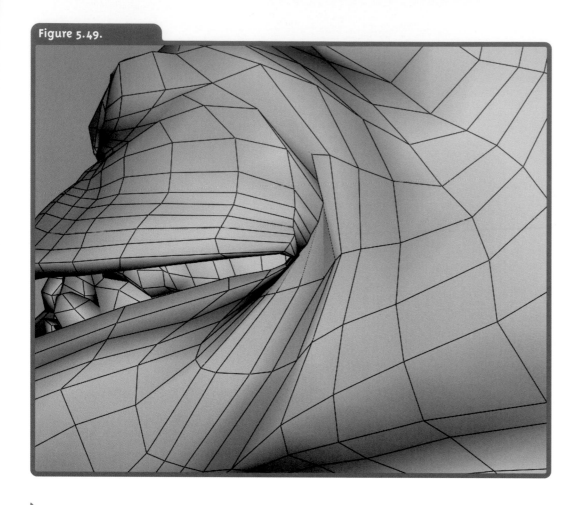

Incorporating the Head into the Body Rig:

Thus far, we've only been dealing with Bobo's static head. The final step in this entire setup is to transfer the animation from the static head to the actual head on Bobo's body (if he had a body). The actual head is the one that has rotations in the neck and is also the head that will be rendered. The best way to transfer the animation from the static head to the actual head is to pipe it through a blendshape node. Thankfully, in Maya, this process is really straightforward, because Maya allows blendshapes between groups, as long as the groups contain identical geometry.

Open **mocapExercise10A.ma.** Here you will find Bobo's actual head rigged below the grid with a simple FK setup. There are only 4 joints and 3 controls in this setup FIGURE 5.50.

The head mesh is smooth bound to the 2 neck joints and the head joint. All the face parts are smooth bound to the head joint only. FIGURE 5.51 shows the skin weights.

If you play the timeline, you'll notice that I animated the motion of the head (not very well, I admit). The head moves but the face does not. To incorporate the animation of the face on top of this movement of the head, we're going to use a blendshape node. Open the Hypergraph. Select Bobo_Group first, then shift-select Bobo_ActualHeadGroup. Notice that the two groups contain identical geometry, which is necessary for the blendshape to work FIGURE 5.52.

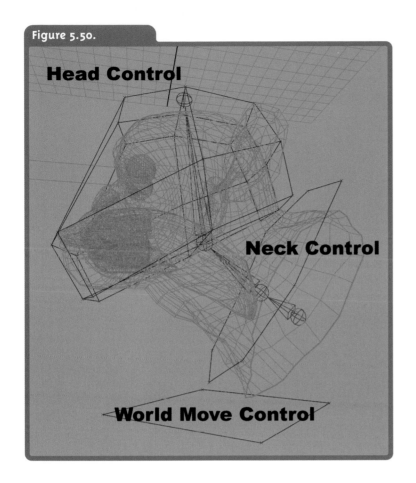

Figure 5.50.

Head Control

Neck Control

World Move Control

With the two groups selected, create a blendshape with the default options. In the blendshape node, turn the Bobo_Group blendshape to 1. Play the timeline. The animation from the face has been successfully transferred to the actual head rig that will be rendered.

To finish off this rig, I've added a Smooth Mesh on/off attribute that toggles the node state of the polySmooth nodes via set driven key. This Smooth Mesh attribute is located in the diamond-shaped World Move Control. Open mocapExercise10B.ma to play with Bobo's finished rig.

As you can see, we're done FIGURE 5.53!

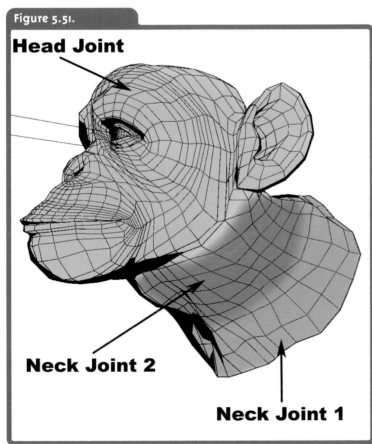

Figure 5.51.

Head Joint

Neck Joint 2

Neck Joint 1

Figure 5.52.

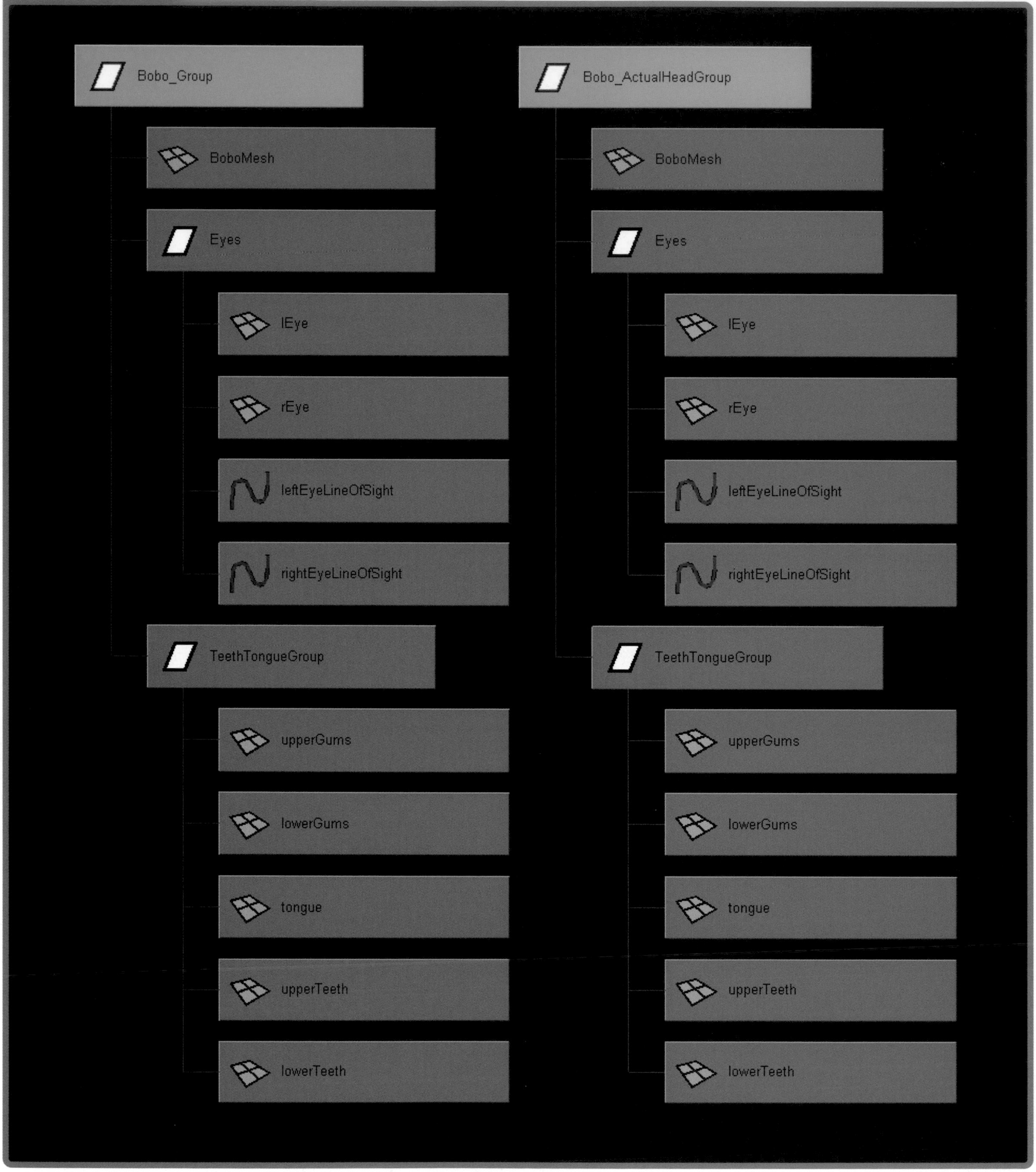
Bobo_Group
BoboMesh
Eyes
lEye
rEye
leftEyeLineOfSight
rightEyeLineOfSight
TeethTongueGroup
upperGums
lowerGums
tongue
upperTeeth
lowerTeeth
Bobo_ActualHeadGroup
BoboMesh
Eyes
lEye
rEye
leftEyeLineOfSight
rightEyeLineOfSight
TeethTongueGroup
upperGums
lowerGums
tongue
upperTeeth
lowerTeeth

Figure 5.53.

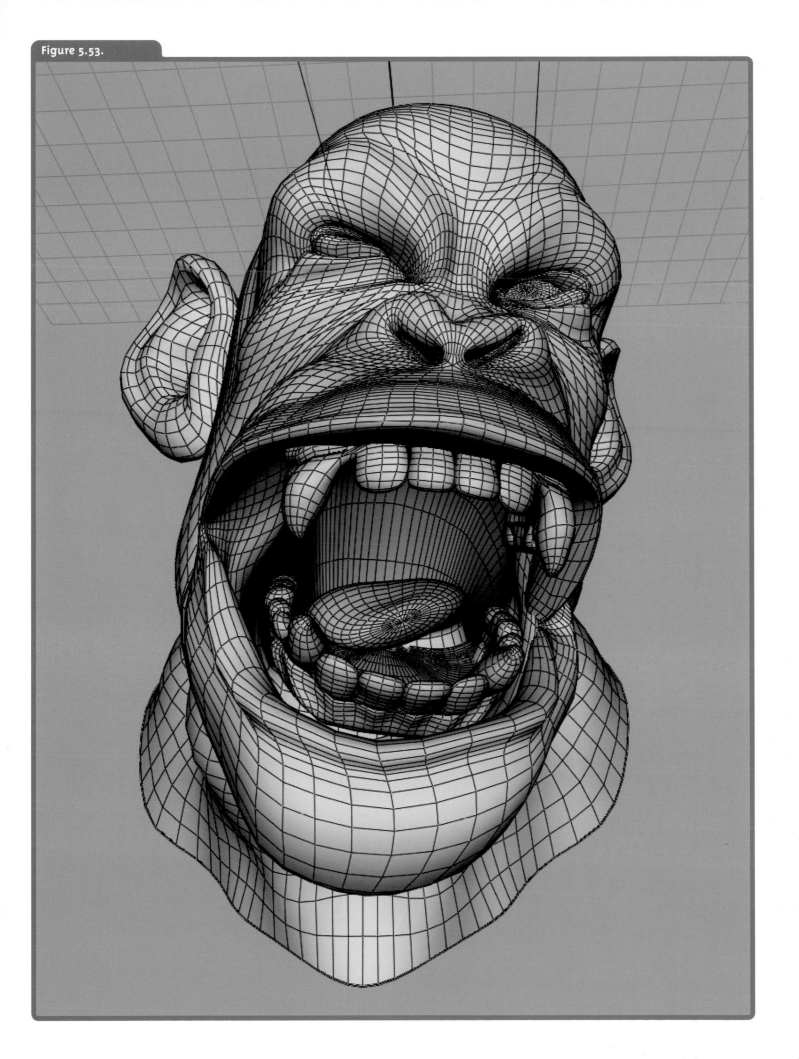

In this section, we're going to comment on the cgTkFacialMocapConnect script used to connect the mocap data locators to the facial muscles locators. This script is in the family of scripts where code generates other code. For an example of this script in use, please see the section on Connecting the Mocap Data to the Muscles.

For readabiliiy, the order of the procedures has been reversed. For example, the UI procedure would usually be the last, but here, it is the first.

The following help header explains in detail what the script does and how to use it.

```
Code
/*
SCRIPT:  cgTkFacialMocapConnect.mel
VERSION: 1.0

DESCRIPTION:

This script constrains multiple pairs of objects at once--all odd
selections to all even selections. It is useful when connecting motion
capture data to your rig. It works for both skeleton-to-skeleton and
locators-to-locators rigs. In other words, it works for both orient and
point constraints.

The script will output the commands to the script editor, allowing you
to create a shelf button for later use. You can also choose to create a
shelf button immediately.

The output looks something like this:

        //CONSTRAIN START
        //Frame check
        if (`currentTime -q` != 1) error "You must be at frame 1.";
        catch(`pointConstraint -mo locator4 nurbsSphere4`);
        catch(`pointConstraint -mo locator3 nurbsSphere3`);
        catch(`pointConstraint -mo locator2 nurbsSphere2`);
        catch(`pointConstraint -mo locator1 nurbsSphere1`);
        //CONSTRAIN END

To ensure that all connections and disconnection are made on the same
keyframe, I have included a frame check that hard-codes the current
frame into the command. All connections and disconnection should always
be made in the neutral pose, usually at frame 1.

HOW TO USE:

Execute 'cgTkFacialMocapConnect' to bring up the UI.

Orient Constrain with Offset:

        Usually used for a skeleton-to-skeleton mocap rig.
        One by one, select the mocap joint first and the corresponding
rig joint second. You can have as many pairs as you need--the script will
orient constrain with offset all odd selections to all even selections.
Press 'Orient Constrain with Offset'.

Point Constrain with Offset:

Usually used for a locators-to-locators mocap rig or to constrain the
root joint of a skeleton-to-skeleton rig. One by one, select the mocap
```

```
data locator first and the corresponding face rig locator second. You
can have as many pairs as you need--the script will point constrain with
offset all odd selections to all even selections. Press 'Point Constrain
with Offset'.

Delete Constraints:

        Select all the objects that you want to delete constraints
on.

        Press 'Delete Constraints'.
*/
```

This is the UI procedure. The UI for cgTkFacialMocapConnect looks like FIGURE 5.54.

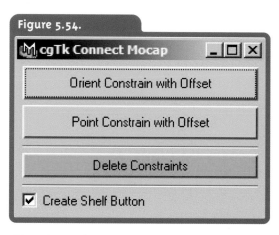

Figure 5.54.

This UI is very basic. It contains 3 buttons and a checkbox, arranged in a columnLayout.

```
Code
////////////////////////////
//UI
global proc cgTkFacialMocapConnect() {

        if (`window -query -exists cgTkFacialMocapConnectUI`) {
                deleteUI cgTkFacialMocapConnectUI;
                windowPref -remove cgTkFacialMocapConnectUI;
        }

        window
                -title "cgTk Connect Mocap"
                -w 230
                -resizeToFitChildren true
                -sizeable true
                cgTkFacialMocapConnectUI;

columnLayout -adjustableColumn true -rowSpacing 5 ...
                                        -columnOffset "both" 5;
```

Notice that the commands for both the Orient Constrain button and the Point Constrain button, are calling the same procedure, cgTkFacialMocapConstrain, but with a different argument for the constraint type.

```
Code
button
        -bgc 0.7 1.0 0.7 //light green
        -h 30
        -l "Orient Constrain with Offset"
        -c "cgTkFacialMocapConstrain ...
                (`checkBox -q -v shelfButtonCheckBox`, \"orient\")"
        -ann "Orient constrains (with offset) every odd selection...
                                to every even selection.";
```

```
button
        -bgc 0.7 1.0 0.7 //light green
        -h 30
        -l "Point Constrain with Offset"
        -c "cgTkFacialMocapConstrain ...
                (`checkBox -q -v shelfButtonCheckBox`, \"point\")"
        -ann "Point constrains (with offset) every odd selection ...
                                        to every even selection.";

separator;

button
        -bgc 1.0 0.7 0.7 //light red
        -l "Delete Constraints"
        -c "cgTkFacialMocapDeleteConstraints
                        (`checkBox -q -v shelfButtonCheckBox`)"
        -ann "Deletes constraints on all selected objects.";

separator;

checkBox
        -v on
        -l "Create Shelf Button"
        -align "left"
        shelfButtonCheckBox;

showWindow cgTkFacialMocapConnectUI;

}
```

This is the constrain procedure. It takes two arguments: whether the user wants a shelf button to be created and what kind of constraints the user wants to create.

```
//////////////////////////
//Constrain proc
global proc string cgTkFacialMocapConstrain
(
 int $shelfButton, //on/off
 string $constraintType     // "point" or "orient"
)
{
 string $selection[] = `ls -sl`;

 //Error checking
 if (size($selection) < 2) error "You must select at least 2 objects";
```

Here the modulus (%) operator is used to determine the remainder. It basically says that if the remainder of the number of selected objects divided by 2 is not 0, then it must not be an even number of objects. If so, an error is returned.

```
if ((size($selection) % 2) != 0)
        error "You must select an even number of objects";

//Declare the command string
string $command = "\n//CONSTRAIN START\n";
```

Here the frame check procedure is called and the resulting string is appended to the command string. The += operator is used to append a string to an existing string. You can read it as: $string = ($string + "new string");

```
//Frame check
$command += cgTkFacialMocapFrameCheck();
```

This is the main for loop. As you can see, the counter is incremented by 2, not by 1. Remember, we are constraining pairs of objects, odd selections to even selections.

```
for ($i = 0; $i < size($selection); $i = $i + 2)
{
        string $oddSelection = $selection[$i];
        string $evenSelection = $selection[$i + 1];
```

The magic happens here. The constraint command is constructed. The type of constraints, Orient or Point, is determined by the $constraintType argument. Also notice we are using the catch statement. This way, if some of the objects have been renamed or deleted when these command are executed, Maya will skip those objects and not stop the execution of the script.

```
//Append to the command string
$command += ("catch(`" + $constraintType + ...
  "Constraint -mo " + $oddSelection + " " + $evenSelection + "`);\n");
        }

//Append to the command string
$command += "//CONSTRAIN END\n\n";
```

Evaluating the command string is the same as executing its contents. Therefore, at this point, the objects are constrained.

```
//Connect mocap
eval($command);
```

The textToShelf command is used to send the command string to a shelf button.

```
//If shelf button is on
if ($shelfButton == 1) textToShelf "Constrain" $command;
```

The command string is printed to the Script Editor and returned by the procedure as well.

```
//Confirmation
print $command;
print "Objects constrained successfully! ...
                                Open Script Editor for details...";

return $command;

}
```

This is the delete constraints procedure. It has one argument; whether the user wants to create a shelf button or not. This procedure is very similar to the Constrain procedure above.

```
//////////////////////////
//Delete Constraints proc
global proc string cgTkFacialMocapDeleteConstraints(int $shelfButton)
{
        //Get selection
        string $selection[] = `ls -sl`;

        //Declare the command string
        string $command = "\n//DELETE CONSTRAINTS START\n";

        //Frame check
        $command += cgTkFacialMocapFrameCheck();
```

The bulk of the command is constructed in this for loop.

```
for ($object in $selection)
{
  //Append to the command string
  $command += ("catch(`delete -constraints " + $object + "`);\n");

}

//Append to the command string
$command += "//DELETE CONSTRAINTS END\n\n";

//Delete constraints
eval($command);

//If shelf button is on
if ($shelfButton == 1) textToShelf "Delete Constraints" $command;

//Confirmation
print $command;
print "Constraints deleted successfully! ...
                                Open Script Editor for details...";

return $command;;

}
```

This is the frame check procedure. It is used to ensure that the user always connects the mocap in the neutral pose, usually at frame 1. The procedure constructs an if command and returns it to the above two procedures that use it.

```
//////////////////////////
//Frame Check proc
global proc string cgTkFacialMocapFrameCheck()
{
  //Declare the command string
  string $command = "//Frame check\n";
```

The current frame is determined and stored in the $frame variable. Then the if command is constructed. It basically says that if the current frame is not what it was when the objects were originally constrained, then the user must return to that frame first and try again.

```
//Frame check
int $frame = `currentTime -q`;
$command += ("if (`currentTime -q` != " + $frame + ") ...
              error \"You must be at frame " + $frame + ".\";\n");

return $command;

}
```

The main thing to notice about this simple script is that the use of the UI is optional. The procedures do not necessarily rely on the UI to get the information they need—the arguments could be typed in manually and the procedures will still work. When the UI and the implementation procedures are completely separated, the implementation procedures could potentially be used elsewhere, not just in the context of this script.

Final Thoughts:

We've come a very long way. While you should now have a thorough understanding of how to rig a face for motion capture, realize that the workflow I described in this chapter is but one out of a multitude of available options.

You already know how to do all that was described: constraining, using influence objects, using sculpt deformers, etc. A good rigger is able to combine all these different tools to create a *workflow*. In this way a rigger is like a chef. A chef uses different ingredients to create a dish. But only when the *recipe* for the dish is written down can the dish be mass produced.

Perhaps, in the future, a television show will emerge called *Iron Rigger*, on which, master riggers from around the world will compete each week to rig a secret...something. Maybe then, the world will come to appreciate the fascinating, obscure art of rigging. We can dream...

On the DVD:

Be sure to watch all playblasts and renders of Bobo.

For an informative look at the entire motion capture session, please view the featurette on the DVD.

Also included is a test render from an excellent unrealized project—a computer animated version of Frank Miller's Sin City, starring Andy Serkis as Marv! This project was directed by Remington Scott. I used a similar rig for Marv as I did for Bobo.

Acknowledgements:

At this time, all of us at CG Toolkit would like to personally thank everyone involved in this chapter for their generosity and hard work.

Specifically:

- Remington Scott — Motion Capture Session Director
- Eric Aten — Actor
- Glen Southern — Texture Artist

Motion Analysis Corporation - www.motionanalysis.com

- Matt Bauer - General Manager
- Christopher Johnson - Motion Capture Technician
- James Bowers - Production Assistant
- Larry Jacks - Account Executive
- Anet Hambarsumian - Post Production Manager
- Bo Wright - Motion Capture Technician
- Kristopher Evans - Motion Capture Technician
- Mario Perez - Motion Capture Technician

Thank you all!

Chapter 6
Finishing Techniques

In a typical animated production, almost anything can (and usually does) happen to a character. It would be an exercise in futility to attempt to account for every possible action a character might take. As a technical director, your rigs should focus on those actions which are most common. Actions such as raising an arm, bending an elbow or delivering dialog. That being said, situations will arise where a character must be capable of doing something completely unusual.

This is especially true of cartoon characters who are routinely dropped, punched, poked or abused in some manner. In the majority of cases, these actions require little or no extra attention. But every once in a while, a shot will arise which requires some tweaking of the deformations or custom rigging.

Consider this example: Two star-crossed lovers are sharing a quiet moment. The scene's climax depicts an intimate moment where the man caresses the women's cheek with his finger. To draw the audience into the scene, this shot would likely make use of an extreme close-up. With the female's face in full view, it might look strange if the man's finger did not create a slight indentation as it slides down her cheek. It's not hard to imagine a scenario where a character's mesh must undergo some type of unexpected deformation.

In addition to character work, there are countless cases where background props will require special tweaks to react to the action of a particular shot. Consider this scenario: A fat CG-animator comes home from working on a computer all day and plops into his sofa. The sofa squishes under the weight of the character and forms several wrinkles and folds. Displaying this type of interaction between the character and the couch will help sell the weight of the character.

This type of 'finishing' work, as it is known as, while not very glamorous, is quite important and requires its own workflows. This chapter is a collection of techniques that you may find useful for dealing with these not-so-odd situations that seem to arise all too often. We will also explore the process of finishing a character and preparing it for rendering. In a nutshell, this chapter is about fitting everything together and adding the finishing touches.

More specifically, we will be covering:

- The Myth of the 'Perfect' Rig
- Baking Vertex Animation / Shot Sculpting
- Deformation Tweaking Techniques
- Preparation/Simulation of a Shot with the Minx
- A Word About Fur/Cloth Interaction

The Myth of the Perfect Rig:

Any experienced character rigger can tell you that there is no such thing as a 'perfect' rig. A rig that behaves perfectly in every situation is, quite honestly, impossible. That being said, a rig *can* and should do a pretty good job of sticking together through most maneuvers.

Recognizing that a 'perfect' rig is nothing more than a myth is an important concept. Knowing this, it should be obvious that situations *will* arise where a rig requires some modification in order to perform a specific task. This is often referred to as 'shot rigging' because these modifications typically correspond with a specific shot in an animated production. Perhaps more important than recognizing this necessity is knowing *how* to implement it. Situations will arise where a character will be asked to do something that your 'general' rig is not capable of performing. The following list demonstrates the most common solutions to these problems:

Update the Rig File: If the fix is something simple, like adding a new facial blendshape, then it might be best to implement this by simply updating the rig files. The addition of the new blendshape will not damage the existing animation and shouldn't present any further difficulties.

Create a Shot-Specific Rig: If the change is quite drastic, like a character losing an arm, then it should be implemented in a completely new rig file. Depending on the nature of the fix, this usually requires the creation of a new animation and deformation rig file. In some cases, it may only require a change to one or the other. For example, imagine a shot where a character is blasted by an explosion. We want the post-explosion character's hair to be blown back and covered in soot (in true cartoon fashion). These changes could be implemented in the render/deformation rig and do not require changes to the animation rig.

Shot Sculpt: Some shots require a character to interact with the scene in such a way as to cause unexpected deformations. It's not uncommon for a character to be poked, squished, or pushed around. In these cases, it might be best to manually sculpt the deformations by hand. This is often referred to as 'shot sculpting'. This is covered in detail in the next section.

Updating or creating a new rig file is usually the preferred method for adding shot-specific deformations to a character. Sometimes, even after tweaking some deformations for a specific shot, you may find that there are a few vertices that just won't behave FIGURE 6.1. You could always create a series of blendshapes (or some other elaborate combination of deformers) to fix these glitches, but wouldn't it be nice to just manually grab the offending vertices and push them around? This is what shot sculpting is all about; gaining absolute control over every vertex on the deforming mesh.

Using a Finishing Pipeline:

Shot sculpting is part of a larger idea commonly referred to as a finishing pipeline. Quite simply, this is the last stage of preparation that every model will go through before being lit and rendered. You might be wondering, what does a finishing pipeline *actually* do to prepare a mesh for being rendered? Is this stage even necessary?

The necessity of this final step depends, in large part, on the particulars of the production. After learning about what can be done at the finishing stage, it should be apparent whether or not your next production will benefit from it. Basically, the finishing stage involves baking the animation of the vertices into a cache of sorts. This has several advantages, the most important of which is a major decrease in the complexity of the scene file.

When all of the meshes in your scene are baked, it means that their deformations are being driven by a single input. This is a *huge* advantage. The joints, blendshapes, lattices, clusters, cloth solvers, muscle simulations or whatever else might have been affecting the mesh are no longer necessary. Once a mesh is baked, all of it's history can and should be removed from the scene file. Usually, this will leave you with nothing but the mesh itself and a single input node FIGURE 6.2. This makes the lighting and rendering phase much smoother.

Figure 6.2.

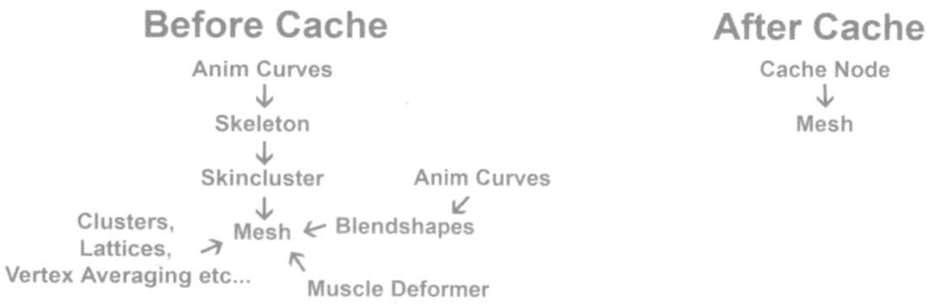

Before Cache
Anim Curves
↓
Skeleton
↓
Skincluster   Anim Curves
↓   ↙
Clusters,   Mesh ← Blendshapes
Lattices,   ↗   ↖
Vertex Averaging etc...   Muscle Deformer

After Cache
Cache Node
↓
Mesh

Decreasing scene complexity may be reason enough to adopt a mesh baking solution, but the advantages don't stop there. In a fully-fleshed finishing pipeline, there exists not only a method of caching the deformations, but also the ability to tweak the vertices and save the results into the cache (rather than adding additional history). This allows absolute control over the final deformations without the need to add complexity to the scene. We are effectively trading the flexibility of history-creating, deformer/dynamics-driven deformations for the speed and accuracy of per-point, cache-driven deformations.

There can be disadvantages to creating deformations in this manner. Obviously, it would be an exercise in futility to attempt to animate a mesh using shot sculpting exclusively. Maya's deformers are designed

Figure 6.1.

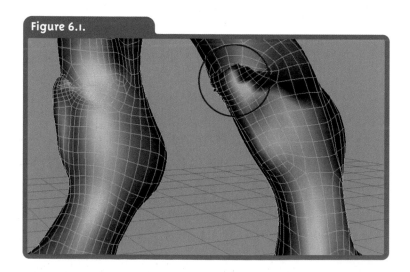

to affect hundreds of vertices in a predictable and adjustable manner. Shot sculpting is precise, but prohibitively slow and tedious. The finishing stage should be reserved for only very minute tweaks (like popping vertices, or minor interpenetrations). It should not be relied upon to fix sloppy skin weights or poorly solved cloth simulations.

Shot sculpting is a great tool for tweaking, but using it as a crutch for poorly designed deformations is a sure way to guarantee headaches.

The following table demonstrates several different methods of baking mesh animation:

Method	How to Use	Pros/Cons
Bake Simulation	Select the mesh and choose Edit > Keys > Bake Simulation. Check the control points option. FIGURE 6.3	This method sets a keyframe on the translation of every vertex for each frame. This produces extremely large scene files and is prohibitively slow for caching purposes. While it might not be useful for caching, it can be used for shot sculpting. By setting keyframes on the vertices, the mesh may be tweaked as needed. Once shot sculpted, the mesh may be cached once again using a more efficient technique. This method is covered in detail in the previous chapter where we use it to smooth the deformations on a motion captured facial rig.

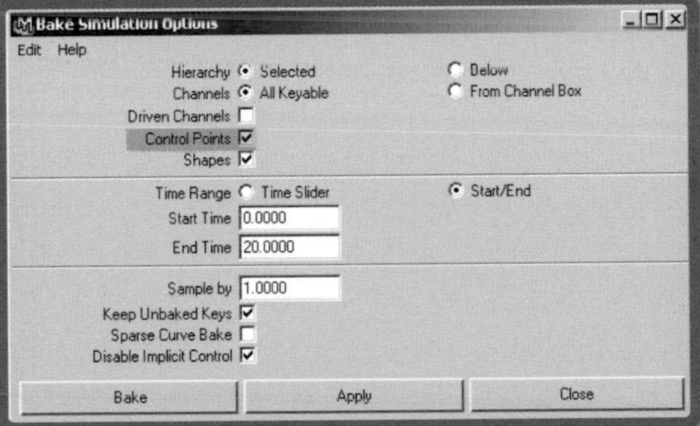

Figure 6.3.

Method	How to Use	Pros/Cons
Blendshape Method	Duplicate the mesh on each frame to produce a series of in-between blendshapes. Usually automated by a script. FIGURE 6.4 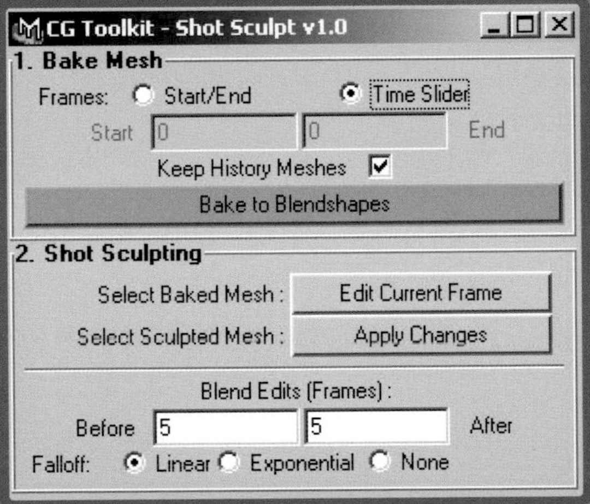	The blendshape method is demonstrated in detail later in this chapter. The blendshape method produces moderate file sizes that may suit your caching needs (although more efficient techniques exist). The main advantage of the blendshape method is that the deformations are stored in the scene file itself. This technique is best reserved for pipelines that occasionally need a caching solution and do not want to worry about external cache file dependencies.

Figure 6.4.

Method	How to Use	Pros/Cons
Particle Disk Cache	Convert the mesh to a soft body so that each vertex has a corresponding particle. Then save a particle disk cache. FIGURE 6.5	This method is rarely used. It provides absolutely no method of shot sculpting the deformations and relies on keeping the mesh as a soft body. It creates an individual cache file for each frame (.pdc). In a nutshell, this technique works, but is far from ideal.

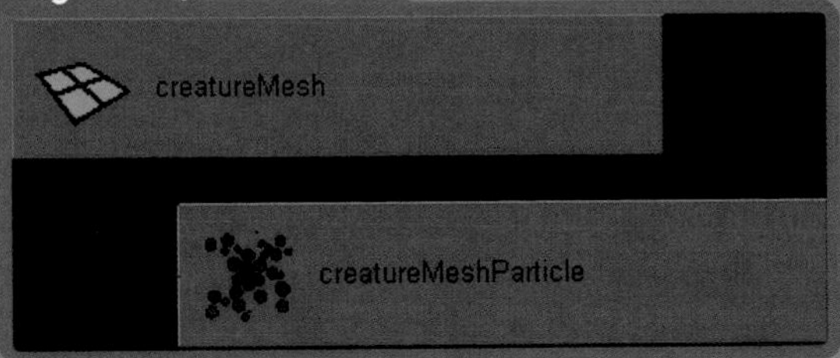

Figure 6.4.

Method	How to Use		Pros/Cons
Jiggle Cache	Add a jiggle deformer to the mesh and then use the jiggle deformer's cache. FIGURE 6.6		This method is useful for caching deformations. It creates a single cache file (.mcj). It doesn't provide a method of shot sculpting, but the cache file is much more efficient than any other native caching techniques. A cache of about 150 frames on a mesh of about 10k vertices will produce a cache file of roughly 200mb. Still quite large, but it can be read at a reasonable speed.
3rd Party / In-House Plugin	Plugins typically bake the mesh into a single binary cache file. FIGURE 6.7		The best solution for caching deformations is through the use of a proprietary plug-in. Because all of the native Maya techniques have severe limitations (usually related to speed and efficiency), this is the perfect opportunity for Maya's API to be put to work. The 'ideal' vertex caching plug-in is discussed below.

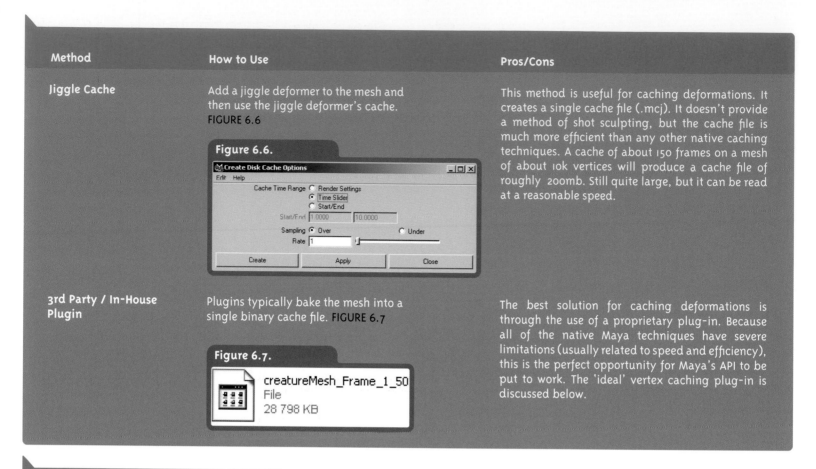

Figure 6.6.

Figure 6.7.

creatureMesh_Frame_1_50
File
28 798 KB

The 'Ideal' Vertex Caching Solution:

Normally, we don't discuss particular solutions unless we can prove their usefulness with an example. Unfortunately, we can't include a working example of a vertex caching plug-in, so instead we will explain how the ideal solution should behave (if you were to make it yourself). I think it is important to provide you with an understanding of what an ideal vertex caching solution should be like.

Firstly, this solution should take the form of a compiled Maya plug-in and not a MEL script. As seasoned TDs can attest, MEL is a superb tool for automating processes, especially those that must be repeated many times over. That being said, MEL is still an *interpreted* language and as such, its execution speed can be severely inhibited to the point of making it unsuitable for some applications. When it comes to vertex caching, MEL is simply not 'up-to-par'. To really get serious about caching deformations, you must use a compiled C++ application written with Maya's API.

Most studios that use Maya as the backbone of their 3d animation pipeline already have an in-house solution for vertex caching (and sometimes shot sculpting too). Typically, these solutions implement the following features:

A Simple, Efficient, Binary File Format: The mesh cache file format should be as simple as possible. All it needs to store are the positions (3 doubles) of each vertex on the mesh at each frame. Any data not related to the motion of the vertices would be superfluous and should be excluded in the interest of keeping the file as efficient as possible. If you give the file a header, be sure to include a version number so that future changes to the format can be handled smoothly.

Flexibility: The ability to manage the cache files by adding/removing and blending caches can be very useful. Many vertex caching solutions allow for multiple caches to be blended into a single mesh and controlled with weight maps (to specify which part of the mesh is affected by what cache). This is useful for cloth simulations where, for example, a sleeve animation from one cache may be blended onto the shirt from another cache.

Shot Sculpting: There should exist a method of tweaking the vertices on a specific frame and blending those tweaks into surrounding frames with user-definable falloff. Shot sculpting can be achieved by first caching the deformations, then applying animated deformers to the cached mesh (as needed to fix any trouble spots). Once the fixes are made, the mesh may be cached again to bake all of the shot sculpting back into the cache. Again, it is important to note that shot sculpting should not be relied on to fix large problems with the deformations.

A Deformer-Driven Connection: Usually the plug-in takes the form of a custom deformer that is applied to the mesh and connected to an external cache file. The deformer reads the vertex positions from the cache file and then drives the displacement of the mesh.

I have seen many different vertex caching plug-ins, but they all share basically two features, a simple file format and a method of plugging the position data into the mesh (usually via a deformer). While I have yet to find a commercially available plug-in based solution for vertex caching *and* shot sculpting, I have found a few solutions that may be of interest (opposite page):

VertexCache by www.imaginecube.com: This plug-in costs a measly $79 USD and provides a method of caching deformations. In my personal tests, the plug-in performed quite well and cached a large mesh over hundreds of frames without a hitch. It does not, however, have any shot sculpting features. A demo of the plug-in is available from the website.

cMuscleSystem by www.cometdigital.com: In addition to it's amazing muscle-skinning toolset, this plug-in provides a method of caching meshes to an external ASCII file. In addition to the caching feature, this plug-in includes many other useful deformation tools.

Because the 'ideal' finishing pipeline tools are not (currently) commercially available, individual studios have resorted to developing their own solutions. As expensive and annoying as that may be, in-house solutions have the advantage of being tailor-made to suit your particular production.

To get you started in designing a custom-built finishing pipeline, we have created a MEL script that implements some basic shot sculpting functionality. The script is certainly powerful enough to be used on it's own, although it's MEL-based nature prevents it from being a truly production-level tool. MEL is a great tool for rapid prototyping and proof of concept. With that in mind, consider our shot sculpting script as a stepping stone to a fully featured API-based plug-in.

A Sample Shot Sculpting / Finishing Tool:

Let's take a quick look at how the cgTkShotSculpt.mel script works. With the script installed, execute cgTkShotSculpt from the command line to bring-up the interface. As you can see, it is divided into two sections: baking/caching and shot sculpting FIGURE 6.8.

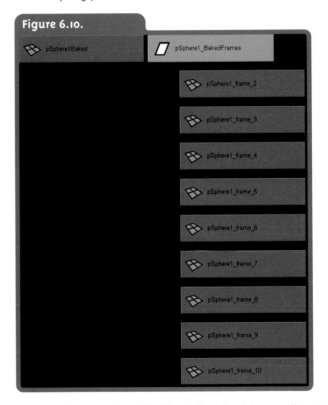

Figure 6.8.

The first step is used to bake a mesh's deformations into a blendshape node. The user selects a mesh object (only polygons supported), specifies the frame range and hits the bake button. The script executes the cgTkBakeToBlendshape procedure which does the following:

1. The scene is played-back from the start to the end frame (as specified by the user). At each frame, the mesh is duplicated FIGURE 6.9.

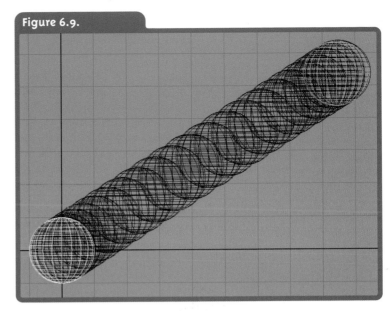

Figure 6.9.

2. If 'Keep History Meshes' is checked, the script places all the duplicates into a group FIGURE 6.10 , otherwise each mesh/frame is added as an in-between blendshape and deleted before the loop continues to the next frame. Deleting the meshes as you go uses far less RAM, but disables the shot sculpting features.

Figure 6.10.

> pSphere1Baked   pSphere1_BakedFrames
> pSphere1_frame_2
> pSphere1_frame_3
> pSphere1_frame_4
> pSphere1_frame_5
> pSphere1_frame_6
> pSphere1_frame_7
> pSphere1_frame_8
> pSphere1_frame_9
> pSphere1_frame_10

3. When the procedure is finished, the blendshape will contain a target in-between shape for each frame. To animate the mesh, the weight value of the in-between shape is keyframed FIGURE 6.11. Finally, the original mesh is hidden leaving only the baked mesh visible.

Figure 6.11.

INPUTS
meshBakedBlendshape
tweak2
          Envelope 1
     pSphere1_frame_24   0.391304

Now that the mesh has been effectively 'baked' into blendshapes, the other deformers that were previously driving the deformations may be removed from the scene. When saved, the scene file size will be noticeably larger, indicating that the deformations are indeed stored explicitly.

This is how the blendshape baking method works. As we've already discussed, it's not the best method of caching deformations, but it does have a few advantages. It keeps the cache data in the scene file itself (eliminating the need for external dependencies) and it allows for some post-baking, editing of the mesh (by utilizing the history connections to the blendshape targets). This is important because it enables some basic shot sculpting functionality.

When the history meshes are not deleted (ie. when the checkbox is checked), the original target shapes still exist in the scene after the baking is finished. Any edits to these meshes will propagate through the blendshape node into the baked mesh itself. If we were to compare this type of functionality to the 'ideal' shot sculpting solution outlined earlier, the history meshes are basically like the cache file itself. They house the deformations that are being applied to the mesh via the blendshape deformer (albeit in a fairly inefficient way). The shot sculpting features of this script affect the target meshes in the same way that the ideal solution would affect a cache file. Keep this in mind while we continue to explore our MEL prototype.

Once the mesh has been baked, the shot sculpting features can be accessed in the bottom section of the UI. The shot sculpting workflow goes like this:

1. The user scrubs to the frame where they wish to fix a deformation. They select the baked mesh and click the Edit Current Frame button. This creates a duplicate of the mesh to use for modeling fixes FIGURE 6.12.

2. Once the fixes are modeled into the duplicate mesh, the user selects the duplicate and clicks the Apply Changes button.

3. This button calls the 'cgTkCompareMesh' procedure which compares the fixed mesh with the baked mesh (at the same frame). The positions of the vertices are compared, and any displacements are recorded into a float array (which acts like a vector array) FIGURE 6.13.

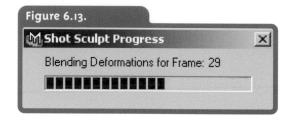

Figure 6.13.

4. This float array is passed to the cgTkDeformMesh procedure which applies these displacements to a history mesh (the mesh that is the target shape for the current frame). The magnitude of the displacements are adjusted by a falloff parameter that is specified by the user. This allows the tweaks to the blended into the surrounding frames.

The effect of the fourth step is that the fixes that were modeled into the duplicate, magically appear on the baked mesh itself. This happens because the displacements that were made to the duplicate mesh, were applied to the original target shape that is being fed through the blendshape node back into the baked mesh itself. That may seem like a convoluted method of editing the baked mesh, but what's interesting here is that since these fixes are recorded as an array of displacements, they can be blended into the surrounding frames! This means that you only have to sculpt the fix for a single frame, and then either add that fix to multiple frames or blend it with a falloff (either linear or exponential).

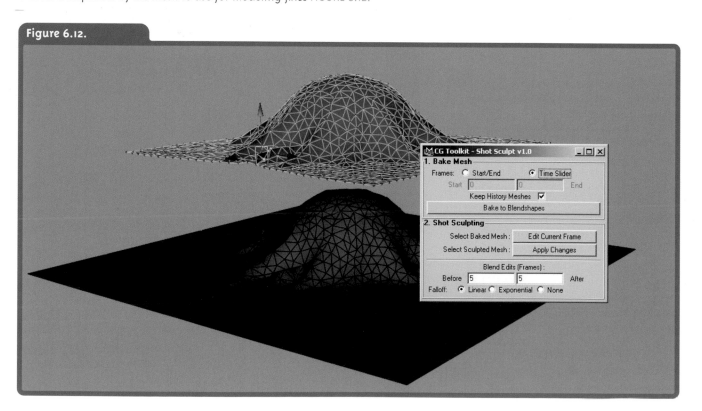

Figure 6.12.

The ability to blend deformation fixes across multiple frames is what shot sculpting is all about. In a real production, there will be plenty of instances where a character's skin pinchs, warps or skews for a few frames. In these cases, it can be extremely difficult to model the fix on each frame while maintaining some kind of uniformity. That is, modeling the fix manually for each frame tends to create 'wobbly' looking vertices due to the small differences in each frame. Obviously, having some method of applying the same fix across multiple frames would be preferable.

Having seen the benefit of blendable shot sculpting, let's discuss where the MEL script could be improved. The MEL script has two problems that prevent it from being an ideal solution:

1. It's slow. Blending a deformation fix across multiple frames brings-up a progress window that can come to a crawl as the number of vertices on the mesh surpasses any appreciable amount. For example, it can take a matter of minutes to blend a single fix across 20 frames on a mesh with 3k vertices. And if it doesn't turn out exactly how you had intended, it can take just as long to undo the changes.

2. The blending can't be animated. The MEL script allows for linear, exponential or no falloff, but provides no method of adjusting the 'strength' of the fix beyond that. Ideally, the fix should be blended into the surrounding frames through the use of an animation curve. This would give you the ability to apply the fix to any frames that need it, while blending it in/out where necessary.

It should now be apparent exactly how/why shot sculpting is useful. In the process of learning about shot sculpting, we have also abolished the myth of the 'perfect' rig. So now that you know perfect rigs don't exist, how are we supposed to create perfect deformations? Of course, the answer is with shot sculpting, which simply provides a method of patching the imperfections that can be left behind by large-scale deformations.

Before we leave this topic to focus on other finishing techniques, I want to re-iterate the fact that shot sculpting is *only* useful when applied on-top of well designed deformations. In the same way that a carpenter applies lacquer to smooth a piece of wood, shot sculpting should only be used to fix minor glitches (aka, small deformations).

Finishing a Shot with the Minx:

So far we have covered all of the specifics involved in creating advanced character effects like fur/hair and cloth. But this is only part of the picture. This section will help solidify those concepts by bringing everything together in a single example. We will be covering the preparation and simulation of a 40-frame shot of the Minx jumping up and down FIGURE 6.14.

In the process, we are going to complete the following steps (in order):

1. Start by copying the animation from the animation rig to a file (.jca) on the hard drive.
2. Prepare the high-res scene (with cloth and fur/hair) before we copying the animation from the .jca file back onto the skeleton.
3. Setup and animate the spikes using the cgTkDynChain.mel script.

4. Setup and animate the cloth using Maya Cloth.
5. Transfer the cloth animation to the render garment (with a wrap deformer) and bake the deformations (using cgTkShotSculpt.mel).
6. Tweak and cache the hair systems that are driving the fur.

The completion of these seven steps will mark the end of our cloth and fur/hair training. Once we have gone through this process, you should be left with a complete understanding of how the different pieces of the puzzle fit together. Please note that some steps could be done in a different order, while others are obviously arranged in a specific order for a reason. Regardless, the reasoning behind each step and its order in the list will become apparent as you follow along.

Rather than conveying this section in the form of a really long, step-by-step exercise, we will guide you through the process and discuss the specifics along the way. All relevant scene files are available on the DVD and will be mentioned where necessary for those who wish to follow along.

Figure 6.14.

Step One: Copy Animation

For this step, we will be utilizing a script from The Art of Rigging Vol I called, jcAnimCS.mel. This script copies animation from a skeleton to an ASCII file on the user's hard drive. This file contains the keyframes and tangent information for the entire animation clip. We can then transfer this animation data from the ASCII file, to the skeleton in the high-res rig file. Before continuing, please copy the jcAnimCS.mel script file from the DVD to your Maya scripts directory.

With the script installed, execute jcAnimCS from the command line. This will bring-up the interface for the script FIGURE 6.15. All of the functionality of this script can be accessed through this interface. For a complete breakdown of how this script is used (as well as a line-by-line explanation of how it works) please take a look a chapter five in The Art of Rigging Vol I. We will cover its use in the context of only our specific needs.

Figure 6.15.

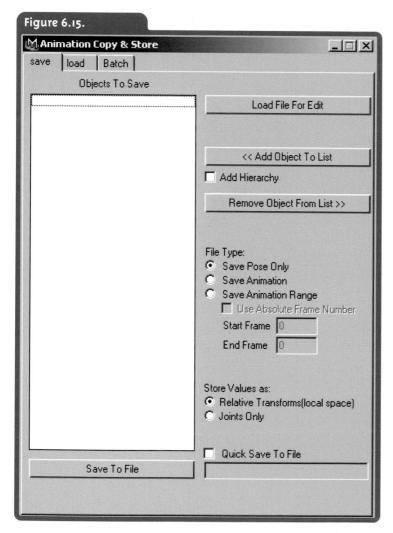

Start by opening the animation rig file from the DVD (exercise5.1_Start.mb). This scene contains the Minx's low-res rig which has been animated from frame 1 to 27. During that time, the Minx springs from a crouched position and leaps into the air before landing again about 20 frames later FIGURE 6.16. Nothing overly complex, but this animation has some very quick movements. As we already know, quick movements tend to wreak havoc on dynamic simulations, especially cloth. For that reason, the dynamics in this scene will require some special attention.

Figure 6.16.

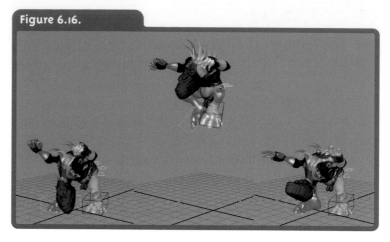

Let's get started. Select Edit > Quick Select Sets > Bound Joints. This set includes all of the joints in the Minx's skeleton that are bound to the skin. It's always a good idea to use a selection set so that you don't waste your time selecting hundreds of pieces every time you want to copy some animation. With the selection made, open the jcAnimCS window and click the 'Add Object to List' button. This populates the list with all of the joints in the Minx's skeleton FIGURE 6.17.

Figure 6.17.

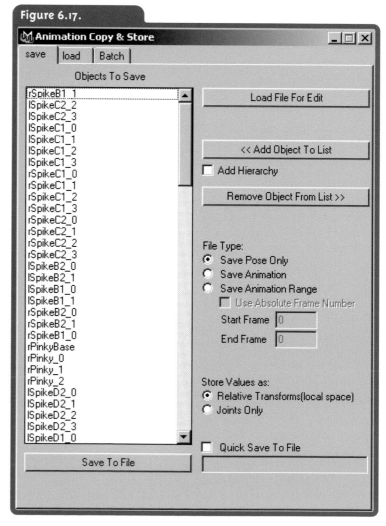

Now to write the animation data to disk, go to the middle of the Save tab and check the 'Save Animation' option. This will save the animation on every object in the list for every frame in the scene. To write the data to disk, click the 'Save To File' button and specify a directory/fileName (ie. c:/minxJump.jca). This will bring-up a progress window indicating how long it will take (usually less than a minute) FIGURE 6.18.

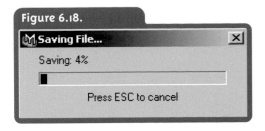

Figure 6.18.

Saving File...

Saving: 4%

Press ESC to cancel

Step Two: Paste Animation

When the script is finished, it will spit-out a .jca file that contains all of the animation data FIGURE 6.19 . Load the high-res scene (exercise5.1_ A.mb) from the DVD. This file contains the Minx's deformation rig as well as the cloth and fur. Before we copy the animation into this scene, let's set a key on all the joints at frame -10. Set the current frame to -10 and choose Edit > Quick Select Set > Bound Joints to select all of the joints. Now select the translate and rotate attributes in the channel box and set a key. At this point, the animation will blend from frame -10 at the bind pose to frame 0 where the animation clip begins. This will create a ten frame buffer for our cloth solver to catch-up to the starting pose of the animation (which is different from the bind pose of our character). If the starting pose were translated further from the origin, we would increased the size of the frame buffer (perhaps to -50) to give the cloth more time to blend into the start of the animation.

Figure 6.19.

minxJump.jca
JCA File
765 KB

Now switch to the Load tab in the script window. This tab is used to transfer animation from a .jca file to objects in the current scene. Click the 'Load Objects from List' button to bring-up a file browser. Load the .jca file that contains the Minx's jump animation (minxJump.jca on the DVD). This will parse through the animation file and populate the list with items whose animation is stored in the file FIGURE 6.20. The script does allow for the user to specify what target objects to copy the animation to, but as long as the naming remains identical we can use the Auto Map Objects feature. Check this box to tell the program to automatically find the corresponding object in the scene file to copy animation to.

To finish the animation transfer, click the Copy Source to Targets button. This brings-up a progress window indicating how long the copying progress will take. After a few moments, the script will finish leaving us with the exact animation from the low-res scene copied into the high-res scene. I encourage you to watch the included video lecture to watch this process. Transferring animation shouldn't become a bottleneck in your pipeline as long as everything is properly prepared. Use this checklist to ensure your own experience with this technique goes as smoothly as possible:

■ Ensure that the skeleton in the source and target scene files are named identically. Manually re-targeting the animation is an extra step you shouldn't have to worry about.

■ Create a selection set of all of the objects you wish to copy animation for. This is a huge time saver when the rig consists of hundreds of

joints and/or controllers with animation on them.

■ Create a global animation node (see previous chapter) to help consolidate disparate rig elements.

■ Keep your scene files clean! A well organized scene will help prevent problems related to naming conflicts which can be especially nasty when transferring animation.

Save the scene file (exercise5.1_B.mb) before continuing with the rest of the finishing process.

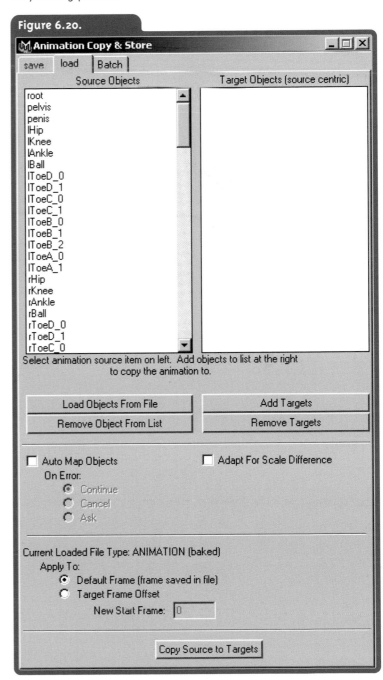

Figure 6.20.

Step Three: Animate the Spikes

With the animation transferred, we need to setup and animate the spikes on the Minx's back so that they flop around. Please recall that the spikes are rigged with 3-4 joint chains. To animate these chains with dynamics, we will be utilizing a MEL script from The Art of Rigging Vol I called cgTkDynChain.mel. Please copy this script to the Maya scripts directory before continuing.

Now open exercise5.1_B.mb. This scene contains the Minx's high-res rig with the animation copied. Template the layer with the Minx's skin geometry and turn on the joints layer. Notice the joint chains running through his spikes. These are going to be setup using the MEL script. Execute cgTkDynChain from the command line to bring-up the script's interface FIGURE 6.21.

Figure 6.21.

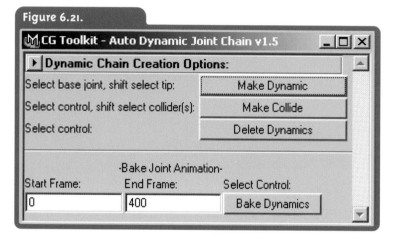

We won't be covering all of the specifics of this script in this lesson (please refer to chapter three in The Art of Rigging Vol I), but it's not difficult to use. Select a base joint, shift select a tip joint and hit the 'Make Dynamic' button. This will setup a spline IK system with a dynamic hair curve. It also creates a sphere object at the tip of the chain with controls for the behavior of the dynamics (ie. gravity, stiffness, etc.).

Setup all of the spikes using the MEL script (you can ignore the last two spikes, they are too short to move anyway). This should result in the creation of ten dynamic chains. Play the scene (or open exercise5.1_C.mb) and watch as the spikes flop around dynamically. By default, the spikes will completely lose their shape due to the lack of stiffness in the dynamic chains FIGURE 6.22. To give them some strength, select the sphere controller and crank-up the stiffness to a value of 1.0. You may notice that even at full stiffness, the dynamic chains are having difficulty maintaining shape during the extremely fast movement of the jump. This is the perfect time to utilize the Start Curve Attract feature. Grab all of the hairSystem nodes that were created with the dynamic chains (this can be done with a single marquee selection in the hypergraph). Now open the channel box and set the Start Curve Attract to a value of 0.6. Set the stiffness back to a value of 0.01 and replay the animation.

Figure 6.22.

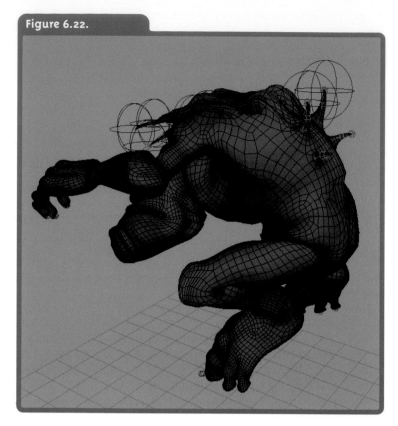

At this point, the spikes should flop around a bit, but still maintain their shape through the fast motion. Being happy with the motion, let's bake it directly into keyframes so that we don't have to calculate the hair dynamics anymore. Drag select all of the chain controllers (the spheres created by the script) and hit the 'Bake Dynamics' button in the script interface. Bake the first 40 frames of animation FIGURE 6.23.

Figure 6.23.

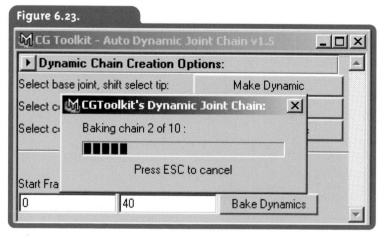

With the animation baked, there is no need to keep the dynamic chains in the scene file. Select all of the controller spheres and click the 'Delete Dynamics' button. This cleans-up all of the nodes the script created and leaves the scene as tidy as you found it. That's all there is to animating the spikes. The entire process should take about 2-5 minutes.

Step Four: Animate the Cloth

Open exercise5.1_E.mb to see the Minx with the finished skeletal animation. Now we're ready to animate his clothing. The cloth garment is not, by default, setup for animation. The reason for this is simple: When setting-up cloth animation, it can help to know exactly what attributes are set to what values. This makes the behavior of the cloth much more predictable. For this reason, the cloth will be setup from scratch on a shot-by-shot basis. That may sound tedious, but the entire process should only take a few minutes.

To start with, grab the simulation garment and choose Cloth > Create Cloth Object FIGURE 6.24. Ignore the warning message that says "Cloth cannot solve because run-up is not supported...". This occurs because our animation starts in the negative frames (-10). Let's adjust the solver so that it begins solving at the beginning of the animation, before the character blends into its crouching position. Set the Start Frame on the solver node to -10.

The garment has already been draped on the character. For this reason, it is not necessary to relax the garment at the beginning of the simulation. Set the Relax Frame Length to a value of 0. Recall that the relaxation phase is useful for pulling a garment together after sewing panels together. Since we are using a regular polygonal cloth object (and not a panel-based garment) that has already been draped, this feature is not necessary. Fortunately, you will be reminded very quickly if you forget this vital step. Indeed, if relaxation were not disabled, the garment would stretch out of shape in the first 5 frames

Assuming we want the Minx's garment to animate as though it were about 80cm in length, we must adjust the Solver Scale attribute. Recall that the proper solver scale attribute can be calculated by dividing the real world size (80cm) by the Maya size (8cm). Set the Solver Scale to a value of 10 (80/8). Now the garment should react with a realistic sense of weight.

That concludes the setup for the solver node. Open exercise5.1_F.mb to see the properly adjusted solver. Now let's finish the cloth setup by creating some collisions. Select the Minx's mesh and choose Cloth > Create Collision Object. Set the Collision Offset and Collision Depth attributes to a value of 0.1 FIGURE 6.25.

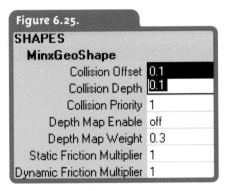

Figure 6.25.

SHAPES
 MinxGeoShape

Collision Offset	0.1
Collision Depth	0.1
Collision Priority	1
Depth Map Enable	off
Depth Map Weight	0.3
Static Friction Multiplier	1
Dynamic Friction Multiplier	1

Ensure that the playback speed is set to Play Every Frame and then run the simulation. The cloth should react appropriately as the Minx blends into his crouching pose. Shortly thereafter, around frame 3, the character bursts into a jump. At this point the action is so fast, the solver will certainly fail and the cloth will crumple into a big mess FIGURE 6.26.

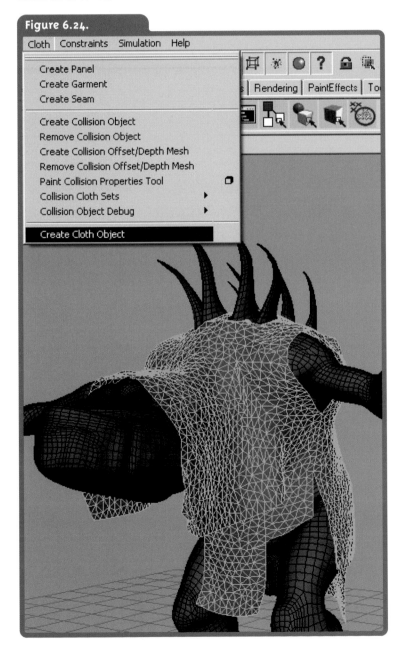

Figure 6.24.

Cloth   Constraints   Simulation   Help

Create Panel
Create Garment
Create Seam

Create Collision Object
Remove Collision Object
Create Collision Offset/Depth Mesh
Remove Collision Offset/Depth Mesh
Paint Collision Properties Tool
Collision Cloth Sets
Collision Object Debug

Create Cloth Object

Rendering | PaintEffects | To

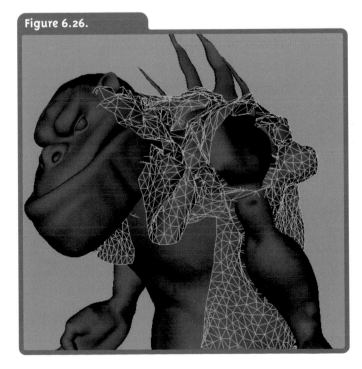

Figure 6.26.

At this point, a novice might scream and run away, but this behavior is quite typical of extremely fast motions. To give the solver more time to work-out the cloth position during this fast motion, we can increase the Frame Samples attribute on the solver node. Increase this from a value of 1 to 5. Now rewind the scene, delete the old cache and re-simulate.

This time around, the increased frame samples will inevitably slow the simulation to a crawl, but at least it will work FIGURE 6.27. If you are lazy like me, now would be a good time to grab a tea (or coffee if you're into that sort of thing) while the simulation solves. For really long simulations, it might be useful to animate the Frame Samples so that the simulation accuracy increases only where necessary. A modest workstation should be able to calculate about 50 frames of the cloth animation in a matter of minutes.

Figure 6.27.

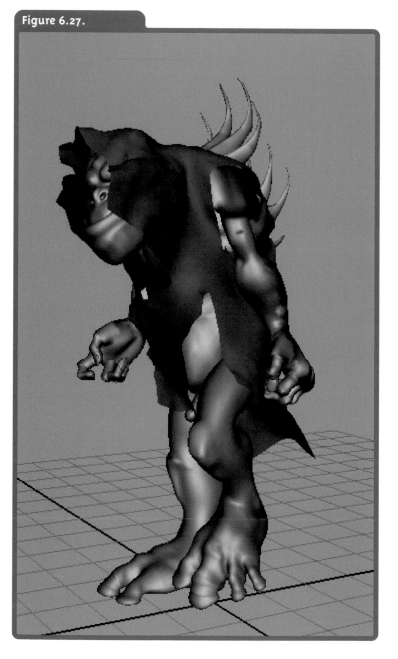

Stage Five: Setup Render Garment

Open exercise5.1_G.mb to see the finished cloth simulation. Now we need the render garment to follow along. Unhide the render cloth layer, rewind to the start frame and then wrap deform the thick cloth to the simulation cloth. In the wrap deformer settings, set the Max Distance to 0.2 and the Influence Type to Points FIGURE 6.28. The thicker cloth should now deform along with the render cloth.

Figure 6.28.

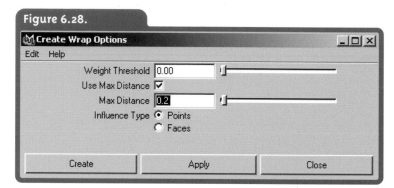

At this point, you can tweak the cloth animation as much as is necessary. To save yourself time, it helps to have the render camera in the scene so that you can tweak only the cloth that will be seen in the final render. To do this, simply scrub to a frame where you want to make a minor tweak. Sculpt the changes into the simulation garment and choose Simulation > Update Cloth State FIGURE 6.29. This will save your changes into the cloth cache.

Figure 6.29.

When you are happy with how it looks, you can bake the cloth animation to blendshapes if you want. To do this, install the cgTkShotSculpt script and execute its name from the command line. Now select the render garment and hit the Bake to Blendshapes button. Bake the mesh from frame 0 to 40 FIGURE 6.30. To prepare the render garment for being rendered, apply a bit of vertex averaging (Polygons > Average Vertices) and a single smooth (Polygons > Smooth). This will yield a nice smooth, thick garment ready to be rendered! FIGURE 6.31.

You can delete the simulation garment and all of the cloth nodes; the animation is now stored in the blendshape node. We're almost done preparing this shot for being rendered. To finish this exercise, let's take care of the Minx's fur.

Figure 6.30.

To create a hair cache, simply select the hairSystem and choose `Hair > Create Cache` FIGURE 6.33. When you are happy with the motion of the fur, sit back and relax because... we're all done! Save the file and pat yourself on the back. The Minx is now ready to be lit and rendered.

Figure 6.31.

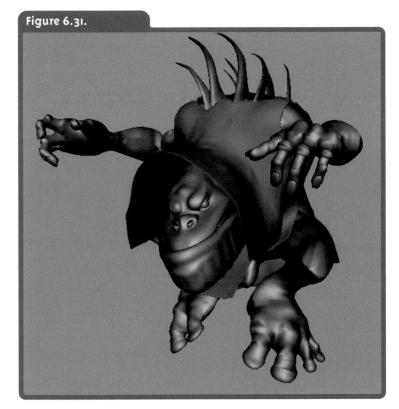

Figure 6.32.

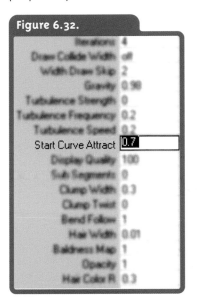

Figure 6.33.

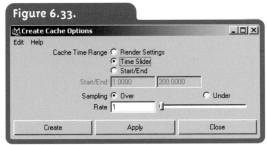

Stage Six: Tweak the Fur Motion

Open exercise5.1_G.mb to see the finished cloth animation. Hide the cloth layer and unhide the hair curves and fur layers. Setup the camera and do a quick playblast to see the fur motion or check out the furJump AVI from the DVD.

At the default settings, the fur should hold-up quite well. As with all dynamic animation, extremely quick motions tend to wreak havoc on the stability of the solution. In this case, however, the hair curves have had their Start Curve Attract attributes set to a reasonable values FIGURE 6.32. This is forcing the hair curves to keep their shape through even the fastest motions.

In this case, it turns out, the hair doesn't require any special attention. Just remember that if the hair curves are flopping about uncontrollably, you may need to dig into the hypergraph and find the hairSystem nodes. Adjusting the Start Curve Attract and Stiffness attributes will usually solve the problem. If the hair begins to jitter, you might want to tweak the Damping as well. Refer to the Hair chapter for more information on the specific effects of each attribute on the hairSystem node.

When you are happy with the motion of the fur, we need to create a hair cache. You could leave it as is, but a cache will ensure a consistent solution and prevent the hair from being recalculated at rendertime.

A Quick Note on Fur/Cloth Interaction

You may notice that the fur passes through the cloth during animation. These type of minor penetrations are guaranteed to crop-up in all but the most static of poses. Getting cloth and fur to interact with each other (while avoiding nasty crashes) presents an interesting problem. You have basically two options here; only one of which is likely to suite your needs:

1.Setup Fur Collisions: Let me start by saying that, while being the most obvious solution, collisions are simply not going to work in most situations. Setting the hair curves to collide with the cloth (or any other interacting pieces) will guarantee the hair curves don't collide with the cloth. But, the problem is that the hair curves are usually placed too sparsely throughout the fur to provide accurate collisions. For obvious reasons, its not inconceivable that the fur could (and probably will) crash through the cloth wherever the hair curves aren't thick enough.

2.Fake it: This is, by far, the better option. Rather than using brute force to prevent the fur from colliding through interacting pieces (like cloth, belts, hats etc...), we can utilize a compositing trick to hide the offending fur. Simply render a separate pass of the character with the fur turned off. Then place this layer on top of the fur+cloth layer and paint a mask wherever the fur penetrates. Obviously, penetrations should be kept to a minimum, but this technique works well for those inevitable minor glitches.

Final Thoughts:

So many productions run into bottlenecks at the finishing stage. It seems that this step in the animation pipeline, while important, receives very little attention in the form of discussion or training. Finishing work is never glamorous. But I suspect it doesn't get much attention in the mainstream simply because finishing is generally only employed in high-end animated productions (whatever that means!).

Shot sculpting is a level of detail you may never need, but that doesn't mean your production can't benefit from a smoother finishing pipeline. Unfortunately, we were unable to provide a comprehensive solution with this chapter (in the form of a Maya plugin). That being said, the ample discussion and MEL prototype should be enough to give any API savvy programmer a great head start.

After discussing how shot sculpting works, we explored a sample animated shot with the Minx. Its not always clear how all the pieces of a character should fit together; especially when the character employs so many dynamic elements (spikes, cloth, fur and hair curves). We hope that this chapter presented a sample scenario from which your own productions can benefit.

Interview with Remington Scott:

Remington Scott has supervised computer generated performance animation for visionary feature film directors including Peter Jackson, Hironobu Sakaguchi, Sam Raimi, Bryan Singer, Robert Zemeckis and the Wachowski brothers. His career has spanned over 20 years and includes key roles in the Oscar winning visual effects teams for "The Lord of the Rings: The Two Towers" and "Spider-man 2". Other films include "Final Fantasy: The Spirits Within", "The Animatrix: The Final Flight of the Osiris", "Superman Returns", "Spider-man 3", and "Beowulf".

Image 1

CG Toolkit: Could you tell us a bit about your background?

My father is a world renowned magician who directed visual effects for commercials in the 1970's. Everything back then was 'smoke and mirrors' and his skills as a magician made for a successful career. Much of my early childhood memories were of being on-set for commercials. I spent my time on-set drawing and made fast friends with the art directors. My early education came from these experiences and mentors. I knew I was going to be an artist at a very young age.

In my teens I made some stop motion animation shorts, a couple of successful video games and enjoyed painting. I was very interested in developing my artistic skills so I enrolled in a Fine Arts program at the School of Visual Arts in NYC and received my BFA. The knowledge I've gained from that experience comes into play every day.

CG Toolkit: How did you get started in the 3D industry?

I began working professionally with computer imagery and animation in high school when I co-created the first digitized home video game, "WWF: Superstars of Wrestling" (1986). That game proved that one could use an alternate technology to create realistic graphics rather than using the accepted medium, which at that time were animated sprites. We were just thinking outside the box and ultimately created one of the first 'multimedia' products.

Shortly thereafter, a video game publishing company started up in the next town over from where I lived on Long Island. The company was Acclaim. They were grossing hundreds of millions annually from successful games such as "Mortal Kombat", which utilized digitized characters. I was brought on board to direct the bluescreen action.

In the early 90's when the transition from 2D digitized imagery to 3D animation was beginning, Acclaim made a commitment to a rather new technology called 'Motion Capture' to create animations for their games and full-motion videos. It was there that, as an Interactive Director in the Advanced Technology Group, I had the opportunity to work extensively with mocap. The Acclaim Motion Capture studio was the first motion capture facility worldwide dedicated to entertainment. One of Acclaims high watermarks included motion capturing the first realistic digital double for a feature film in "Batman Returns".

CG Toolkit: Did you always know you wanted to work with motion capture, or did it just sort of "happen"?

In the early 90's when we were developing motion capture as a viable digital performance medium at Acclaim, I realized that this was an extremely powerful technology for the entertainment industry. I remember, back then, thinking that by using this technology we could finally breath life into realistic digital humans.

I thought there was going to be a Motion Capture boom, everyone would understand it and it would be everywhere. I couldn't be more wrong. It was reviled by mainstream animators and any major project that utilized motion capture seemed to have failure written all over it. Few in Hollywood would touch it or consider it for their projects claiming that it was too difficult to work with.

Then I got a call from a producer representing a Japanese video game company that wanted to make a full length motion captured feature film. It made total sense that the first motion captured film would come from 'outside' Hollywood from a Japanese video game company since they were technology savvy and early adopters. They were visionary in that they wanted to make an animated film that wasn't a 'cartoon'; they wanted to create digital characters that were realistic in their human emotions, physicality and spirituality. The company was Square and the film was "Final Fantasy: The Spirits Within". I managed the motion capture department and was a director on the film.

Word got out that a motion capture project was in the works and other visionaries started to come by the studio and gain interest. These people included James Cameron and the Wachowski Bros. who hired us to make the theatrically released short film "The Matrix: Final Flight of the Osiris".

When Weta won the Oscar for Visual Effects for *The Lord of the Rings: The Two Towers* for "using a computer motion capture system to create the split personality character of Gollum and Smeagol,"* I consider that as a turning point for motion capture. As the Motion Capture Supervisor on *LOTR:TTT* I believe that Peter Jackson's and Andy Serkis' enthusiasm for the art and craft of motion capture were the driving forces for the successful translation of one of the 20th century's greatest literary characters into a digital persona.

CG Toolkit: Could you briefly describe the motion capture pipeline at Sony Imageworks?

Sony Imageworks has dedicated the industry's brightest talent, both artistically and technically for their motion capture productions. The motion capture work that is being done at Imageworks has got to be some of the most demanding to date, and each successive motion capture project increases its scope and magnitude.

Some shows include full body and face simultaneous motion capture for principle digital characters, some use motion capture for crowds and some for highly detailed realistic facial animation. Depending on the show, the motion capture is recorded using an advanced proprietary studio with more cameras than you can shake a few hundred sticks at. Or the motion capture may even be outsourced from a vendor. Primary tools include Diva, MotionBuilder and Maya with much additional internal software development for each package.

CG Toolkit: What are some of your responsibilities as a Motion Capture Director?

I believe my personal success is accomplished through in-depth experience of all aspects of the motion capture production, from pre-production through post and finaled shots. Without a thorough understanding of the complete overview of the production and animation process, the result is at risk.

The hats I've worn have been as Director, Supervisor, Animation Director, Senior Technical Director and Producer. Depending on the scale of the project my responsibilities change. Regardless of title, my ultimate goal is to record an actor's performance and find the most effective way to make that performance come to life in the soul of the digital character. I believe that success is achieved when the digital character's persona is unique and the actor shines through, a feat achieved through equal parts artistic vision and technical understanding.

CG Toolkit: Describe your typical day at Sony Imageworks. Is there such a thing as a typical day?

There is no typical day. This past year, during some downtime, I had the opportunity to work on an R&D concept with Mark Sagar. We ended up authoring a patent for Sony that allows for the recording of an actor's eye rotation utilizing electrical potential. It's called 'imageEye' and has been developed for production for *Beowulf*.

I spend the majority of my time working on developing realistic digital facial actions and animations.

CG Toolkit: In your opinion, what is the future for motion capture?

This is my favorite question because I've thought about this a lot and have had the opportunity to watch the toolset of digital human acquisition and motion capture advance from its infancy. The direction of development I'm seeing is inspiring.

CG Toolkit: So where is this heading?

Communication will utilize motion capture, integrating with the average consumer's life in many ways. I believe that image recognition and facial data recording will play an important role in teleconference data compression and online communication. In the near future we'll see HD resolution cameras connected to our home computers and game consoles that record our expressions and transfer that onto digital personas. In the long term- keep an eye out for this technology adapting to cell phones and mobile devices.

In film, pre-visualization companies will use motion capture libraries to build pre-vis actions quicker and more efficiently. For production, capture systems will continue to grow in size using hundreds of cameras per zone. We'll see this continue for a brute force approach to face and body capture. However, there will be more elegant solutions regarding localized capture systems that revitalize the art and streamline production. We've only scratched the surface of digital performances in feature films. Visionary directors will continue to push the envelope for character action to develop new perspectives for stories.

The interactive arena will continue to make strides towards more realistic digital humans. Feature film pipelines and production methodologies for digital human acquisition will amalgamate into game production. The big hurdle for video game designers is to integrate emotionally rich characters into the interactive experience so the player can relate on a deeper, poignant level. This will occur through detailed facial expressions and realistic communication to the digital persona.

One thing is for sure, we are at the infancy of the art and science of motion capture and digital human acquisition.

CG Toolkit: Thank you very much for sharing your thoughts on digital human recording and motion capture. Keep-up the great work and best of luck in your future endeavors.

There is no doubt that this field will play an important role in the coming years. We at CG Toolkit look forward to seeing how this exciting technology will impact our lives.

*Keanu Reeves, Actor and Presenter, 75th Academy Awards.

MotionAnalysis

Motion Analysis Corporation is the undisputed world-wide leader and provider of optical motion-capture systems in entertainment, video games, film, broadcast, virtual reality, medicine, sports and research. The company was formed in 1982 and has its headquarters in Santa Rosa, California.

Motion Analysis' Eagle Digital System was used for facial capture in Peter Jackson's "KING KONG".

Contact Information:
Motion Analysis Corporation
3617 Westwind Boulevard
Santa Rosa, California 95403
707.579.6500
www.motionanalysis.com
info@motionanalysis.com

The studio division of Motion Analysis is located in the heart of Hollywood. Working with the best in the business, our studio is at the forefront of motion capture in Feature Film, Television, Gaming and more.

For information on our services, visit our website at: www.mastudios.com

Internships are available. Send inquires to info@mastudios.com

Contact Information:
323.461.3835 main line
323.461.1380 sales

Interview with Gabor Marinov, Andras Tarsoly from Digic Pictures:

Digic Pictures– As a relative newcomer to the high-end visual FX scene, *Digic Pictures* has firmly established themselves in the upper-echelon of high-quality digital animation studios. Based out of Budapest, Hungary, *Digic* comprises of fewer than twenty very talented individuals. Unlike many other smaller studios, *Digic* still hires 'specialized' artists rather than generalists. This regimented skill-set has given artists at *Digic* (sometimes with no serious computer experience) the opportunity to create the stunning imagery and surreal beauty seen throughout their work. Their recent work includes visual effects shots for *Terminator 3: Rise of the Machines* as well as cinematics for the *Armies of Exigo* and *Warhammer: Mark of Chaos* videogames. The technological backbone of their pipeline includes *Alias Maya, Pixar's Renderman, SyFlex, Eyeon Digital Fusion, D2 Nuke* and *Pixologic's Zbrush.*

Interview with Gabor Marinov, Visual FX Supervisor /Producer:

CG Toolkit: Digic Pictures is one of the few visual FX studios producing work for Hollywood movies outside of California. Do you find being in Hungary makes it challenging to keep-up with the rest of the industry? Many artists feel that their environment is an important source of inspiration. How has the picturesque scenery of Budapest affected your work, if at all?

Budapest is a beautiful city indeed. Every day, on my way to the Digic office, I see the banks of Danube, which has been proclaimed to be a part of the World Heritage by UNESCO. The sight of the bridges built in various ages that span across the river, and the St. Gellert hill are fantastic. I've even incorporated the hazy, looming image of the riverbank into a few shots of Armies of Exigo which I've composited.

I live in a beautiful part of the city, where my window opens to the nearly two thousand years old, restored Roman Military Camp ruins. Yes, Budapest is a very inspiring place to live in.

I think our physical distance from Hollywood is no longer an issue. We can exchange a huge amount of information very quickly with anyone anywhere in the world. Siggraph papers and other publications allow us to keep up with the latest technical developments worldwide.

Hungary's economy is growing very quickly and the government supports the film makers (even the digital ones) with huge tax discounts.

Image 1

We have a wonderful academic education system for Computer Science and Art, so I think the stage is set for a digital rebirth of the once world famous Hungarian animation.

CG Toolkit: Being a producer working on such high-profile projects as Terminator 3: Rise of the Machines and Warhammer, you must get a great sense of satisfaction from your job. What is the most rewarding part of working at a studio like Digic? Where do you draw your motivation from?

Digic is all about quality and that's also my personal motivation. It is very rewarding at Digic to see how a variety of gifted artists with totally different backgrounds are working together for a common goal. The whole company is built around and driven by the idea of "quality". Of course I'm never satisfied with the results. I keep searching for new ways to raise the bar...

Image 2

Image 3

CG Toolkit: 'Raising the bar' is really the ultimate goal of many productions. Modern audiences are increasingly exposed to high quality animation in movies, cinematics and even television. Extremely powerful animation software is now widely available, ultimately leading to fewer roadblocks for smaller studios. Amongst this onslaught of competition, how does a studio, like Digic, stand out? Considering that almost any effect is now possible, what exactly constitutes 'raising the bar' these days?

There is a unique duality in creating a computer animated film. On one hand, the end result is an artwork that serves the same fundamental purpose as any since the beginning of cave paintings; that is, awakening or amplifying various feelings in the audience. On the other hand, the

Image 4

tools we are using are incredibly complex, often requiring advanced mathematics and the mentality of an engineer. This situation is a bit like having one of our great classical painters unable to handle brushes. Imagine if he was forced to communicate with one or more engineers who had to physically apply the paint to the canvas according to the master's set of instructions. Nearly every computer graphics firm struggles to hire a staff which possesses artistic and engineering skills, which, combined, can be very scarce.

At Digic, we realized that our films become successful if they're created by artists. The goal of our engineers is to create tools that enable these artists to bring forth their vision with the least amount of technicality. Thus, we put a lot of energy into developing our own custom software. The Digic team is extremely talented in both aspects, but more importantly, everybody shares that same mentality and value system.

I believe that our thinking is what makes Digic unique, and the easier we make the "use of the brush" in the future, the better our films will become.

CG Toolkit: Digic is making waves in the CG industry with it's film-quality cinematics. Other studios with similar backgrounds are now trying to produce their own full-length feature animations. Admittedly, there has never been a full-length feature animation in the style of the Warhammer or Exigo cinematics. With the increasing interest in science fiction and fantasy films, do you think the public would be ready for something like that? What do you see in Digic's future?
I believe that this is a very interesting path to explore, but because we are bound to various confidentiality agreements, I cannot discuss it much further. :)

Image 5

Interview with Andras Tarsoly, Character Technical Director:

CG Toolkit: Digic has created some astounding character animation for The Armies of Exigo videogame cinematics. Each character is meticulously detailed with hundreds of tiny bits that dangle from their garments. Surely the animators are not responsible for all of these pieces! Can you describe the typical workflow for adding such immense detail? How do these complex rigs flow through your pipeline and what technologies drive them?

The main idea behind Digic's pipeline for highly detailed characters (which is based on Alias Maya) is to create a separate rig for every main function. This usually means five rigs ('anim', 'deform', 'dynamic', 'face' and 'render') that can be connected to each other to share data.

Image 6

Image 7

The 'anim' rig stores all the primary motion, whether it is motion capture, keyframe animation, or a mixture of the two. The 'deform' rig describes all the deformations of a character, which may even include approximated muscle simulation. The 'dynamic' rig performs all the physical simulations, like cloth or hair. The 'face' rig is used for all the facial animation; and the final stage of the pipeline, the 'render' rig will then gather the data from all the other rigs and pass it on to PRMan for rendering.

A character's complexity and its required rigs are decided on during the conceptual design phase. When required, we also build specialized rigs or create several versions of a given rig in addition to the ones above. This flexible structure allows independent development and parallel

workflow of the individual rigs for complicated characters. It saves us significant production time compared to a more linear approach.

CG Toolkit: One can't help but notice that *The Armies of Exigo* and *Warhammer* cinematics make brilliant use of cloth animation. From full-body cloaks, to flapping capes, Digic has created it all. How do you fit such an immense amount of cloth into your pipeline? Is the cloth added as a last touch? How do you handle the complexity of the detailed rigs that must interact with the cloth?

Digic uses SyFlex exclusively for all the cloth-type dynamics simulations. These span from multi-layered cloth to small attachments like ribbons, straps, cords or even ghosts swimming through the air. Thanks to the reliability, speed and flexibility of SyFlex, we often use it for dynamic

Image 10

Image 8

Image 9

CG Toolkit: Many of our readers are interested in alternative skin deformation techniques. In the hands of a skilled artist, simple blendshapes and smooth skinning can produce amazing results. You mentioned having a skin simulation rig in the 'experimental phase'. What advantages would this offer? Could you elaborate on exactly what this system involves?

It is very hard to create the slippery, puckery behavior of skin using traditional methods. Smooth-skinning and pose-based deformations produce good results, however still not enough to bring a character to life. Unwanted vertex movements will always be apparent using traditional skinning methods.

The key to our method is to apply the simulation of the skin in a separate step, onto the "muscled" and already moved surface. The whole simulation is created by a separate rig that connects to the pipeline

Image 11

Image 12

simulations of simple rigid bodies as well. We also have a fast and easy-to-use skin movement simulation rig in the experimental phase. It is built on SyFlex, using our previously developed muscle system.

The cloth simulation performs its calculations with special collision geometry, created for the above mentioned dynamic rig. The cloth itself is usually simulated with a simplified- but still very dense mesh, which is then used to deform the final cloth that appears in the renders. The simulation version does not have any details that would be superfluous to the movement, like extra edges that define the seams and borders of the garment.

Dynamic simulations are some of the last stages of the animation workflow. They are performed after the animation has been locked down. Fortunately, the speed of SyFlex allows last minute changes of the motion in order to improve quality.

by the already mentioned method. This rig collects the necessary data from the deform phase, executes the simulation, and with the results creates the final movement of the skin.

The movement simulation of the skin as well as the simulated mesh and the partial or full linking of the skinned mesh is done by SyFlex. The emerging movement data is finally used by the 'render' rig.

Image 15

Image 13

CG Toolkit: It is amazing to hear how the world's leading animation studios are tackling modern productions. CG Toolkit would like to thank Digic Pictures, Gabor Marinov and Andras Tarsoly for giving us some insight into their work.

Armies of Exigo cinematics, image courtesy of Digic Pictures.
© 2005 Cinergi Interactive LLC. All rights reserved.

CG Toolkit: Working with advanced character rigs, you must have a very good understanding of the limitations of current animation techniques. Like everything in this industry, character rigging will change over time. What do you see for the future of character rigging? What 'uber feature' should be included in future software to make your job easier?

In the future, modular rigging will probably speed up the work. There are already automated rigging scripts/software which make it possible to create complete character setups in a matter of minutes. The advantage of these solutions is you get quick results without having to understand much of what is happening underneath the surface.

Image 14

I don't think that there is a specific 'uber feature'. Every project is different from the one before it, and so is every character. Sometimes a realistic movement of the skin is important, and sometimes the character will be completely covered with armor. Different scenarios require different approaches, we never run out of new challenges and solutions.

Perhaps the only 'uber feature' that I would like to see universally, is faster computers and software. If the same amount of work would require less time, we could spend more time perfecting setups.

CREATIVE POWER